Lecture Notes in Computer Science   14213

FoLLI Publications on Logic, Language and Information
Subline of Lecture Notes in Computer Science

More information about this series at https://link.springer.com/bookseries/558

Daisuke Bekki · Koji Mineshima ·
Elin McCready
Editors

Logic and Engineering of Natural Language Semantics

19th International Conference, LENLS19
Tokyo, Japan, November 19–21, 2022
Revised Selected Papers

 Springer

Editors
Daisuke Bekki
Ochanomizu University
Tokyo, Japan

Koji Mineshima 🔾
Keio University
Tokyo, Japan

Elin McCready
Aoyama Gakuin University
Tokyo, Japan

ISSN 0302-9743   ISSN 1611-3349 (electronic)
Lecture Notes in Computer Science
ISBN 978-3-031-43976-6   ISBN 978-3-031-43977-3 (eBook)
https://doi.org/10.1007/978-3-031-43977-3

This Springer imprint is published by the registered company Springer Nature Switzerland AG
The registered company address is: Gewerbestrasse 11, 6330 Cham, Switzerland

Paper in this product is recyclable.

Preface

Logic and Engineering of Natural Language Semantics (LENLS) is an annual international conference on theoretical and computational linguistics covering topics ranging from syntax, semantics, and pragmatics to the philosophy of language and natural language processing.

The 19th LENLS conference was held November 19–21, 2022 in a hybrid format. Sessions were held at Ochanomizu University (Nov. 13, 14) and the University of Tokyo (Nov. 15), and also online. It was the first time in three years that the conference was held in person, and it was a pleasure to see the participants' faces after such a long time.

A total of 21 research presentations and 3 invited talks were given, covering a wide range of topics, and this post-proceedings volume includes a selection of the 13 research papers. The total number of submissions were 34, each of which is peer reviewed by at least two reviewers. The review process was double-blind.

The number of registered on-site and online participants was 61 and 52, respectively (including some overlap), and the total number was higher than in previous years. Thanks to the development of technologies for hybrid conferences, we were able to facilitate a relatively seamless interaction between the on-site and online participants.

The 19th LENLS conference marks a major milestone, becoming an official conference endorsed by the Association for Logic, Language and Information (FoLLI). Going forward, selected papers will be published as post-proceedings in the FoLLI series. To discuss what this means for us, we would first like to take a brief look back at the history of LENLS.

The first LENLS conference was held in 2003, organized by two researchers, Prof. Norihiro Ogata and Dr. Elin McCready. At that time, Prof. Ogata was a researcher focusing on formal semantics and natural language processing, while Dr. McCready was a postdoctoral researcher at Osaka University. The other founding members were Prof. Yoshimoto, Prof. Nakayama, Prof. Yabushita, and Prof. Mori, most of whom were also program committee members at LENLS19.

I met Prof. Ogata, Dr. McCready, and others at my first LENLS conference (LENLS5) in Asahikawa in 2008. Prof. Ogata believed that LENLS needed younger members, and on the way back from a conference dinner, he persuaded me to take on the role of chair for LENLS6. When I told him that this was my first time participating in LENLS and I didn't know anything about the organization, he laughed and said, "Don't worry, I have the know-how. I'll take care of all the behind-the-scenes work myself."

Unfortunately, that was the last conversation I had with Prof. Norihiro Ogata. He passed away in August of the same year.

I still remember the shock, sadness, and feelings of loss and even confusion. We dealt with our grief by organizing a memorial workshop. We also talked and decided that we should continue LENLS for his sake, and I decided to honor his request to serve as chair of LENLS6. However, I no longer had access to Prof. Ogata's know-how. So, we had to start by reconstructing it.

LENLS had originally been organized as a satellite workshop of JSAI-isAI, that is, the International Symposia on AI (isAI) hosted by the Japanese Society for Artificial Intelligence (JSAI). Around that time, JSAI had set a goal to expand its conferences beyond Japan to reach an international audience and had launched JSAI-isAI as one of several international workshops by public invitation. Post-proceeding volumes consisting of selected papers were published by Springer, and LENLS followed suit until LENLS18.

Building on the values that are important and cherished among LENLS participants —values that were, in fact, inherited from Prof. Ogata—we aim to resolve the conflict between the liberal use of advanced mathematical tools and the discovery of interesting linguistic phenomena. This means that the interests of the audience are often biased toward either mathematical frameworks or linguistic phenomena. For example, a sharp linguistic viewpoint that is not yet fully formulated may be undervalued by an audience with strong mathematical interests. At the same time, we may hesitate to introduce the latest mathematical tools to an audience with strong linguistic interests. Prof. Ogata created a forum where both the mathematical options and the profound stories about linguistics and philosophy are acceptable: If semantics is a branch of natural science, then there should be more freedom in theory building; if semantics is a branch of philosophy, then there should be more freedom in notion building.

We have embraced Prof. Ogata's philosophy and tried our best to fulfill his vision. Whether we have succeeded or not, LENLS has nevertheless continued to grow over the years, first, because of the attention it has attracted through the excellent research papers presented and cited, and second, thanks to the growing reputation of LENLS as an open forum for debate. The participants at LENLS are a diverse crowd from the fields of formal semantics, mathematical logic, analytic philosophy, and computational linguistics. However, we respect and show interest in each other's fields, and because the research presentations are mixed and discussed, it is not uncommon for overly conservative ideas to be subverted; indeed, we are eager to learn about so-called "non-standard" ideas.

Not a small number of participants have realized that this perspective of LENLS has much in common with the philosophy of FoLLI. LENLS has graduated from its status as a JSAI-affiliated workshop and become a full-fledged international society under FoLLI. The publication of the post-proceedings as part of the FoLLI series by Springer, as in the past, is the fulfillment of a long-held dream for the organizers. I would like to thank Larry Moss, the FoLLI 2022 chair, as well as Michael Moortgat and Valentin Goranko, the FoLLI 2022 co-chairs, for their invaluable support throughout this process.

What would Prof. Ogata say if I told him how much LENLS has grown and changed? I imagine he would say, "I want to contribute, too. I've been developing an interesting research idea and there is a mathematical mechanism such that..."

May 2023   Daisuke Bekki

In the original version of this book the first name of the editor was misspelled. The first name has been corrected. The correction to the book is available at https://doi.org/10. 1007/978-3-031-43977-3_14

LENLS19 Organization

Workshop Chair

Daisuke Bekki   Ochanomizu University, Japan

Workshop Co-chairs

Koji Mineshima   Keio University, Japan
Elin McCready   Aoyama Gakuin University, Japan

Program Committee

Alastair Butler	Hirosaki University, Japan
Patrick D. Elliott	Heinrich-Heine University of Dusseldorf, Germany
Naoya Fujikawa	University of Tokyo, Japan
Yuric Hara	Hokkaido University, Japan
Robert Henderson	University of Arizona, USA
Hitomi Hirayama	Keio University, Japan
Magdalena Kaufmann	University of Connecticut, USA
Yoshiki Mori	University of Tokyo, Japan
David Y. Oshima	Nagoya University, Japan
Katsuhiko Sano	Hokkaido University, Japan
Osamu Sawada	Kobe University, Japan
Ribeka Tanaka	Ochanomizu University, Japan
Wataru Uegaki	University of Edinburgh, UK
Katsuhiko Yabushita	Naruto University of Education, Japan
Tomoyuki Yamada	Hokkaido University, Japan
Shunsuke Yatabe	Ochanomizu University, Japan
Kei Yoshimoto	Tohoku University, Japan

Local Organizers

Yuta Takahashi	Ochanomizu University, Japan
Ribeka Tanaka	Ochanomizu University, Japan
Yoshiki Mori	University of Tokyo, Japan
Naoya Fujikawa	University of Tokyo, Japan

Sponsored By

- The Association for Logic, Language and Information (FoLLI)
- "AI systems that can explain by language based on knowledge and reasoning" project (Grant Number JPMJCR20D2), funded by JST CREST Programs "Core technologies for trusted quality AI systems"

Contents

Cumulative Reading, QUD, and Maximal Informativeness

Linmin Zhang[1,2](✉) (iD)

[1] NYU Shanghai, Shanghai, China
[2] NYU-ECNU Institute of Brain and Cognitive Science, Shanghai, China
zhanglinmin@gmail.com, linmin.zhang@nyu.edu
https://sites.google.com/site/zhanglinmin/

Abstract. Motivated by our intuitive interpretation for two kinds of cumulative-reading sentences, this paper argues for a novel **QUD-based view of maximal informativeness**. For a sentence like *Exactly three boys saw exactly five movies* (Brasoveanu 2013), it addresses an underlying QUD like *how high the film consumption is among boys* and provides a most informative answer with mereological maximality. However, for a sentence like *In Guatemala, at most 3% of the population own at least 70% of the land* (Krifka 1999), it addresses rather a QUD like *how skewed wealth distribution is in Guatemala* and provides a most informative answer with the maximality of the ratio between the amount of wealth and its owner population. I implement the analysis of these cumulative-reading sentences within a dynamic semantics framework (à la Bumford 2017). I also compare the current QUD-based view of maximal informativeness with von Fintel et al. (2014)'s entailment-based view and discuss a potentially broader empirical coverage (see also Zhang 2022).

Keywords: Cumulative reading · QUD · Maximal informativeness

1 Introduction

Sentence (1) has a distributive reading (see (1a)) and a cumulative reading (see (1b)). This paper focuses on its **cumulative reading**.

(1)   Exactly three boys saw exactly five movies.

     a. There are in total 3 boys, and for each atomic boy, there are in total 5 movies such that he saw them.   **Distributive reading**
          ↝ In total, there are 15 movie-seeing events, and the cardinality of distinct movies involved is between 5 and 15.

This project was financially supported by the Shanghai Municipal Education Commission (the Program for Eastern Young Scholars at Shanghai Institutions of Higher Lerning, PI: L.Z.). I thank the organizers, anonymous reviewers, and audience of LENLS 19. Errors are mine.

D. Bekki et al. (Eds.): LENLS 2019, LNCS 14213, pp. 1–17, 2023.
https://doi.org/10.1007/978-3-031-43977-3_1

b.   The cardinality of all boys who saw any movies is 3, and the cardinality of all movies seen by any boys is 5.   **Cumulative reading**
↝ In total, the cardinality of distinct movies involved is 5, and there are between 5 and 15 movie-seeing events.

Our intuition for the cumulative reading of (1) crucially involves the notion of **maximality**. As described in (1b), the two modified numerals (see the underlined parts of (1)) denote and count the **totality** of boys who saw any movies and the **totality** of movies seen by any boys.

In Brasoveanu (2013)'s compositional analysis of the cumulative reading of (1), two mereology-based maximality operators are applied simultaneously (at the sentential level) to derive the truth condition that matches our intuition.

In this paper, I further investigate the nature and source of this maximality. In particular, I follow Krifka (1999) to show that there are natural language cumulative-reading sentences that cannot be naturally interpreted with mereological maximality.

In a nutshell, I propose that (i) although the cumulative reading of (1) involves multiple modified numerals, it actually does not involve multiple independent maximality operators, but only one, and (ii) this maximality operator is not necessarily mereology-based, but rather informativeness-based, with regard to the resolution of a contextually salient degree QUD (Question under discussion). Thus Brasoveanu (2013)'s analysis for (1b) can be considered a special case within a more generalized theory on maximal informativeness.

The rest of the paper is organized as follows. Section 2 presents Brasoveanu (2013)'s mereological-maximality-based analysis of cumulative-reading sentences like (1). Then Sect. 3 presents Krifka (1999)'s discussion on a case that challenges a direct extension of Brasoveanu (2013)'s analysis. In Sect. 4, I propose to adopt the notion of QUD-based maximality of informativeness and show how this new notion of maximality provides a unified account for the data addressed by Brasoveanu (2013) and Krifka (1999). Section 5 compares the current QUD-based view with von Fintel et al. (2014)'s entailment-based view on maximality of informativeness. Section 6 further shows a wider empirical coverage for the notion of QUD-based maximality of informativeness. Section 7 concludes.

2   Brasoveanu (2013)'s Analysis of Cumulative Reading

Cumulative-reading sentences involve modified numerals, which bring **maximality** (see e.g., Szabolcsi 1997, Krifka 1999, de Swart 1999, Umbach 2006).

The contrast in (2) shows that compared to **bare numerals** (here *two dogs*), **modified numerals** (here *at least two dogs*) convey maximality, as evidenced by the infelicity of the continuation *perhaps she fed more* in (2b). Thus, the semantics of *two* in (2a) is **existential**, but the semantics of *at least two* in (2b) is **maximal**, indicating the cardinality of the **totality** of dogs fed by Mary.

(2)   a.   Mary fed two dogs. They are cute. Perhaps she fed more.
       b.   Mary fed at least two dogs. They are nice. #Perhaps she fed more.

According to Brasoveanu (2013), the semantics of the cumulative reading of (1) involves the **simultaneous** application of two maximality operators.

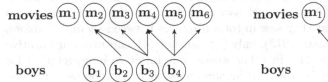 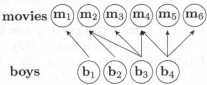

Fig. 1. The genuine **cumulative** reading of (1) is **true** in this context.

Fig. 2. The genuine **cumulative** reading of (1) is **false** in this context.

(3)   Exactly three^u boys saw exactly five^v movies.   (= (1))
Cumulative reading of (1):   (Brasoveanu 2013)

$$\sigma x \sigma y[\text{BOY}(x) \wedge \text{MOVIE}(y) \wedge \text{SEE}(x,y)] \quad \wedge |y| = 5 \wedge |x| = 3$$

the mereologically maximal x and y satisfying these restrictions   cardinality tests

(σ: maximality operator; for notation simplicity, cumulative closure is assumed.)

As sketched out in (3), Brasoveanu (2013) casts his analysis in dynamic semantics. The semantic contribution of modified numerals is two-fold. They first introduce plural discourse referents (drefs), x and y (assigned to u and v respectively). Then after restrictions like BOY(x), MOVIE(y), and SEE(x,y) are applied onto these drefs, modified numerals contribute maximality tests and cardinality tests. As shown in (3), two maximality operators σ are applied simultaneously to x and y at the global/sentential level, picking out the mereologically maximal x and y that satisfy all the relevant restrictions. Finally, these mereologically maximal x and y are checked for their cardinality, so that eventually the sentence addresses the cardinality of all the boys who saw any movies (which is 3) and the cardinality of all the movies seen by any boys (which is 5).

Crucially, the genuine cumulative reading characterized in (3) is distinct from the non-attested pseudo-cumulative reading shown in (4), where *exactly three boys* takes a wider scope than *exactly five movies*:

(4)   **Unattested pseudo-cumulative reading of (1):**
$$\sigma x[\text{BOY}(x) \wedge \underbrace{\sigma y[\text{MOVIE}(y) \wedge \text{SEE}(x,y)]}_{\text{the mereologically maximal } y} \wedge |y| = 5] \wedge |x| = 3$$

the mereologically maximal x

i.e., The maximal plural individual x satisfying the restrictions (i.e., atomic members of x are boys and each of them saw some movies, and x saw a total of 5 movies between them) has the cardinality of 3.

⤳ **True** for Fig. 2! (see $b_2 \oplus b_3 \oplus b_4$ and $b_1 \oplus b_2 \oplus b_4$, and there is no larger boy-sum satisfying these restrictions.)

The analysis shown in (4) can be ruled out by the contrast between our intuitive judgments: sentence (1) is judged true under the context shown in Fig. 1 but false under the context shown in Fig. 2. However, the truth condition characterized in (4) is actually true under the context shown in Fig. 2, where boy-sums $b_2 \oplus b_3 \oplus b_4$ and $b_1 \oplus b_2 \oplus b_4$ each saw a total of 5 movies, and there are no larger boy-sums such that they saw in total 5 movies between them. Therefore, as concluded by Brasoveanu (2013), only (3), but not (4), captures our intuitive interpretation of sentence (1). In other words, our intuitive interpretation for the cumulative reading of (1) (see (3)) involves no scope-taking between the two modified numerals (see also Krifka 1999, Charlow 2017 for more discussion).

Although Brasoveanu (2013) and relevant discussions in existing literature have shown that the reading of (4) is empirically non-attested and needs to be ruled out, they do not explain **why** (4) is not attested. In this sense, the simultaneity of applying two maximality operators seems a stipulation.

3   A Challenging Case Discussed by Krifka (1999)

Krifka (1999) uses sentence (5) to address his observations on cumulative reading.

(5)   In Guatemala, <u>at most 3%</u> of the population own <u>at least 70%</u> of the
         land.   ($\approx$ (13) and (27) of Krifka 1999)

First, the intuitively most natural interpretation of (5) also indicates that there is no scope-taking between the two modified numerals here:

'The problem cases discussed here clearly require a representation in which NPs are not scoped with respect to each other. Rather, they ask for an interpretation strategy in which all the NPs in a sentence are somehow interpreted in parallel, which is not compatible with our usual conception of the syntax/semantics interface which enforces a linear structure in which one NP takes scope over another.'   (Krifka 1999)

Then Krifka 1999 further points out that the simultaneous mereology-based maximization strategy that works for data like (1) does not work for (5):

'Under the simplifying (and wrong) assumption that foreigners do not own land in Guatemala, and all the land of Guatemala is owned by someone, this strategy would lead us to select the alternative *In Guatemala, 100 percent of the population own 100% of the land*, which clearly is not the most informative one among the alternatives – as a matter of fact, it is pretty uninformative. We cannot blame this on the fact that the NPs in (27) (i.e., (5) in the current paper) refer to percentages, as we could equally well express a similar statistical generalization with the following sentence (assume that Guatemala has 10 million inhabitants and has an area of 100,000 square kilometers):

(28)   In Guatemala, 300,000 inhabitants own 70,000 square kilometers
          of land.

Again, the alternative *In Guatemala, 10 million inhabitants own 100,000 square kilometers of land* would be uninformative, under the background assumptions given.

What is peculiar with sentences like (27) is that they want to give information about the bias of a statistical distribution. One conventionalized way of expressing particularly biased distributions is to select a small set among one dimension that is related to a large set of the other dimension. Obviously, to characterize the distribution correctly, one should try to decrease the first set, and increase the second. In terms of informativity of propositions, if (27) is true, then there will be alternative true sentences of the form *In Guatemala, n percent of the population own m percent of the land*, where *n* is greater than *three*, and *m* is smaller than *seventy*. But these alternatives will not entail (27), and they will give a less accurate picture of the skewing of the land distribution.'   (krifka 1999)

In short, Krifka (1999)'s discussion on (5) suggests that in accounting for cumulative-reading sentences, (i) a direct application of simultaneous mereology-based maximization strategy does not always work, and (ii) what kind of concern interlocutors aim to address via the use of a cumulative-reading sentence matters for sentence interpretation, and in particular, the interpretation of the interplay between modified numerals.

4   Proposal: QUD-Based Maximal Informativeness

As suggested by Krifka (1999), QUD should matter in our intuitive interpretation of cumulative-reading sentences. Based on this idea, I start with an informal discussion on the underlying QUD in interpreting cumulative-reading sentences (Sect. 4.1). Then I propose a QUD-based view on maximality of informativeness (Sect. 4.2) and develop a compositional analysis for cumulative-reading sentences like (1) and (5) within a dynamic semantics framework (Sect. 4.3), à la Bumford (2017) and in the same spirit as Brasoveanu (2013).

4.1   Cumulative-Reading Sentences and Their Underlying QUD

Here I first show that numerals or measure phrases provide quantity/measurement information, but quantity/measurement information alone does not determine how we interpret an uttered sentence and reason about its informativeness. The same sentences (e.g., (6) and (7)) can lead to different patterns of meaning inference, depending on a potentially implicit **degree QUD**.

In (6), the measurement information provided by *7 o'clock* directly addresses *what time it is* (see (6a)). However, it is not (6a), but rather an underlying **degree question**, that determines whether (6) is interpreted as *it's as late as 7 o'clock* (≈ already 7 o'clock) or *it's as early as 7 o'clock* (≈ only 7 o'clock).

If the underlying QUD is *how late it is* (see (6b)), then (6) is interpreted as *it's as late as 7 o'clock*, conveying a stronger meaning than *it's 6/5/... o'clock* by indicating a higher degree of **lateness**. Thus, to resolve *how late it is*, we consider a temporal scale from earlier to later time points, and **higher informativeness** correlates with **later** time points, i.e., the **increase** of numbers.

On the other hand, if the underlying QUD is *how early it is* (see (6c)), then (6) is interpreted as *it's as early as 7 o'clock*, conveying a stronger meaning than *it's 8/9/... o'clock* by indicating a higher degree of **earliness**. Thus, to resolve *how early it is*, we consider rather a temporal scale from later to earlier time points, and **higher informativeness** correlates with **earlier** time points, i.e., the **decrease** of numbers.

(6)   It's 7 o'clock.

    a.   What time is it?   **Neutral**: no evaluativity
    b.   QUD: How late is it?   (6) ⤳ It's <u>as late as</u> 7 o'clock
        In addressing (6b), *It's as late as 7:00* $>_{\text{info}}$ *It's as late as 6:00*
    c.   QUD: How early is it?   (6) ⤳ It's <u>as early as</u> 7 o'clock
        In addressing (6c), *It's as early as 7:00* $>_{\text{info}}$ *It's as early as 8:00*

Similarly, along a scale of length, we intuitively feel that *John is 5 feet tall* is stronger than *John is 4 feet tall*. This intuition is actually based on the degree QUD – *How tall is John*. However, it is not guaranteed that measurement sentences containing a higher number are always more informative. Depending on whether the underlying degree QUD is (7b) or (7c), (7) can be interpreted as *John is <u>as tall as</u> 5 feet* and more informative than an alternative sentence with a smaller number, or (7) can be interpreted as *John is <u>as short as</u> 5 feet* and more informative than an alternative sentence with a larger number.[1]

(7)   John measures 5 feet.

    a.   How many feet does John measure?   **Neutral**: no evaluativity
    b.   QUD: How tall is John?   (7) ⤳ He is <u>as tall as</u> 5 feet
        In addressing (7b), *John is as tall as 5′* $>_{\text{info}}$ *John is as tall as 4′*
    c.   QUD: How short is John?   (7) ⤳ He is <u>as short as</u> 5 feet
        In addressing (7c) *John is as short as 5′* $>_{\text{info}}$ *John is as short as 6′*

Therefore, as illustrated by (6) and (7), in the interpretation of sentences containing numerals, it is not always the case that the use of larger numbers leads to higher level of informativeness. Rather, the inference on informativeness

---

[1] Degree questions like *how <u>tall</u> is John* are more default (i.e., less marked) than *how <u>short</u> is John*. Thus, we naturally feel that *John measures 5 feet* (or *John is 5 feet tall*) is stronger (i.e., more informative) than *John measures 4 feet* (or *John is 4 feet tall*). However, I make a distinction between **being more informative** and **entailment** and avoid the term 'entailment' here. As shown in (i), (ia) is stronger than but does not directly entail (ib). See also Sect. 5 for more discussion.

(i)   a.   John is above 6 feet tall. $\lambda w.\text{HEIGHT}(\text{JOHN})(w) \subseteq [6', +\infty)$
    b.   John is between 4 and 5 feet tall. $\lambda w.\text{HEIGHT}(\text{JOHN})(w) \subseteq [4', 5']$

hinges on (i) an underlying degree QUD (along with the direction of the scale associated with the degree QUD) and (ii) how numerals are used to resolve the degree QUD. Sometimes the use of smaller measurement numbers leads to higher informativeness in resolving degree QUDs (e.g., (6c) and (7c)).

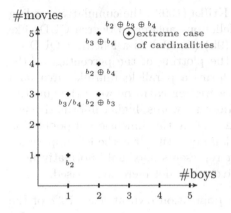

Fig. 3. QUD: How much is the overall film consumption among boys? The cardinalities of some boy-sums and movie-sums in the context of Fig. 1 are plotted as dots. The extreme case that addresses the degree QUD in the most informative way is represented by the right-uppermost dot, i.e., the one corresponding to the boy-sum $b_2 \oplus b_3 \oplus b_4$ and the 5 movies they saw between them.

Fig. 4. QUD: How skewed is wealth distribution? The plotting of the percentages of the population and their owned land should form a parallelogram-like area. The extreme case that addresses the degree QUD in the most informative way is represented by the left uppermost corner, which means that 3% of the population own 70% of the land.

The above observation can be extended to cumulative-reading sentences that contain multiple numerals: the interpretation of a sentence and our inference on its informativeness depend on its underlying degree QUD.

In particular, when multiple numerals are used together to address a degree QUD, their interplay brings new patterns for connecting numbers and meaning inference on informativeness. Higher informativeness does not correlate with the increase or decrease of a **single number**, but **an interplay among numbers**.

According to our intuition, the cumulative-reading of sentence (1) addresses and can be a felicitous answer to QUDs like (8a) or (8b), but it does not address QUDs like (8c) or (8d).[2] Therefore, as illustrated in Fig. 3, **higher informativeness** correlates with the **increase along both the dimensions** of boy-cardinality and movie-cardinality, and the right-uppermost dot on this two-dimensional coordinate plane represents maximal informativeness. I.e., maximal informativeness amounts to simultaneous mereology-based maximality.

---

[2] (8c) and (8d) do not even sound like natural questions for some native speakers.

(8)   Exactly three boys saw exactly five movies.   (= (1))
   a.   QUD: How many boys saw how many movies?
   b.   QUD: How much is the overall film consumption among boys?
   c. $\not\leadsto$??How many boys saw exactly five movies (between them)?
   d. $\not\leadsto$??How many movies did exactly three boys see (between them)?

On the other hand, as pointed out by Krifka (1999), the cumulative-reading of sentence (5) addresses and can be a felicitous answer to degree QUDs like (9a), but it does not address QUDs like (9b) (cf. (8a) as a felicitous QUD for (8)). Therefore, as illustrated in Fig. 4, the plotting of the percentage of the population and their entire owned land forms a parallelogram-like area, and **higher informativeness** correlates with a **higher ratio** between the quantity of owned land and its owner population. In other words, higher informativeness correlates simultaneously with the **decrease** along the dimension of population and the **increase** along the dimension of land quantity. It is the left-uppermost corner of this parallelogram-like area that represents maximal informativeness. In this case, obviously, maximal informativeness is not mereology-based.

(9)   In Guatemala, at most 3% of the population own at least 70% of the land.   (= (5))
   a.   QUD: How skewed is wealth distribution in Guatemala?
   b. $\not\leadsto$ How many people own how much land in Guatemala?

In brief, although the interpretation of both types of cumulative-reading sentences is based on maximal informativeness, they are different with regard to how maximal informativeness is computed from numbers, and crucially, this computation is driven by an underlying degree QUD.

Further evidence comes from the monotonicity of numerals used in these cumulative-reading sentences. In the case represented by (1)/(8), the two numerals cannot have opposite monotonicity, while in the case represented by (5)/(9), the presence of two numerals with opposite monotonicity is perfectly natural (e.g., in (5)/(9), the use of a downward-entailing expression, *at most 3%*, along with the use of an upward-entailing expression, *at least 70%*). Evidently, in the former case, the two numerals contribute to the informativeness of a sentence in a parallel way, while in the latter case, the two numerals contribute to the informativeness of a sentence in opposite ways.

It is worth mentioning that **multi-head comparatives** (see von Stechow 1984, Hendriks and De Hoop 2001) also provide empirical support for (i) a degree-QUD-based interpretation and informativeness inference as well as (ii) the connection between QUDs and the pattern of monotonicity.

As illustrated in (10)–(12), the underlying QUD determines how the changes of quantity/measurement contribute to sentence interpretation.

In contrast, (13) sounds degraded because with the use of *fewer dogs* and *more rats*, the sentence fails to suggest a QUD that it can felicitously address: (i) the evaluation in terms of the quantity and quality of preys and (ii) the quantity of dogs as successful predators are at odd with each other in conveying coherent meaning.

(10)   Less land produces more corn than ever before.   (von Stechow 1984,
       Hendriks and De Hoop 2001)
       QUD: How is the productivity rate increased?
       ⤳ Correlating with the **decrease** of input and the **increase** of output

(11)   Nowadays, more goods are carried faster. (Hendriks and De Hoop 2001)
       QUD: How is the efficiency of transportation increased?
       ⤳ Correlating with the **increase** of both amount and speed

(12)   More dogs ate more rats than cats ate mice.   (von Stechow 1984,
       Hendriks and De Hoop 2001)
       QUD: How are dogs more successful predators than cats?
       ⤳ Comparison along two dimensions address the QUD in a parallel way

(13)   *Fewer dogs ate more rats than cats ate mice.   (Hendriks and De Hoop
       2001)

4.2 A QUD-Based Maximality Operator

Based on the informal discussion in Sect. 4.1, I propose a **QUD-based maxi-mality operator** and implement it within a dynamic semantics framework:

(14) $\mathbf{M}_{u_1,u_2,\ldots} \overset{\text{def}}{=}$
       $\lambda m.\lambda g. \{h \in m(g) | \neg \exists h' \in m(g). G_{\text{QUD}}(h'(u_1, u_2, \ldots)) >_{\text{info}} G_{\text{QUD}}(h(u_1, u_2, \ldots))\}$
       (Type of m: $g \to \{g\}$; Type of $\mathbf{M}$: $(g \to \{g\}) \to (g \to \{g\})$)

As shown in (14), I assume meaning derivation to be a series of updates from an information state to another, and an information state m (of type $g \to \{g\}$) is represented as a function from an input assignment function to an output set of assignment functions (see also Bumford 2017).

The QUD-based maximality operator $\mathbf{M}_{u_1,u_2,\ldots}$ works like a filter on information states. With the application of $\mathbf{M}_{u_1,u_2,\ldots}$, the discourse referents (drefs, which are assigned to $u_1, u_2, \ldots$) that lead to the maximal informativeness in resolving a QUD will be selected out.

More specifically, the definition of $\mathbf{M}_{u_1,u_2,\ldots}$ includes an operator G_{QUD}, which, when applied on drefs, returns a value indicating informativeness. This informativeness amounts to a measurement in addressing a contextually salient degree QUD: e.g., in the case of (8) (see Fig. 3), *how much the overall film consumption is among boys*; in the case of (9) (see Fig. 4), *how skewed wealth distribution is in Guatemala*. In this sense, G_{QUD} can be considered a measure function.

4.3 Analyzing Cumulative-Reading Sentences

The step-by-step semantic derivation for the core example (1) is shown in (15). (15a) first shows the introduction of plural drefs and relevant restrictions.

Given that this sentence is interpreted with a contextually salient QUD like *how high film consumption is among boys* (see (8) and Fig. 3), higher informativeness amounts to higher degree of consumption level (e.g., with $d_1 > d_2$, *the consumption level is* d_1*-high* is more informative than *the consumption level is* d_2*-high*). Thus the measurement of informativeness amounts to the measurement of cardinalities of both plural drefs (see (15b)).

Maximal informativeness is achieved when the mereologically maximal drefs (i.e., $b_2 \oplus b_3 \oplus b_4$ and $m_2 \oplus m_3 \oplus m_4 \oplus m_5 \oplus m_6$ in Fig. 1) are assigned (see (15c)).

(15)   <u>Exactly three^u</u> boys saw <u>exactly five$^\nu$</u> movies.   (= (1))

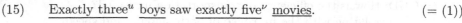
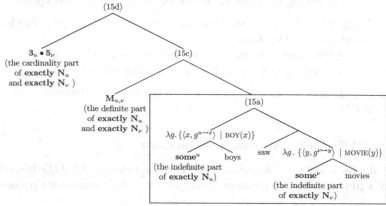

a. $p = [\![\text{some}^u \text{ boys saw some}^\nu \text{ movies}]\!] =$

$$\lambda g . \left\{ g_{u \mapsto x}^{\nu \mapsto y} \middle| \text{MOVIE}(y), \text{BOY}(x), \text{SAW}(x,y) \right\}$$

(i.e., the introduction of plural drefs x and y and restrictions)

b. $G_{\text{QUD}} = \lambda x . \lambda y . |x| + |y|$

(i.e., Based on the QUD, maximizing informativeness amounts to simultaneously maximizing x and y.)

c. $\mathbf{M}_{u,\nu}(p) =$

$$\lambda g . \left\{ g_{u \mapsto x}^{\nu \mapsto y} \middle| \begin{array}{c} y = \iota y . [\text{MOVIE}(y) \wedge \underbrace{\exists x [\text{BOY}(x) \wedge \text{SAW}(x,y)]}_{\text{some boys saw } y} \\ \wedge \underbrace{\forall y' \neq y [\text{MOVIE}(y') \wedge \exists x [\text{BOY}(x) \wedge \text{SAW}(x,y')] \rightarrow y' \sqsubset y]}_{y \text{ is mereologically maximal}}] \\ x = \iota x . [\text{BOY}(x) \wedge \underbrace{\exists y [\text{MOVIE}(y) \wedge \text{SAW}(x,y)]}_{x \text{ saw some movies}} \\ \wedge \underbrace{\forall x' \neq x [\text{BOY}(x) \wedge \exists y [\text{MOVIE}(y) \wedge \text{SAW}(x,y)] \rightarrow x' \sqsubset x]}_{x \text{ is mereologically maximal}}] \end{array} \right\}$$

(i.e., the drefs x and y that lead to maximal informativeness are picked out ⤳ mereologically maximal x and y are picked out.)

d. $[\![(1)]\!]$ $= \quad [\![\text{exact } 3^u \text{ boys saw exactly } 5^\nu \text{ movies}]\!] \quad =$

$\mathbf{M}_{u,\nu}(p)$, if $\begin{array}{l} |x| = 3, \\ |y| = 5 \end{array} =$

$$\lambda g . \left\{ g_{u \mapsto x}^{\nu \mapsto y} \middle| \begin{array}{l} y = \iota y . [\text{MOVIE}(y) \wedge \exists x [\text{BOY}(x) \wedge \text{SAW}(x,y)] \\ \wedge \forall y' \neq y [\text{MOVIE}(y') \wedge \exists x [\text{BOY}(x) \wedge \text{SAW}(x,y')] \rightarrow y' \sqsubset y] \\ x = \iota x . [\text{BOY}(x) \wedge \exists y [\text{MOVIE}(y) \wedge \text{SAW}(x,y)] \\ \wedge \forall x' \neq x [\text{BOY}(x) \wedge \exists y [\text{MOVIE}(y) \wedge \text{SAW}(x,y)] \rightarrow x' \sqsubset x] \end{array} \right\},$$

if $|x| = 3$ and $|y| = 5$

(i.e., the cardinalities of mereologically maximal x and y are checked.)

The step-by-step semantic derivation of the core example (5) is shown in (16). The crucial difference between the analysis in (15) vs. (16) consists in their QUD, i.e., G_{QUD}, as reflected in (15b) vs. (16b).

Given that (5) is interpreted with a QUD like *how skewed wealth distribution is in Guatemala* (see (9) and Fig. 4), higher informativeness amounts to higher degree of skewedness. Thus the measurement of informativeness amounts to the ratio between the quantity of drefs (see (16b)).

Maximal informativeness is achieved when the quantity of a dref y satisfying LAND(y) $\wedge$ OWN(x, y) divided by the quantity of a dref x satisfying HUMAN(x) $\wedge$ OWN(x, y) yields the maximal ratio/quotient (see (16c)).

Finally, modified numerals *at most 3%* and *at least 70%* impose cardinality tests on the drefs selected out from the step in (16c) (see (16d)).

(16)   At most 3%^{u} of the population own at least 70%^{v} of the land.   (=(5))

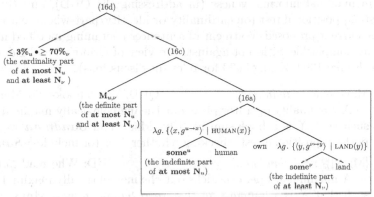

a. $p = [\![\text{some}^u \text{ population own some}^v \text{ land}]\!] =$

$$\lambda g. \left\{ \left. \begin{matrix} {}^{\nu \mapsto y} \\ g^{u \mapsto x} \end{matrix} \right| \text{LAND}(y), \text{HUMAN}(x), \text{OWN}(x, y) \right\}$$

(i.e., the introduction of drefs x and y and restrictions)

b. $G_{\mathrm{QUD}} = \lambda x. \lambda y. |y| \div |x|$

(i.e., Based on the QUD, maximizing informativeness amounts to maximizing the ratio between the quantity of y and x.)

c. $\mathbf{M}_{u,\nu}(p) =$

$$\lambda g. \left\{ \left. \begin{matrix} {}^{\nu \mapsto y} \\ g^{u \mapsto x} \end{matrix} \right| \begin{matrix} \langle x, y \rangle = \langle \iota x, \iota y \rangle \text{ such that} \\ \text{LAND}(y) \wedge \text{HUMAN}(x) \wedge \text{OWN}(x, y) \\ \wedge \neg \exists y' \sqsupset y[\text{LAND}(y') \wedge \text{OWN}(x, y')] \\ \underbrace{\qquad\qquad}_{y \text{ is the maximal land owned by } x} \\ \wedge \neg \exists x' \sqsupset x[\text{HUMAN}(x') \wedge \text{OWN}(x', y)] \\ \underbrace{\qquad\qquad}_{x \text{ is the maximal owner of } y} \\ \wedge \forall x'' \forall y''[\text{LAND}(y'') \wedge \text{HUMAN}(x'') \wedge \text{OWN}(x'', y'') \\ \wedge \neg \exists y''' \sqsupset y''[\text{LAND}(y''') \wedge \text{OWN}(x'', y''')] \\ \underbrace{\qquad\qquad}_{y'' \text{ is the maximal land owned by } x''} \\ \wedge \neg \exists x''' \sqsupset x''[\text{HUMAN}(x''') \wedge \text{OWN}(x''', y'')] \to \frac{|y|}{|x|} \ge \frac{|y''|}{|x''|}] \\ \underbrace{\qquad\qquad}_{x'' \text{ is the maximal owner of } y''} \end{matrix} \right\}$$

(i.e., the drefs x and y that lead to maximal $\frac{|y|}{|x|}$ are picked out.)

    d. $\llbracket (5) \rrbracket =$
        $\llbracket$ at most $3\%^u$ of the population own at least $70\%^\nu$ of the land$\rrbracket =$
        $\mathbf{M}_{u,\nu}(p)$, if $|x| \subseteq (0, 3\%], |y| \subseteq [70\%, 1]$
        (i.e., the cardinalities of selected x and y are checked.)

Here I would also like to address an issue raised by an anonymous reviewer: is it valid to use QUD in the derivation of (truth-conditional) meaning of a sentence? Works like Grindrod and Borg (2019) point out that the framework of QUD is pragmatic, mainly accounting for phenomena like the use of prosodic focus in question-answer congruence, and further extension to account for truth-conditional meaning is illegitimate.

As sketched in the following examples (17)–(19), modified numerals actually parallel exactly with items that bear prosodic focus: their interpretation all involve (i) a certain QUD, (ii) the application of a maximality operator that results in maximal informativeness (in addressing the QUD), and (iii) a further post-suppositional test (on cardinality or identity/part-whole relationship). Thus the current proposed treatment of sentences containing modified numerals is actually compatible with, not against, the view of Grindrod and Borg (2019) (see also Krifka 1999; Zhang 2023 for relevant discussions).

(17)   Mary read $[Sandman]_F^u$.   QUD: What books did Mary read?
        ⇝ A maximality operator picks out the mereologically maximal dref X, such that X is a book-sum read by Mary, and **Sandman** works as a post-suppositional test, checking whether X is (or includes) **Sandman**.

(18) $[Mary]_F^u$ read *Sandman*.   QUD: Who read *Sandman*?
        ⇝ A maximality operator picks out the mereologically maximal dref X, such that X is a human-sum that read *Sandman*, and **Mary** works as a post-suppositional test, checking whether X is (or includes) **Mary**.

(19)   Mary fed at least two^u dogs. $(= (2b))$
        QUD: how many dogs did Mary feed?
        ⇝ A maximality operator picks out the mereologically maximal dref X, such that X is a dog-sum fed by Mary, and **at least two** checks the cardinality of this maximal X, whether $|X| \geq 2$.

5   Discussion: Comparison with von Fintel et al. (2014)

Under the current analysis, it is a contextually salient degree QUD (i.e., what interlocutors care about, their ultimate motivation behind their utterance, see Roberts 2012) that determines how informativeness is actually measured (see the implementation of G_{QUD} in (15b) vs. (16b)). This degree-QUD-based informativeness measurement, G_{QUD}, further determines how the maximality operator $\mathbf{M}_{u_1,u_2,...}$ filters on drefs and how (modified) numerals affect meaning inference.

The notion of **degree-QUD-based** maximality of informativeness proposed here is in the same spirit as but more generalized than the **entailment-based** one proposed by von Fintel et al. (2014) (which primarily aims to account for the interpretation of *the*; see also Schlenker 2012). According to von Fintel et al. (2014), informativeness ordering is based on entailment relation (see (20)).

(20)   von Fintel et al. (2014)'s notion of informativeness ordering:
        For all x, y of type α and property ϕ of type $\langle s, \langle \alpha, t \rangle \rangle$, $x \geq_\phi y$ iff
        $\lambda w. \phi(w)(x)$ entails $\lambda w. \phi(w)(y)$.   (von Fintel et al. (2014): (3b))

Thus as shown in (21), depending on the monotonicity of properties, maximal informativeness corresponds to maximum or minimum values.

(21)   a.   For **upward monotone** properties (e.g., λd. Miranda is d tall),
              maximal informativeness means **maximum** values:
              e.g., *Miranda is* 1.65 *m tall* entails *Miranda is* 1.60 *m tall.*
        b.   For **downward monotone** properties,
              maximal informativeness means **minimum** values:
              e.g., given that $m > n$, *n walnuts are sufficient to make a pan of baklava* entails *m walnuts are sufficient to make a pan of baklava.*

Compared to von Fintel et al. (2014), the notion of QUD-based maximal informativeness developed in the current paper is more generalized in two aspects.

First, the current QUD-based view on maximality of informativeness can be easily extended from dealing with a single value to a combination of values.

As shown in Sect. 4, in cumulative-reading sentences where multiple numerals are involved, maximal informativeness does not directly correspond to whether the uttered numbers are considered maximum or minimum values. In example (5), as observed by Krifka (1999), each of the numerals (i.e., *at most 3%* and *at least 70%*) alone cannot be maximum or minimum values. It is how the combination of these uttered numbers contributes to resolve an implicit, underlying QUD that leads to the achievement of maximal informativeness.

Second, and more importantly, the current degree-QUD-based view on maximality of informativeness can overcome the issue that sometimes we intuitively feel that one sentence has a stronger meaning (or is more informative) than another, but the former does not directly entail the latter.

In (21a), *Miranda is 1.65 m tall* means that the height of Miranda reaches the measurement of 1.65 m, i.e., $\lambda w. \text{HEIGHT}(\text{MIRANDA})(w) \geq 1.65$ m. Thus it does entail *Miranda is 1.60 m tall* – $\lambda w. \text{HEIGHT}(\text{MIRANDA})(w) \geq 1.60$ m.

The two sentences mentioned in footnote 1 (repeated here as (22)) should be interpreted in a way parallel to the two sentences in (21a). Actually we do have a natural intuition that (22a) has a stronger meaning than (22b). However, it is evident that (22a) does not directly entail (22b).

(22)   a.   John is above 6 feet tall. $\lambda w. \text{HEIGHT}(\text{JOHN})(w) \subseteq [6', +\infty)$
        b.   John is between 4 and 5 feet tall. $\lambda w. \text{HEIGHT}(\text{JOHN})(w) \subseteq [4', 5']$

Under the current degree-QUD-based view on maximality of informativeness, I tease apart (i) the height measurement (typically with units like feet, meters, etc.) and (ii) the degree of tallness. Presumably, items of different comparison class can share the same scale for height measurement (e.g., the height of humans, giraffes, and mountains can be measured along the same scale and with the same units). However, the degrees of tallness and the comparison between them hinge on the notion of comparison class (e.g., toddlers are usually compared with other toddlers in terms of tallness). Thus it is evident that although '$\lambda w.\text{HEIGHT}(\text{JOHN})(w) \subseteq [6', +\infty)$' does not entail '$\lambda w.\text{HEIGHT}(\text{JOHN})(w) \subseteq [4', 5']$', under a degree QUD like *to what extent is John tall*, the measurement '$[6', +\infty)$' represents a higher degree in addressing this degree QUD and is thus more informative than '$[4', 5']$'. Therefore, our intuition that (22a) has a stronger meaning than (22b) can be accounted for.

For the core example (1), it is also worth noting that under the scenario of Fig. 1, although *exactly 3 boys saw exactly 5 movies* holds true, *exactly 1 boy saw exactly 4 movies* does not hold true (in Fig. 1, no boys saw more than 3 movies). Thus, this example also shows that it is problematic to build informativeness ordering directly upon the entailment relation between uttered sentences and their alternatives (derived by replacing uttered numbers with other numbers). However, *exactly 3 boys saw exactly 5 movies* does indicate a higher film consumption level (or a more prosperous situation) than the consumption level indicated by *exactly 1 boy saw exactly 4 movies*. Thus, the uttered sentence indicates a higher informativeness in addressing an underlying QUD than its alternatives. In this sense, with the use of a degree QUD, the current proposal provides a more generalized view on informativeness than an entailment-based one.

6   Extension: QUD-Based Informativeness and *even*

Beyond cumulative-reading sentences (and measurement sentences like (22)), here I use the case of *even* to show a broader empirical coverage of the proposed QUD-based view on maximality of informativeness (see also Zhang 2022).[3]

According to the traditional view on *even*, its use brings two presuppositions (and presuppositions are considered a kind of entailment): (i) **entity-based additivity** (see (23a)) and (ii) **likelihood-based scalarity** (see (23b)).

(23)   (It's not the case that) even [Mary]$_F$ came.

      a.   (23) $\models$ Someone other than Mary came.

      b.   (23) $\models$ Compared to others, Mary was unlikely to come.

However, it seems that the notion of entailment is too strong to characterize the meaning inferences with regard to the use of *even*. As illustrated by an example from Szabolcsi (2017), under the given scenario in (24), the use of an *even*-sentence in (25) is perfectly natural, but it challenges the traditional entailment-based view on our natural inferences for *even*-sentences. First,

---

[3] I thank an anonymous reviewer for raising this issue, which has led me to see this kind of connection that I missed before.

as shown in (25a), the presuppositional requirement of additivity is not met, because Eeyore was the only one who took a bite of thistles and spit them out. Second, if no one other than Eeyore took a bite of thistles, it seems also questionable to claim that the likelihood of the truth of the prejacent is lower than that of X *spit thistles out* ($X \in$ Alt(Eeyore)), as shown in (25b).

(24)   **Scenario:** Imagine Pooh and friends coming upon a bush of thistles. Eeyore (known to favor thistles) takes a bite but spits it out.

(25)   (Those thistles must be really prickly!) Even [Eeyore]$_F$ spit them out!

    a.   (25) $\not\models$ Someone other than Eeyore spit thistles out.

    b.   (25) $\not\models$ Compared to others, Eeyore was unlikely to spit thistles out.

Zhang (2022) proposes a degree-QUD-based analysis for the use of *even* (see Greenberg 2018 for a similar view). The use of *even* is always based on a contextually salient degree QUD (for (25), *how prickly are those thistles*). The prejacent of *even* (here *Eeyore spit those thistles out*) provides information to resolve this degree QUD with an increasingly positive answer, and compared with alternatives, this prejacent is also considered maximally informative in resolving this degree QUD. I.e., here compared to X *spit those thistles out* ($X \in$ Alt(Eeyore)), *Eeyore spit those thistles out* is maximally informative in resolving the degree question *how prickly are those thistles*.

Therefore, as illustrated in (26), the presupposition of *even* contains two parts. First, in all the accessible worlds where the prejacent is true, the range of the prickliness measurement of thistles, I_p, exceeds the threshold d_{stdd} (i.e., the degree QUD is resolved by the prejacent with a positive answer). Second, compared to I_q (i.e., the range of the prickleness measurement of thistles informed by an alternative statement X *spit thistles out*), I_p is maximally informative.[4]

(26)   The degree-QUD-based presupposition of *even* proposed by Zhang (2022):

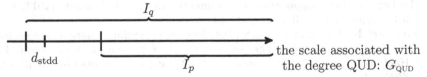

$$I_p = \text{Max}_{\text{info}}[\lambda I.[\forall w' \in \text{Acc}(w) \cap p[G_{\text{QUD}}(x_{\text{QUD}})(w') \subseteq I]]],$$
$$I_q = \text{Max}_{\text{info}}[\lambda I.[\forall w'' \in \text{Acc}(w) \cap q[G_{\text{QUD}}(x_{\text{QUD}})(w'') \subseteq I]]].$$

It is interesting to see that our interpretation for both cumulative-reading sentences and focus-related sentences can be based on the same degree-QUD-based mechanism of informativeness and demonstrate the maximality of informativeness.

---

[4] In Zhang (2022), I implement my analysis based on intervals, instead of degrees (see also Abrusán 2014; Schwarzschild and Wilkinson 2002; Zhang and Ling 2021).

7   Conclusion

Starting from the discussion on our intuitive interpretation for two kinds of cumulative-reading sentences, this paper proposes a degree-QUD-based view on the maximality of informativeness. The informativeness of a sentence basically stands for how the sentence resolves a contextually salient degree QUD.

For cumulative-reading sentences like *Exactly three boys saw exactly five movies*, its informativeness means the degree information in addressing *how high the film consumption level is among boys*, and the uttered numbers reflects mereological maximality. Then for cumulative-reading sentences like *In Guatemala, at most 3% of the population own at least 70% of the land*, its informativeness means rather the degree information in addressing *how skewed wealth distribution is in Guatemala*, and the uttered numbers reflects the maximality of the ratio between land and their owner population.

It seems that the current QUD-based view on the maximality of informativeness can overcome some issues that challenge the existing entailment-based view on informativeness and provide a broader empirical coverage. A further development of the current proposal to account for other related phenomena, especially with regard to the interpretation of numerals and focus items (e.g., *even*), as well as a more detailed discussion on its theoretical implications are left for future research.

References

Abrusán, M.: Weak island effects. OUP (2014). https://doi.org/10.1093/acprof:oso/9780199639380.001.0001

Brasoveanu, A.: Modified numerals as post-suppositions. J. Semant. **30**, 155–209 (2013). https://doi.org/10.1093/jos/ffs003

Bumford, D.: Split-scope definites: relative superlatives and Haddock descriptions. Linguist. Philos. **40**, 549–593 (2017). https://doi.org/10.1007/s10988-017-9210-2

Charlow, S.: Post-suppositions and semantic theory. J. Semant. (2017, in Press). https://ling.auf.net/lingbuzz/003243

von Fintel, K., Fox, D., Iatridou, S.: Definiteness as maximal informativeness. In: Crnič, L., Sauerland, U. (eds.) The Art and Craft of Semantics: A Festschrift for Irene Heim, vol. 2, pp. 175–179. Cambridge (2014). https://semanticsarchive.net/Archive/jZiNmM4N/

Greenberg, Y.: A revised, gradability-based semantics for even. Nat. Lang. Semant. **26**(1), 51–83 (2018) https://doi.org/10.1007/s11050-017-9140-0

Grindrod, J., Borg, E.: Questions under discussion and the semantics/pragmatics divide. Philos. Q. **69**(275), 418–426 (2019). https://doi.org/10.1093/pq/pqy058

Hendriks, P., De Hoop, H.: Optimality theoretic semantics. Linguist. Philos. **24**, 1–32 (2001). https://www.jstor.org/stable/25001802

Krifka, M.: At least some determiners aren't determiners. In: Tuner, K. (eds) The semantics/pragmatics interface from different points of view, vol. 1, 257–291. Elsevier (1999). https://semantics.uchicago.edu/kennedy/classes/w14/implicature/readings/krifka99.pdf

Roberts, C.: Information structure: towards an integrated formal theory of pragmatics. Semant. Pragmat. **5**, 6:1–69 (2012). https://doi.org/10.3765/sp.5.6

Schlenker, P.: Informativity-based maximality conditions. Snippets. **26**, 18–19 (2012). https://www.ledonline.it/snippets/allegati/snippets26007.pdf

Schwarzschild, R., Wilkinson, K.: Quantifiers in comparatives: a semantics of degree based on intervals. Nat. Lang. Semant. **10**, 1–41 (2002). https://doi.org/10.1023/A: 1015545424775

von Stechow, A.: Comparing semantic theories of comparison. J. Semant. **3**, 1–79 (1984). https://doi.org/10.1093/jos/3.1-2.1

de Swart, H.: Indefinites between predication and reference. Proc. SALT **9**, 273–297 (2006). https://doi.org/10.3765/salt.v9i0.2823

Szabolcsi, A.: Strategies for scope taking. In: Szabolcsi, A. (eds) Ways of Scope Taking, pp. 109–154. Springer, Cham (1997). https://doi.org/10.1007/978-94-011-5814-5_4

Szabolcsi, A.: Additive presuppositions are derived through activating focus alternatives. Proc. Amsterdam Colloquium **21**, 455–464 (2017). https://semanticsarchive. net/Archive/jZiM2FhZ/AC2017-Proceedings.pdf

Umbach, C.: Why do modified numerals resist a referential interpretation. Proc. SALT **15**, 258–275 (2006). https://doi.org/10.3765/salt.v15i0.2931

Zhang, L.: The presupposition of even. Proc. SALT **32**, 249–269 (2022). https://doi. org/10.3765/salt.v1i0.5355

Zhang, L.: Post-suppositions and uninterpretable questions. Proc. TLLM, 167–187 (2023). https://doi.org/10.1007/978-3-031-25894-7_9

Zhang, L., Ling, J.: The semantics of comparatives: A difference-based approach. J. Semant. **38**, 249–303 (2021). https://doi.org/10.1093/jos/ffab003

Events and Relative Clauses

Oleg Kiselyov[✉] [ID] and Haruki Watanabe

Tohoku University, Sendai, Japan
oleg@okmij.org

Abstract. This work is the continuation of the development of polynomial event semantics (a dialect of Neo-Davidsonian event semantics), using the FraCaS textual entailment corpus as a whetstone. This time we grapple with various, often complicated, relative clauses.

Relative clauses have hardly been analyzed before in event semantics. Although simple cases are straightforward, challenges arise when a clause contains quantification, coordination or negation. We deal with such complications in the present paper, focusing on entailments.

1 Introduction

This work is the continuation of [5–7] on polynomial event semantics and textual entailment.

Deciding entailments 'by pure logic' – without resorting to meaning postulates – is one of the most attractive features of event semantics. However, beyond the classical "Brutus stabbed Caesar violently", one quickly runs into problems. One is quantification, described and dealt with in [5,7]; another is negation [6]. Then there are relative clauses, which are rarely considered in event semantics. In fact, the recent survey [10] and the extensive study [3] give, among the multitude of examples, not a single analysis of a sentence with a relative clause.

A relative clause appears already in the very first problem in the FraCaS textual inference problem set [4,9]:

> There was an Italian who became the world's greatest tenor.

Such a simple case was analyzed in [7]. But even a slightly more complicated problem 018 below requires quite a non-trivial entailment reasoning involving the relative clause.

(1)	Every European has the right to live in Europe.
(2)	Every European is a person.
(3)	Every person who has the right to live in Europe can travel freely within Europe.
(4)	Every European can travel freely within Europe.

As in all FraCaS problems, the goal is to determine the entailment of the last sentence (in our case, (4)) from the others. We must stress that FraCaS collects

D. Bekki et al. (Eds.): LENLS 2019, LNCS 14213, pp. 18–30, 2023.
https://doi.org/10.1007/978-3-031-43977-3_2

not only positive examples of expected entailments, but also negative examples where entailment does not hold – and also "yes and no" cases where entailment comes through only on some readings. Our goal is hence not only to derive entailments where expected, but also to explain why entailment does not hold in negative examples, as well as to reproduce several readings where present.

FraCaS has quite a few problems similar to the above, with copula relative clauses (problems 005, 006, 028) and quantifiers like 'most' (problem 074). Object relative clauses also appear (e.g., problems 133 and 344):

> There is someone whom Helen saw answer the phone.
>
> ITEL maintains all the computers that GFI owns.

There are further complications, with quantified or coordinated relative clauses:

(5)   There was one auditor who signed all the reports.

(6)   There is a car that John and Bill own.

(7)   There is a representative that Smith wrote to every week.

We take FraCaS as a whetstone of a semantic theory, as a necessary application – but by no means sufficient. For example, NPs of the following form are quite common, but do not appear in FraCaS:

(8)   two students who skipped three classes

(9)   every student who skipped no classes

(10)   a student who didn't skip all classes

One should be able to analyze them and derive entailments. A reviewer has pointed further interesting examples, such as

(11)   land he had created and lived in

The present paper gives analysis of all such sentences and NPs, focusing on entailments.

2   Background

First a brief reminder of polynomial event semantics. It deals with events, notated e, such as 'having become the world's greatest tenor' or 'being Italian' or 'having the right to live in Europe' (we denote the latter set of events as RtIE). It should be clear that we take events in a broad sense (as detailed in [10]): associated not only with actions but also states. Besides events, there are also individuals, notated i, such as john, and relations between events and individuals (written as rel') such as

$$\mathsf{subj}' = \{(e, i) \mid \mathsf{ag}(e) = i\} \qquad \mathsf{obl}' = \{(e, i) \mid \mathsf{th}(e) = i\}$$

where ag and th are thematic functions (for subjects and direct objects, resp.). Their names are mere the nod to the tradition in the event semantics literature (see §7).

If rel′ is a relation of events to individuals,

$$\mathsf{rel'}/i \triangleq \{e \mid (e, i) \in \mathsf{rel'}\}$$

is the set of events related to i. In particular,

$$\mathsf{subj'}/\mathsf{john} = \{e \mid (e, \mathsf{john}) \in \mathsf{subj'}\} = \{e \mid \mathsf{ag}(e) = \mathsf{john}\}$$

is the set of events whose subject is john. The semantics of a simple sentence such as "John has the right to live in Europe" is given compositionally as

$$[\![\text{John has the right to live in Europe}]\!] =$$

(12) $$\mathsf{subj'}/\mathsf{john} \cap \mathsf{RtlE}$$

Subject, predicate, complements all denote event sets, and the whole sentence is their intersection. In particular, our sentence denotes – or, is witnessed by – the events of having the right to live in Europe whose subject is John. The denotation is hence an event set – or the formula representing it, as (12), which one may think of as a query of the record of events in the world. A sentence is true in that world just in case the result of the query is a non-empty event set.

The denotation of the subject is also determined compositionally, by applying subj′ to the denotation of NP, in our case, john.

If d_1 and d_2 are two denotations (queries), we say d_1 entails d_2 (in symbols: $d_1 \implies d_2$) just in case for any record of events (for any world), whenever d_1 delivers a non-empty set of witnessing events, so does d_2. If d_1 and d_2 entail each other, they are called equivalent.

2.1   Coordination and Quantification

We often deal not with individuals but with sets of individuals such as Student or European, which are the denotations of common nouns. Determiners pick which individuals from this set to consider. Correspondingly, they call for generalization: the introduction of (internal) choice $\sqcup$ (for narrow-scope existentials and indefinites), external choice $\oplus$ (wide-scope ones) and grouping $\otimes$. Thus john$\sqcup$bill is a choice between John and Bill, whereas john$\otimes$bill is a group of John and Bill: both have to be involved, not necessarily in the same action however. Likewise, event sets are generalized to *polyconcepts*, such as $d_1 \otimes d_2$ for two disjoint event sets d_1 and d_2, which specifies that an event from d_1 *and* an event from d_2 must have transpired. Grouping is quite different from intersection $\cap$ (generalized to $\sqcap$ for polyconcepts), which describes common events. In particular, if d is a singleton event set, then $d \otimes d = \bot$ (the empty polyconcept), but $d \sqcap d = d$.

We define for convenience

$$\mathcal{E}c = \sqcup_{j \in c}\, j \qquad \mathcal{I}c = \oplus_{j \in c}\, j \qquad \mathcal{A}c = \otimes_{j \in c}\, j$$

The meaning of "All Europeans/Every European" is then $\mathcal{A}$ European; on the other hand, [A European] (narrow scope) is $\mathcal{E}$ European. Therefore, (1), repeated below

(1)   Every European has the right to live in Europe.

has as its denotation

$$(\text{subj}'/\,\mathcal{A}\text{European}) \sqcap \text{RtlE}$$
$$= \mathcal{A}(\text{subj}'/\,\text{European}) \sqcap \text{RtlE}$$
(13) $= \bigotimes_{i \in \text{European}} (\text{subj}'/\,i \cap \text{RtlE})$

where $\sqcap$ is the generalization of set intersection $\cap$ to polyconcepts; $\text{subj}'/$ is likewise generalized to apply to sets of individuals and poly-individuals – as homomorphism.

The distribution laws detailed in [7] lead to (13), which asserts there is a group of non-empty events of having right to live in Europe, and each European is a subject of some event in that group.

The notion of entailment extends to polyconcepts: The polyconcept d_1 entails d_2 just in case $d_1 \neq \bot \implies d_2 \neq \bot$. For example, [7] described several equational laws of polyconcepts, among whose is

$$x \otimes \bot = \bot \otimes x = \bot$$

from which it logically follows that

(14) $x \otimes y \neq \bot \implies x \neq \bot$

That is, (13) entails $\text{subj}'/\,i \cap \text{RtlE}$ for any individual $i \in \text{European}$. In other words, if John is European, (1) entails that "John has the right to live in Europe".

2.2 Negation

The central idea of polynomial event semantics is that the sentence denotation is a query (formula), which when applied to the record of events in a world, selects the events that support, or witness, the sentence. If that set of events turns out empty, the sentence is not supported (in that world). Negation hence presents a problem: what is the witness for the absence of support?

Our resolution [6] is to consider counter-examples. The denotation of a sentence with negation or negative quantification is also a query, but what it selects is interpreted as counter-examples. If the set of counter-examples is empty, the corresponding sentence is not contradicted. To distinguish counter-example-selecting queries and polyconcepts, they are marked with the $\neg$ sign.

For example, the denotation of (15) below is (16), which can be re-written to (17) according to the laws of [6].

(15)   John didn't skip the PE class.

(16) $\text{subj}'/\,\text{john} \sqcap \neg\,\text{Skip} \sqcap \text{ob1}'/\,\text{peClass}$

(17) $= \neg\,(\text{subj}'/\,\text{john} \sqcap \text{Skip} \sqcap \text{ob1}'/\,\text{peClass})$

Likewise, the denotation for (18) is (19):

(18)   John didn't skip every class.

(19) $\neg \bigotimes_{i \in \mathsf{Class}} (\mathsf{subj}'/\mathsf{john} \sqcap \mathsf{Skip} \sqcap \mathsf{ob1}'/i)$

Indeed, the counter-example for (18) would be a group of John skipping class events, for each class.

Negation calls for further generalization of entailment. If d_1 and d_2 are poly-concepts marked as negative, $d_1 \implies d_2$ just in case $d_2 \neq \bar{\bot} \implies d_1 \neq \bar{\bot}$: whenever d_2 is contradicted, then so is d_1. We thus obtain that (15) entails (18).

Suppose that Attend and Skip are disjoint event sets. Then if "John attended the PE class" is supported, "John didn't skip the PE class" cannot be contradicted. For the sake of such entailments, we introduce (see [6, 7])

(20) $\mathrm{justified}(d) = \begin{cases} d = \bar{\bot} & \text{if } d \text{ is marked as negative} \\ d \neq \bot & \text{if } d \text{ is not negatively marked} \end{cases}$

which lets us define entailment most generally: d_1 entails d_2 just in case $\mathrm{justified}(d_1)$ logically entails $\mathrm{justified}(d_2)$. For example, we may now derive that "John attended the PE class" entails (18).

3   Subject Relative Clauses

The problem is hence determining the meaning of "who has the right to live in Europe." If RtlE is the set of events of having the right to live in Europe, then who has that right is the subject of these events. Thus the denotation of our subject relative clause, to be notated as $\overline{\mathsf{subj}}'/\mathsf{RtlE}$, is the set of individuals

(21) $\overline{\mathsf{subj}}'/\mathsf{RtlE} \triangleq \{\mathsf{ag}(e) \mid e \in \mathsf{RtlE}\}$

Then (3), recalled below,

(3)   Every person who has the right to live in Europe
                    can travel freely within Europe.

has as its denotation

(22) $\mathsf{subj}'/\mathcal{A}\left(\mathsf{Person} \cap (\overline{\mathsf{subj}}'/\mathsf{RtlE})\right) \sqcap \mathsf{CtfE}$

where CtfE is the set of events of having the possibility to freely travel within Europe. This analysis is more or less what was described in [7], but recast now in simpler terms. It takes us quite far: many more FraCaS problems can be analyzed similarly.

However, relative clauses with quantifiers, coordination or negation present a problem. Again we need to generalize. Remembering the definition of the subj$'$ relation, we may re-write (21) as

$$\overline{\text{subj}}'/\text{RtIE} \triangleq \{\text{ag}(e) \mid e \in \text{RtIE}\}$$
$$= \{i \mid e \in \text{RtIE}, (i, e) \in \text{subj}'\}$$
$$= \{i \mid \text{subj}'/i \cap \text{RtIE} \neq \varnothing\}$$

One may notice that subj$'/i \cap$ RtIE is exactly the meaning of "i has the right to live in Europe". That is, "who has the right to live in Europe" is the set of those i in the domain of the subj$'$ who make the sentence true (in the world of the discourse). The denotation of a subject relative clause "who C" may hence be defined as

(23) $[\![\text{who } C]\!] \triangleq \overline{\text{subj}}'/[\![C]\!] = \{i \mid \text{subj}'/i \cap [\![C]\!] \neq \varnothing\}$

This is already helpful, to solve FraCaS 018, which is, recall

(1)   Every European has the right to live in Europe.
(2)   Every European is a person.
           Every person who has the right to live in Europe
(3)   can travel freely within Europe.
(4)   Every European can travel freely within Europe.

For (1) we have earlier obtained the denotation (13), which says that subj$'/i \cap$ RtIE is non-empty for all $i \in$ European. Then (23) immediately gives European $\subset \overline{\text{subj}}'/\text{RtIE}$; in words: the set of who has the right to live in Europe includes all Europeans. Likewise, (2) gives European $\subset$ Person, leading to European $\subset$ (Person $\cap \overline{\text{subj}}'/\text{RtIE}$). Then, by monotonicity of $\mathcal{A}$, (22) entails subj$'/(\mathcal{A}$European$) \sqcap$ CtfE, which is the denotation of (4). The entailment of (4) from the other sentences of the problem indeed holds.

Definition (23), unlike (21), now easily generalizes to the case when the denotation of the rest of the clause d is not an event set but a polyconcept with choice or grouping:

(24) $[\![\text{who } C]\!] \triangleq \overline{\text{subj}}'/[\![C]\!] = \{i \mid \text{subj}'/i \sqcap [\![C]\!] \neq \bot\}$

The generalization lets us analyze quantified and coordinated relative clauses such as (5)-(7). For example, for (5), repeated below,

(5)   There was one auditor who signed all the reports.

we obtain the denotation ($\mathcal{E}$Be is an existence event, see [7])

$$\text{subj}'/\mathcal{E}\left(\text{Auditor} \cap \overline{\text{subj}}'/(\text{Sign} \sqcap \text{ob1}'/\mathcal{A}\text{Report})\right) \sqcap \mathcal{E}\,\text{Be}$$

where, to remind, $\overline{\text{subj}}'/(\text{Sign} \sqcap \text{ob1}'/\mathcal{A}\text{Report})$ is a set of those individuals i such that

$$[\![i \text{ signed all the reports}]\!] = \text{subj}'/i \sqcap \text{Sign} \sqcap \text{ob1}'/\mathcal{A}\text{Report}$$

is justified. By the very construction, the scope of the universal does not extend past its clause. We return to this example in §5 and show a more intuitive, and useful for entailment, analysis.

4 Other Relative Clauses

The approach introduced in §3 easily extends to object, locative, etc. relative clauses. A good example to illustrate is as follows, also containing an interesting case of coordination:[1]

> The land over which he sped was
>   the land he had created and lived in: his valley.

We concentrate on one constituent:

(25)   land he had created and lived in

Section 2 already introduced the relation ob1$'$ between an action and its direct object; analogous to it is the relation inloc$'$ between an action and an individual denoting location. Let Land be the set of such location-individuals. Similarly to (24) we may then define

$$(26) \qquad [\![\text{which } C]\!] \triangleq \overline{\text{ob1}}'/[\![C]\!] \triangleq \{i \mid \text{ob1}'/i \sqcap [\![C]\!] \neq \bot\}$$

$$(27) \qquad [\![\text{in which } C]\!] \triangleq \overline{\text{inloc}}'/[\![C]\!] \triangleq \{i \mid \text{inloc}'/i \sqcap [\![C]\!] \neq \bot\}$$

which gives us

$$[\![\text{land he had created}]\!] = \text{Land} \cap \overline{\text{ob1}}'/(\text{subj}'/\text{He} \sqcap \text{Created})$$
$$(28) \qquad = \text{Land} \cap \{i \mid \text{subj}'/\text{He} \sqcap \text{Created} \sqcap \text{ob1}'/i \neq \bot\}$$

$$[\![\text{land he had lived in}]\!] = \text{Land} \cap \overline{\text{inloc}}'/(\text{subj}'/\text{He} \sqcap \text{Lived})$$
$$(29) \qquad = \text{Land} \cap \{i \mid \text{subj}'/\text{He} \sqcap \text{Lived} \sqcap \text{inloc}'/i \neq \bot\}$$

where He is a particular individual to which the pronoun "he" is resolved. The repetitiveness and boilerplate are apparent: generalization is in order.

We have been assigning the denotation to a sentence in a surface form – at least, how it appeared so far. In reality, we take as input a parse tree, with Penn-treebank–like annotations (see [2]). For example, "land he had created" and "land he had lived in" are represented as:

(30) $\text{land}_N\, [_{\text{IP-REL}}\, [_{\text{NP-SBJ}}\, \text{he}_{\text{PRO}}]\, \text{had}_{\text{HVD}}\, [_{\text{NP-OB1}}\, \text{T}]\, \text{created}_{\text{VVN}}]$

(31) $\text{land}_N\, [_{\text{IP-REL}}\, [_{\text{NP-SBJ}}\, \text{he}_{\text{PRO}}]\, \text{had}_{\text{HVD}}\, \text{lived}_{\text{VVN}}\, [_{\text{PP-LOC}}\, \text{in}_{\text{P-ROLE}}\, [_{\text{NP}}\, \text{T}]]]$

---

[1] from Clifford Irving, The Valley (1961) – sentence 170 of susanne_N02 included in [2].

where T is the trace. Denotations (28) and (29) then clearly correspond to the annotated trees (30) and (31), resp. In fact, they are built as follows:

$$[\![\text{land}_N]\!] = \text{Land} \quad [\![\text{created}_{VVN}]\!] = \text{Created} \quad [\![\text{lived}_{VVN}]\!] = \text{Lived}$$

$$[\![_{NP\text{-}SBJ}\,\text{he}_{PRO}]\!]\!] = \text{subj}'/\,[\![\text{he}_{PRO}]\!] = \text{subj}'/\,\text{He}$$

$$[\![_{NP\text{-}OB1}\,i]\!]\!] = \text{ob1}'/\,i \quad [\![_{PP\text{-}LOC}\,\text{in}_{P\text{-}ROLE}\,[_{NP}\,i]]\!]\!] = \text{inloc}/\,i$$

(32) $$[\![_{IP\text{-}REL}\,C]\!]\!] = \{i \mid [C/i] \neq \bot\}$$

where C/i means replacing the trace with i. (Aspect/tense is out of scope, and the auxiliary had$_{HVD}$ is ignored.) Connections of any constituents are uniformly represented as the intersection ($\cap$ or $\sqcap$) of their denotations. Therefore, for the original clause (25) we have:[2]

(33) $$[\![(25)]\!] = \text{Land} \cap \{i \mid \text{subj}'/\,\text{He}\,\sqcap$$
$$((\text{Created} \sqcap \text{ob1}'/\,i) \otimes (\text{Lived} \sqcap \text{inloc}/\,i)) \neq \bot\}$$

which lets us do entailments. For example, from (28) and (14), we obtain that

$$[\![(25)]\!] \subset [\![\text{the land he created}]\!]$$

There remains a puzzle, however: (32) seems postulated, with the operation C/i of trace substitution coming out of the blue. It is also hardly compositional. We now describe how (32) comes about, and how to derive denotations (28), (29) and (33) and others like them rigorously and compositionally. We will also see what is the denotation of trace after all.

4.1   Relative Algebra

Recall, to give denotations in the polynomial event semantics we use the algebra of polyconcepts (denoted by the metavariable d) with the operations $\bot$, $\oplus$, $\otimes$, $\sqcap$ and $\sqcup$. Strictly speaking, there are two algebras: their operations are the same, but generators differ: individuals vs. event sets. The two algebras are homomorphic: the operations subj$'/\cdot$, ob1$'/\cdot$, etc. are the homomorphisms.

We now introduce yet another algebra – called relative algebra – whose carrier are relations between individuals and polyconcepts: sets of pairs (i, d) where i is an individual ranging over $\mathbb{I}$, the set of all individuals. The operations of the relative algebra are the lifted operations on polyconcepts: $\bot$ of relative algebra is $\{(i, \bot) \mid i \in \mathbb{I}\}$, and

$$\{(i, d_1) \mid i \in \mathbb{I}\} \sqcap \{(i, d_2) \mid i \in \mathbb{I}\} = \{(i, d_1 \sqcap d_2) \mid i \in \mathbb{I}\}$$

and similarly for the other operations. Relative algebra is clearly homomorphic to a polyconcept algebra: for each polyconcept d there is a corresponding (we say, 'lifted') element of the relative algebra:

$$d \rightarrow \{(i, d) \mid i \in \mathbb{I}\}$$

---

[2] The annotated form is https://oncoj.orinst.ox.ac.uk/cgi-bin/tspc.sh?tree=170_susa nne_N02@21\&mode=clip.

with the algebra operations commuting with lifting, as we already observed. Relative algebra also has elements that are not lifted polyconcepts. Among them is so-called t^r:

$$t^r \triangleq \{(i,i) \mid i \in \mathbb{I}\}$$

Let $[\![C]\!]_{rel}$ be the denotation of a clause/constituent C in terms of relative algebra. It is built compositionally, mostly from the lifted denotations of its sub-constituents; the exception is the denotation of trace, which is t^r. The denotation of a relative clause is then

(34) $$[\![{}_{\text{IP-REL}} \, C]\!] \triangleq \{i \mid (i,d) \in [\![C]\!]_{rel}, d \neq \bot\}$$

This is the compositional analogue of (32): with it and the denotation of trace as t^r, we may build denotations of arbitrary relative clauses. In particular, the denotation of (25) works out to be exactly (33).

5   Relative Clauses, Database Joins, and Trace as a Wide-Scope Indefinite

We now show two other, related, points of view on relative clauses. One treats relative clauses as database joins. The other regards trace as a wide-scope indefinite, and separates out the relative clause into an independent sentence, to which the original sentence anaphorically refers.

Relative clauses are NP modifiers: for example, in "land (that) he created", the relative clause modifies the common noun "land". As described earlier, polynomial event semantics derives the compositional denotation

(35) $[\![\text{land}_N \, [_{\text{IP-REL}} \text{ he created T}]]\!] = [\![\text{land}_N]\!] \cap [\![[_{\text{IP-REL}} \text{ he created T}]]\!]$

(The denotation of the relative clause is also derived compositionally per (34).) Since the trace is related to "land", one may wonder about a way to reflect that relation in the denotation. Although this breaks compositionality to some (small) extent, the insight seems worth it.

Among operations of the (relative) polyconcept algebra, $\oplus$ stands out: it distributes across/commutes with any other operation. For example, letting d_{hc} be $\text{subj}'/\text{He} \sqcap \text{Created}$,

(36) $[\![\text{He created a}_W \text{ land}]\!] = d_{hc} \sqcap \text{ob1}'/\mathcal{I}\text{Land}$

$$\equiv d_{hc} \sqcap \text{ob1}'/ \left(\bigoplus\nolimits_{j \in \text{Land}} j \right) = \bigoplus\nolimits_{j \in \text{Land}} (d_{hc} \sqcap \text{ob1}'/j)$$

where a_W is a wide-scope indefinite. Let

$$\delta_{ij} = \begin{cases} i & \text{if } i = j \\ \bot & \text{otherwise} \end{cases} = i \sqcap j$$

which is a bona fide polyconcept. Let us introduce a 'lifted' $\mathcal{I}$:

$$\mathcal{I}^r S \triangleq \left\{ \left(i, \bigoplus\nolimits_{j \in S} \delta_{ij}\right) \mid i \in \mathbb{I} \right\}$$

and note that

(37) $\{(i, d_{hc}) \mid i \in \mathbb{I}\} \sqcap \text{ob1}' / \mathcal{I}^r \text{Land}$

$$= \{(i, \bigoplus_{j \in \text{Land}} (d_{hc} \sqcap \text{ob1}' / \delta_{ij})) \mid i \in \mathbb{I}\}$$

looks like a relative algebra denotation of some clause, which we call C_{hcal} for the time being. Treating it as if it were a relative clause

$$[\![\text{IP-REL} \, C_{hcal}]\!] = \{i \mid (i, d) \in [\![C_{hcal}]\!]_{rel}, d \neq \bot\}$$

$$= \{i \mid \bigoplus_{j \in \text{Land}} (d_{hc} \sqcap \text{ob1}' / \delta_{ij}) \neq \bot\}$$

$$= \{i \mid i \in \text{Land}, d_{hc} \sqcap \text{ob1}' / i \neq \bot\}$$

$$= \text{Land} \cap [\![\text{IP-REL} \text{ he created T}]\!]$$

gives an interesting result: on one hand, the denotation of "land he created" may be computed compositionally per (35), from $[\![\text{land}_N]\!]$ and the denotation of the proper relative clause (with trace interpreted as t^r). On the other hand, the entire $[\![\text{land}_N \, [\text{IP-REL} \text{ he created T}]]\!]$ can be computed in one scoop, as the denotation of a "relative clause" C_{hcal}, as we have just shown. What is C_{hcal} then? Comparing (37) with (36) we notice they are almost the same: only the former uses relative algebra, and instead of a_W, denoted by $\mathcal{I}$, we have something else, denoted by $\mathcal{I}^r$. One may call it a_W^r: a wide scope indefinite to which one may refer to. We thus obtained that "land he created" – the relative clause together with the modified noun – is related to an independent sentence "he created a_W^r land". In fact, it is a set of referents created by the indefinite a_W^r of that sentence.

Hence, speaking in database terms, relative clause is a join. Using a FraCaS example, the denotation of (3) may be regarded as a database join, of "A person has the right to live in Europe." with "can travel freely within Europe" on subject. Such database join may be illustrated by a (bit contrived) paraphrase: "Some people have the right to live in Europe. Every one of them can travel freely within Europe." That is, the relative clause is moved out into a separate sentence, with the trace filled with a (wide-scope) indefinite. The original sentence anaphorically refers to that indefinite. One can generalize: "It builds up muscles people thought didn't exist." to paraphrase as "People thought some muscles didn't exists. It builds up them."

This replacement of trace with the indefinite leads to a variety of analyses. Returning to (5), repeated below,

(5)   There was one auditor who signed all the reports.

we obtain the denotation

$\text{subj}' / \mathcal{E} [\![\text{auditor who signed all the reports}]\!] \sqcap \mathcal{E} \, \text{Be}$

where $\mathcal{E} \text{Be}$ is an existence event (see [7]). This denotation is equivalent to $[\![\text{auditor who signed all the reports}]\!]$, which is equivalent to $[\![a_W^r \text{ auditor signed all the reports}]\!]$. In other words, (5) is equivalent to, or mutually entails, "One particular auditor/the same auditor signed all the reports" – which is what FraCaS problem 196 is all about.

Similarly, we obtain that (6) is equivalent to "John and Bill own the same car". For problem 308, we obtain (7) is equivalent to "Smith wrote to a representative every week." on the wide-scope reading of the indefinite – with no entailment for the narrow-scope reading.

6   Negation in Relative Clauses

Negation calls for one more generalization of (24) and related denotations:

$$[\![\text{who } C]\!] \triangleq \overline{\text{subj}}'/[\![C]\!] = \{i \mid \text{justified}(\text{subj}'/i \sqcap [\![C]\!])\}$$

We calculate, for example

$$[\![\text{student who didn't skip all classes}]\!]$$
$$= \text{Student} \cap \overline{\text{subj}}'/[\![\text{didn't skip all classes}]\!]$$
$$= \text{Student} \cap \{i \mid \text{justified}(\text{subj}'/i \sqcap (\neg \text{Skip} \sqcap \text{ob1}'/\mathcal{A}\text{Class}))\}$$
$$= \text{Student} \cap \{i \mid \text{justified}(\neg(\text{subj}'/i \sqcap \text{Skip} \sqcap \text{ob1}'/\mathcal{A}\text{Class}))\}$$
$$= \text{Student} \cap \{i \mid \neg(\text{subj}'/i \sqcap \text{Skip} \sqcap \text{ob1}'/\mathcal{A}\text{Class}) = \bar{\perp}\}$$
$$= \text{Student} \cap \{i \mid \text{subj}'/i \sqcap \text{Skip} \sqcap \text{ob1}'/\mathcal{A}\text{Class}) = \perp\}$$

by unrolling definitions and applying the distributive laws of negation touched upon in Sect. 2.2. Comparing with

$$[\![\text{students who skipped all classes}]\!]$$
$$= \text{Student} \cap \{i \mid \text{justified}(\text{subj}'/i \sqcap \text{Skip} \sqcap \text{ob1}'/\mathcal{A}\text{Class})\}$$
$$= \text{Student} \cap \{i \mid \text{subj}'/i \sqcap \text{Skip} \sqcap \text{ob1}'/\mathcal{A}\text{Class} \neq \perp\}$$

we easily see that the two sets are complementary. Likewise, "student who skipped no classes" is the complement of the set of students who skipped a class.

7   Related Work, Discussion and Conclusions

Semantic and syntactic analyses are often tightly coupled: e.g., lexical entries are assigned syntactic categories or features, as well as semantic interpretations (often as lambda-terms). Examples include various categorial-grammar–based analyses (see [8] for the latest example), minimalist grammars ([12] for the latest), etc. As a result, semantic analysis is coupled to a particular parsing technique. In contrast, we, like Butler's Treebank semantics [1], start with an already parsed sentence: to be precise, Penn-treebank–like annotated tree (see [2] for details on annotations). The annotations can be assigned manually or by any appropriate parser (e.g., Stanford CoreNLP [1]). Starting from an annotated sentence is also common in dependency-tree–based approaches, see [11]. (Our approach can also be adapted to dependency trees).

Closest to our work is the dependency-tree semantics of Tian et al. [11], who also represent the meaning of a sentence as an abstract query. The paper [11] briefly mentions relative clauses, analyzed along the lines of (21). Our and dependency-tree semantics diverge when it comes to quantification and coordination: we depart relational algebra for polyconcepts, expressing grouping and choice.

Analyses of relative clauses in event semantics are rare. One of the few is the relatively recent [12, §4.2.1 and §6], which uses Minimalist Grammar coupled with a continuation-based approach (in the spirit of [3]).

As a nod to the tradition, Sect. 2 mentioned thematic functions ag and th when defining the subj′ and obl′ relations. These relations are meant to be grammatical subject and object relations, with ag specifying the grammatical subject of an action carried by a verb, rather than the semantic agent. After all, event semantics is widely praised for avoiding meaning postulates as far as possible and deriving entailments from the structure alone. Likewise, the focus of FraCaS is textual entailment without relying on world knowledge. We, too, concentrate on the structure: Just as verbs have arguments, events – records in a world database – have attributes. The functions ag and th, etc. merely refer to these attributes. As a consequence, we treat active and passive VP as completely separate, and do not consider entailments between active and passive forms of the same verb. In the future, we may introduce a postulate that, say, for any event $e \in$ See there exists an event $e' \in$ BeSeen such that $\mathsf{ag}(e') = \mathsf{th}(e)$ and $\mathsf{intstr}(e') = \mathsf{ag}(e)$. One may also deal with passive constructions syntactically: convert passive construction to active at parsing time (see Prithiviraj Damodaran's Styleformer based on Stanford CoreNLP.)

In conclusion, we demonstrated handling of relative clauses in polynomial event semantics, from simple to coordinated and quantified. The approach handles the subject, object, locative, etc. relative clauses. Extension to tense/time is straightforward. Future work is the mechanical implementation of the approach to derive the entailments automatically.

Acknowledgments. We are very grateful to the reviewers and the participants of LENLS19 for their insightful comments and questions. We particularly appreciate the interesting examples to analyze (Sect. 4) pointed out by a reviewer. This work was partially supported by a JSPS KAKENHI Grant Number 17K00091.

References

1. Butler, A.: From discourse to logic with stanford CoreNLP and treebank semantics. In: Sakamoto, M., Okazaki, N., Mineshima, K., Satoh, K. (eds.) JSAI-isAI 2019. LNCS (LNAI), vol. 12331, pp. 182–196. Springer, Cham (2020). https://doi.org/10.1007/978-3-030-58790-1_12

2. Butler, A.: The treebank semantics parsed corpus (TSPC). https://entrees.github.io (2022)
3. Champollion, L.: The interaction of compositional semantics and event semantics. Linguist. Philos. **38**(1), 31–66 (2015)
4. Cooper, R., et al.: Using the framework. Deliverable D16, FraCaS Project (1996)
5. Kiselyov, O.: Polynomial event semantics. In: Kojima, K., Sakamoto, M., Mineshima, K., Satoh, K. (eds.) JSAI-isAI 2018. LNCS (LNAI), vol. 11717, pp. 313–324. Springer, Cham (2019). https://doi.org/10.1007/978-3-030-31605-1_23
6. Kiselyov, O.: Polynomial event semantics: negation. In: Okazaki, N., Yada, K., Satoh, K., Mineshima, K. (eds.) JSAI-isAI 2020. LNCS (LNAI), vol. 12758, pp. 82–95. Springer, Cham (2021). https://doi.org/10.1007/978-3-030-79942-7_6
7. Kiselyov, O., Watanabe, H.: QNP textual entailment with polynomial event semantics. In: Yada, K., Takama, Y., Mineshima, K., Satoh, K. (eds.) JSAI-isAI 2021. LNCS (LNAI), vol. 13856, pp. 198–211. Springer, Cham (2023). https://doi.org/10.1007/978-3-031-36190-6_14
8. Kubota, Y., Levine, R.D.: Type-Logical Syntax. The MIT Press, Cambridge, MA (2020)
9. MacCartney, B.: The FRACAS textual inference problem set. https://nlp.stanford.edu/~wcmac/downloads/fracas.xml
10. Maienborn, C.: Event semantics, chap. 8, pp. 232–266. Semantics - Theories, De Gruyter Mouton (2019). https://doi.org/10.1515/9783110589245-008
11. Tian, R., Miyao, Y., Matsuzaki, T.: Logical inference on dependency-based compositional semantics. In: ACL (1), pp. 79–89. The Association for Computer Linguistics (2014). http://aclweb.org/anthology/P/P14/
12. Tomita, Y.: Solving event quantification and free variable problems in semantics for minimalist grammars. In: Proceedings of the 30th Pacific Asia Conference on Language, Information and Computation, PACLIC 30: Oral Papers, pp. 219–227. ACL, Seoul, South Korea (2016), https://aclanthology.org/Y16-2020/

The Semantic Markedness of the Japanese Negative Preterite: Non-existence of (Positive) Eventualities vs. Existence of Negative Eventualities

David Y. Oshima$^{(\boxtimes)}$ (iD)

Graduate School of Humanities, Nagoya University, Nagoya 464-8601, Japan
davidyo@nagoya-u.jp
http://www.hum.nagoya-u.ac.jp/~oshima

Abstract. In Japanese, the use of a negative preterite (past-perfective) clause ("...V *nakatta*") is discourse-pragmatically constrained, and oftentimes a negative nonpast-nonperfective clause ("...V-*te inai*") is used where a preterite clause is expected. At the descriptive level, a negative preterite can be characterized as conveying that the described eventuality was plausible (though did not happen) at some past time. This work argues that the Japanese negative preterite predicate invariably expresses the existence (occurrence) of a "negative eventuality", as opposed to the non-existence (non-occurrence) of eventualities, and that the "plausibility implication" is a side effect of this feature. It will be furthermore argued that, while Japanese nonpast-tensed clauses generally specify that the topic time is some nonpast time, this does not necessarily apply to nonpast-nonperfective clauses, making it possible for a negative nonpast-nonperfective clause to express the non-existence of eventualities in a past topic time.

1 Introduction

In Japanese, the use of a negative preterite (also called "past perfective" or "simple past") clause is discourse-pragmatically constrained, and oftentimes a negative nonpast-nonperfective (present-nonperfective) clause with -*te* IRU[1] is used where a preterite clause is expected (Matsuda 2002, Yamashita 2004, Kusumoto 2016).

To illustrate, the preterite in ($1B_a$) sounds unnatural, conveying something to the effect that the speaker *could have* hired a new nurse; a nonpast-nonperfective clause is not pragmatically loaded in the same way, as seen in ($1B_b$) (the initial vowel of the auxiliary IRU is often dropped in colloquial speech).[2]

---

[1] IRU is a "nonperfective" auxiliary that may receive a wide array of interpretations, including resulting state, progressive, habitual, and perfect (Sect. 4).

[2] The abbreviations in glosses are: Acc = accusative, Attr = attributive, Aux = auxiliary, BenAux = benefactive auxiliary, DAux = discourse auxiliary, Dat = dative,

D. Bekki et al. (Eds.): LENLS 2019, LNCS 14213, pp. 31–50, 2023.
https://doi.org/10.1007/978-3-031-43977-3_3

(1)   (A and B are medical practitioners.)

A: Anta no   tokoro, sengetsu   atarashii kangoshi yatotta?
   you Gen place   last.month new.Npst nurse   hire.Pst
   'Did you hire a new nurse at your clinic last month?'

B$_a$: ??E? [**Yatowanakatta**]$_{preterite}$ yo.   Nande?
   Intj hire.Neg.Pst   DPrt why
   'Huh? I didn't hire anyone. Why?'

B$_b$: E? [**Yatotte (i)nai**]$_{nonpast.nonperfective}$ yo.   Nande?
   Intj hire.Ger NpfvAux.Neg.Npst   DPrt why
   'Huh? I didn't hire anyone. Why?'

(2) illustrates that a negative preterite can be naturally used in a context where it was previously plausible (from the interlocutors' viewpoint) that the logical contradiction of the propositional content would hold true.

(2)   A: Senshuu mensetsu shita hito,   doo natta?   Yatou
   last.week interview do.Pst person how become.Pst employ.NPst
   koto   ni   shita no?
   matter Cop.Inf do.Pst DAux
   'What happened to that person who you interviewed last week? Did you decide to hire him?'

B: Iya, ano hito   wa (kekkyoku) **yatowanakatta**.
   no that person Th after.all   employ.Neg.Pst
   'No, I did not hire him(, after all).'

To provide further illustration, (3B$_a$) with a preterite predicate cannot, and (3B$_b$) with a nonpast-nonperfective predicate can, be naturally followed by (4a). Both (3B$_a$) and (3B$_b$) can be naturally followed by (4b).

(3)   A: Yuube   nomikai   ni   itta?
   last.evening drinking.party Dat go.Pst
   'Did you go to the drinking party last evening?'

B$_a$: Iya, [**ikanakatta**]$_{preterite}$.
   no go.Neg.Pst
   'No, I did not go.'

B$_b$: Iya, [**itte   nai**]$_{nonpast.nonperfective}$.
   no   go.Ger NpfvAux.Neg.NPst
   'No, I did not go.'

(adapted from Kusumoto 2016:117)

DPrt = discourse particle, Gen = genitive, Ger = gerund, Inf = infinitive, Intj = interjection, ModAux = modal auxiliary, Neg(Aux) = negation/negative auxiliary, NegGer = negative gerund, NpfvAux = non-perfective auxiliary, Npst = nonpast, Pl = plural, Plt(Aux) = polite(ness auxiliary), Pfv = perfective, Prs = present, Psv = passive, Th = thematic *wa* (topic/ground marker).

(4) a. Nomikai   ga   atta   nante,   shiranakatta yo.
        drinking.party Nom exist.Pst such.a.thing.as know.Neg.Pst DPrt
        'I didn't know that there was a drinking party.'
    b. Taichoo ga   amari yoku   nakatta   kara.
        condition Nom quite good.Inf NegAux.Pst because
        '(The reason is that) I was not feeling very well.'

It can be said that, in Japanese, as long as negative clauses are concerned, the nonpast nonperfective is the default way to describe a situation in the past. The negative preterite, on the other hand, is subject to what can be called the "plausibility requirement".

This work argues that the Japanese negative preterite predicate invariably expresses the existence (occurrence) of a "negative eventuality", as opposed to the non-existence (non-occurrence) of eventualities, and that the plausibility requirement can be accounted for as a side effect of this feature. It will be furthermore argued that, while Japanese nonpast-tensed clauses generally specify that the topic time (in Klein's 1994 sense) overlaps with or follows the topic time, this does not necessarily apply to nonpast-nonperfective clauses, making it possible for a negative nonpast-nonperfective clause to represent the non-existence of eventualities in a past topic time.

2 Existence of Negative Eventualities vs. Non-existence of (positive) Eventualities

It has been widely acknowledged in the literature that a negative clause may describe the existence (occurrence) of a negative eventuality, rather than the non-existence (non-occurrence) of eventualities (Krifka 1989; de Swart 1996; Przepiórkowski 1999; Bernard & Champollion 2018; Fábregas & González Rodríguez 2020; Higginbotham 2000; Zaradzki 2020). Among the most compelling pieces of evidence for "negative eventualities" are: (i) that a negative clause can be a complement of a perception verb like SEE, as in (5), and (ii) that a negative clause may occur in slots like "What happened is . . . ", " . . . took place", and " . . . is what they did", as in (6).

(5) The police officer saw Ken **not** stop for the traffic light.
     (similar examples discussed in Przepiórkowski 1999:240, Zaradzki 2020:485, among others)

(6) a. What happened next was that the consulate **didn't** give us our visa.
                                    (de Swart 1996:229)
    b. **Niedopelnienie** obowiązków służbowych przez Kowalskiego
        not.fulfilment.Pfv duties   professional by   K.
        miało miejsce w roku 1983.
        had place   in year 1983
        'Kowalski's not fulfilling his professional duties took place in 1983.'
                                    (Polish; Przepiórkowski 1999:242)

c.   **No** vender casas   durante un año fue   lo   que   hizo Juan
not sell.Inf house.Pl for   one year be.Pst that what did J.
para que lo   despidieran.
so   that he.Acc they.fire.Pfv.Pst
'Not to sell houses for one year is what Juan did to get fired.'
(Spanish; Fábregas & González Rodríguez 2020:740)

The ontological nature of a "negative eventuality" has been a matter of extensive debate. This work adopts Bernard & Champollion's (2018) idea that each set of eventualities P expressible with a clause nucleus has a negative counterpart, **Neg**(P), which contains all and only those eventualities which preclude—i.e., cannot co-exist in the same world with—every eventuality in P. When P is eventualities whereby Mary leaves, for example, **Neg**(P) is something like eventualities whereby Mary stays. Eventualities constituting P and **Neg**(P) will respectively be referred to as "P eventualities" and "anti-P eventualities".

The incompatibility of an eventuality (a P eventuality) and its negative counterpart (an anti-P eventuality) may be accounted for with an axiom like (7), which mirrors the Law of Contradiction in classical logic.

(7)   **Axiom of Negation**
$[\exists e[e \in P] \rightarrow \neg\exists e[e \in \mathbf{Neg}(P)]]$ & $[\exists e[e \in \mathbf{Neg}(P)] \rightarrow \neg\exists e[e \in P]]$

Bernard & Champollion (2018) assign a meaning along the following lines to English *not*;[3] subscript E stands for "eventive", and v is the type for eventualities.

(8) $\mathrm{not}_E \mapsto \lambda P_{\langle v,t \rangle}[\mathbf{Neg}(P)]$

Reference to anti-eventualities helps develop reasonable semantic representations for sentences like (5) and (6). It is an event of "anti-stopping" that is described as having been seen by a police officer, it is an event of "anti-visa-issuance" that is described as having happened, and so forth.

Now, if a negative clause may describe a negative eventuality, does it always do so? Does, say, the English adverb *not* always represent something like (8), or can it represent the classical Boolean negation, i.e. (9) where P stands for "propositional", as well?

(9) $\mathrm{not}_P \mapsto \lambda p[\neg p]$

With Przepiórkowski (1999), Fábregas & González Rodríguez (2020), and Zaradzki (2020), I maintain that clausal negation may receive two distinct readings corresponding to propositional negation (= (9)) and eventive negation (= (8)). In a sentence like (10), the negation occurs in the complement of a perception verb and is forced to receive the eventive reading. In a sentence like (11), on the other hand, English *not* may, in theory, be either eventive or propositional.

---

[3] This is grossly simpler than Bernard & Champollion's original formulation, which implements the continuation approach to syntax/semantic interface.

(10)   Ken saw Mary not$_E$ dance.
         'There was a negative eventuality where Mary did not dance, and Ken
         saw it.'

(11)   Mary did not$_{P/E}$ dance.
         a.   'There was no eventuality where Mary danced.'
         b.   'There was a negative eventuality where Mary did not dance.'

A negative clause involving propositional negation can be said to express the
non-occurrence of eventualities (NOE), and one involving eventive negation the
occurrence of a negative eventuality (ONE). (11a) and (11b) are respectively
paraphrases of the NOE and ONE readings of the sentence *Mary did not dance*.

I furthermore suggest that reference to a negative eventuality (corresponding to a dynamic event; see Sect. 4.3 for the case of stative eventualities)—i.e.,
the ONE reading of a (dynamic) negative clause—is highly constrained, and is
available only when the occurrence of a corresponding positive eventuality is or
was expected or at least plausible.

It has been commonly acknowledged that generally negative sentences are
pragmatically more marked than their affirmative counterparts (Tian & Breheny
2019 and references therein). However, there seems to be a significant difference in the degree of markedness between sentences with regular (propositional)
negation and ones with eventive negation. In a context where there has been no
expectation for Mary to take a picture, let alone a picture of an eggplant, the
negative sentence in (12a) would be a fairly strange thing to say. It nevertheless is judged as a true statement, if indeed Mary did not take a picture of an
eggplant. The same goes with (12b), where the perception report as a whole is
negated.

(12)   I observed Mary for three hours...
         a.   She did not take a picture of an eggplant.
         b.   I did not see her take a picture of an eggplant.

(13) situated in the same context, on the other hand, does not merely sound
odder than (12a,b), but seems not to be true. It is not clear if it even counts as a
false statement—it has a flavor of presupposition failure (see Miller 2003:297–299
and Zaradzki 2020:485 for relevant remarks).

(13)   (I observed Mary for three hours...) #I saw her not take a picture of
         an eggplant.

(14) illustrates the (extra) markedness of eventive negation with a construction
other than the direct perception report. Utterances like (14a) sound not only
odd but also are perceived as non-true; (14b) sounds comparatively less odd and
seems to count as a true statement.

(14)   I observed Mary for three hours. ...
         a.   #One thing she did was to not take a picture of an eggplant.
         b.   One thing she didn't do was to take a picture of an eggplant.

(15), which has a structure parallel to that of (14), sounds rather natural, it being commonsensically plausible that Mary could have fulfilled the described action.

(15)   One (stupid) thing Mary did was to not take her boss's warnings seriously.

In sum, it seems fair to suppose that eventive negation is much more pragmatically constrained than that of propositional negation, and to posit the following generalization:

(16)   **Constraint on Eventive Negation**
The use of eventive negation is felicitous only if it is common ground that the occurrence of a relevant positive ("pre-negated") eventuality has or had been plausible.

3   Proposal: The Japanese Preterite is Not Compatible with Propositional Negation

3.1   The Japanese Tense System

Japanese has a two-way distinction of tense: past and nonpast (also called present). The nonpast tense is marked with an inflectional ending: $-(r)u$ for (affirmative) verbs and $-i$ for adjectives, including negative predicates derived out of a verb with the suffix $-(a)na$ (e.g. *utawanai* in (28a)). The past tense is marked with the marker $-ta$, which I take to be a particle following an infinitive predicate (Oshima 2014).

A nonpast-tensed dynamic predicate as a rule describes an event taking place after the relevant temporal anchoring point (typically the time of utterance), putting aside the habitual/generic interpretation. A nonpast-tensed stative predicate by default describes a state co-temporal with the anchoring point, but may also describe one that holds after it.

(17)   (nonpast)
a.   Ken wa ashita   Mari ni   au.
K.   Th tomorrow M.   Dat see.Npst
'Ken will see Mari tomorrow.'
b.   Ken wa {ima/ashita}   wa Tokyo ni   iru.
K.   Th now/tomorrow Th T.   Dat exist.Npst
'Ken {is/will be} in Tokyo {now/tomorrow}.'

A past-tensed predicate, whether it is dynamic or stative, locates the described eventuality in the past relative to the anchoring point.

(18)   (past)
a.   Ken wa kinoo   Mari ni   atta.
K.   Th yesterday M.   Dat see.Pst

'Ken saw Mari yesterday.'
b. Ken wa kinoo   Tokyo ni   ita.
K.   Th yesterday T.   Dat exist.Pst
'Ken was in Tokyo yesterday.'

I assume that a tense poses a restriction on the topic time in Klein's (1994) sense. (19) illustrates the case of the Japanese past tense marker *-ta*. **TT** and **TU** represent the topic time and the time of utterance, respectively. The logical predicate **At** is defined in (20) (cf. Condoravdi 2002:70). τ represents the temporal trace function (Krifka 1989:97). $\subseteq$ stands for the temporal inclusion. The material between braces represents non-proffered (not-at-issue) content.

(19)   -ta (past) $\mapsto \lambda P[\lambda e\{\mathbf{TT} < \mathbf{TU}\}[\mathbf{At}(e,\mathbf{TT})$ & $P(e)]$

(20) $\mathbf{At}(e,t) =_{def} \begin{cases} \tau(e) \supseteq t & \text{if } e \text{ is stative} \\ \tau(e) \subseteq t & \text{otherwise} \end{cases}$

I furthermore adopt the view that the Japanese nonpast tense does not code a temporal meaning, and it indicates "nonpastness" merely as an implicature arising from the absence of a past marker (cf. Sauerland 2002 on the English present tense). This supposition is not essential to the central claims of the present work, but it helps account for the distribution of the nonpast nonperfective to be discussed in Sect. 4 below.

(21)   -(r)u, -i (nonpast) $\mapsto \lambda P[\lambda e[\mathbf{At}(e,\mathbf{TT})$ & $P(e)]]$

One piece of evidence that the Japanese nonpast tense does not code temporal meaning is the observation that complex predicates carrying both a nonpast-tense feature and a past-tense feature, such as (22b,c), are interpreted as past-tensed, as if the nonpast-tense feature "gave way" to the past-tense feature.

(22)   a.   Nenakatta.   (plain/negative/nonpast)
sleep.Neg.Pst
'(*pro*) did not sleep.'
b.   Nemasen   deshita.   (polite/negative/past)
see.Plt.Neg.Npst PltAux.Pst
'(*pro*) did not sleep.'
c.   Nenakatta   desu.   (polite/negative/past)
see.Neg.Pst PltAux.Npst
'(*pro*) did not sleep.'

The literal meanings of a past-tensed clause and a nonpast-tensed clause will look like (23) and (24).

(23)   Ken wa Mari ni atta. (= (18a)) $\mapsto$
$\exists e\{\mathbf{TT} < \mathbf{TU}\}[\tau(e) \subseteq \mathbf{TT}$ & $\mathbf{see}(e)$ & $\mathbf{Actor}(e) = \mathbf{ken}$ &
$\mathbf{Undergoer}(e) = \mathbf{mari}]$

(24)   Ken wa Mari ni au. ($\approx$ (17a)) $\mapsto$
         $\exists e[\tau(e) \subseteq \mathbf{TT}$ & $\mathbf{see}(e)$ & $\mathbf{Actor}(e) = \mathbf{ken}$ & $\mathbf{Undergoer}(e) = \mathbf{mari}]$

The meanings of the rest of the constituents, and how they are combined with
the meaning of a tense, are assumed to be as follows:

(25)   a.   Ken wa Mari ni aw (the clause nucleus) $\mapsto$
               $\lambda e[\mathbf{see}(e)$ & $\mathbf{Actor}(e) = \mathbf{ken}$ & $\mathbf{Undergoer}(e) = \mathbf{mari}]$
         b. $OP_\exists \equiv \lambda P[\exists e[P(e)]]$

(26)   a. $OP_\exists([\![\text{-ta}]\!]([\![\text{Ken wa Mari ni aw}]\!]))$
         b. $OP_\exists([\![\text{-u}]\!]([\![\text{Ken wa Mari ni aw}]\!]))$

At the pragmatic level, the meaning in (24) is enriched into (27), where the
implicated component is shaded.

(27) $\exists e\{\mathbf{TU} \leq \mathbf{TT}\}[\tau(e) \subseteq \mathbf{TT}$ & $\mathbf{see}(e)$ & $\mathbf{Actor}(e) = \mathbf{ken}$ &
         $\mathbf{Undergoer}(e) = \mathbf{mari}]$

3.2 The Incompatibility of the Past Tense and the Propositional Negation

I propose that the negation in a Japanese negative preterite is invariably eventive, so that, for example, (28b) allows only the ONE reading while (28a) is
ambiguous. The plausibility requirement for the negative preterite can be seen
as an outcome of this feature (cf. (13)/(14)).

(28)   a.   Ken wa utawanai.
               K.   Th sing.Neg.Npst
               'Ken will not sing.'
         b.   Ken wa utawanakatta.
               K.   Th sing.Neg.Pst
               'Ken did not sing.'

(29)   a.   Ken wa utaw (the clause nucleus) $\mapsto \lambda e[\mathbf{sing}(e)$ & $\mathbf{Actor}(e) = \mathbf{ken}]$
         b.   -(a)na(kat)$_P$ (propositional negation) $\mapsto \lambda p[\neg p]$
         c.   -(a)na(kat)$_E$ (eventive negation) $\mapsto \lambda P_{\langle v,t\rangle}[\mathbf{Neg}(P)]$

(30)   a.   the NOE reading of (28a)
               $[\![\text{-ana}_P]\!](OP_\exists([\![\text{-i}]\!]([\![\text{Ken wa utaw}]\!]))) \Rightarrow$
               $\neg\exists e\{\mathbf{TU} \leq \mathbf{TT}\}[\mathbf{At}(e,\mathbf{TT})$ & $\mathbf{sing}(e)$ & $\mathbf{Actor}(e) = \mathbf{ken}]$
         b.   the ONE reading of (28a)
               $\exists e\{\mathbf{TU} \leq \mathbf{TT}\}[\mathbf{At}(e,\mathbf{TT})$ & $\mathbf{Neg}(\lambda e'[\mathbf{sing}(e')$ & $\mathbf{Actor}(e') =$
               $\mathbf{ken}])(e)]$

(31)   a.   the NOE reading of (28b) (unavailable)
               $[\![\text{-anakat}_P]\!](OP_\exists([\![\text{-ta}]\!]([\![\text{Ken wa utaw}]\!]))) \Rightarrow$
               $\neg\exists e\{\mathbf{TT} < \mathbf{TU}\}[\mathbf{At}(e,\mathbf{TT})$ & $\mathbf{sing}(e)$ & $\mathbf{Actor}(e) = \mathbf{ken}]$
         b.   the ONE reading of (28b)
               $OP_\exists([\![\text{-ta}]\!]([\![\text{-anakat}_E]\!]([\![\text{Ken wa utaw}]\!]))) \Rightarrow$

$$\exists e\{\mathbf{TT} < \mathbf{TU}\}[\mathbf{At}(e,\mathbf{TT}) \;\&\; \mathbf{Neg}(\lambda e'[\mathbf{sing}(e') \;\&\; \mathbf{Actor}(e') = \mathbf{ken})(e)]$$

The lack of the NOE interpretation of the negative preterite likely has to do with the grammatical status/position of the past marker -*ta*. Historically, the marker -*ta* developed from the auxiliary TARI, an archaic marker of perfect (Ogihara & Fukushima 2015). When a sentence with TARI is negated, the negation occurs to its right, as in (32), where *tar*, the stem of TARI, is followed by *anu*, a negative-attributive suffix (Kondo 2003).

(32) [...] aete koto to mo **omoitaranu**   keshiki   nite [...]
      at.all matter as even think.*tar*.Neg.Attr appearance with
      '[The merchant (who was robbed by a group of thieves) was standing
      on the ridge,] appearing not to think of it (= the robbery) as a big deal
      [...]'
      (from *Konjaku Monogatari Shuu*, estimated to be written around the
      beginning of the 12th century)

The contemporary past marker -*ta* no longer retains its status as an inflecting word, and can only be preceded by negation. Some scholars, including Bloch (1946), Teramura (1984), and Tsujimura (2007), consider that -*ta* is—i.e. has grammaticalized into—an inflectional suffix directly following the predicate stem (the "attachment-to-stem" analysis). Others, including Shibatani (1990) and Shirota (1998), suppose that -*ta* is a particle or auxiliary that, like its predecessor TARI, follows an infinitive form, an inflected form capable of heading a subordinate clause on its own, as in (33a,b) (the "attachment-to-infinitive" analysis).

(33) a. Ken wa Mari ni **ai**,   hon o   watashita.
          K.   Th M.   Dat see.Inf book Acc hand.Pst
          'Ken saw Mari and handed her the book.'
      b. Sora ga **hare**,   kion   ga   agatta.
          sky Nom clear.up.Inf atmospheric.temperature Nom   rise.Pst
          'The sky having cleared, the temperature rose.'

The infinitive form of a Type I verb (i.e. a verb whose stem ends with a consonant), such as AU 'see, meet' (the stem = *aw*) and ODORU 'dance' (the stem = *odor*), is formed by appending -*i* to the verb base (which may incur a phonotactically motivated sound change of the stem; e.g. *aw* + *i* ⇒ *ai*). I take -*i* here to an epenthetically inserted vowel, although it can alternatively be regarded as an inflectional suffix. The infinitive form of a Type II verb (i.e. a verb whose stem ends with a vowel), such as NERU 'sleep' (the stem = *ne*) and HARERU 'clear up, get sunny' (the stem = *hare*), is string-identical to the stem.

In Oshima (2014), I argued that -*ta* can be (though usually is not) separated from the verb to its left by an accent-phrase boundary, as in (34b), and argues that this lends support for the attachment-to-infinitive analysis; in (34a,b), braces indicate accent-phrase boundaries and downward arrows indicate accent falls.

(34)   Moshi   hareta   to   shite   mo,   ...
        hypothetically get.sunny.Pst Comp do.Ger though
        'Even if it {had gotten/should get} sunny, ...'
        a.   ...{ha$^\downarrow$ re ta to} ... (the default phrasing pattern)
        b.   ...{ha$^\downarrow$ re} {ta$^\downarrow$ to} ... (an alternative phrasing pattern)

The verb to the left of -*ta* may be regarded either as the "host" or "complement" of -*ta*, depending on the premises regarding syntactic structure and headedness. I will regard it as a host for the sake of concreteness, but the choice here does not have direct bearings on the discussion.

The nonpast markers -(*r*)*u* and -*i*, as well as the negative-nonpast marker -*en*, on the other hand, can sensibly regarded as inflectional suffixes. (35) and (36) illustrate the compositions of the nonpast- and past-tensed plain (nonpolite) negative predicates whose base is *aw* 'see, meet' posited in Oshima (2014). Plus signs and slashes respectively indicate word-internal morpheme boundaries and word boundaries; "⇒" represents sound change, including the insertion of an epenthetic vowel, incurred by (morpho-)phonological rules. Subscript *inf* is meant to clarify the status of the expression as an inflected infinitive form.

(35)   plain negative nonpast form
        a.   Awanai. '(*pro$_i$*) will not see (*pro$_j$*).'
        b.   [[*aw* (verb base) + *ana* (negative suffix deriving an adjective out of a verb)] + *i* (nonpast-tense suffix)]

(36)   plain negative past form
        a.   Awanakatta. '(*pro$_i$*) did not see (*pro$_j$*).'
        b.   [[[*aw* (verb base) + *ana* (negative suffix deriving an adjective out of a verb)] + *kar* (suffix deriving a verb out of an adjective)]$_{inf}$ / *ta* (past-tense particle)]
              ⇒ *awanakatta*

The key point here is that -*ta* is separated from its host, which contains the negation, by a word boundary, while -*i* belongs to the same word as its host.

By and large the same goes with polite counterparts of nonpast- and past-tensed negative predicates. In nonpast ones, the tense feature occurs within the same word as the negation; in past ones, this is not the case.

(37)   polite negative nonpast form
        a.   Aimasen. '(*pro$_i$*) will not see (*pro$_j$*).'
        b.   [[*aw* (verb base) + *mas* (bound base)] + *en* (negative nonpast-tense suffix)]
              ⇒ *aimasen*

(38)   polite negative past form (variant #1)
        a.   Aimasen deshita. '(*pro$_i$*) did not see (*pro$_j$*).'
        b.   [[[*aw* (verb base) + *mas* (bound base)] + *en* (negative nonpast-tense suffix)] / [[*des* (politeness auxiliary base)]$_{inf}$ / *ta* (past-tense

particle)]]

⇒ *aimasen deshita*

(39)   polite negative past form (variant #2)

    a.   Awanakatta desu. '(*pro_i*) did not see (*pro_j*).'

    b.   [[[[*aw* (verb base) + *ana* (negative suffix deriving an adjective out of a verb)] + *kar* (suffix deriving a verb out of an adjective)]$_{inf}$ / *ta* (past-tense particle)] / [*des* (politeness auxiliary base) + *u* (nonpast-tense suffix)]]

    ⇒ *awanakatta desu*

It seems quite plausible that the word boundary blocks negation in the host to take scope over -*ta*, thereby inducing the differing scopal behaviors of the nonpast and past tense markers.

(40)   **possible patterns**: Neg > Nonpast, Nonpast > Neg, Past > Neg
        impossible pattern: Neg > Past

Due to their semantic types, propositional negation ($\langle t, t \rangle$) must be applied after the closure of the eventuality variable, hence taking scope over the tense; eventive negation ($\langle vt, vt \rangle$), on the hand, may take scope under the tense ($\langle vt, vt \rangle$). The impossibility of the "Neg > Past (-*ta*)" pattern implies that the negation occurring in a preterite can only be eventive.

4   The Nonpast Nonperfective as an "Alternative Preterite"

The puzzle of the limited discourse-configurational distribution of the negative preterite has a flip side: the unexpectedly wide distribution of the negative nonpast nonperfective. I suggest that the Japanese nonpast nonperfective sometimes receives a "preterite-like" interpretation.

4.1   The -*te* IRU form in its Perfect Use

The opposition between the so-called -*te* IRU form (nonperfective form), and the simple form (perfective form) has been recognized to be central to the aspect system of Japanese. The -*te* IRU form receives a wide array of interpretations, including (i) resulting state (also called resultative perfect), (ii) progressive, and (iii) habitual (e.g. Kudo 2020). Among the various uses of -*te* IRU, the one that most directly concerns the purposes of the current work is the one labeled "perfect" in such works as Shirai (2000) and Kudo (2020) (alternative labels for this use include "existential perfect", "experience (*keiken*)", and "retrospection (*kaisoo*)").

Providing examples like (41a–c), Teramura (1984:131) maintains that the function of -*te* IRU in its perfect use is to describe "an event in the past that has significance on the present time (*genzai ni igi o motsu kako no jishoo*)".

(41) a. Ano hito   wa takusan no   shoosetsu o   **kaite**
          that person Th many   Cop.Attr novel   Acc write.Ger
          iru.
          NpfvAux.Npst
          'That person has written many novels.'
      b. (a police officer to a medical examiner, who has conducted an
          autopsy on a woman)
          Otoko wa tasukarimashita. Onna   wa nani o   **nonde**
          man   Th survive.Plt.Pst   woman Th what Acc take.Ger
          imasu   ka?
          NpfvAux.Plt.Npst DPrt
          'The man [who was with the woman and found unconscious] sur-
          vived. What [medicine] did the woman take?'
      c. Kasai Zenzo wa Akutagawa jisatsu no   yokunen,
          K.   Z.   Th A.   suicide Gen following.year
          Showa   3 nen 7 gatsu ni **shinde iru**.
          the.Showa.era 3 year 7 month Dat die.Ger NpfvAux.Npst
          '[The novelist] Kasai Zenzo died in July 1927 (Showa 3), the follow-
          ing year of the suicide of [the novelist] Akutagawa.'
                  (Teramura 1984:126,132,133; (b) is originally from a novel)

A nonpast-tensed -*te* IRU form in its perfect use has a meaning rather similar
to that of the corresponding preterite, much like how an English present-perfect
clause is similar in meaning to its preterite counterpart (e.g., *Ken has read the
book* vs. *Ken read the book*). Given this, it is tempting to suppose that a -*te*
IRU form occurring in a direct answer to a past-tensed interrogative, such as the
instance in (1B$_b$), receives the perfect interpretation (I will dismiss this view
below, however).

I assume that the -*te* IRU perfect is by and large synonymous to the English
HAVE -*ed* perfect. Here I adopt Parsons's (1990) resultativity-based analysis of
the perfect aspect, according to which it describes the resultant state of an
eventuality, i.e., an abstract state whereby some eventuality's "having occurred".
The meaning of *i* (the stem of IRU) in its perfect use is taken to be something
like (42); **RS** stands for "resultant state".

(42)   i (perfect) $\mapsto \lambda P[\lambda e[\exists e'[e = \mathbf{RS}(e') \& P(e')]]]$

Nonpast/past-tensed perfect clauses (43a,b) will be taken to have the meanings in (44a,b) respectively, with the derivational process schematized in (45)
(the gerund marker -*te* is considered to be semantically vacuous).

(43)   Ken wa Mari ni   atte   {a. iru   / b. ita   }.
        K.   Th M.   Dat see.Ger   NpfvAux.Npst   NpfvAux.Pst
        'Ken {a. has (or will have) / b. had} seen Mari.'

(44) a. $\exists e\{\mathbf{TU} \leq \mathbf{TT}\}[\tau(e) \supseteq \mathbf{TT} \& \exists e'[e = \mathbf{RS}(e') \& \mathbf{see}(e') \& \mathbf{Actor}(e')$
          $= \mathbf{ken} \& \mathbf{Undergoer}(e') = \mathbf{mari}]]$

   b. $\exists e\{\mathbf{TT} < \mathbf{TU}\}[\tau(e) \supseteq \mathbf{TT}\ \&\ \exists e'[e = \mathbf{RS}(e')\ \&\ \mathbf{see}(e')\ \&\ \mathbf{Actor}(e')$
        $= \mathbf{ken}\ \&\ \mathbf{Undergoer}(e') = \mathbf{mari}]]$

(45)   OP$_\exists$([-ru/-ta]([i]([Ken wa Mari ni atte])))

4.2 The Nonpast Nonperfective as an "Alternative Preterite"

Some instances of nonpast-nonperfective predicates appear to receive a "past-like" interpretation that is to be distinguished from the perfect interpretation.

Under the assumption that the nonperfective auxiliary in (46B$_b$) indicates the perfect aspect, the meanings of the boldfaced parts of (46B$_{a,b}$) should look like (47a,b).

(46)   (A big soccer game was broadcast on TV the evening before.)
       A: Kinoo,   sakkaa mita?
            yesterday soccer see.Pst
            'Did you watch the soccer game yesterday?'
       B$_a$: Un, **mita**. Sono tame   ni   zangyoo   mo kotowatta
            yes see.Pst that purpose Dat overtime.work also resufe.Pst
            n   da.
            DAux Cop.Npst
            'Yes, I watched it. I refused to work overtime for that purpose.'
       B$_{a'}$: #Un, **mite** (i)ru.   Sono tame   ni   zangyoo
            yes see.Ger NpfvAux.Npst that purpose Dat overtime.work
            mo kotowatta n   da.
            also resufe.Pst DAux Cop.Npst
            'Yes, I watched it. I refused to work overtime for that purpose.'
       B$_b$: Iya, **mite** **nai**.   Mitakatta   kedo,
            no see.Ger NpfvAux.Neg.Npst see.want.Pst though
            zangyoo   ga   atte.
            overtime.work Nom exist.Ger
            'No, I did not watch it. I wanted to watch it, but I had to work overtime.'
(47)   a. $\exists e\{\mathbf{TT} < \mathbf{TU}\}[\tau(e) \subseteq \mathbf{TT}\ \&\ \mathbf{watch}(e)\ \&\ \mathbf{Actor}(e) = \mathbf{Speaker}\ \&$
           $\mathbf{Undergoer}(e) = \mathbf{the\text{-}game}]$
       b. $\neg\exists e\{\mathbf{TU} \leq \mathbf{TT}\}[\exists e'[\tau(e) \supseteq \mathbf{TT}\ \&\ e = \mathbf{RS}(e')\ \&\ \mathbf{watch}(e')\ \&$
           $\mathbf{Actor}(e') = \mathbf{Speaker}\ \&\ \mathbf{Undergoer}(e') = \mathbf{the\text{-}game}]]$

It is implausible, however, that the relevant parts of (46B$_a$) and (46B$_b$) are construed as being "about" different temporal scenes, the topic time set in the past (relative to the utterance time) and in the nonpast respectively. Affirmative response (46B$_a$) to question (46A) cannot be naturally replaced with its nonpast-nonperfective variant, i.e. (46B$_{a'}$), suggesting that the topic time has to be set in the past in this context. There is no evident reason that the same does not happen when a negative response is made to the same question.

It is noteworthy that some instances of *affirmative* nonpast-nonperfective clauses, too, seem to make reference to a past topic time. Such instances are commonly found in written historical and biographical accounts, as exemplified with (48), a part of a Wikipedia article on Mahatma Gandhi[4] (see also (41c) from Teramura 1984).

(48)   Korera ichiren no   undoo   no tame ni, Gandhi wa
        these serial Cop.Attr movement Gen cause Dat G.   Th
        tabitabi   toogoku sareta   (kei   rokkai). Tatoeba   1922
        frequently imprison do.Psv.Pst in.total six.times for.example 1922
        nen 3 gatsu 18 nichi ni   wa, ni-nen-kan no   fufukujuu
        year 3 month 18 day   Dat Th 2-year-for Cop.Attr disobedience
        undoo   no tame ni, roku-nen-kan no   chooekikei   no
        movement Gen cause Dat 6-year-for   Cop.Attr imprisonment Gen
        hanketsu o **ukete**   **iru**.
        judgment Acc receive.Ger NpfvAux.Npst

        'Gandhi was frequently imprisoned (six times in total) for this series
        of movements. For example, on March 18, 1922, he **was sentenced** to
        six-year imprisonment for a two-year long civil disobedience movement.'

I suggest that, on top of its perfect(, resultative, progressive, …) use(s), IRU has a "quasi-past" use, which specifies that the topic time is in the past.

(49)   i (quasi-past) $\mapsto \lambda P[\lambda e\{\mathbf{TT} < \mathbf{TU}\}[P(e)]]$

The topic-time restriction posed by IRU in its quasi-past use conflicts with, and hence suppresses, the "nonpastness" implicature that a nonpast predicate usually induces.

To illustrate, (50a) and (50b) each have two possible logical translations (putting aside the ONE interpretations of (50b)): (51a,b) for (50a) and (52a,b) for (50b). (51b) and (52b) can be characterized as the "alternative preterite" reading. Note that "i" and "-i" respectively refer to the nonperfective auxiliary stem and the nonpast tense suffix following an adjectival stem.

(50)   a. Ken wa Mari ni atte   iru.
            K. Th M.   Dat see.Ger NpfvAux.Npst

            'Ken has (or will have) seen Mari.' / 'Ken saw Mari.'
        b. Ken wa Mari ni atte   inai.
            K. Th M.   Dat see.Ger NpfvAux.Neg.Npst

            'Ken has (or will have) not seen Mari.' / 'Ken did not see Mari.'

(51)   OP$_\exists$([[-ru]]([[i]]([[Ken wa Mari ni atte]])))
        a. $\exists e\{\mathbf{TU} \leq \mathbf{TT}\}[\tau(e) \supseteq \mathbf{TT}$ & $\exists e'[e = \mathbf{RS}(e')$ & $\mathbf{see}(e')$ & $\mathbf{Actor}(e')$
            $= \mathbf{ken}$ & $\mathbf{Undergoer}(e') = \mathbf{mari}]]$ (nonpast perfect)

---

[4] https://w.wiki/3D$7 (accessed on October 1, 2021).

     b. $\exists e\{\mathbf{TT} < \mathbf{TU}\}[\tau(e) \subseteq \mathbf{TT}$ & $\mathbf{see}(e)$ & $\mathbf{Actor}(e) = \mathbf{ken}$ & $\mathbf{Undergoer}(e) = \mathbf{mari}]$ ("alternative preterite")

(52) $[\![\text{-}na_P]\!](\text{OP}_\exists([\![\text{-i}]\!]([\![i]\!]([\![\text{Ken wa Mari ni atte}]\!]))))$

     a. $\neg\exists e\{\mathbf{TU} \leq \mathbf{TT}\}[\tau(e) \supseteq \mathbf{TT}$ & $\exists e'[e = \mathbf{RS}(e')$ & $\mathbf{see}(e')$ & $\mathbf{Actor}(e') = \mathbf{ken}$ & $\mathbf{Undergoer}(e') = \mathbf{mari}]]$ (nonpast perfect)

     b. $\neg\exists e\{\mathbf{TT} < \mathbf{TU}\}[\tau(e) \subseteq \mathbf{TT}$ & $\mathbf{see}(e)$ & $\mathbf{Actor}(e) = \mathbf{ken}$ & $\mathbf{Undergoer}(e) = \mathbf{mari}]$ ("alternative preterite")

On the (a) interpretation, (50a,b) are "about" a temporal scene where the resultant state of an event whereby Ken sees Mari, described by the pre-tensed clause, held or did not hold. On the (b) interpretation—i.e. the alternative-preterite interpretation—(50a,b) are "about" the temporal scene where an event whereby Ken sees Mari occurred or did not occur. I take (46B$_b$), as well as the second sentence in (48), to receive the alternative-preterite interpretation.[5]

There is additional language-internal evidence that IRU may indicate pastness: it serves to indicate temporal anteriority in some types of conditional clauses in which a tensed clause cannot occur. Japanese has several markers of conditional clauses, including $(r)eba$, $tara$, and $naraba$. $(R)eba$ and $tara$ respectively follow a verbal base and a verb in its infinitive form (Oshima 2014), and thus neither can be combined with a tensed clause; $naraba$, on the other hand, follows a tensed clause.

(53)   a.   Pan ga   mada {i. areba   / ii. *aru(r)eba   / iii.
          bread Nom still   exist.eba exist.Npst.$(r)eba$
          aru   naraba}, sore o   taberu.
          exist.Npst $naraba$ that Acc eat.Prs
          'If there is some bread left, (I) will eat it.'

     b.   Moshi   ashita   Ken ga   {i. kitara   / ii.
          hypothetically tomorrow K. Nom   come.$tara$
          *kurutara   / iii. kuru   naraba}, Mari wa yorokobu
          come.Npst.$tara$ come.Npst $naraba$ M. Th rejoice.Prs
          daroo.
          ModAux
          'If Ken comes tomorrow, Mari will be delighted.'

---

[5] A past-tensed nonperfective clause, such as (i), does not allow a preterite-like interpretation, unlike its nonpast-tensed counterpart. I take this to be simply because the quasi-past interpretation of i is blocked because it would lead to sheer semantic redundancy, i and $-ta$ both specifying "$\mathbf{TT} < \mathbf{TU}$".

(i)   Ken wa Mari ni atte ita.
       K. Th M. Dat see.Ger NpfvAux.Npst
       'Ken had seen Mari.'

In conditional constructions with $(r)eba$ and *tara*, if the antecedent describes a possibly true situation in the past (relative to the utterance time), the predicate must involve IRU.[6]

(54)   "I wonder if the rat will eat the rat poison ..."

    a.   Moshi   {tabetara/tabereba}, sugu   shinu
        hypothetically eat.*tara*/eat.*reba*   immediately die.Npst
        daroo.
        ModAux
        'If it eats it, it will die immediately.'

    b.   #Moshi   tabete {itara/ireba},
           hypothetically eat.Ger NpfvAux.*tara*/NpfvAux.*reba*
        sugu   shinu   daroo.
        immediately die.Npst ModAux
        'If it ate it, it will die immediately.'

(55)   "I wonder if the rat ate the rat poison ..."

    a.   #Moshi   {tabetara/tabereba}, moo   shinde
          hypothetically eat.*tara*/eat.*reba*   already die.Ger
        iru   daroo.
        NpfvAux.Npst ModAux
        'If it eats it, it must be already dead.'

    b.   Moshi   tabete {itara/ireba},   moo
        hypothetically eat.Ger NpfvAux.*tara*/NpfvAux.*reba* already
        shinde iru   daroo.
        die.Ger Npfv.Npst ModAux
        'If it ate it, it must be already dead.'

(55b) is more naturally paraphrased with (56a) with a preterite *naraba*-conditional clause than with (56b) with a nonpast-nonperfective one.

(56)   "I wonder if the rat ate the rat poison ..."

    a.   Moshi   tabeta naraba, moo   shinde iru
        hypothetically eat.Pst *naraba* already die.Ger NpfvAux.Npst
        daroo.
        ModAux

---

[6] This pattern does not straightforwardly carry over to counterfactual conditionals with a "fake past" in the matrix clause.

(i)   "That smart rat did not eat the rat poison ..."
    Moshi   {i. tabetara / ii. tabete itara   }, moo   shinde
    hypothetically   eat.*tara*   eat.Ger NpfvAux.*tara*   already die.Ger
    ita   daroo.
    NpfvAux.Pst ModAux
    'If it had eaten it, it would have been already dead.'

'If it ate it, it must be already dead.'

b.   ??Moshi   tabete iru   naraba, moo   shinde
       hypothetically eat.Ger NpfvAux.NPst *naraba* already die.Ger
       iru   daroo.
       NpfvAux.Npst ModAux
       '(lit.) If it has eaten it, it must be already dead.'

It is thus natural to suppose that IRU in the antecedent of (55b) indicates pastness in the way the past marker *ta* does in environments where it can occur, such as the antecedent of (56a).

It is worth noting that a rather similar phenomenon is seen in English: the HAVE -*ed* construction, which typically expresses the perfect aspect, can be deployed to express mere temporal anteriority in environments where finite past forms cannot occur, as in (57b):

(57)   a.   They have fixed the printer (#yesterday).
         b.   They may have fixed the printer yesterday. (≈ It is possible that they fixed the printer yesterday.)

I suggest that, the -*ta* preterite being the default/unmarked means of describing a situation in the past, the quasi-past meaning of *i* is mobilized only for special purposes. One is to compensate for the inability of a negative preterite to describe the non-occurrence of eventualities. Another, typically seen in formal writings, is to signal a marked discourse relation (rhetorical relation), such as exemplification or supplementation, between the clause and the surrounding discourse segments, as in (48). Yet another is to form a (*r*)*eba* or *tara*-conditional clause describing a past situation.

4.3   Negative Preterites with a Stative Base

When the base of a predicate is stative (a stative verb, an adjective, or a nominal predicate), the addition of -*te* IRU is blocked, or has no or only a subtle semantic effect.

(58)   a.   Sono hon wa toshoshitsu ni   {a. aru   / b. *atte
              that book Th library   Dat   exist.Npst   exist.Ger
              iru   }.
              NpfvAux.Npst
              'That book is in the library.'
         b.   Sono jisho   wa toshoshitsu ni   {a. nakatta   / b.
              that dictionary Th library   Dat   absent.Pst
              *nakute   ita   }.
              absent.Ger NpfvAux.Pst
              'That dictionary was not in the library.'

c.   Resutoran wa ima yasumi {a. da   / b. *de
     restaurant Th now closed   Cop.Npst   Cop.Inf
     iru   }.
     NpfvAux.Npst
     'The restaurant is closed now.'

d.   Ken no   shuchoo wa jijitsu to   {a. kotonaru   / b. kotonatte
     K. Gen claim   Th fact   with   differ.Npst   differ.Ger
     iru   }.
     NpfvAux.Npst
     'What Ken claims differs from the actual facts.'

A negative preterite form with a stative base does not implicate the plausibility of the logical contradiction of the propositional content in the past; the naturalness of (59B)/(60B) illustrates this point.

(59)   (B, a demolition contractor, comes back after checking out an abandoned mansion.)

A: Otakara toka atta?
     treasure etc. exist.Pst
     'Was there treasure or something?'

B: **Nakatta** yo. Sonna mono aru   wake   nai
     absent.Pst DPrt such   thing exist.Npst reason not.exist.Npst
     daro.
     DAux
     'No, there wasn't. You know there's no way there is such a thing.'

(60)   A: Resutoran, yasumi datta?
             restaurant closed Cop.Pst
             'Was the restaurant closed?'

        B: E? Iya, **yasumi ja   arimasen   deshita**.
             Intj no   closed   Cop.Inf Aux.Plt.Neg(.Npst) PltAux.Pst
             Dooshite desu   ka?
             why   Cop.Plt.Npst DPrt
             'Huh? No, it was not closed. Why?'

It is not clear to me if this implies that a negative preterite with a stative base allows the NOE interpretation. It seems plausible that for a negative predicate with a stative base, the ONE reading is not marked, or even is preferred to the NOE reading, and thus is not pragmatically constrained in the same way as that of a negative predicate with a dynamic base is. This supposition is motivated by the observation that "anti-states" can often be lexically coded, unlike "anti-(dynamic-)events". In the case of English, for an adjective expressing stative concept S, it tends to be possible to derive, with prefixes like *non-* and *in-*, another adjective expressing "anti-S" (e.g., *non-American, inappropriate*). The same does not go with verbs, which generally express a dynamic event.

Consequently, the lack of the plausibility implication in an utterance like (60B) does not necessary undermine the generalization that -*ta* cannot be outscoped by (propositional) negation to its left.

5 Conclusion

It was argued that in Japanese, as long as situations in the past are concerned, "non-occurrence of eventualities (NOE)" and "occurrence of a negative eventuality (ONE)" are coded differently. NOE is invariably coded with a nonpast-nonperfective form, and ONE is typically coded with a preteritie (past-perfective) form. It was also proposed that a nonpast-nonperfective form may indicate that the topic time is in the past, thereby inducing an "alternative-preterite" interpretation.

While various pieces of evidence have been put forth in the literature for the existence of negative eventualities as linguistically expressible objects, explicit markers or constructions favoring one of the NOE and ONE interpretations and deterring the other have hardly been discussed. The analysis presented in this work suggests that examination of Japanese data, and search for phenomena comparable to the Japanese regular-preterite/alternative-preterite opposition in other languages, have good potential to deepen our understanding of "negative eventualities".

References

Bernard, T., Champollion, L.: Negative events in compositional semantics. In: Proceedings of Semantics and Linguistic Theory, vol. 28, pp. 512–532 (2018). https://doi.org/10.3765/salt.v28i0.4429

Bloch, B.: Studies in colloquial Japanese I: inflection. J. Am. Orient. Soc. **66**, 97–130 (1946). https://doi.org/10.2307/596327

Condoravdi, C.: Temporal interpretation of modals: modals for the present and for the past. In: Beaver, D.I., Martínez, L.D.C., Clark, B.Z., Kaufmann, S. (eds.) The Construction of Meaning, pp. 59–88. CSLI Publications, Stanford (2002)

Fábregas, A., Rodríguez, R.G.: On inhibited eventualities. Nat. Lang. Linguist. Theory **38**, 729–773 (2020). https://doi.org/10.1007/s11049-019-09461-y

Higginbotham, J.: On events in linguistic semantics. In: Higginbotham, J., Pianesi, F., Varzi, A.C. (eds.) Speaking of Events, pp. 18–52. Oxford University Press, Oxford (2000). https://doi.org/10.1093/acprof:oso/9780199239313.003.0002

Klein, W.: Time in Language. Routledge, London (1994)

Kondo, A.: Jodooshi "ri/tari" ni hiteiji ga kasetsu suru baai. Kokugogaku Kenkyuu **42**, 1–13 (2003)

Krifka, M.: Nominal reference, temporal constitution and quantification in event semantics. In: Bartsch, R., van Benthem, J., van Emde Boas, P. (eds.) Semantics and Contextual Expression, pp. 75–115. Foris, Dordrecht (1989). https://doi.org/10.1515/9783110877335-005

Kudo, M.: Tense and aspect in discourse. In: Jacobsen, W.M., Takubo, Y. (eds.) Handbook of Japanese Semantics and Pragmatics, pp. 423–448. Walter de Gruyter, Berlin (2020). https://doi.org/10.1515/9781614512073-008

Kusumoto, T.: Kako no hitei jitai o arawasu shite inai ni okeru hanashite no shinteki taido to hyoogen kooka. Area and Culture Studies **92**, 48–64 (2016)

Matsuda, F.: "Kakoji ni ... shita ka?" ni taisuru hitei no hentoo keishiki: Shite inai to shinakatta no sentaku ni kanshite. Nihongo Kyoiku J. Jpn. Lang. Teach. **113**, 34–42 (2002)

Miller, P.: Negative complements in direct perception reports. In: Proceedings of Chicago Linguistic Society 39, vol. 1, pp. 287–303 (2003)

Ogihara, T., Fukushima, T.: Semantic properties of the so-called past tense morpheme in Late Late Middle Japanese. J. East Asian Linguis. **24**, 75–112 (2015). https://doi.org/10.1007/s10831-014-9124-8

Oshima, D.Y.: On the morphological status of - te, - ta, and related forms in Japanese: evidence from accent placement. J. East Asian Linguis. **23**(3), 233–265 (2014). https://doi.org/10.1007/s10831-014-9120-z

Parsons, T.: Events in the Semantics of English: A Study in Subatomic Semantics. MIT Press, Cambridge (1990)

Przepiórkowski, A.: On negative eventualities, negative concord, and negative yes/ no questions. In: Matthews, T., Strolovitc, D. (eds.) Semantics and Linguistic Theory, vol. 9, pp. 237–254. CLC Publications, Ithaca (1999). https://doi.org/10.3765/salt.v9i0.2828

Sauerland, U.: The present tense is vacuous. Snippets **6**, 12–13 (2002)

Shibatani, M.: The Languages of Japan. Cambridge University Press, Cambridge (1990)

Shirai, Y.: The semantics of the Japanese imperfective - teiru. J. Pragmat. **32**(3), 327–361 (2000). https://doi.org/10.1016/S0378-2166(99)00051-X

Shirota, S.: Nihongo keitairon. Hituzi Shobo, Tokyo (1998)

de Swart, H.: Meaning and use of *not...until*. J. Semant. **13**(3), 221–263 (1996). https://doi.org/10.1093/jos/13.3.221

Teramura, H.: Nihongno no sintakusu to imi, vol. II. Kurosio Publishers, Tokyo (1984)

Tian, Y., Breheny, R.: Negation. In: Cummins, C., Katsos, N. (eds.) The Oxford Handbook of Experimental Semantics and Pragmatics, pp. 195–207. Oxford University Press, Oxford (2019). https://doi.org/10.1093/oxfordhb/9780198791768.013.29

Tsujimura, N.: An introduction to Japanese linguistics, 2nd edn. Blackwell, Malden (2007)

Yamashita, Y.: Tensu no "ta" to asupekuto no "ta". J. Int. Student Center Hokkaido Univ. **8**, 1–13 (2004)

Zaradzki, L.: Verbal negation. In: Proceedings of Sinn und Bedeutung 24, vol. 2, pp. 485–502 (2020). https://doi.org/10.18148/sub/2020.v24i2.911

Granularity in Number and Polarity Effects

Eri Tanaka[1]([✉])[iD] and Kenta Mizutani[2][iD]

[1] Osaka University, 1-5 Machikaneyamacho, Toyonaka, Osaka, Japan
`tanaka.eri.hmt@osaka-u.ac.jp`
[2] Aichi Prefectural University, 1522-3 Ibaragabasama, Nagakute-shi, Aichi, Japan
`kmizutani@for.aichi-pu.ac.jp`

Abstract. This paper offers a granularity-based account of the fact that round and non-round numbers may exhibit polarity effects when they are appended by even-type focus particles. The key observation is that non-round numbers appended by *mo* 'even' in Japanese cannot be in the scope of negation, while round numbers exhibit no restriction in scopal relation. Adopting the scope theory of *mo* and a theory of granularity ([6, 10]), we propose that an asymmetric entailment relation holds between propositions with a non-round and a round number and this entailment relation invites a proposition with a coarser granularity into the set of alternatives in computing the scalar presupposition of *mo*. Given that the scalar presupposition of *mo* with numerals is only sensitive to asymmetric entailment, we argue that the availability of asymmetric entailment from the prejacent to this additional alternative proposition is responsible for the polarity effects. We also discuss the related issues such as polarity effects observed in explicit approximators (e.g. *about, approximately*) and numerals with the contrastive topic marker *wa*.

Keywords: Round and non-round numbers · Granularity · Focus particles · Polarity effects

1 Introduction

The recent literature on the polarity phenomena has revealed that vagueness and granularity have an impact on the polarity effect (e.g., [14] on approximators such as *approximately* and *about*, [1] on *some* NP and minimizers). This work is yet another contribution to this trend, reporting an unnoticed contrast between round and non-round numbers when associated with focus particles in Japanese. Our analysis predicts that this phenomenon is sensitive to what granularity is assumed in the context and to whether non-round and round numbers are in competition in the relevant context.

We would like to express our gratitude to Stephanie Solt and anonymous reviewers of LENLS 19 for their invaluable comments on an earlier version of the paper. This work is supported by JSPS Grant-in-Aid 21K00525.

D. Bekki et al. (Eds.): LENLS 2019, LNCS 14213, pp. 51–66, 2023.
https://doi.org/10.1007/978-3-031-43977-3_4

2 Data

It has been acknowledged that *mo* 'even' in Japanese invites different implications when it appears in positive or negative sentences, just like its counterpart in English. The positive version of (1a), for example, implies that Question 2 is hard, while with the negative version of (1a), Q2 is understood to be easy. [1]

(1) a.
    John-wa toi   2-mo {toita/toka-nakat-ta}.
    John-TOP Question 2-mo {solved/solve-NEG-PAST}
    'John even solved Question 2.'

   b.   John solved Q2, <u>which is hard</u>.

   c.   John didn't solve Q2, <u>which is easy</u>.

When *mo* is appended to numerals, as in (2a)–(2b), the implications are about how large the interlocutors consider them to be. The positive sentence in (2a) denotes a situation where John solved five problems, and implicates that '5' is considered to be large.

(2) a.   John-wa mondai-o   5-mon-mo toita
          John-TOP problem-ACC 5-CL-mo   solved
          'John even solved five problems. (And 'five' is considered to be large.)'

   b.   John-wa mondai-o   5-mon-mo toka-nakat-ta.
          John-NOM questions-ACC 5-CL-mo   solve-NEG-PAST
          'John didn't even solve five problems.'

(2b) is ambiguous: in one reading, it is true in a context where the number of problems John solved does not reach 5 (=(3a)), while in the other reading, it becomes true in a context where the number of problems John didn't solve is five (=(3b)). These readings are associated with different implications: in Context A, '5' is understood to be small, while in Context B, the same number is considered to be large. We call these two readings small and large number readings, respectively.[2]

---

[1] *Mo* has several usages as exemplified below. We will confine ourselves to the scalar usage with a similar meaning to 'even' in this paper. We do not make any specific assumption about the issue of whether these different usages come from a single source or not.

  (i) Taro-mo, Taro-mo Jiro-mo, Dare-mo-ga ..., Dare-mo ...nai
     Taro-too, Taro-and Jiro-and, who-mo-NOM ..., who-mo ...NEG
     'Taro also', 'Taro and Jiro', 'Everyone...' 'No one ...'

[2] [9] notes that there is yet another reading for (2b), where truth-conditionally, John solved fewer than five problems and '5' is implicated to be large. We will not consider this reading here, but our analysis can explain why this reading is legitimate both with round and non-round numbers.

(3) a. **Context A**: John has 20 problems to solve, and he solved fewer than five, and '5' is considered small.   **small number reading**

   b. **Context B**: John has 20 problems to solve, and he solved 15 of them, which means that there are five problems that he didn't solve, and '5' is considered to be a large number.   **large number reading**

Even in English behaves differently from its Japanese counterpart in negative sentences. It induces a small-number reading (=Context A), and the large-number reading is very hard to get, if not impossible.[3]

(4) a. John didn't even solve five problems.
       John solved fewer than five problems and '5' is considered to be small.

   b. Not even five people came to the party.
       Fewer than five people came and '5' is considered to be small.

We observe that this ambiguity mysteriously disappears when we use a different number. The key observation here is that the small-number readings available for (2b) and (4) become mysteriously unavailable when the number included is a non-round one, such as 48, while the positive sentence does not exhibit any contrast between 50 and 48, as shown in (5a)–(5b)(see [3]).[4]

(5) a. John-wa {50/48}-mon-mo toita.
       John-TOP 50/48-CL-mo   solved
       'John even solved 50/48 problems.'

   b. John-wa {50/48}-mon-mo toka-nakat-ta.
       John-TOP 50/48-CL-mo   solve-NEG-PAST
       'John didn't even solve 50/48 problems.'

   c. ✓ John solved fewer than 50 problems, and 50 is a small number.
       ✓ There are 50 problems that John didn't solve, and 50 is a large number.

   d. # John solved fewer than 48 problems, and 48 is a small number.
       ✓ There were 48 problems that John didn't solve, and 48 is a large number.

---

[3] Nakanishi [8, 185] notes that the large-number reading is indeed not impossible in English, as shown in (i):
(i) Al, Bill and Conan always read everything they are assigned, but this time, they each had some books that they didn't read. Al didn't read [one]$_F$ book, Bill didn't read [three]$_F$ books and Conan ended up not even reading [five]$_F$.

[4] Ijima [3] takes the sentence with 48 in (5b) is unacceptable. We found this description unsatisfactory because the 48-version of the sentence does have a legitimate interpretation with the large-number reading.

This judgment is replicated in English *even*, in which *even* with numbers in negative sentences only has a small number reading.

(6) a.   John didn't even solve {50/??48} problems.

     b.   Not even {50/??48} people came to the party.

Another interesting aspect of this phenomenon is context sensitivity: in (7), '25' is judged to be weird, because in this case, the conspicuous unit of measure is 12. In other words, in this unit of measure, 25 cannot be a 'round' number.

(7)   24 vs. 25 h
       Han'nin-no   minoshirokin yokyuu-no   denwa-kara   mada {24/#25}
       culprit-GEN   ransom   demand-GEN   call-from   yet   {24/25}
       jikan-mo tat-tei-nai.
       hours-mo pass-ASP-NEG
       (lit.) 'Even 24/25 h haven't passed yet since the culprit called to demand ransom money.'

The obvious question here is what makes 'non-round' numbers awkward in the negative context with *mo*. We propose that this contrast arises when the non-round numbers compete with round numbers in the satisfaction of the presupposition induced by *mo*.

3   The Scope Theory of *Mo* 'Even'

We follow [7] and [8] in that Japanese *mo* is best analyzed in terms of the Scope Theory of *even*-items ([4]). In this theory, *mo* introduces a scalar presupposition without contributing to the assertive content, and its scalar meaning is defined by unlikeliness.[5]

(8) $[\![mo]\!]^{w,c} = \lambda p.\ p(w) = 1$, defined if $\forall q \in C\ [q \neq p \rightarrow q >_{likely} p]$
                                                          Scalar Presupposition

It has been argued that the hard/easy implications observed in (1a) are due to this scalar presupposition ([4]). Nakanishi [7] argues that the small and large readings also come from the scalarity of *mo*, with crucial assumptions that numeral expressions are interpreted to be one-sided, 'at least n', and that the unlikeliness is equated with asymmetric entailment, as in (9).[6]

---

[5] *Even*-items including *mo* may also introduce an additive presupposition (=(i)), but we will put this component aside in this paper.

   (i) $\exists q \in C\ [q \neq p \wedge q(w) = 1]$ **Additive Presupposition** .

[6] We do not claim that the unlikeliness of *mo* is *always* based on asymmetric entailment: this simply makes a wrong prediction. In (i), for example, it has to be

(9)   Let p and q be propositions.
       p is less likely than q iff p entails q but not vice versa.

Under this setting, *John solved n problems* asymmetrically entails a proposition *John solved m problems*, where $m < n$.

The scope theory of *mo* espouses that *mo* moves to a propositional level at LF, even if it is appended to a numeral or a DP. This produces the following LFs for the sentences in (2a)–(2b):

(10)   a.   (2a): [mo [John solved five$_F$ problems]]   large number

       b.   (2b): [mo [¬ [John solved five$_F$ problems]]]   small number

       c.   (2b): [mo [five$_F$ problems [¬ John solved t]]]   large number

The LF in (10a) satisfies the presupposition of *mo* when the set of alternative propositions, C, consists of the propositions that are entailed by the prejacent. This means that the numerals included in the alternative propositions (other than the prejacent) are lower than 5. Since the prejacent proposition includes the largest number among the propositions in C, the large-number reading results.

(11)   a. $[\![(10a)]\!]^{w,c}$ is defined if $\forall q \in C.$ [q $\neq$ [[John solved five problems]]
             $\rightarrow$ [[John solved five problems]] $<_{likely}$ q]

       b.   C = { John solved n problems | n $\leq$ 5 }

In (10b), *mo* scopes over negation, which in turn takes scope over the numeral. To satisfy the presupposition of *mo*, the alternatives in C should be the ones that have a smaller number than 5, since the negation flips the entailment. This leads to the small number reading.

(12)   a. $[\![(10b)]\!]^{w,c}$ is defined if $\forall q \in C$ [q $\neq$ [[¬ John solved five problems]]
             $\rightarrow$ [[¬ John solved five problems]] $<_{likely}$ q]

       b.   C = { ¬ John solved n problems | n $\geq$ 5 }

The configuration in (10c) again results in a large number reading. Since the negation takes a narrower scope than the numeral, the following entailment

---

the case that *Taro came to the party* is less expected than, say, *Mary came to the party*, which is not in entailment relation with the former.
(i) Taro-mo paatii-ni   kita.
    Taro-mo party-DAT came.
    'Even Taro came to the party.'
What seems to be the case is that in the case of *mo* appended to numerals, the unlikeliness based on other than asymmetric entailment is not available.

relation holds: if there are five problems that John didn't solve, it is true that there are four problems that John didn't solve. This leads to the large-number reading.

(13) a. $[\![(10c)]\!]^{w,c}$ is defined if ...

$\forall q \in C \, [q \neq [\![$ there are five problems that John didn't solve $]\!]$

$\rightarrow [\![$ there are five problems that John didn't solve $]\!] <_{\text{likely}} q]$

b. C = { there are n problems that John didn't solve | n ≤ 5 }

It should be noted here that in the scope theory of *even*-items, these items have to take scope over negation to yield appropriate interpretations. In Japanese, this is independently motivated by the general property of focus particles, which take a wider scope than negation.[7] Take *dake* 'only', for example. In (14) below, the only interpretation possible is an interpretation where *only* takes a wider scope than negation.[8]

(14) Taro-wa toi   2-dake toka-nakat-ta.
      Taro-TOP question 2-only solve-NEG-PAST
      (lit.) 'Taro didn't solve only question 2.'
      'It is not the case that Taro solved only question 2.' $*\neg >$ only
      'It is only question 2 that Taro didn't solve.' $\checkmark$ only $> \neg$

The data that concerns us here is now understood in the following way: the contrast between the round and non-round numbers arises when *mo* takes a proposition in which negation takes scope over numerals (=(15b)).

(15) a. LF: [mo [...50/48...]]

b. LF: [mo [¬ [...50/#48...]]]

c. LF: [mo [50/48 [¬ ...]]]

---

[7] In footnote 2 we pointed out that (2b) has the third reading. The scopal relation involved in this reading should be [¬ > mo > n]. This apparent inconsistency to what we claim here is resolved if we consider this reading to be actually a case of external negation. A piece of evidence for this view comes from the fact that this use requires a preceding discourse that refers to the number, as in (i).

(i) A: How many students are enrolled in your class this semester? 50 students have enrolled in mine.

B: 50-nin-mo tooroku si-tei-mas-en.
   50-CL-mo register do-ASP-POLITE-NEG
   (lit.) 'Even 50 students hasn't enrolled (in my class.).'

[8] See [12] for morpho-syntactic reasoning of this obligatory wide-scope reading of focus particles.

This generalization is supported by the fact that the contrast is not observed when *mo* takes a narrower scope than other 'negative' operators. In Japanese, *mo* does not move across a clause boundary ([8]), which is evidenced by the lack of the 'easy' reading in (16). If *mo* takes a proposition within which a 'negative' operator does not take scope over a numeral, it is predicted that there will be no contrast between 50 and 48 observed. This prediction seems to be borne out, as shown in (17).

(16)

    [[Taro-ga toi   2-mo toita]-towa] odoroki-da.
    Taro-NOM question 2-mo solved-COMP surprise-COPULA
    'It's surprising that Taro even solved question 2.'

                                      Question 2 is hard/*easy

(17)   a.   [[Taro-ga {50/48}-mon-mo toita]-towa] odoroki-da.
            Taro-NOM {50/48}-CL-mo   solved-COMP surprise-COPULA
            'It is surprising that Taro even solved 50/48 problems.'

                                     50/48 is a large number.

      b.   [Moshi Taro-ga   {50/48}-mon-mo toita-ra]   kurasu-de
            if   Taro-NOM {50/48}-CL-mo   solved-CONDITIONAL class-in
            ichiban-ni nar-eru-daroo.
            no.1-DAT   become-can-will
            'If Taro even solved 50/48 problems, he will be the best student in
            the class.'   50/48 is a large number.

In the next section, we explain why the generalization in (15) holds, based on granularity.

4 Proposal

4.1 Granularity in Number

Before moving to our proposal, we first lay out how round and non-round numbers are treated in this paper.

We have described '50' can be a round number, while '48' is not. In other words, we understand '48' as a precise number when we say 'Taro solved 48 problems,' while '50' in 'Taro solved 50 problems.' can be understood to denote an exact number Taro solved or an approximate number he solved. Krifka [6] formulates this in terms of the Coarsest Scale Principle in (18): That '50' is on the coarser and finer scales in (19) makes it possible to have an approximate interpretation.

(18)   The Coarsest Scale Principle
If a measure expression α occurs on scales that differ in granularity, then uttering α implicates that the most coarse-grained scale on which α occurs is used. ([6, 119-120])

(19)   <-40———————————————50———————————————60->
<-40–41–42–43–44–45–46–47–48–49–50–51–52–53–54–55–56–57–58–59–60->

We follow [10] and [14] in that granularity is formulated as a contextual parameter of interpretation. A granularity function, $\mathbf{gran_i}$ is a function that maps a number, n to the interval $[n - 1/2 \times i \leq n \leq n + 1/2 \times i\,]$, where i represents the granularity level. Under this formulation, for example, '50' on the coarser scale in (19) denotes the interval from [45–55], and '48' on the finer scale in (19) denotes the interval from [47.5-48.5].

(20)   a. $[\![\,50\,]\!]^g = \mathbf{gran_{10}}(50) = [45\text{-}55]$

     b. $[\![\,48\,]\!]^g = \mathbf{gran_1}(48) = [47.5\text{-}48.5]$

We can now define the relative coarseness of granularity functions, as in (21). $\mathbf{gran_1}$ is finer than $\mathbf{gran_{10}}$ since the former returns a narrower interval when it is applied to a number than when the latter is applied to the same number.

(21)   Relative coarseness of granularity functions
gran is finer than **gran'** iff for any number n,
$\max(\mathbf{gran}(n)) - \min(\mathbf{gran}(n)) < \max(\mathbf{gran'}(n)) - \min(\mathbf{gran'}(n))$

Under this interpretation of granularity, if there is a context where you can truthfully say (22a), then there should be a context where you can truthfully say (22b). This relation holds when the interval denoted by $\mathbf{gran_1}(48)$ falls within the one denoted by $\mathbf{gran_{10}}(50)$.

(22)   a. $[\![$ John solved 48 problems. $]\!]^{w,c} = 1$, iff
Taro solved (at least) $\mathbf{gran_1}(48)$ = Taro solved at least [47.5-48.5] problems.

     b. $[\![$ John solved 50 problems. $]\!]^{w,c} = 1$, iff
Taro solved (at least) $\mathbf{gran_{10}}(50)$ = Taro solved at least [45-55] problems.

The relation between these two is one of entailment: if (22a) is true in a context, then (22b) has to be true in another context. This notion of entailment is thus formulated as follows:

(23)   Let **gran** be finer than **gran'** and n and m be variables for numbers.
For any number n, if there is a context c and a number m such that
if $\mathbf{gran}(n) \subset \mathbf{gran'}(m)$, then $[\![\phi(n)]\!]^{c,\mathrm{gran}} = 1 \Rightarrow [\![\phi[n/m]]\!]^{c,\mathrm{gran'}} = 1$,
where ϕ does not contain $\neg$.

(23) is, in effect, the condition for rounding numbers. Thus '48' can be rounded to '50', but not vice versa.

4.2   Polarity Effects Explained

In the previous section, we made a crucial assumption that the unlikeliness of *mo*, when appended to numerals, is equated with asymmetric entailment. In other words, *mo* appended to numerals is sensitive to entailment relation between its possible alternatives. We propose that an alternative set C contains a proposition with a coarser granularity when it satisfies the relation in (23) with the prejacent. In simpler terms, when the numeral in the prejacent can be rounded to another numeral, then C has to include the proposition with the round number as one of the alternative propositions.

Let us now proceed to how this proposal accounts for our data. Consider first the affirmative cases. Since *mo* does not contribute to the assertive content, we will only consider whether the scalar presupposition is satisfied. (24a) has the prejacent proposition that may be truthfully denoted by a proposition with a round number. Thus the set of alternative propositions in (25b) has to include that proposition (=the underlined one), in addition to the propositions with the same granularity level. Since the prejacent 'John solved 48_{gran1} problems.' entails all the other propositions in C, the scalar presupposition of *mo* is satisfied.

(24)   a.   John-wa 48-mon-mo toita.
John-TOP 48-CL-mo   solved
'John even solved 48 problems.'

b.   John-wa 50-mon-mo toita.
John-TOP 50-CL-mo   solved
'John even solved 50 problems.'

(25)   a. $[\![(24a)]\!]^{w,c}$ is defined, if
$\forall q \in C[q \neq [\![\text{John solved 48 problems}]\!]^{w,c}$
$\rightarrow [\![\text{John solved 48 problems}]\!]^{w,c} <_{\mathrm{likely}} q]$

b.   C = { John solved 48_{gran1} problems, John solved 47_{gran1} problems, John solved 46_{gran1} problems, ... John solved $\underline{50_{\mathrm{gran10}}\ \text{problems}}$ }

c.   'John solved 48_{gran1} problems' entails 'John solved 50_{gran10} problems.'

the scalar presupposition satisfied

(24b), in turn, does not include alternatives with different granularity levels, since the prejacent does not entail, say, 'John solved 48_{gan1} problems.' The computation of the scalar presupposition goes through as usual, with either of C_1 or C_2.

(26) a. $[\![(24b)]\!]^{w,c}$ is defined, if
$\forall q \in C\ [[\![\text{John solved 50 problems}]\!]^{w,c} <_{\text{likely}} q]$

b. $C_1 = \{$ John solved 50_{gran1} problems, John solved 49_{gran1} problems, John solved 48_{gran1} problems, ... $\}$
the scalar presupposition satisfied

c. $C_2 = \{$ John solved 50_{gran10} problems, John solved 40_{gran10} problems, John solved 30_{gran10} problems, ... $\}$
the scalar presupposition satisfied

In the case of negative sentences, two LF are possible, (27b) and (27c).

(27) a.   (=(5b))
John-wa   50/48-mon-mo   toka-nakat-ta.
John-TOP 50/48-CL-mo   solve-NEG-PAST
'John didn't even solve 50/48 problems.'

b. LF_1: [mo [¬ [John solved 48 problems]]]

c. LF_2: [mo [48 problems [¬ John solved t]]]

Let us first consider the wider scope negation reading with '48'. Since '48' is a number that conforms to the relation in (23), C has to include a proposition with a different granularity as its member (=the underlined one in (28b)). Since we espouse the 'at least' semantics of numerals, the prejacent does not entail '¬ John solved 50_{gran10} problems.' (see (29)). This leads to the unsatisfied presupposition, and thus the unacceptability results.

(28) a. $[\![(27b)]\!]^{w,c}$ is defined, if
$\forall q \in C\ [q \neq [\![\text{¬ John solved 48 problems}]\!]^{w,c}$
$\rightarrow [\![\text{¬ John solved 48 problems}]\!]^{w,c} <_{\text{likely}} q]$

b. $C = \{$ ¬ John solved 48_{gran1} problems, ¬ John solved 49_{gran1} problems, ¬ John solved 50_{gran1} problems, ...
¬ John solved 50_{gran10} problems $\}$

c.   '¬ John solved 48_{gran1} problems.' does not entail '¬ John solved 50_{gran10} problems.'   **the scalar presupposition unsatisfied**

(29)   John didn't solve $50_{\text{gran}10}$

$$\overbrace{\hspace{3cm}} \quad \text{---}48\text{---}$$
$$[45\text{---}55]$$

With the numeral taking wider scope, as in (27c), the proposition 'there are $50_{\text{gran}10}$ problems that John didn't solve.' has to be added to the set of alternatives, but this time it does not do any harm: Just like the affirmative case, 'there are $48_{\text{gran}1}$ problems that John didn't solve' entails 'there are $50_{\text{gran}10}$ problems that John didn't solve'. The scalar presupposition of *mo* is satisfied in this reading.

Our proposal that a proposition with a different granularity level is added to the set of alternatives when we compute the scalar presupposition of *mo* thus predicts the contrast between the round and non-round numbers we observed in Sect. 2.

4.3   Some Predictions

The current proposal is based on the idea that a numeral + *mo* sounds awkward when it can be rounded without making the sentence false. This reasoning leads to the prediction that if a numeral is not rounded to another one, then it does not exhibit awkwardness. This prediction is actually borne out, as shown in (30b). According to the definition in (23), '3' cannot be rounded to any number with, say, gran_{10}:

(30) a. **Context**: John had 20 problems to solve, and he only solved two of them.

  b. John-wa mondai-o   3-mon-mo toka-nakat ta.
      John-wa problems-ACC 3-CL-mo   solve-NEG-PAST
      'John didn't even solve three problems.' $\checkmark \neg > 3$

Another consequence of the proposal is that if the context in question makes it easier to access a particular measure of the unit, the numerals that would not show a contrast in other contexts may exhibit a difference in acceptability. (7), repeated here as (31) below, is just the case: In (31), the conspicuous measure of the unit is 12, and thus 25 can be replaced by 24, without making the (affirmative) sentence false.

(31) Han'nin-no minoshirokin yokyuu-no   denwa-kara mada {24/#25}
      culprit-GEN ransom   demand-GEN call-from   yet   {24/25}
      jikan-mo tat-tei-nai.
      hours-mo pass-ASP-NEG
      'Not even 24/25 h have passed yet since the culprit called to demand ransom money.'

Putting a proposition with a different granularity level into a set of alternatives when the number can be rounded to another one thus explains apparently mysterious contrasts between round and non-round numbers in negative sentences.

5 Discussion

This section presents some issues that arise from our analysis.

5.1 Approximately N

Solt [14] observes that numerals modified by 'approximators' such as *approximately, about, roughly* avert negative contexts:

(32)   Lisa { has/*doesn't } have {about/roughly/approximately} 50 sheep.
                                                                    [14,91]

Japanese behaves in the same way, in that the reading where the modified numeral has a narrower scope than negation is not available in (33).

(33)   Lisa-wa mondai-o   oyoso 50-mon toka-nakat-ta.
        Lisa-TOP problems-ACC about 50-CL   solve-NEG-PAST
        'There are 50 problems that Lisa didn't solve.'
                                             *¬ > about 50, ✓about 50 >¬

The possible scopal relation is confined to the one where negation takes a narrower scope when modified numerals appended by *mo*:

(34)   John-wa mondai-o   oyoso 50-mon-mo toka-nakat-ta.
        John-TOP problems-ACC about 50-CL-mo   solve-NEG-PAST
        'John didn't even solve about 50 problems.'
                                    *mo > ¬ > about 50, ✓mo > about 50 > ¬

Our analysis does not seem to predict this distribution. Let us assume that the approximators restrict possible granularity functions to the coarsest possible in the given context (cf. [10, 13]). Since this does not require a proposition with a different granularity in its alternatives, the scalar presupposition of *mo* should be satisfied.

(35)   ⟦ about 50 ⟧^{g} = **gran**(50), where **gran** is the coarsest functions available in the context.

(36)   a. $[\![\neg$ John solved about 50 problems-mo $]\!]^{w,c}$ is defined if
$\forall q \, [q \neq [\![\neg$ John solved about 50 problems $]\!]^{w,c}$
$\rightarrow [\![\neg$ John solved about 50 problems $]\!]^{w,c} <_{likely} q]$

     b. $C = \{ \neg$ John solved about 50 problems, $\neg$ John solved about 60 problems, $\neg$John solved 70 problems, ... $\}$

Solt [14] argues that the PPI-hood of numerals modified by approximators comes from the conversational principle in (37) ([5]) when they are in competition with bare numerals in their structural terms. Under her denotations of modified and bare numerals, these two may not be better than the other from the informational perspective, but the latter is definitely simpler in form and thus better in this respect. So if the speaker uses a proposition with a modified numeral, she/he implicates that an alternative proposition with a bare numeral cannot be asserted.

(37)   Conversational principle: Do not use ϕ if there is another sentence $\phi' \in$ ALT(ϕ) such that both (i) ϕ' is better than ϕ and (ii) ϕ' is weakly assertable.

Suppose we understand that *about 50 problems* denotes the interval around (precisely) '50'. In that case, the negative sentence with the modified numeral causes a contradiction, while the affirmative does not cause any trouble: asserting that John didn't solve [50-k, 50+k] problems implicates the speaker cannot assert that John didn't solve 50 problems, which in turn means that John solved 50 problems.

We might thus explain the oddness of (34) with wide-scope negation reading by resorting to the PPI-hood of modified numerals.

5.2   Contrastive Topic Marker *Wa* and Numerals

Ijima ([3]) has made another observation that when a non-round number is appended by the contrast topic marker *wa*, the sentence becomes odd whether it is in an affirmative or negative context:

(38)   a.   John-wa   mondaio-o   {50/??48}-mon-wa   toita.
          John-TOP   questions-ACC   {50/??48}-CL-CT   solved.
          'John solved (at least) {50/48} problems.'

     b.   John-wa   mondaio-o   {50/??48}-mon-wa   toka-nakat-ta.
          John-TOP   questions-ACC   {50/??48}-CL-CT   solve-NEG-PAST.
          'John didn't solve (at least) {50/48} problems.'

Let us first adopt a scalar analysis of *wa* ([11]). Sawada [11] claims that *wa* works as a mirror image of *mo* 'even', proposing the following semantics.

(39) $[\![wa_{CT}]\!]^{w,c} = \lambda p.\ p(w) = 1$, defined if

    a. $\exists q\ [q \in C \wedge q \neq p \wedge \neg\ q(w)=1]$ Anti-Additive Presupposition

    b. $\forall q\ [q \in C \wedge q \neq p \rightarrow q <_{likely} p]$ Scalar Presupposition

The scalar presupposition in (39b) requires that the prejacent p should be the most likely among the set of alternative propositions C (i.e., p is entailed by all the other alternatives in C.)

If we apply this denotation of *wa* to (38a), we will get the following results:

(40) a. $[\![$ John solved 48-wa problems $]\!]^{w,c}$ is defined if

      b. $\exists q\ [q \in C \wedge q \neq [\![$ John solved 48 problems $]\!]^{w,c} \wedge \neg\ q(w)=1]$

      c. $\forall q\ [q \in C \wedge q \neq [\![$ John solved 48 problems $]\!]^{w,c} \rightarrow q <_{likely} [\![$ John solved 48-mo problems $]\!]^{w,c}]$

      d.   C = { John solved 48_{gran1} problems, John solved 49_{gran1} problems, John solved 50_{gran1} problems, ... <u>John solved 50_{gran10} problems.</u> }

Just like the other examples with '48', the alternative set includes a proposition with a different granularity (=the underlined one in (40d)), which is entailed by the prejacent 'John solved 48-wa problems'. The scalar presupposition is not thus satisfied and the infelicity is predicted as desired.

Unfortunately, the same analysis cannot be extended to the negative sentence in (38b): we predict that the scalar presupposition of *wa* is *satisfied* in this case.

(41) a. $[\![$ John didn't solve 48-wa problems $]\!]^{w,c}$ is defined if

      b. $\exists q\ [q \in C \wedge q \neq [\![\neg$John solved 48 problems $]\!]^{w,c} \wedge \neg\ q(w)=1]$

      c. $\forall q\ [q \in C \wedge q \neq [\![\neg$John solved 48 problems $]\!]^{w,c} \rightarrow q <_{likely} [\![\neg$ John solved 48-mo problems $]\!]^{w,c}]$

      d.   C = { ..., $\neg$ John solved 46_{gran1} problems, $\neg$John solved 47_{gran1} problems, $\neg$John solved 48_{gran1} problems, <u>$\neg$John solved 50_{gran10} problems.</u> }

In the negative environment, the entailment relationship is reversed, and the underline proposition above entails the prejacent. Thus, the prejacent is the most likely in C, and the scalar presupposition is satisfied.

Let us now adopt a non-scalar analysis of *wa* ([2]). Hara ([2]) also proposes that *wa* introduces defindness condition without contributing to the assertion, which requires the existence of at least one stronger proposition than the assertion. Furthermore, this produces an uncertainty implicature where it is possible that the stronger proposition is false.

(42) a. $[\![\text{wa}]\!]^{w,c} = \lambda p.\ p(w) = 1$, defined if $\exists q \in C\ [\ q \Rightarrow p \wedge p \not\Rightarrow q]$

   b.   Implicates: $\Diamond \neg\ q$

The application of this analysis to our case does not give us what we want: since there is at least one stronger alternative in C in (42c), say, John solved 50_{gran1} problems, this should not cause any problems, even if we have an alternative with different granularity.

(43) a. $[\![\,\text{John solved 48-wa problems}\,]\!]^{w,c}$ is defined if

   b. $\exists q\ [q \in C \wedge q \to [\![\,\text{John solved 48 problems}\,]\!]^{w,c} \wedge [\![\,\text{John solved 48 problems}\,]\!]^{w,c} \not\to q]$

   c. $C = \{$ John solved 48_{gran1} problems, Jon solved 49_{gran1} problems, John solved 50_{gran1} problems, ... John solved $\underline{50_{\text{gran10}} \text{ problems}}$ $\}$

The same holds of the negation, and thus we cannot explain the distribution of '48' with *wa*.

The above discussions indicate that unlike the cases with *mo*, the incompatibility of *wa* with non-round numbers is not due to the entailment relation between round and non-round numbers. Thus, we need a different, non-entailment-based analysis, and we speculate that the uncertainty implicature induced by *wa* is at odds with the fine granularity of non-round numbers. In (38a) and (38b), the speaker implicates that she or he does not have perfect knowledge about numbers greater/smaller than 48 but at the same time, she or he uses the non-round number, indicating that she or he has sufficient knowledge to choose the fine granularity scale. Given that the choice of the precise scale increases the speaker's certainty, non-round numbers seem to be incompatible with the contrastive topic marker *wa*. However, we leave the detailed exposition of this analysis for future work.

6   Conclusion

This paper has discussed an unfamiliar polarity effect observed with non-round and round numbers appended by *mo* and proposes that a proposition with a non-round number has to include a proposition with a number with a coarser granularity. It is important to note here that the contrast reported here is not confined to Japanese *mo*: as we noted above English exhibits the same contrast. This indicates that this phenomenon could be robust across languages, which we have to leave for future work. We hope that our work will contribute to the understanding of the roles of granularity in polarity effects, which has gained a lot of attention in recent literature.

References

1. Goncharov, J., Wolf, L.: Deriving polarity from granularity. In: Proceedings of SALT, vol. 31, pp. 683–702 (2021)
2. Hara, Y.: Grammer of Knowledge Representation: Japanese Discourse Items at Interfaces. Ph.D. thesis, University of Delaware (2006)
3. Ijima, M.: Suuryooshi to wa to mo (quantifiers and wa and mo). In: Tsukishima Hiroshi sensei koki kinen kokugogaku ronshu (A Festschrift for Professor Hiroshi Tsukishima on his 70th birthday), pp. 1041–1062. Kyuuko shoin (1995)
4. Karttunen, L., Peters, S.: Conventional implicature. Syntax Semant. **11**, 1–56 (1979)
5. Katzir, R.: Structurally-defined alternatives. Linguist. Philos. **30**, 669–690 (2007)
6. Krifka, M.: Approximate interpretations of number words: a case for strategic communication. In: Hinrichs, E., Nerbonne, J. (eds.) Theory and evidence in semantics, pp. 109–132. CSLI Publications, Stanford (2009)
7. Nakanishi, K.: Even, only, and negative polarity in Japanese. In: Proceedings of SALT, vol. 16, pp. 138–155 (2006)
8. Nakanishi, K.: Scope of Even: A cross-linguistic perspective. In: Proceedings of NELS , vol. 38, pp. 179–192 (2009)
9. Nakanishi, K.: Focus particle 'mo' appended to numerals and negation (suushi toritate-no 'mo' to hitei). In: Kato, Y., Yoshimura, A., Imani, I. (eds.) Negation and Linguitic Theory (Hitei to Gengo Riron), pp. 260–284. Kaitakusha (2010)
10. Sauerland, U., Stateva, P.: Scalar vs. epistemic vagueness: evidence from approximators. In: Proceedings of SALT, vol. 17, pp. 228–245 (2007)
11. Sawada, O.: The Japanese contrastive Wa: a mirror image of EVEN. In: Proceedings of Berkeley Linguistic Society, vol. 34, pp. 281–292 (2008)
12. Shibata, Y.: Negative structure and object movement in Japanese. J. East Asian Linguis. **24**(3), 217–269 (2015). https://doi.org/10.1007/s10831-014-9131-9
13. Solt, S.: An alternative theory of imprecision. In: Proceedings of SALT, vol. 24, pp. 514–533 (2014)
14. Solt, S.: Approximators as a case study of attenuating polarity items. In: Hucklebridge, S., Nelson, M. (eds.) Proceedings of NELS, vol. 48, pp. 91–104 (2018)

Contrafactives and Learnability: An Experiment with Propositional Constants

David Strohmaier[1] and Simon Wimmer[2]([envelope])

[1] Department of Computer Science and Technology, ALTA Institute, University of Cambridge, Cambridge, UK
ds858@cam.ac.uk
[2] Institut für Philosophie und Politikwissenschaft, Technische Universität Dortmund, Dortmund, Germany
simon.wimmer@tu-dortmund.de

Abstract. Holton has drawn attention to a new semantic universal, according to which no natural language has contrafactive attitude verbs. Because factives are universal across natural languages, Holton's universal is part of a major asymmetry between factive and contrafactive attitude verbs. We previously proposed that this asymmetry arises partly because the meaning of contrafactives is significantly harder to learn than that of factives. Here we extend our work by describing an additional computational experiment that further supports our hypothesis.

Keywords: Contrafactives · Factives · Semantic universals · Neural networks · Learnability

1 Introduction

Richard Holton [8] has drawn attention to a novel semantic universal, according to which no natural language has contrafactive attitude verbs. Contrafactives are the mirror image of factive attitude verbs, such as *know, remember, see*, and *regret*. Although both factives and contrafactives entail a belief, contrafactives differ from factives in presupposing the falsity, as opposed to truth, of their declarative complements. To illustrate, suppose we extend our language with the contrafactive *contra*. Now, whilst both *Dan knows that Maggie is dancing*

This paper reports on research supported by Cambridge University Press and Assessment, University of Cambridge. We thank the NVIDIA Corporation for the donation of the Titan X Pascal GPU used in this research. Simon Wimmer's work on this paper was supported by a postdoc stipend of the Fritz Thyssen Foundation. We thank audiences in Bochum, Dortmund, Essen, Tokyo, and Utrecht, and anonymous reviewers for LENLS19 and AC23 for discussion of related material. David Strohmaier designed and ran both computational experiments, Simon Wimmer brought philosophical and linguistic discussions to bear on their design and interpretation.

D. Bekki et al. (Eds.): LENLS 2019, LNCS 14213, pp. 67–82, 2023.
https://doi.org/10.1007/978-3-031-43977-3_5

and *Dan contras that Maggie is dancing* entail that Dan believes that Maggie is dancing, the former presupposes that she is, the latter that she is not. This difference in presuppositions between the factive and contrafactive surfaces in several diagnostics; for instance:

1. # Umut knows that it's raining, but it isn't.
2. # Umut contras that it's raining, and it actually is.
3. (a) Does Eylem know that we've won?
   (b) Eylem doesn't know that we've won.
   → We've won.
4. (a) Does Eylem contra that we've won?
   (b) Eylem doesn't contra that we've won.
   → We haven't won.

The diagnostic in 1 and 2 shows that the inference to the truth/falsity of the verb's declarative complement cannot be cancelled; the diagnostic in 3 and 4 suggests that the inference generally (cf., e.g., [13, p. 218]) projects through entailment-cancelling environments, such as question and negation.

That no natural language has contrafactives raises the question: why do natural languages universally have factives, such as *know* [6], but universally lack contrafactives? Importantly, the key issue here would remain, even if some counterexamples to Holton's universal were eventually found. For even if there were some contrafactives, an asymmetry between factives and contrafactives would persist: factives would be abundant, contrafactives scarce.

Our aim here is to uncover one reason for the asymmetry between factives and contrafactives. Drawing on recent discussions of other semantic universals [26–28], we explore the hypothesis that the asymmetry between factives and contrafactives arises partly because the meaning of a contrafactive is harder to learn than that of a factive. Our hypothesis is inspired by the intuitive idea that languages have words for meanings that are easier to acquire and use compositional methods to express meanings that are harder to learn [27, p. 4]. We tested our hypothesis by conducting two computational experiments using artificial neural networks. We previously reported the results of the first experiment in [30], but there also noted some limitations of that experiment. Our second experiment, whose results we report here for the first time, addresses these limitations. We find that both of our computational experiments support our hypothesis that the meaning of a contrafactive is harder to learn than that of a factive.

We begin by discussing some putative counterexamples to Holton's universal. Section 3 motivates our hypothesis by extending lessons from factive and non-factive theory of mind as well as the acquisition of belief and desire verbs to contrafactives. Section 4 describes our computational experiments.

2 Counterexamples

An important feature of a contrafactive we have yet to mention is that, according to Holton, it is an "atomic propositional attitude verb" [8, p. 248].[1] Thus, the inference to the falsity of its declarative complement is not the result of a compositional method. This means that [1]'s Spanish *creerse* 'wrongly believe' (as well as [24]'s Puerto Rican Spanish *creerse*) does not count as a contrafactive. *Creerse* performs much as *contra* on our diagnostics, with the exception of what [1, pp. 66-8] calls "polarity reversal under negation". And this exception, they note, could be due not to a lack of the presupposition of a contrafactive, but to syntactic neg-raising, i.e. an interpretation of the negation within, as opposed to outside, the scope of *creerse*.

5. (a) # Juan se cree que Ana tiene 30 años ...y tiene razón!
        'Juan REFL believes that Ana is 30 years old ...and he is right!'
    (b) Se cree Juan que está lloviendo?
        'Does Juan REFL believe that it is raining?'   → It's not raining
    (c) Juan no se cree que está lloviendo.
        'Juan doesn't REFL believe that it is raining.'   → It's raining.

However, *creerse* is built by adjoining the reflexive pronoun *se* to the non-factive verb *creer* 'believe'.[2] And, since adjoining the reflexive pronoun has similar effects in the case of Spanish *pensarse* and French *s'imagine*, [1, p. 72] suggests that the inference to the falsity of *creerse*'s declarative complement results, at least partially, from composing the meanings of *se* and *creer*. Hence, *creerse* is not atomic, and so not a contrafactive.

Holton's restriction of contrafactives to atomic propositional attitude verbs is one reason why he would not count English *disprove* as a contrafactive, contrary to [12, p. 271].[3] For even if *disprove* presupposed the falsity of its declarative complement, which is questionable (see diagnostics below), that inference would result from a compositional method: adjoining the negative prefix *dis* to *prove* reverses *prove*'s inference to the truth of its declarative complement.[4]

---

[1] Holton adopts two further conditions expressions musts satisfy to count as contrafactives. In parallel with *know*, he would regard *contra* as a mental state verb and as responsive (embedding declarative and interrogative complements). For present purposes, however, we set these conditions aside. We take the question of why no natural language has a verb with the features noted in the text to be of independent interest, and expect the work we present here to also go some way toward addressing why no natural language has a verb that satisfies all of Holton's conditions.

[2] Although a non-factive (e.g. *believe* or *think*) entails a belief too, it contrasts with factives and contrafactives in triggering neither an uncancelleable inference to the truth/falsity of its declarative complement nor an inference to truth/falsity that projects through entailment-cancelling environments.

[3] Another reason is that *disprove* neither entails a belief that its declarative complement is true nor is a mental state verb, though Hyman explicitly questions the mental state condition, making appeal to that condition dialectically ineffective.

[4] [12] also lists *pretend* and *lie* as counterexamples to Holton's universal. But in [8, p. 247], Holton denies that *pretend* is a contrafactive as its falsity inference is cancellable and in [9], he argues that *lie* does not embed declarative complements.

6. (a) # Anna disproved that we are in the matrix, and we actually are.
   (b) Did Anna disprove that she was responsible?   ↛ She was not responsible.
   (c) Anna did not disprove that she was responsible.   ↛ She was not responsible.

The example of *creerse* illustrates that languages without contrafactives can still express, at least approximately, the meaning of a contrafactive by use of compositional methods. In combination with our hypothesis, viz. that it is significantly harder to learn the meaning of a contrafactive than the meaning of a factive, this helps to provide a further part of the explanation of why natural languages lack contrafactives. Given the difficulty of acquiring their meaning, speakers of natural languages are more likely to be content with expressing their meaning by use of compositional methods (cf. [27, p. 4]).[5]

[8, pp. 245-9, 262-4] considered several apparent counterexamples to his universal found in non-Indo-European languages. However, as far as we know, none is a genuine contrafactive. Take the Mandarin verb *yǐwéi*, which [25] treats as a contrafactive. [5] has argued that this verb carries a post-supposition that the declarative complement must not be added to the common ground, rather than a presupposition that its declarative complement is false. This post-supposition is preserved under some entailment-cancelling environments. In particular, it projects through questions: on the assumption that the speaker either believes that there is or that there is not a test tomorrow, 7b triggers an inference to the falsity of *yǐwéi*'s declarative complement. However, the falsity inference is cancellable (7a) and fails to project through negation (7c).

7. (a) Rénmén yǐwéi tā shì yìwànfùwēng ...ér tā díquè shì
       'People are under the impression that she's a billionaire ...and she actually is.'
   (b) Lìlì yǐwéi míngtiān yǒu kǎoshì ma?   → There's no test tomorrow.
       'Is Lili under the impression that there's a test tomorrow?'
   (c) Lìlì bìng-bù yǐwéi míngtiān yǒu kǎoshì.   ↛ There's no test tomorrow.
       'Lily definitely doesn't think there's a test tomorrow.'

Further apparent non-Indo-European counterexamples that Holton considers are [24]'s Turkish verbs *san* and *zannet*, glossed as 'believe (falsely)'. However, Holton's native speaker informants disagreed over whether these are contrafactives. And our informant strongly denies that they are.[6] She observes that the inference to the falsity of their complements can be cancelled:

8. (a) Simon yağmur yağdığını sanıyor/zannediyor ve gerçekten yağmur yağıyor.
       'Simon believes (falsely) that it's raining, and it is raining.'

Although *san* and *zannet* contrast slightly with the more neutral *dusun* 'believe', this might be explained by assimilating them to *yǐwéi*. For *yǐwéi* also contrasts slightly with the more neutral *rènwéi* 'believe'. In effect, the data we have is consistent with *san* and *zannet* merely post-supposing that their complements must not be added to the common ground.

---

[5] Most likely there are further reasons for the absence of contrafactives. In future work, we will survey how the costs and benefits of contrafactives tally up.

[6] We thank Dilara Malkoc for discussion of the Turkish data.

A final non-Indo-European verb we might be tempted to treat as a counterexample to Holton's universal, but not noted by Holton, is *liah8-tsun2* in
Taiwanese Southern Min. [10] glosses this verb as 'think (counterfactually)' and
argues that it presupposes the falsity of its declarative complement. However,
as they note, the inference to the falsity of its declarative complement can be
cancelled (9a). Using machinery from [16], they argue that this does not falsify
their claim that *liah8-tsun2* presupposes the falsity of its declarative complement. But even if this is so, the possibility does undermine *liah8-tsun2*'s status
as a mirror image of a factive; for the inference triggered by a factive cannot
be cancelled in the way in which *liah8-tsun2*'s inference can be cancelled. In
addition, *liah8-tsun2* is ungrammatical embedded under negation (9b). Thus,
the inference it triggers cannot project through negation. This is yet another
way in which *liah8-tsun2* fails to be the mirror image of a factive. In sum, then,
liah8-tsun2 should not be regarded as a contrafactive.

9. (a) gua2 liah8-tsun2 i1 si7 huan1-a2. siong2-be7-kau3, i1 tsiann5-sit8 si7!
       'I thought that he was an aborigine; to my surprise, he really is!'
   (b) *i1 bo5 liah8-tsun2 a1-ing1 tsa1-hng1 kah4 ong5-sian1-sinn1 tso3-hue2.
       'He didn't mistakenly think that Aing was with Mr. Wang yesterday.'

3   Motivating Our Hypothesis

Before we turn to our computational experiments, we want to provide an intuitive
motivation for our claim that factives are easier to learn than contrafactives. This
motivation is inspired by [20]'s work on differences between factive and non-
factive mental state attribution (see also [17,19]). We describe this motivation
in greater detail in [30], and merely provide a brief sketch here.

Since factives presuppose the truth of their declarative complements, a factive attitude ascription (with a declarative complement) commits a speaker to
the truth of its declarative complement. And since factives entail a belief, the
ascription entails that its subject too is committed to the truth of its declarative
complement. For this reason, factive attitude ascriptions are constrained, and so
simplified, by an overlap of what the speaker and the subject of their ascription
take the world to be like: the speaker can simply copy-paste their own take of
what the world is like to represent that of the subject of their ascription.

Ascription of non-factive and contrafactive attitudes is not constrained in
this way. Non-factives do not presuppose the truth of their declarative complements. So, a non-factive attitude ascription does not commit its speaker to
the truth of its declarative complement; but it does entail that its subject is
committed to the truth of that complement. For this reason, the ascription by
itself leaves open whether the ways its speaker and its subject take the world to
be overlap. Contrafactives, of course, presuppose the falsity of their declarative
complements. Thus, a contrafactive attitude ascription commits its speaker to
the falsity of its declarative complement; yet it still entails that its subject is
committed to the truth of that complement. Given this, the contrafactive attitude ascription represents the ways its speaker and its subject take the world to

be as incompatible. In sum, then, neither non-factive nor contrafactive attitude ascriptions are constrained, and so simplified, by an overlap of what the speaker and the subject of their ascription take the world to be like.

Importantly, the presence or absence of the constraints on factive and contrafactive attitude ascriptions just described is arguably (at least partly) due to the meaning of factives and contrafactives. But given this, we expect the meaning of a contrafactive to be harder to acquire than that of a factive.

By the same reasoning, we also expect the meaning of a contrafactive to be slightly easier to learn than that of a non-factive. The way the speaker takes the world to be constrains, albeit only slightly, their contrafactive, but not their non-factive, attitude ascriptions. If, say, our speaker takes Maggie to be dancing, they cannot consistently claim that Dan contras that Maggie is dancing, but can consistently claim that Dan believes it. The way the speaker takes the world to be rules out the contrafactive attitude ascription for them, but not the non-factive attitude ascription. In this sense, our speaker's view of the world contributes mere noise to non-factive attitude ascription; noise they must learn to ignore.

Other Factors. Given that, just like factives, non-factives such as *think* are universal across natural languages [6], the result that the meaning of a non-factive is slightly harder to acquire than that of a contrafactive can seem puzzling. However, for at least two reasons, the added difficulty of acquiring the meaning of a non-factive just described need not make non-factives less common.

First, other factors can make it significantly more important to learn the meaning of a non-factive. Non-factives are neutral regarding the truth-value of their declarative complements. For this reason, ascribing non-factive attitudes allows us to explain and predict others' actions, even if we have no view of what the world is (not) like or want to stay neutral on that issue for some other reason (e.g. a disagreement with an interlocutor). Non-factives also allow us to rationalize what others do by pointing to what, from their point of view, was to be said in favour of their action, regardless of what was to be said for or against their action from our own point of view [3]. Thus, speakers have significant reasons to acquire the meaning of a non-factive that do not generalize to the meaning of a contrafactive. As we will explore in future work, this is plausibly just one way in which the benefits of acquiring the meaning of a non-factive outweigh those of acquiring the meaning of a contrafactive. We thus expect languages to universally feature non-factives, even if the meaning of a non-factive is slightly harder to learn than that of a contrafactive.

Second, as we [30] noted previously, other factors, which go beyond how a speaker's view of the world constrains their attitude ascriptions, can make the meaning of a contrafactive *overall* harder to learn than that of a non-factive. One factor we expect to play this role is that, unlike in the case of contrafactive attitude ascriptions and their declarative complements, key pragmatic properties of non-factive attitude ascriptions and their declarative complements match. To understand this factor, consider the pragmatic syntactic bootstrapping model of how infants acquire attitude verb meanings [7].

To illustrate the model, take belief and desire verbs, e.g. *think* and *want*. In English, the first typically take a complement in finite tense, e.g. *it's raining*, whilst the second typically take an infinitival complement, e.g. *you to have a milkshake*. The syntactic differences between the complements of belief and desire verbs connect to differences in the pragmatic properties of belief and desire ascriptions. Belief ascriptions are widely used to make indirect assertions. The point of using *I believe that it's raining* can be, and often is, to make a hedged assertion that it is raining. This pragmatic property matches one had by the ascription's complement. Given its finite tense, the complement is a declarative clause and so is primarily used to make assertions. The meaning of belief verbs is inferred from the match of the pragmatic properties of belief ascriptions and their complements. Given this match, a belief ascription must, in some sense, commit its subject to the truth of its declarative complement.

By contrast, desire ascriptions are widely used to make indirect requests. The point of *I want you to tell me the time* can be, and often is, to indirectly request that the listener tell me the time. This pragmatic property matches one had by the ascription's complement: its fragment *Tell me the time* is primarily used to make requests. The meaning of desire verbs is inferred from the match of the pragmatic properties of desire ascriptions and a fragment of their complements. Given this match, a desire ascription must, in some sense, commit its subject to having a preference for the truth of its complement.

On this model of how the meaning of belief verbs is acquired, we expect the meaning of a contrafactive to be more difficult to learn than that of a non-factive. One cannot infer the meaning of a contrafactive from a match between pragmatic properties of contrafactive attitude ascriptions and their complements. Syntactically, the complement of a contrafactive is the same as that of a belief verb. So, it is primarily used to make assertions. But, since a contrafactive presupposes the falsity of its declarative complement, a contrafactive attitude ascription cannot be used to make an assertion, hedged or not. It can at best be used to indirectly deny the content of its complement. Given this mismatch of the pragmatic properties of contrafactive attitude ascriptions and their complements, we expect it to be quite difficult to acquire the meaning of a contrafactive, especially to learn that a contrafactive attitude ascription commits its subject to the truth, rather than falsity, of its declarative complement.

4   Experiments

To test our expectation that the meaning of a contrafactive is harder to acquire than that of a factive, we conducted two computational experiments using artificial neural networks, specifically Transformer encoders with Binary Cross Entropy Loss from the pyTorch library. Transformers, based upon the so-called attention mechanism that allows contextualised processing of word information, are the foundation of current state-of-the-art results in natural language processing [4,21,31]. Recent work also suggests that, despite not being originally designed for cognitive plausibility, Transformer-based networks show greater convergence with human processing than other approaches [2,23]. They therefore form the best currently available basis for obtaining results that reflect learnability for human language learners.

That being said, there likely are ways in which our results do not perfectly reflect learnability for human language learners. For one, human language learning seems to require significantly less data than is required to train our networks. Still, there is reason to think that if we presented neural networks with data in a similar order in which a child is presented with data, these networks would need significantly less data to learn target expressions [11]. So, we expect that this difference between human language learning and the way our network learns is, at least in principle, no barrier to using our results to draw conclusions about human language learning. For another, our networks are trained by backpropagation, a method usually taken to be cognitively implausible. However, there have been attempts to argue that algorithms similar to backpropagation could be implemented by human brains [14,15,22]. So, whilst using backpropagation is problematic, it remains open how much doubt this casts on our argument.

First Experiment. In our first experiment, we trained our network to predict the truth-value of factive, non-factive, and contrafactive attitude ascriptions, given a representation of a small world and a representation of the small world as the attitude holder takes it to be (which may or may not be accurate).[7] Our network used position embeddings and sequence embeddings to encode word order and distinguish the three types of input (attitude ascription, world representation, mind representation). Its predictions were expressed in a probability within [0,1] that the target ascriptions are true. An assignment of 1 to an ascription can be understood as claiming that the ascription is definitely true. By contrast, an assignment of 0 is to be understood as claiming that the ascription is definitely not true, which leaves open whether the ascription is false or undefined due to presupposition failure. We did not train the network to distinguish these two cases and plan to fill this gap in a follow-up experiment.

The artificial language in which our target ascriptions were formulated and which the neural network learned can be interpreted as a fragment that describes propositions about the relative locations of two objects to each other plus the attitude taken towards these propositions. The small world can be conceived of as a 3-by-3 grid containing 3 objects. All objects differ in shape and they sometimes differ in colour. A typical statement in the artificial language can be glossed as *contra red triangle above blue square*, so long as we bear in mind that the network lacks any real world knowledge about triangles, squares, etc.[8]

Generally speaking, the results of our experiment show the Transformer-encoder to perform better on factives than contrafactives. While the performance on non-factives was even worse, this is to be expected both from our previous

---

[7] We did not train our network to handle ascriptions in entailment-cancelling environments. We plan to fill this gap in a follow-up experiment.

[8] Further details and a comparison of this experiment with others in the literature can be found in [30]. A link to our paper, the code for our network, and further information are available on GitHub [29].

discussion in Sect. 3 and the architecture of our network. Our network always processes both a mind and a world representation, although the latter only contributes noise in the case of non-factives. We suspect that, as humans acquire non-factives, they learn (to deploy) a better input-gating mechanism than our model to filter out this noise. Further, our network is not sensitive to pragmatic properties of attitude ascriptions or their complements. Below we focus on results that bear on the comparison between factives and contrafactives.

We evaluated 51 hyperparameter settings in an initial search performing five-fold cross-validation on the training data.[9] We then applied the setting that performed best in the hyperparameter search, i.e. the one with the highest overall accuracy, to a hold-out test set. The results on this set showed higher performance for factives than contrafactives. But the difference in accuracy was small (97.8% vs. 97.6%), as the model was trained on such a large data set (633,981 examples) that it successfully learned all attitude verbs.

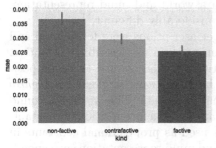

Fig. 1. Mean absolute error on test set (Color figure online)

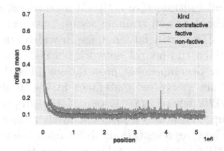

Fig. 2. Rolling mean loss smoothed over 10,000 instances during training

Looking at accuracy, however, discards some information, since for an ascription that is true (not true), a prediction (not) above 0.5 is treated as accurate. By contrast, mean absolute error also considers how far the prediction strayed from the correct values of 0 (not true) and 1 (true). The differences for the mean absolute error are still small, but more striking. A permutation significance test (resamples = 9,999) shows that the error is significantly larger for contrafactives than factives ($p < 0.01$), see Fig. 1.[10] The training for the factive also proceeded faster than for the contrafactive, see Fig. 2, providing further support for a difference in how hard it is to learn the meaning of a contrafactive as opposed to factive. To give some numbers for intuition, after 100,000 training examples the average loss for the factive is 0.39, while the average loss for the contrafactive is 0.54.

---

[9] A list of the available as well as the best-performing hyperparameters can be found in our online appendix on GitHub [29].

[10] Here and below we used the permutation test included in the scipy library.

Post-experimental analysis suggests that many of the network's remaining errors have the following source. Evaluating a sentence like *contra red triangle above blue square* proves difficult if the world or mind representation contains a red triangle next to a blue square, rather than one of the objects being missing altogether. The network was paying excessive attention to whether objects named in the artificial language sentences were present, ignoring whether the described relationship between the objects held. Put differently, the network struggles with reading the spatial relations from the linear enumeration of the 3-by-3 grid's 9 cells. This can be interpreted as a difficulty of dealing with word order, which is well-documented for Transformer models in the NLP literature [18]. Given this, our next experiment had the network learn a simpler artificial language.

Second Experiment. We use the same neural architecture as before, and again train our Transformer encoder to predict the truth-value of factive, non-factive and contrafactive attitude ascriptions, given a world and mind representation. The data and training setup, however, are considerably different.[11]

The artificial language in which our target ascriptions were formulated and which the neural network learned can be interpreted as describing primitive, non-decomposable propositions plus the attitude taken toward those propositions. A typical statement in the artificial language can be glossed as *contra p110*, where *p110* is one of 120 propositional constants. The world and mind representations consist of further representations of a propositional constant. These representations differ from the tokens used as propositional constants in attitude ascriptions. For instance, the world and mind representation corresponding to *p110* can be glossed as r_p110. We decided not to formulate the world and mind representations in the same vocabulary as attitude ascriptions because these representations could, e.g., be given in a distinct language of thought.

The new experiment also introduces a placeholder verb into our artificial language. This verb is the mirror image of a non-factive: whilst the truth of a non-factive attitude ascription does not depend on the world representation, the truth of a placeholder statement does not depend on the mind representation. Thus, a typical statement with our placeholder verb can be glossed as *p110 obtains*; this statement is true if and only if the world representation is r_p110. Placeholder statements like this are used exclusively in a pre-training set; by contrast, the main training set and hold-out test set only contain attitude ascriptions.

Balancing the data so that the model learns the general distribution of truth-values is not straightforward. For instance, there is only one way to make the factive attitude ascription *factive p110* true: world and mind representation must both be r_p110; but there are 119 ways to make the corresponding contrafactive attitude ascription true: the only constraint is that the mind representation is r_p110 and the world representation is not. Just as there is an imbalance between attitude verbs, there is also an imbalance within some attitude verbs, especially factives: although there is only one way to make *factive p110* true, there are

---

[11] The code for this network and further details are also available on GitHub [29].

121*119 ways to make it not true. This issue also arises for the pre-training data, since there are 120 ways to make *p110 obtains* true—the mind representation does not matter—, but 119*120 ways to make it not true. We address this problem by sampling extra instances of the underrepresented truth-values for the pre-training and training data.

For the first experiment, balancing the data on the basis of truth-values in this way led to a problematic imbalance. This was due to the different ways in which the truth-value of our ascriptions depended on the presence of objects in our 3-by-3 grid. *Factive red triangle above blue square* was true only if the red triangle was above the blue square, but *contra red triangle above blue square* was true only if there was no red triangle or it was not above the blue square (e.g., because there was none). The truth-conditions of a contrafactive attitude ascription can thus be understood as disjunctive. And notably, the satisfaction of the second of these disjuncts depends on word order: for the red triangle to be above the blue square, the token for the red triangle has to occur in the first (second) third of the sequence and the blue square in the second (third) third of the sequence describing our 3-by-3 grid.

Transformer models, however, struggle with word order. Hence, the different ways the truth-conditions for contrafactives can be satisfied should arguably be treated as different cases for Transformer models. On this basis, it could be argued that to give the network a fair chance of acquiring our attitude verbs equally well, it would be necessary to balance these relevantly different cases in our data. Effectively, we had to choose between balancing true factive and true contrafactive attitude ascriptions, and so just on the basis of truth-value, or balancing true factive attitude ascriptions with each sub-group of true contrafactive attitude ascriptions. But neither choice is obviously correct.

Our new experiment avoids this problem by having a simpler artificial language, replacing ordered descriptions of a 3-by-3 grid with primitive, non-decomposable representations of propositional constants. Of course, *factive p110* is still true iff world and mind representation are r_p110, while for *contra p110* the only constraint is that the mind representation is r_p110 and the world representation is not. But importantly, this difference in truth-conditions does not connect to the problem Transformers have with word order. Since humans do not struggle with word order, any influence of this problem for Transformers on our results casts doubt on whether they reflect learnability for human language learners. Fortunately, given primitive, non-decomposable representations of propositional constants, our new network is processing much shorter sequences of tokens, so that difficulties due to word order are minimized.

Generally, the training and test data are split according to propositional constants. Randomly selected 30% of propositional constants and corresponding representations are reserved for the test set (which consists of 3,405,889 examples). More specifically, they and their corresponding representations (e.g. *p110* and r_p110) never occur in the main training data (3,528,000 examples). This split ensures that our model does not overfit to the specific propositional constants and corresponding representations it sees in learning the meaning of our attitude verbs, but acquires functions that generalize well to cases it has not seen before. To complicate the situation further, we also need to split the pre-training data into one version for the hyperparameter search (1,171,296 examples), which excludes the selected 30% of propositional constants and corresponding representations, and another for the final evaluation (3,427,200 examples), which includes them. The reason for this split is that we do not want to overfit our selection of hyperparameters to the 30% selected propositional constants and corresponding representations, but nonetheless need to pre-train on them so the network can learn their embeddings for the final evaluation.

This last point brings us to a difficulty for our model that the introduction of our placeholder verb resolves. The network has to learn the embeddings for the propositional constants and corresponding representations that we have reserved for the test set. Put roughly, the model needs to learn that a use of *p110* is true if and only if the world representation is r_p110. Because we use different tokens for these two expressions, the model must learn that they are connected. However, since we do not want to overfit the attitude verbs on our propositional constants, the network cannot learn the embeddings on attitude ascriptions.[12] Instead, it learns them on placeholder statements.

In effect, our network first learns the meaning of an attitude verb's complement, e.g. that *p110* is true iff the world representation is r_p110, regardless of what the mind representation is, by learning to predict the truth-value of *p110 obtains.* Our network can then use the meaning of the complement it acquired in inferring the meaning of our attitude verbs. But some attitude verbs stray farther from the meaning of the complement than others. In particular, *non-factive p110* merely inverts the role of mind and world representations, whilst *contra p110* requires as much of the mind-representation as *non-factive p110*, but also that the world representation is not r_p110. Given this, we expect our second experiment to differ from the first on whether non-factives perform even worse than contrafactives. Although our network still processes a mind and a world representation, and the latter only contributes noise for non-factives, it is now sensitive to some properties that make the meaning of a contrafactive harder to learn than that of a non-factive. This is because the data and training setup reflect, in one respect, the pragmatic syntactic bootstrapping model's order of explanation: like infants, our network acquires attitude verb meanings partly based on its understanding of attitude verb complements.

For our hyperparameter search we again performed a five-fold cross validation, but with 130 hyperparameter settings. We primarily consider results from the model trained using the best hyperparameters, including the selected random seed. Call this the *selected model*. Improving on our earlier experiment, we reran the best hyperparameter settings with 66 random seeds in addition to the 1 random seed that performed best in our hyperparameter search.

---

[12] We could also expand the main training set for the final evaluation, i.e. add the excluded instances of the propositional constants and corresponding representations. However, our approach tests the model's ability to generalise more strictly, as we require it to generalise to attitude ascriptions it has not seen before.

The results on the test set show a significant difference between ascriptions that are true and those that are not true. Both the selected model and other random seeds perform worse with true ascriptions than with those that are not true, see Table 1. Still, the network's accuracy on true ascriptions is generally above chance, and it only struggles with true factive ascriptions of which there are extremely few cases, suggesting that our network has to some extent learned our attitude verb meanings. Although the selected model's accuracy on ascriptions that are not true is indistinguishable across attitude verbs once rounded to one decimal point, its performance with true factive attitude ascriptions stands out. However, we should bear in mind how just few of these ascriptions were in the test set: 30% of 120, so just 40. Moreover, this result is not robust across other random seeds. The accuracy is higher for true factive attitude ascriptions than true contrafactive attitude ascriptions for just 4 of 67 seeds. Across the 67 seeds, mean accuracy for true factive ascriptions is considerably lower. Similarly, for mean absolute error, true factive attitude ascriptions score lower (=better) given the selected model, but the result reverses once we look at other random seeds. We observe no such effect for factive attitude ascriptions that are not true: averaging across seeds, they have the highest accuracy and lowest MAE. Since the ambiguous results for true ascriptions can be explained by how few factive attitude ascriptions were in the test set, we conclude that looking at the test set neither supports nor undermines our hypothesis that the meaning of contrafactives is harder to learn than that of factives.

Table 1. Accuracy and mean absolute error (MAE) by attitude verb and truth-value for selected model and mean of all 67 seeds

verb	truth-value	acc. selected	acc. mean	MAE selected	MAE mean
factive	not true	100%	99.7%	0.000	0.003
	true	77.8%	42.1%	0.246	0.579
contrafactive	not true	100%	99.6%	0.000	0.004
	true	73.7%	68.2%	0.263	0.318
non-factive	not true	100%	99.5%	0.000	0.005
	true	72.5%	68%	0.276	0.318

As an alternative to looking at the test set, we can look at how fast training for our attitude verbs proceeded: how did the training loss change over time? While we use the loss from the training data instead of accuracy on test data over time, our investigation of the loss curve resembles similar discussion in [27]. Our approach reduces the computational costs of the investigation, because we do not repeatedly evaluate on the test set during the training; instead we have distinct training and test phases. In addition, since we only consider early stages of training, concerns about overfitting, which would motivate looking at the test set, are not significant; more on this below. Hence, we use the loss directly as a measure of learning progress.

The loss curves for the complete training show a clear general picture: Loss drops faster for factives (see Figs. 3 and 4). For further analysis, we consider the loss before its convergence and treat the loss functions for different attitude verbs as having converged when the rolling mean loss (window-size 500) has fallen below the threshold of 0.1 for both factives and contrafactives. Given this, we focus on the first 4,707 training instances for each verb. A permutation significance-test (resamples = 9,999) suggests that the mean of the loss for factives and contrafactives differed significantly ($p < 0.005$). Since accuracy and MAE of the selected model did not appear to be robust across random seeds, we worried that the difference in the mean of the loss between factives and contrafactives too is not robust across random seeds. Fortunately, however, it is. For all of the 67 seeds, the mean loss for the first 4707 factive attitude ascriptions is lower than the mean loss for the first 4,707 contrafactive attitude ascriptions.

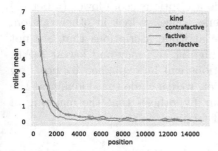

Fig. 3. Rolling mean loss for first 15,000 instances smoothed over 500 instances during training.

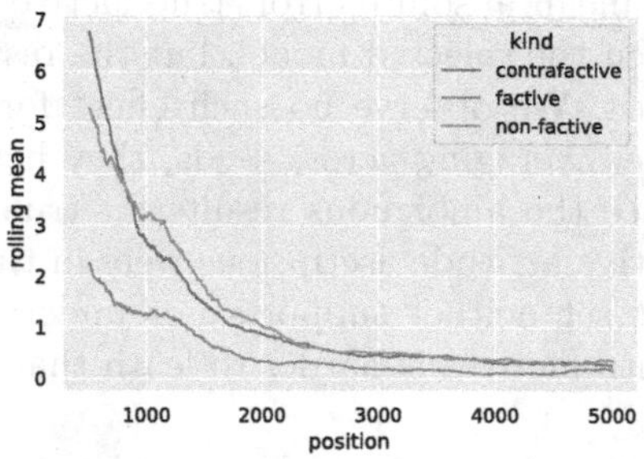

Fig. 4. Rolling mean loss for first 5,000 instances smoothed over 500 instances during training.

A residual worry might be that the lower loss of factive attitude ascriptions is due to the oversampling, for training purposes, of true instances of factive attitude ascriptions. Given this oversampling, the network sees the same instance multiple times and might overfit even in the early stages of training. To test for this, we can isolate the untrue instances amongst our 4,707 training instances and check whether factive attitude ascriptions still have a smaller loss than contrafactive ones. This is the case for 60 of the 67 random seeds, suggesting that the result is relatively robust even under more extreme conditions.

In contrast to our earlier experiment, we now see no important difference between contrafactive and non-factive attitude ascriptions. While the MAE for true non-factives is larger than that for contrafactives in our selected model, this difference vanishes for the mean MAE (see Table 1). An inspection of the loss curves further supports not putting too much emphasis on this result. The mean loss of the first 4,707 non-factive instances is lower than the mean loss of the first 4,707 contrafactive instances for 61 of the 67 random seeds explored. This suggests that the meaning of a non-factive is easier to learn. And this is what we expected, given that our new model is sensitive to some properties that make the meaning of a contrafactive harder to learn than that of a non-factive.

5 Conclusion

Natural languages universally have factives, but lack contrafactives. We proposed that this asymmetry is partly due to a difference in learnability: the meaning of a contrafactive is significantly harder to learn than that of a factive. To support our suggestion, we reported the results of two computational experiments. In closing, let us emphasize the scope of our discussion. Our aim here was to highlight one broad reason for the difference in frequency between factives and contrafactives in natural languages. But, most likely, this is not the only reason. We mentioned one other likely reason in Sect. 2, viz. the possibility of using compositional methods to closely approximate the meaning of a contrafactive, and plan to identify further reasons in future work.

References

1. Anvari, A., Maldonado, M., Soria Ruiz, A.: The puzzle of reflexive belief construction in Spanish. Proc. Sinn und Bedeutung **23**(1), 57–74 (2019). https://doi.org/10.18148/sub/2019.v23i1.503
2. Caucheteux, C., King, J.R.: Brains and algorithms partially converge in natural language processing. Commun. Biol. **5**(1), 134 (2022). https://doi.org/10.1038/s42003-022-03036-1
3. Davidson, D.: Actions, reasons, and causes. In: Davidson, D. (ed.) Essays on Actions and Events, pp. 3–19. Oxford University Press, Oxford (2001)
4. Devlin, J., Chang, M.W., Lee, K., Toutanova, K.: BERT: Pre-training of Deep Bidirectional Transformers for Language Understanding, May 2019. arXiv:1810.04805 [cs]
5. Glass, L.: The Negatively Biased Mandarin Belief Verb yǐwéi*. Studia Linguistica n/a(n/a) (2022). https://doi.org/10.1111/stul.12202
6. Goddard, C.: Universals and variation in the lexicon of mental state concepts. In: Words and the Mind: How words capture human experience. Oxford University Press, Oxford (2010)
7. Hacquard, V., Lidz, J.: On the acquisition of attitude verbs. Ann. Rev. Linguist. **8**(1), 193–212 (2022). https://doi.org/10.1146/annurev-linguistics-032521-053009
8. Holton, R.: I-Facts, factives, and contrafactives. Aristotelian Soc. Supplementary **91**(1), 245–266 (2017). https://doi.org/10.1093/arisup/akx003
9. Holton, R.: Lying about. J. Philos. **116**(2), 99–105 (2019). https://doi.org/10.5840/jphil201911625
10. Hsiao, P.Y.K.: On counterfactual attitudes: a case study of Taiwanese Southern Min. Lingua Sinica **3**(1), 4 (2017). https://doi.org/10.1186/s40655-016-0019-7
11. Huebner, P.A., Sulem, E., Cynthia, F., Roth, D.: BabyBERTa: learning more grammar with small-scale child-directed language. In: Proceedings of the 25th Conference on Computational Natural Language Learning, pp. 624–646 (2021). https://doi.org/10.18653/v1/2021.conll-1.49
12. Hyman, J.: II-knowledge and belief. Aristotelian Soc. Supplementary **91**(1), 267–288 (2017). https://doi.org/10.1093/arisup/akx005

13. Kadmon, N.: Formal Pragmatics: Semantics, Pragmatics, Presupposition, and Focus. Blackwell, Malden (2001)
14. Lillicrap, T.P., Cownden, D., Tweed, D.B., Akerman, C.J.: Random synaptic feedback weights support error backpropagation for deep learning. Nat. Commun. **7**(1), 13276 (2016). https://doi.org/10.1038/ncomms13276
15. Lillicrap, T.P., Santoro, A., Marris, L., Akerman, C.J., Hinton, G.: Backpropagation and the brain. Nat. Rev. Neurosci. **21**(6), 335–346 (2020). https://doi.org/10.1038/s41583-020-0277-3
16. McCready, E.: The Dynamics of Particles. Ph.D. thesis, University of Texas at Austin (2005). https://repositories.lib.utexas.edu/bitstream/handle/2152/1779/mccreadyjre33399.pdf
17. Nagel, J.: Factive and nonfactive mental state attribution. Mind Lang. **32**(5), 525–544 (2017). https://doi.org/10.1111/mila.12157
18. Pham, T., Bui, T., Mai, L., Nguyen, A.: Out of Order: How important is the sequential order of words in a sentence in Natural Language Understanding tasks? In: Findings of the Association for Computational Linguistics: ACL-IJCNLP 2021, pp. 1145–1160. Online (2021). https://doi.org/10.18653/v1/2021.findings-acl.98
19. Phillips, J., et al.: Knowledge before Belief. Behavioral and Brain Sciences, pp. 1–37 (2020). https://doi.org/10.1017/S0140525X20000618
20. Phillips, J., Norby, A.: Factive theory of mind. Mind Lang. **36**(1), 3–26 (2021). https://doi.org/10.1111/mila.12267
21. Rogers, A., Kovaleva, O., Rumshisky, A.: A primer in BERTology: what we know about how BERT works. Trans. Assoc. Comput. Linguist. **8**, 842–866 (2020). https://doi.org/10.1162/tacl_a_00349
22. Scellier, B., Bengio, Y.: Equilibrium propagation: bridging the gap between energy-based models and backpropagation. Front. Comput. Neurosci. **11**, 24 (2017). https://doi.org/10.3389/fncom.2017.00024
23. Schrimpf, M., et al.: The neural architecture of language: integrative modeling converges on predictive processing. Proc. Natl. Acad. Sci. **118**(45), November 2021. https://doi.org/10.1073/pnas.2105646118
24. Shatz, M., Diesendruck, G., Martinez-Beck, I., Akar, D.: The influence of language and socioeconomic status on children's understanding of false belief. Dev. Psychol. **39**(4), 717–729 (2003). https://doi.org/10.1037/0012-1649.39.4.717
25. Shuxiang, L.: Eight Hundred Words in Contemporary Chinese. Commercial Press, Beijing (1999)
26. Steinert-Threlkeld, S.: An explanation of the veridical uniformity universal. J. Semant. (2019). https://doi.org/10.1093/jos/ffz019
27. Steinert-Threlkeld, S., Szymanik, J.: Learnability and semantic universals. Semantics Pragmatics **12** (2019). https://doi.org/10.3765/sp.12.4
28. Steinert-Threlkeld, S., Szymanik, J.: Ease of learning explains semantic universals. Cognition **195** (2020). https://doi.org/10.1016/j.cognition.2019.104076
29. Strohmaier, D.: Contrafactives: Exploration of a Grid World, November 2022. https://github.com/dstrohmaier/contrafactives_grid_world
30. Strohmaier, D., Wimmer, S.: Contrafactives and Learnability. In: Proceedings of the 23rd Amsterdam Colloquium. Amsterdam (2022)
31. Vaswani, A., et al.: Attention is All you Need. In: 31st Conference on Neural Information Processing Systems, pp. 1–11 (2017)

Formalizing Argument Structures with Combinatory Categorial Grammar

Shinnosuke Isono$^{(\boxtimes)}$, Takuya Hasegawa, Kohei Kajikawa , Koichi Kono, Shiho Nakamura, and Yohei Oseki

University of Tokyo, Komaba, Meguro-ku, Tokyo, Japan
{isono-shinnosuke,takuya-hasegawa,kohei-kajikawa,koichi-kono,
ssd1120ho728,oseki}@g.ecc.u-tokyo.ac.jp

Abstract. We present a formalization of the *constructivist* analysis of argument structure in Combinatory Categorial Grammar (CCG). According to the constructivist analysis, often couched in terms of Distributed Morphology (DM), arguments are introduced in the syntax rather than specified by the lexical argument structure of the verb. We argue that formalizing constructivism in CCG not only provides the basis for a model of incremental processing of argument structure but also a principled account for the locality constraints on contextual allomorphy observed in the DM literature.

Keywords: Combinatory Categorial Grammar · argument structure · morphology

1 Introduction

Combinatory Categorial Grammar (CCG) [33] is a lexicalized theory of grammar in which syntactic derivations are carried out by applying a small set of combinatory rules that operate on categories that constituents are associated with. A major advantage of the theory is that it can be directly incorporated into a parsing model as it allows (largely) left-to-right structure building based on the surface string. CCG thus conforms to the Strict Competence Hypothesis, which states that the language processor needs only mechanisms provided by the competence grammar to build structures [33].

The current study deals with a challenge to the analysis of verbal argument structure that is typically employed in CCG. In such an analysis, the argument structure is specified by the category of the verb. For example, (2) is a CCG

We would like to thank the audience of Logic and Engineering of Natural Language Semantics 19 (LENLS19) and the anonymous reviewers of the abstract and the post-proceedings for insightful comments. We also thank Carlee Iritani for proofreading the manuscript. Any remaining errors are our own.

D. Bekki et al. (Eds.): LENLS 2019, LNCS 14213, pp. 83–99, 2023.
https://doi.org/10.1007/978-3-031-43977-3_6

analysis of the Japanese sentence (1) based on [2].[1] Here, the category of *kowasu* 'break' is specified as $S\backslash NP_{ga}\backslash NP_o$, which means that the verb takes two NPs to its left (as indicated by the backslashes; see Sect. 2 for details) marked with nominative case (*ga*) and accusative case (*o*), respectively.

(1)   John-ga   kabin-o   kowasu.
      John-NOM vase-ACC break
      'John breaks the vase.'

(2)   John-ga   kabin-o   kowasu
      $T/(\overline{T\backslash NP_{ga}})$ $T/(\overline{T\backslash NP_o})$ $(S\backslash\overline{NP_{ga}})\backslash NP_o$
$$\frac{\qquad\qquad\qquad\overline{S\backslash NP_{ga}}\quad >}{S}>$$

In mainstream generative grammar, the same line of analysis is realized by assuming that verbs have a list of arguments (θ-grid) as one of their lexical properties, and that list is "projected" to the verb phrase headed by the verb (e.g., [10]). (3a) is such an analysis for the verb phrase in (1).

(3)   a.   VP   b.   VoiceP

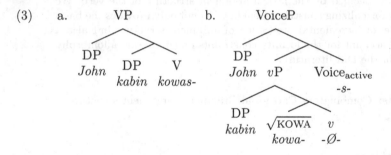

However, there is an alternative view on argument structure called *constructivism*, often couched in terms of Distributed Morphology (DM) [15]. Constructivism assumes that argument structures are composed in the syntax, rather than in the lexicon. (3b) is a constructivist analysis of (1) based on [30] (also see [16,26]). In this structure, the root √KOWA does not have an inherent argument structure. Instead, the internal and external arguments are introduced by functional heads called *v* and Voice, respectively.[2] In contrast, analyses of the line of (3a) is called *projectionism,* since the lexical argument structure of the verb is projected to the syntax (see [6,17,27] for more discussions on projectionism vs. constructivism).

---

[1] In (2), features irrelevant for the current discussion are omitted. T is a variable ranging over categories.

[2] There is a debate within constructivism over whether the internal argument should be severed from the root. We assume that it should, given that the root can appear without an internal argument (e.g., in deverbal nouns), following [7,24]. See [17,18] for arguments against separation of the internal argument from a root.

Constructivism provides a straightforward explanation for why speakers can interpret innovative combinations of verbs and argument structures [6]. For example, native speakers of English can interpret sentences in (4) even if they have never heard of *siren* being used in these particular constructions, as pointed out by [12]. In constructivism, their interpretations derive from the encyclopedic meaning associated with the root $\sqrt{\text{SIREN}}$ and the compositional semantics of the functional heads that give rise to the respective construction (see works such as [6,7,17,22,27] for more arguments in favor of constructivism).

(4)   a.   The factory horns *sirened* throughout the raid.
      b.   The factory horns *sirened* midday and everyone broke for lunch.
      c.   The police car *sirened* the Porsche to a stop.
      d.   The police car *sirened* up to the accident site.
      e.   The police car *sirened* the daylight out of me.

The theoretical framework of DM is suitable for constructivism. DM adopts the *single engine hypothesis*, according to which "all computation, whether of small (words) or large elements (phrases and sentences), is syntactic" [1] (p. 738). The single engine hypothesis straightforwardly captures the relation between verbal morphology and its consequence on the syntactic argument structure. At the same time, DM captures the irregularity of such argument-introducing morphology by *late insertion*. Late insertion stipulates that the morphological (and semantic) realization of terminal nodes is determined after the syntactic structure is built and can refer to the syntactic context. In (3b), for example, Voice$_{\text{active}}$ is realized as *-s-* in the context of the root $\sqrt{\text{KOWA}}$ (to be interpreted as 'break'); the same head would be realized as *-as-* in the context of $\sqrt{\text{HER}}$ (to be interpreted as 'reduce') [16,30]. This analysis captures the fact that transitivity morphemes in Japanese are separable from the root (cf. *kowa-re-* 'break.intransitive') but varies depending on the root.

While late insertion offers a nice account of such *contextual allomorphy*, it is problematic when a real-time use of language is taken into account. Human sentence processing is known to proceed incrementally from left to right (e.g., [21,34]). However, DM assumes bottom-up structural building (as in Minimalist analyses in general), and this is not just a convention in description. "Late" insertion, along with the phase-based account of context-sensitivity of such insertion, crucially relies on the assumption that syntactic structures are built in a bottom-up manner before any phonological (or semantic) information is supplied. Given the theoretical plausibility of assuming that competence grammar is used in performance in some way [8,9,23,33], such a bottom-up approach bears the burden of explaining how the grammar defined that way can be made compatible with incremental processing [32]. This is the primary motivation of our study: can we capture the constructivist nature of argument structure using a surface-oriented grammar formalism that is compatible with incremental processing? Note that there is some psycholinguistic evidence that the decomposition of argument structure is relevant for real-time processing (e.g., [14,29]).

One preceding study that attempts to rigorously formalize (a fragment of) DM is [35]. This study presents an algorithm that can parse a sequence of output forms into a sequence of terminals (i.e., feature bundles) given DM-style contextual insertion rules. The parsing algorithm is fairly complicated, mainly because it has to look ahead of the context on the right side. Also, Trommer's approach is different from ours in that the Vocabulary Insertion mechanism is not integrated into a mechanism to build syntactic structures.

Turning back to the current study, we thus attempt a formalization of the constructivist analysis in CCG, which is claimed to be compatible with incremental structure building. Although analyses in CCG are non-constructivist as mentioned earlier, we will demonstrate that the constructivist analysis can indeed be translated to CCG. We will further argue that such an analysis provides an explanation for an important feature of the constructivist analysis, the locality-sensitivity of contextual allomorphy. We focus on the Japanese verbal morphology as a test case since it has morphological phenomena that are interesting for the current purpose: agglutinative conjugation with a few irregular verbs, and systematic transitivity alternation with overt morphological marking. The rest of this paper is organized as follows. Section 2 presents an analysis of verbal conjugation in Japanese, which serves as the basis for the analysis of transitive alternation presented in Sect. 3. Section 4 discusses extensions of the current analysis to other morphological phenomena, namely infixation and fusion. Section 5 summarizes the study and discusses remaining issues.

2   Segment-Based Analysis of Japanese Verb Conjugation

The current section develops an analysis of Japanese verb conjugation in CCG. An overview of the Japanese verb conjugation paradigm is presented in Table 1. Most Japanese verbs belong to either the five-grade (*godan*) or mono-grade (*itidan*) conjugation class. In the traditional mora-based analysis, the conjugated forms of a five-grade verb are decomposed into an invariant stem (*to-* in the case of 'fly,' shown in Table 1) and an inflectional ending. The inflectional endings share the initial consonant while differing in the vowel: *-ba-, -bi-, -bu-, -be-, -bo-* in the case of 'fly.' Since these syllables belong to the same row in the traditional Japanese syllabary chart, 'fly' is said to belong to the *ba*-row subclass of the five-grade conjugation. Five-grade verbs can also take an euphonic (*onbin*) form, whose inflectional ending does not share the initial consonant with other forms. The mono-grade conjugation is much simpler. Each form consists of an invariant stem and an inflectional ending shared by all mono-grade verbs, and there is no euphonic variation. There are also some irregular verbs, most notably *suru* 'do' and *kuru* 'come.' Below we limit our discussion to the terminal, negation, and euphonic forms, since these three forms are sufficient to illustrate how the stem, the inflectional ending, and subsequent morphemes are concatenated.

We take Bekki's analysis of Japanese verb conjugation in CCG [2] as our starting point. A CCG consists of categorial lexicon which assigns each lexical item a syntactic category and a logical form, and a set of combinatory rules that combine those categories and logical forms to yield new ones. A syntactic category is either a *basic category* such as S or NP, or a *complex category* such

Table 1. An excerpt from the Japanese verb conjugation paradigm. The strings in parentheses are not considered to be part of the conjugated forms but are endings that these forms typically accompany.

Form	Five-grade 'fly' (ba-row)		Five-grade 'write' (ka-row)	Mono-grade 'see'	Irregular 'come'
Negative	$toba(nai)$	'do not fly'	$kaka(nai)$	$mi(nai)$	$ko(nai)$
Continuous	$tobi$	'fly, and...'	$kaki$	mi	ki
Euphonic	$ton(da)$	'flew'	$kai(ta)$	$mi(ta)$	$ki(ta)$
Terminal/Attributive	$tobu$	'fly$_{nonpast}$'	$kaku$	$miru$	$kuru$
Conditional	$tobe(ba)$	'if ... fly'	$kake(ba)$	$mire(ba)$	$kure(ba)$
Imperative	$tobe$	'fly!'	$kake$	$miro$	koi

as NP/NP or $(S\backslash NP)\backslash NP$, which is recursively built from basic categories and two types of slashes that indicate the directions of arguments. X/Y means that it takes Y as an argument to its right to yield X, while $X\backslash Y$ means that it takes Y to its left to yield X. The combinatory rules that will be used in the current analysis are listed with their semantics in (5). $X, Y, \ldots$ range over categories while $a, f, g, \ldots$ range over λ-terms. $>, <, \ldots$ are the annotations for the combinatory rules to be used in the derivation trees. Basic categories can also have *features*, indicated by superscripts and subscripts. Features are used to represent information such as case, conjugation class, and inflectional forms.

$$
\begin{aligned}
&X/Y : f \quad Y : a &&\Longrightarrow X : fa && (>) \\
&Y : a \quad X\backslash Y : f &&\Longrightarrow X : fa && (<) \\
(5)\quad &X/Y : f \quad Y/Z : g &&\Longrightarrow X/Z : \lambda x.f(gx) && (> \mathbf{B}) \\
&Y\backslash Z : g \quad X\backslash Y : f &&\Longrightarrow X\backslash Z : \lambda x.f(gx) && (< \mathbf{B}) \\
&(Y\backslash W)\backslash Z : g \quad X\backslash Y : f &&\Longrightarrow (X\backslash W)\backslash Z : \lambda z.\lambda w.f((gz)w) && (< \mathbf{B}^2)
\end{aligned}
$$

Bekki's analysis formalizes the mora-based analysis described above using CCG. The selection of the appropriate inflectional ending and subsequent morphemes are achieved by annotating categories with features. (6) shows the analysis of *tobanai* 'do not fly.' Here, $S_{stem}^{v::5::b}$ means the stem of a five-grade verb of ba-row, and $S_{term|attr}^{a}$ means a terminal (*syusi*) or an attributive (*rentai*) form of an adjective (features in the original work that are irrelevant for the current discussion are omitted).

(6)
$$
\dfrac{\dfrac{\underset{\text{to-}}{S_{stem}^{v::5::b}\backslash NP_{ga}} \quad \underset{\text{-ba-}}{S_{neg}^{v::5::b}\backslash S_{stem}^{v::5::b}} }{S_{neg}^{v::5::b}\backslash NP_{ga}}{}^{<\mathbf{B}} \quad \underset{\text{-nai}}{S_{term|attr}^{a}\backslash S_{neg}}}{S_{term|attr}^{a}\backslash NP_{ga}}{}^{<\mathbf{B}}
$$

A mora-based analysis is a reasonable choice if the application to text data is concerned, given that Japanese orthography is mora-based. However, segment-based analysis allows further generalization for the conjugation system of the language by eliminating the classification by row [4]. For example, -a- that appears in *tob-a-nai* is also found in negated forms of other verbs that belong to other rows such as *kak-a-nai* 'do not write' and *yom-a-nai* 'do not read.'

A problem that remains in such a basic segment-based analysis is that the stem thus identified is not stable across the paradigm. The stem for 'fly' can be identified as *tob-* from forms such as *tob-u* 'fly (present)' and *tob-a-nai* 'do not fly.' However, when *tob-* is combined with the past tense morpheme *-ta*, the result is *ton-da* rather than **tob-ta*, which violates the Japanese phonotactics. Such a "change" is regular in the language, and the type of the change is dictated by the final consonant of the stem. In a processing-compatible approach that we are aiming at here, we cannot resort to a rewriting rule such as $b \rightarrow n \; / \; \_ \; [+\text{past}]$ since the derivation must start from the string as it is observed. Instead, we assume that regularly alternating consonants like b/n in *tob-u* vs. *ton-da* are separated from the nonalternating part as an *inflectional consonant* (*Ic*). *To-* demands *-b-* as its inflectional consonant, and this demand is satisfied in the cases of (7a,b).[3] In (7c), on the other hand, *-n-* overrides that demand by taking $V_5^{stem}/Ic_{b|m|n}$ (a stem whose inflectional consonant has not been realized) as an argument.[4] Note also that, unlike Bekki's analysis, we employ V and S as distinct categories to introduce the distinction between verb phrase and tense phrase, that is usually assumed in the Minimalist syntax.

(7)   a.

$$
\begin{array}{ccc}
\overline{\text{to-}} & \overline{\text{-b-}} & \overline{\text{-u}} \\
(V_5^{stem}/Ic_b)\backslash NP_{ga} & V_5^{stem}\backslash(V_5^{stem}/Ic_b) & S_{term|attr}\backslash V_5^{stem}
\end{array}
$$

$$
\frac{\qquad\qquad}{V_5^{stem}\backslash NP_{ga}} <\textbf{B}
$$

$$
\frac{\qquad\qquad\qquad}{S_{term|attr}\backslash NP_{ga}} <\textbf{B}
$$

b.

$$
\begin{array}{cccc}
\overline{\text{to-}} & \overline{\text{-b-}} & \overline{\text{-a-}} & \overline{\text{-nai}} \\
(V_5^{stem}/Ic_b)\backslash NP_{ga} & V_5^{stem}\backslash(V_5^{stem}/Ic_b) & V_{neg}\backslash V_5^{stem} & S_{term|attr}^a\backslash V_{neg}
\end{array}
$$

$$
\frac{\qquad\qquad}{V_5^{stem}\backslash NP_{ga}} <\textbf{B}
$$

$$
\frac{\qquad\qquad\qquad}{V_{neg}\backslash NP_{ga}} <\textbf{B}
$$

$$
\frac{\qquad\qquad\qquad\qquad}{S_{term|attr}^a\backslash NP_{ga}} <\textbf{B}
$$

---

[3] We assume that the inflectional consonant is type-raised as $V_5^{stem}\backslash(V_5^{stem}/Ic_b)$ in the lexicon rather than having a simple category Ic_b and then being type-raised in the derivation. This follows the suggestion of one of the reviewers, who pointed out that the elimination of type-raising rules from the grammar has desirable consequences concerning parsing and long-distance dependencies.

[4] Oleg Kiselyov (p.c.) pointed out that the current analysis does not provide a phonological explanation for why b and m corresponds to n, k and g to i, etc., in the euphonic change. Indeed, there are phonological reasons for the historic sound changes that are responsible for those correspondences. However, we remain agnostic about whether such an explanation is needed in the model of the synchronic I-language of a speaker of modern Japanese.

c.
$$\frac{\dfrac{\overset{\text{to-}}{(V_5^{stem}/Ic_b)\backslash NP_{ga}}\quad \overset{\text{-n-}}{V_{euph::d}\backslash(V_5^{stem}/Ic_{b|m|n})}}{V_{euph::d}\backslash NP_{ga}}{}^{<B}\quad \overset{\text{-da}}{S_{term|attr}\backslash V_{euph::d}}}{S_{term|attr}\backslash NP_{ga}}{}^{<B}$$

The analysis for the mono-grade conjugation under the current approach does not differ from the mora-based analysis of [2] since the morpheme boundaries in this type of conjugation are placed at mora boundaries. Thus, the analyses for *miru* 'see' are as shown in (8). Note the use of a phonologically null item Ø that converts a stem into a conjugated form.

(8)   a.
$$\frac{\overset{\text{mi-}}{(V_1^{stem}\backslash NP_{ga})\backslash NP_o}\quad \overset{\text{-ru}}{S_{term|attr}\backslash V_1^{stem}}}{(S_{term|attr}\backslash NP_{ga})\backslash NP_o}{}^{<B^2}$$

b.
$$\frac{\dfrac{\overset{\text{mi-}}{(V_1^{stem}\backslash NP_{ga})\backslash NP_o}\quad \overset{\text{-Ø-}}{V_{neg|cont|euph::t}\backslash V_1^{stem}}}{(V_{neg|cont|euph::t}\backslash NP_{ga})\backslash NP_o}{}^{<B^2}\quad \overset{\text{-nai}}{S_{term|attr}^a\backslash V_{neg}}}{(S_{term|attr}^a\backslash NP_{ga})\backslash NP_o}{}^{<B^2}$$

c.
$$\frac{\dfrac{\overset{\text{mi-}}{(V_1^{stem}\backslash NP_{ga})\backslash NP_o}\quad \overset{\text{-Ø-}}{V_{neg|cont|euph::t}\backslash V_1^{stem}}}{(V_{neg|cont|euph::t}\backslash NP_{ga})\backslash NP_o}{}^{<B^2}\quad \overset{\text{-ta}}{S_{term|attr}\backslash V_{euph::t}}}{(S_{term|attr}\backslash NP_{ga})\backslash NP_o}{}^{<B^2}$$

There are two major irregular verbs in Japanese, *suru* 'do' and *kuru* 'come.' The segment-based analysis of these verbs differs from the mora-based analysis since the initial consonant (s and k), which is shared by all the conjugated forms, can be separated out. (9) below shows the analyses for *kuru*. The initial consonant k- has the category $V_K^{substem}$ and is selected by the following vowel. A similar analysis is possible for *suru*.

(9)   a.
$$\frac{\dfrac{\overset{\text{k-}}{V_K^{substem}\backslash NP_{ga}}\quad \overset{\text{-u-}}{V_K^{stem::(term|attr)}\backslash V_K^{substem}}}{V_K^{stem::(term|attr)}\backslash NP_{ga}}{}^{<B}\quad \overset{\text{-ru}}{S_{term|attr}\backslash V_K^{stem::(term|attr)}}}{S_{term|attr}\backslash NP_{ga}}{}^{<B}$$

b.
$$\frac{\dfrac{\overset{\text{k-}}{V_K^{substem}\backslash NP_{ga}}\quad \overset{\text{-o-}}{V_{neg}\backslash V_K^{substem}}}{V_{neg}\backslash NP_{ga}}{}^{<B}\quad \overset{\text{-nai}}{S_{term|attr}^a\backslash V_{neg}}}{S_{term|attr}^a\backslash NP_{ga}}{}^{<B}$$

c.

$$\cfrac{\cfrac{\underset{V_K^{substem}\backslash NP_{ga}}{\text{k-}} \quad \underset{V_{euph::t}\backslash V_K^{substem}}{\text{-i-}}}{V_{euph::t}\backslash NP_{ga}}<\textbf{B} \quad \underset{S_{term|attr}\backslash V_{euph::t}}{\text{-ta}}}{S_{term|attr}\backslash NP_{ga}}<\textbf{B}$$

For reasons of space, we do not attempt to formulate a comprehensive analysis of the entire verb conjugation system of Japanese like [2]. Still, the analyses in (7)–(9) cover the three major classes of verb conjugation in the language, and key phenomena found in the paradigm: segment-level agglutination, stem alternation triggered by a suffix, and irregular conjugation. All of these are done in a surface-oriented manner by careful choice of features for the morphemes involved. As suggested, this ensures that the grammar is compatible with left-to-right processing.

3   Constructivist Analysis of Transitivity Alternation

Having established the basic treatment of Japanese verbal conjugation, we now dig deeper into the decomposition of the stem. Japanese has many pairs of intransitive and transitive verbs (or more precisely, stems) that are morphologically related. Verbs in such a pair share the leftmost morpheme, followed by a suffix that marks the transitivity (sometimes null). We will call the leftmost morpheme *base*. Although it may be more intuitive to call it *root*, that term is reserved for the root in the DM sense, as we will see below. A base and a transitivity suffix constitute a stem in the sense defined in the previous section. An example is shown in (10).

(10)   a.   Kabin-ga kowa-*re*-ta.
             vase-NOM break-INTR-PAST
             'The vase broke.'
        b.   Taroo-ga   kabin-o   kowa-*s*-ita.
             Taroo-NOM vase-ACC break-TR-PAST
             'Taroo broke the vase.'

The form of the transitivity suffix is conditioned by the root. [20] classified the pairs into fifteen classes based on the form of the suffixes, as shown in Table 2. An apparent pattern noted in [20] is that suffixes containing s always mark transitive, while those containing r always mark intransitive. Interestingly, e and $\emptyset$ is used to mark both transitive and intransitive, depending on the root.

As mentioned earlier, these transitivity morphemes can be analyzed under DM as realizations of different *flavors* of the functional head that determines the transitivity of the verb, often called Voice, as shown in (11) [30] (also see [16, 26]).The *active* Voice introduces an external argument, resulting in a transitive

Table 2. Classification of transitivity alternation [20]. This summary is based on [30].

Class	Intransitive	Transitive	Meaning	Class	Intransitive	Transitive	Meaning
1	hag-*e*-ru	hag-Ø-u	'peel'	9	tok-*e*-ru	tok-*as*-u	'melt'
2	ak-Ø-u	ak-*e*-ru	'open'	10	nob-*i*-ru	nob-*as*-u	'extend'
3	ham-*ar*-u	ham-*e*-ru	'fit'	11	ok-*i*-ru	ok-*os*-u	'get up'
4	tunag-*ar*-u	tunag-Ø-u	'connect'	12	abi-Ø-ru	abi-*se*-ru	'pour'
5	ama-*r*-u	ama-*s*-u	'remain'	13	obi-*e*-ru	obi-*yakas*-u	'frighten'
6	kowa-*re*-ru	kowa-*s*-u	'break'	14	kom-*or*-u	kom-*e*-ru	'fill'
7	ka-*ri*-ru	ka-*s*-u	'borrow/lend'	15	toraw-*are*-ru	toraw-*e*-ru	'catch'
8	her-Ø-u	her-*as*-u	'decrease'				

structure.[5] The *non-active* Voice, on the other hand, does not introduce an external argument, resulting in an intransitive structure. The transitivity morphemes are regarded as realizations of the respective Voice head. In DM terms, they are inserted to the Voice head after the syntactic structure is built, and the specific morpheme is determined by looking at the syntactic context where the target morpheme is situated. The morphological insertion rules for the active Voice, for example, look like (12a). These rules consist of three parts: the target of insertion (Voice$_{active}$), the morpheme to be inserted (-*s*-, -*as*-, -*os*-, ...), and the local context that restricts the application of the rule, the classification of the root in this case. Similarly, the semantic interpretation for the active Voice is inserted by the rule (12b). Note that this analysis is able to capture the implicational relation that holds between *John broke the vase* and *the vase broke*, as one of our reviewers pointed out; the shared semantics is represented by the *v*P.

(11)　　a. (=3b)

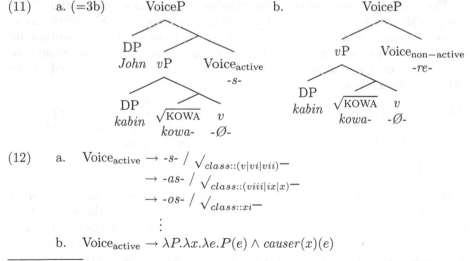

(12)　　a.　Voice$_{active}$ → -*s*- / $\sqrt{}_{class::(v|vi|vii)}$—

　　　　　　　　→ -*as*- / $\sqrt{}_{class::(viii|ix|x)}$—

　　　　　　　　→ -*os*- / $\sqrt{}_{class::xi}$—

　　　　　　　　⋮

　　　b.　Voice$_{active}$ → $\lambda P.\lambda x.\lambda e.P(e) \wedge causer(x)(e)$

---

[5] [30] argues that there are two flavors for the active Voice head that appears in Japanese transitive verbs, which introduce a Causer and Agent respectively. We put aside this point for now and focus on the transitive-intransitive contrast. We note however that this analysis can be easily implemented in the current framework by assuming distinct semantics for each flavor.

The structures in (11) can be translated in CCG straightforwardly as follows:6

(13)

$$
\begin{array}{ccc}
\text{kowa-} & \text{-}\varnothing\text{-} & \text{-s-}
\end{array}
$$

$$
\dfrac{R_{vi}}{\lambda e.kowa(e)} \quad \dfrac{(V_{base::\{1\}}\backslash NP)\backslash R_{\{1\}}}{\lambda P.\lambda x.\lambda e.P(e) \wedge theme(x)(e)} \quad \dfrac{(V_{5::s}^{stem}\backslash NP)\backslash V_{base::(v|vi|vii)}}{\lambda P.\lambda x.\lambda e.P(e) \wedge causer(x)(e)}
$$

$$
\dfrac{V_{base::vi}\backslash NP}{\lambda x.\lambda e.kowa(e) \wedge theme(x)(e)} <
$$

$$
\dfrac{(V_{5::s}^{stem}\backslash NP)\backslash NP}{\lambda x.\lambda y.\lambda e.kowa(e) \wedge theme(x)(e) \wedge causer(y)(e)} <\mathbf{B}
$$

(14)

$$
\begin{array}{ccc}
\text{kowa-} & \text{-}\varnothing\text{-} & \text{-re-}
\end{array}
$$

$$
\dfrac{R_{vi}}{\lambda e.kowa(e)} \quad \dfrac{(V_{base::\{1\}}\backslash NP)\backslash R_{\{1\}}}{\lambda P.\lambda x.\lambda e.P(e) \wedge theme(x)(e)} \quad \dfrac{V_{1}^{stem}\backslash V_{base::vi}}{\lambda P.\lambda e.P(e)}
$$

$$
\dfrac{V_{base::vi}\backslash NP}{\lambda x.\lambda e.kowa(e) \wedge theme(x)(e)} <
$$

$$
\dfrac{V_{1}^{stem}\backslash NP}{\lambda x.\lambda e.kowa(e) \wedge theme(x)(e)} <\mathbf{B}
$$

In these structures, the leftmost element is the root, as indicated by the category R. It is also specified as belonging to the class 6, written vi, following the classification of the root shown in Table 2. The middle element corresponds to the v head in the DM analysis. It selects a root and introduces an NP as the internal argument. It also inherits the class of the root by the *variable* $\{1\}$. The rightmost element corresponds to the Voice head. It selects a verb phrase with the appropriate class feature, introduces the external argument if it is active, and results in a verb stem.

This analysis exemplifies how contextual allomorphy can be treated in CCG, and provides further insights about the nature of allomorphy. The correct morphological form is obtained because the Voice morpheme with the appropriate sound (e.g., -s-) selects the base of the appropriate class. Thus, contextual allomorphy is reduced to mere selection. The allomorphs should be listed in the lexicon, as shown below.

(15) $\text{-s-} \vdash (V_{5::s}^{stem}\backslash NP)\backslash V_{base::(v|vi|vii)} : \lambda P.\lambda x.\lambda e.P(e) \wedge causer(x)(e)$

$\text{-as-} \vdash (V_{5::s}^{stem}\backslash NP)\backslash V_{base::(vii|ix|x)} : \lambda P.\lambda x.\lambda e.P(e) \wedge causer(x)(e)$

$\text{-os-} \vdash (V_{5::s}^{stem}\backslash NP)\backslash V_{base::xi} : \lambda P.\lambda x.\lambda e.P(e) \wedge causer(x)(e)$

$\vdots$

In the list (15), the same logical form and similar categories are repeated. It is apparently less elegant than the DM analysis (12), where the logical form appears only once. Yet we can achieve the same level of abstraction in CCG as in DM by defining a function á la [2] that maps a class feature to a transitivity morpheme, as shown in (16). Then the set of lexical items in (15) are defined succinctly as (17).

$$(16) \quad f(c) \stackrel{def}{=} \begin{cases} \text{-}s\text{-} & (c = v, vi, vii) \\ \text{-}as\text{-} & (c = viii, ix, x) \\ \text{-}os\text{-} & (c = xi) \\ \vdots \end{cases}$$

(17)   For any $c \in dom(f)$,
$$f(c) \vdash (V_{stem}\backslash NP)\backslash V_{base::c} : \lambda P.\lambda x.\lambda e.P(e) \wedge causer(x)(e)$$

Note that the use of feature inheritance is independently justified by adjunction facts. For example, the fragments $[reads\ papers]_{S\backslash NP_{+3sg}}$ and $[read\ papers]_{S\backslash NP_{-3sg}}$ should require a third-person-singular and non-third-person-singular subject respectively, and the categorial specifications of the fragments do this job. A modifier like *carefully* is able to modify both, but the number specification of the verb phrase must be maintained. This is achieved by assigning a variable category $S\backslash NP_{\{1\}}\backslash(S\backslash NP_{\{1\}})$ to *carefully*. Otherwise we would need two almost identical lexical entries for every adverb that adjoins to verb phrases. Thus, although it is a powerful mechanism, the need for feature inheritance by variables is undeniable.

Another interesting implication of the selection-based account of allomorphy concerns the locality constraints on the context that determines the choice of the allomorph. In the DM literature, it has been pointed out that the choice of the allomorph to be inserted to a given terminal node is conditioned by its local context [1,5,26,28]. In other words, insertion rules can only 'see' a certain local context. Linear (string) adjacency has been suggested to be relevant, although there are also cases where strict adjacency is not required [28]. Limitation based on phase-based cyclic spell-out [11] has also been proposed [25]. Consider the Japanese transitivity alternation paradigm again. The phonological realization of the active/non-active Voice is conditioned by the root. The root and the Voice are not adjacent but intervened by a phonologically null v. Still, the insertion to the Voice head can consult the feature of the root, as evident from the paradigm shown in Table 2. Conversely, when the v head is visible, the insertion to the Voice head seems to be unable to consult the root. In Japanese, for example, verbs can be formed by suffixing -m- to an adjectival root. This -m- can be analyzed as realization of v [30]. (18) shows the analyses for *huka-m-e-ru* and *huka-m-ar-u* 'deepen,' which share the root with the adjective *huka-i* 'deep.'

(18)   a.   b.

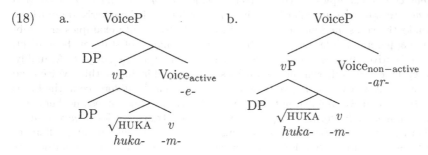

Table 3. An excerpt from the conjugation paradigm of the Greek verb for 'eat,' adopted from [28]. Only the first person singular form is shown.

	Active		Non-active	
	Nonpast	Past	Nonpast	Past
Imperfective	tró-o	é-trog-a	tróg-ome	trog-ómun
Perfective	fá-o	é-fag-a	fago-th-ó	fagó-th-ik-a

Crucially, de-adjectival verbs formed by *-m-* belong to the same alternation class, as evident from forms such as *tuyo-m-e-ru/tuyo-m-ar-u* 'strengthen,' *yowa-m-e-ru/yowa-m-ar-u* 'weaken,' and *taka-m-e-ru/taka-m-ar-u* 'heighten.'[6] This conforms to the suggestion in the DM literature that phonological adjacency is relevant to determine the local context for contextual allomorphy.

However, [28] points to an apparent exception to the locality constraint based on string adjacency in Greek verb conjugation. In Greek, suppletive and irregular alternations of verb stems are conditioned by the *combination* of aspect and voice, as shown in Table 3. Two suffixes can be attached to the stem, and both of them are sensitive to the same voice and aspect features. Thus, *fagóthika* 'eat.nonactive.perfective.past' can be decomposed as *fagó-th-ik-a*, and the first three morphemes are all associated with the non-active voice and the perfective aspect. This means that the insertion of *fagó* to the root must be able to see the features that also contribute to the insertion of *ik,* although *th* intervenes between them. Giving up the decomposition and assuming *fagóthik* to be a single morpheme would miss the generalization that *th* and *ik* appears quite regularly across the Greek verb conjugation. [28] proposes to relax the locality constraint on contextual allomorphy by grouping terminal nodes into 'spans' and let insertion see the adjacent span, rather than the adjacent (non-empty) node, as its context.

The current selection-based approach provides a natural explanation for such complex nature of locality constraints on contextual allomorphy without relying on bottom-up structure building, late insertion, or the notion of span. In CCG, combinatory rules can be applied only for linearly adjacent elements (Principle of Adjacency; [33] p.54). It would then follow that selection-based contextual

---

[6] Apparent counterexamples to this pattern include *ita-m-e-ru/ita-m-u* 'ache' and *kurusi-m-e-ru/kurusi-m-u* 'suffer.' The intransitive forms of these verbs do not have *-ar-*, unlike the verbs mentioned in the main text. These counterexamples are probably only apparent. While the *-ar-* verbs illustrate a change of state of the subject, *ita-m-u* is stative, and *kurusi-m-u* takes an Experiencer as the subject. Arguably, therefore, these verbs differ in the argument structure and include a third Voice head other than what we call non-active here (cf. [3, 13]). Then the difference in the forms is expected. A reviewer pointed out *yuru-m-e-ru/yuru-m-u* 'loosen' as another counterexample; it actually forms a triplet with another intransitive form *yuru-m-ar-u*. A similar explanation may also apply to this case, although the semantic difference between the two intransitive forms is not very clear and seems to be subject to individual variation among native speakers.

allomorphy is only sensitive to linearly adjacent elements. But the feature inheritance mechanism we introduced earlier could circumvent this restriction without any limit: in a string ABC, if B selects A and inherits some of its features, and C selects B, then C is virtually sensitive to A's features. The question is therefore how feature inheritance should be constrained. One possible answer is to postulate a principle that categories must be motivated either semantically or phonologically. A related proposal has been made by Steedman:

(19)   *The Principle of Categorial Type Transparency*
         For a given language, the semantic type of the interpretation together with a number of language-specific directional parameter settings uniquely determines the syntactic category of a category.   ([33], p.36)

That is, categories must be motivated only by semantic types and directionality parameters. This is clearly too strict for the current analysis, since our *class* feature is not motivated semantically. To include morphological considerations in the motivation for categorization, we revise (19) as follows.

(20)   *The Principle of Categorial Type Transparency, revised*
         For any constituent, the semantic type of the interpretation, the morphological class of the entire string, and a number of language-specific directional parameter settings uniquely determine the syntactic category of the constituent.

The intuition is that if B inherits features on A, they must be semantically or morphologically meaningful for the constituent AB (or BA). In the case of transitivity alternation, *kowa-Ø* is allowed to inherit the morphological class feature of *kowa-* since *-Ø-* is the identity element and thus *kowa-Ø* is morphologically indistinguishable from *kowa-*. Conversely, a morphologically visible element blocks inheritance of the morphological feature of the root. This is the case with the Japanese de-adjectival verbs formed by *-m-*. Since *huka-m-* is morphologically different from *huka-*, it cannot inherit the features from *huka-*. On the other hand, if the feature in question is semantic rather than morphological, what is relevant is not the morphological visibility of the intervening element but rather the semantic congruity. In the case of Greek verb stem alternation, the stem, voice, and aspect are all predicates of the event. In other words, each of them adds information to constrain the set of events that the verb denotes. Therefore features that modify the event can be inherited from the stem up to the aspect element.

In sum, the current selection-based approach to contextual allomorphy provides an account for the apparent complexity of the locality constraints on allomorphy in terms of constraints on feature inheritance. Only features that are semantically or morphologically meaningful for the entire constituent can be inherited, and can therefore constrain the choice of the allomorph that selects that constituent. While this account is in line with some of the observations in the DM literature that we discussed here, its empirical plausibility must be tested in a wide range of data in the future.

Table 4. The non-future verb conjugation paradigm of Chamorro, adopted from [19].

	'fly'	'stay'	'stand up'
Singular	gumupu	sumaga	kumuentos
Plural	manggupu	mañaga	manguentos

4 Extensions

Beside transitivity alternation, a characteristic feature of the current analysis is the use of a class of categories that serves for a morphological, but not semantic purpose. We postulated the inflectional consonant category Ic to capture the euphonic alternation between *tob-* and *ton-* (see Sect. 2). Such a morphological category opens a new way to analyze complex morphological phenomena that go beyond simple concatenation of strings. We briefly discuss an extension of this approach. [19][7] proposes to augment Categorial Grammar with a set of "transformational" morphological operations to capture phenomena such as infixation, circumfixation, reduplication, metathesis, umlaut, and so on. We do not have space to discuss all of these phenomena, but let us consider the case of infixation and fusion in Chamorro discussed by [19]. The relevant facts are summarized in Table 4.

The non-future singular form can be analyzed as involving infixation of *-um-*, while the plural form can be analyzed as prefixation of *man-*, followed by a fusion of the n and the first consonant of the stem in the case of *mañaga* (the initial s is fused with n). [19] proposes to deal with such cases with operations specifically designed for them, which involve a destructive rewriting of the stem. In the current analysis, however, standard composition rules and a class of purely morphological categories C suffice. In the case of *saga* 'stay,' *-aga* requires s- on its left, but this requirement is intervened by *-um-* in the singular (21a), and overridden in the plural (21b). Note the resemblance to the analysis of the Japanese euphonic alternation between *tob-* and *ton-* discussed earlier.

$$(21) \quad a. \quad \underbrace{\frac{\text{s-}}{C_s} \quad \frac{\text{-um-}}{(V_{sg}/(V_{sg}\backslash C_{\{1\}}))\backslash C_{\{1\}}} \quad \frac{\text{-aga}}{V\backslash C_s}}_{\dfrac{V_{sg}/(V_{sg}\backslash C_s)}{V_{sg}} >}{<}$$

---

[7] We thank Yusuke Kubota (p.c.) for suggesting [19] as relevant to the current discussion. Another work that deals with morphology with Categorial Grammar is [31], also suggested to us by Yusuke Kubota. The central idea of the work is that morphological operations are functions, and such functions can take another function as their argument. Although many interesting cases discussed there are out of the scope of the current study since they involve suprasegmentals, we believe the approach pursued here — viewing morphemes as functions that take other morphemes, which can be functions themselves — is in line with [31]'s intuition.

b.

$$\cfrac{\cfrac{\text{ma-}}{(V_{pl}/V_{pl})/C_n} \quad \cfrac{\text{-ñ-}}{(V_{pl}/(V_{pl}\backslash C_s))\backslash((V_{pl}/V_{pl})/C_n)}}{V_{pl}/(V_{pl}\backslash C_s)}< \quad \cfrac{\text{-aga}}{V\backslash C_s}}{V_{pl}}>$$

Although this analysis is preliminary and is by no means meant to cover all the relevant morphosyntactic and semantic facts of the Chamorro verb conjugation, it should be sufficient to demonstrate that the current version of CCG, augmented with morphological categories and feature inheritance, is powerful enough to capture morphological phenomena which go beyond simple concatenation. A topic for future work is therefore to explore the potential of the current approach in a broader range of morphological phenomena.

5 Concluding Remarks

We proposed a formalization of the constructivist analysis of verbal argument structure in CCG, in which argument structure is composed in the syntactic derivation, rather than specified in the lexicon. Such a formalization should provide a basis for a constructivist model of argument structure processing since CCG allows incremental, left-to-right structure building. We argued that such an analysis is not only possible but also provides an explanation for the locality constraints on contextual allomorphy observed in the DM literature based on the locality of selection. This explanation is attractive since it reduces contextual allomorphy to the matter of selection, a more fundamental mechanism that is undeniably essential to language.

As both of our reviewers correctly pointed out, a fundamental issue in constructivist analyses is how to constrain the set of argument structures that are allowed with a particular root. In the current framework, possible combinations of argument structures (i.e., argument-introducing items) and roots are defined by features that these items have. To capture the fact that *tabe-* 'eat,' for example, can be combined with the phonologically null transitive morpheme but not with a pronounced transitive morpheme or an intransitive morpheme, one can assign to the root *tabe-* some feature(s) to be selected by the appropriate morpheme. One reviewer suggested that this would be just a 'notational variant' of the projectionist analysis, where *tabe-* is inherently specified as $V\backslash NP\backslash NP$. One possible argument in favor of the constructivist analysis of *tabe-* is that it explains why the first argument is associated with the theme (what is eaten) and the second with the agent (eater). Under the current approach, this fact is explained by hierarchical organization of the argument-introducing elements, which are dictated by features on these categories. The constructivist analysis also enables the role of the arguments to be specified compositionally, rather than lexically (especially the agent role; cf. [22]). Further research is needed to distinguish these two views on empirical grounds.

References

1. Arad, M.: Locality constraints on the interpretation of roots: the case of Hebrew denominal verbs. Nat. Lang. Linguist. Theor. **21**, 737–778 (2003). https://doi.org/ 10.1023/A:1025533719905
2. Bekki, D.: Nihongo bunpoo no keisiki riron (In Japanese). Kurosio, Tokyo (2010)
3. Belletti, A., Rizzi, L.: Psych-verbs and θ-theory. Nat. Lang. Linguist. Theor. **6**(3), 291–352 (1988)
4. Bloch, B.: Studies in colloquial Japanese I: inflection. J. Am. Orient. Soc. **66**(2), 97–109 (1946)
5. Bobaljik, J.D.: The ins and outs of contextual allomorphy. In: University of Maryland Working Papers in Linguistics, pp. 35–71 (2000)
6. Borer, H.: In name only. Oxford University Press, Oxford, UK (2005). https://doi. org/10.1093/acprof:oso/9780199263905.001.0001
7. Borer, H.: The normal course of events. Oxford University Press, Oxford, UK (2005). https://doi.org/10.1093/acprof:oso/9780199263929.001.0001
8. Bresnan, J., Kaplan, R.: Introduction: Grammars as mental representations of language. In: Bresnan, J. (ed.) The Mental Representation of Grammatical Relations, pp. i-lii. MIT Press, Cambridge, MA (1982)
9. Chomsky, N.: Aspects of the Theory of Syntax. MIT Press, Cambridge, MA (1965)
10. Chomsky, N.: Lectures on Government and Binding. Foris, Dordrecht (1981)
11. Chomsky, N.: Derivation by phase. In: Kenstowicz, M. (ed.) Ken Hale: a Life in Language, pp. 1–52. MIT Press, Cambridge, MA (2001)
12. Clark, E.V., Clark, H.H.: When nouns surface as verbs. Language **55**(4), 767–811 (1979). https://doi.org/10.2307/412745
13. Folli, R., Harley, H.: Flavors of v. In: Kempchinsky, P., Slabakova, R. (eds.) Aspectual Inquiries. Studies in Natural Language and Linguistic Theory. vol. 62. Springer, Dordrecht (2005). https://doi.org/10.1007/1-4020-3033-9_5
14. Friedmann, N., Taranto, G., Shapiro, L.P., Swinney, D.: The leaf fell (the Leaf): The online processing of unaccusatives. Linguist. Inq. **39**(3), 355–377 (2008). https://doi.org/10.1162/ling.2008.39.3.355
15. Halle, M., Marantz, A.: Distributed morphology and the pieces of inflection. In: Hale, K., Keyser, S.J. (eds.) The view from Building 20: Essays in linguistics in honor of Sylvain Bromberger, pp. 111–176. MIT Press, Cambridge, MA (1993)
16. Harley, H.: On the causative construction. In: Miyagawa, S., Saito, M. (eds.) The Oxford Handbook of Japanese Linguistics, pp. 20–53. Oxford University Press, Oxford, UK (2008). https://doi.org/10.1093/oxfordhb/9780195307344.013.0002
17. Harley, H.: A Minimalist approach to argument structure. In: Boeckx, C. (ed.) The Oxford Handbook of Linguistic Minimalism, pp. 427–448. Oxford University Press, Oxford, UK (2011). https://doi.org/10.1093/oxfordhb/9780199549368.013. 0019
18. Harley, H.: On the identity of roots. Theor. Linguist. **40**(3–4), 225–276 (2014). https://doi.org/10.1515/tl-2014-0010
19. Hoeksema, J., Janda, R.D.: Implications of process-morphology for categorial grammar. In: Oehrle, R.T., Bach, E., Wheeler, D. (eds.) Categorial Grammars and Natural Language Structures. Studies in Linguistics and Philosophy. vol. 32. Springer, Dordrecht (1988). https://doi.org/10.1007/978-94-015-6878-4_8
20. Jacobsen, W.: The Transitive Structure of Events in Japanese. Kurosio, Tokyo (1992)

21. Kamide, Y., Altmann, G.T.M., Haywood, S.L.: Prediction and thematic information in incremental sentence processing. J. Mem. Lang. **49**, 133–156 (2003). https://doi.org/10.1016/S0749-596X(03)00023-8
22. Kratzer, A.: Severing the external argument from its verb. In: Rooryck, J., Zaring, L. (eds.) Phrase Structure and the Lexicon, pp. 109–137. Kluwer, Dordrecht (1996). https://doi.org/10.1007/978-94-015-8617-7
23. Lewis, S., Phillips, C.: Aligning grammatical theories and language processing models. J. Psycholinguist. Res. **44**(1), 27–46 (2015). https://doi.org/10.1007/s10936-014-9329-z
24. Lohndal, T.: Without specifiers: Phrase structure and events. Ph.D. thesis, University of Maryland, College Park, MA (2012)
25. Marantz, A.: Phases and words. In: Choe, S. (ed.) Phases in the Theory of Grammar, pp. 199–222. Dong-In, Seoul, South Korea (2007)
26. Marantz, A.: Locality domains for contextual allomorphy across the interfaces. In: Matushansky, O., Marantz, A. (eds.) Distributed Morphology Today: Morphemes for Morris Halle, pp. 95–115. MIT Press, Cambridge, MA (2013)
27. Marantz, A.: Verbal argument structure: event and participants. Lingua **130**, 152–168 (2013). https://doi.org/10.1016/j.lingua.2012.10.012
28. Merchant, J.: How much context is enough? Two cases of span-conditioned stem allomorphy. Linguist. Inq. **46**(2), 273–303 (2015). https://doi.org/10.1162/LING_a_00182
29. Momma, S., Slevc, L.R., Phillips, C.: Unaccusativity in sentence production. Linguist. Inq. **49**(1), 181–194 (2017). https://doi.org/10.1162/ling_a_00271
30. Oseki, Y.: Voice morphology in Japanese argument structures (2017). https://ling.auf.net/lingbuzz/003374. submitted manuscript
31. Raffelsiefen, R.: A nonconfigurational approach to morphology. In: Aronoff, M. (ed.) Morphology Now, pp. 133–162. State University of New York Press, Albany, NY (1992)
32. Sag, I.A., Wasow, T.: Performance-compatible competence grammar. In: Borsley, R.D., Börjars, K. (eds.) Non-Transformational Syntax: Formal and Explicit Models of Grammar, pp. 359–377. Blackwell (2011)
33. Steedman, M.: The Syntactic Process. MIT Press, Cambridge, MA (2000)
34. Tanenhaus, M.K., Spivey-Knowlton, M.J., Eberhard, K.M., Sedivy, J.C.: Integration of visual and linguistic information in spoken language comprehension. Science **268**(5217), 1632–1634 (1995). https://doi.org/10.1126/science.7777863
35. Trommer, J.: Morphology consuming syntax' resources: generation and parsing in a minimalist version of Distributed Morphology. In: Proceedings of the ESSLI Workshop on Resource Logics and Minimalist Grammars (1999)

A Proof-Theoretic Analysis
of the Meaning of a Formula
in a Combination of Intuitionistic
and Classical Propositional Logic

Masanobu Toyooka[✉]

Graduate School of Humanities and Human Sciences, Hokkaido University, Sapporo,
Japan
`toyooka.masanobu.t1@elms.hokudai.ac.jp`

Abstract. This paper provides a proof-theoretic analysis of the meaning
of a formula in a combination of intuitionistic and classical propositional
logic, based on the analysis proposed by Restall (2009). Restall showed
that his analysis is applicable to both intuitionistic and classical propositional logic separately, but this paper shows that it is also applicable
to a combination of the two logics called **C + J**. In addition, two points
of improvement of Restall's analysis are mentioned, and they are overcome by employing the method provided by Takano (2018). Moreover,
this paper explains how the analysis of **C + J**, which is based on Restall's
analysis and improved by Takano's method, is related to the bilateralism-
unilateralism debate. It is shown that a unilateral approach is possible
for **C + J**, although Restall's original analysis is based on bilateralism.

Keywords: Sequent Calculus · Combination of Logics · Intuitionistic
Logic · Classical Logic · Semantic Completeness · Bilateralism

1 Introduction and Motivation

1.1 Introduction

This paper provides a proof-theoretic analysis of the meaning of a formula in a combination of intuitionistic and classical propositional logic. A proof-theoretic analysis of meaning is an analysis explaining the meaning of a formula by the notion of
arguments, proofs, or inference rules, not by the notion of truth, models, or validity. Such analyses are studied in, for example, [15, 30, 34, 38, 39, 43]. The analysis
presented in this paper is based on the one proposed by Restall [39], which uses a
sequent calculus. A sequent calculus is a proof theory dealing with an object called
"a sequent," which has the following form: $\Gamma \Rightarrow \Delta$, where Γ and Δ are finite sets
of formulas. The derivability of $\Gamma \Rightarrow \Delta$ is usually interpreted as follows: if all of
the formulas in Γ hold, then some of the formulas in Δ hold. The central idea of
Restall's analysis is to interpret inference rules in a sequent calculus by the notions
of assertion and denial and to obtain a model from the admissibility of these inference rules. Accordingly, in addition to the usual interpretation described above,

D. Bekki et al. (Eds.): LENLS 2019, LNCS 14213, pp. 100–119, 2023.
https://doi.org/10.1007/978-3-031-43977-3_7

Restall [38, 39] provides the following interpretation of the derivability of a sequent by the notions of assertion and denial: it is incoherent to assert all the formulas in Γ and to deny all the formulas in Δ. Corresponding to this interpretation of the derivability of a sequent, inference rules in a sequent calculus are also interpreted by the notions of assertion and denial. Based on these interpretations, the notion of a model is obtained successfully in Restall's analysis.

On the other hand, various combinations of intuitionistic and classical logic are studied in [6, 8–11, 18, 21, 22, 25, 26, 31–33, 35, 49, 50]. In this paper, we regard a logic as a combination of intuitionistic and classical logic if the language of the logic has both intuitionistic and classical operators and if it is a conservative extension of both logics. Although various combinations of intuitionistic and classical logic exist, this paper analyzes the one studied in [10, 11, 18, 22, 49, 50], because for this logic a sequent calculus using an ordinary notion of a sequent was already proposed in [49, 50]. As is noted above, since Restall's original analysis employs a sequent calculus, the existence of a sequent calculus enables us to apply the analysis straightforwardly. In the following, this combination and the sequent calculus for this combination are called $\mathbf{C} + \mathbf{J}$ and $\mathsf{G}(\mathbf{C}+\mathbf{J})$, respectively. The idea of constructing $\mathbf{C} + \mathbf{J}$ is easy to see in the Kripke semantics provided in [11, 18]. This Kripke semantics is obtained by adding to the Kripke semantics for intuitionistic propositional logic the satisfaction relation for a formula whose main connective is classical negation, denoted by "$\neg_c$", described as follows:

$$w \models_M \neg_c A \text{ iff } w \not\models_M A,$$

where $M = \langle W, R, V \rangle$ is a Kripke model for intuitionistic propositional logic and w is a state in W. The sequent calculus for $\mathbf{C} + \mathbf{J}$ is proposed in [49]. This calculus is obtained by adding the right and left rules for intuitionistic implication, denoted by "$\rightarrow_i$," to the propositional fragment of the classical sequent calculus $\mathbf{LK}$. The left rule for "$\rightarrow_i$" added to the propositional fragment of $\mathbf{LK}$ is the one in the intuitionistic multi-succedent sequent calculus $\mathbf{mLJ}$, proposed by Maehara [23], but the right rule should be restricted as follows:

$$\frac{A, C_1 \rightarrow_i D_1, \ldots, C_m \rightarrow_i D_m, p_1, \ldots, p_n \Rightarrow B}{C_1 \rightarrow_i D_1, \ldots, C_m \rightarrow_i D_m, p_1, \ldots, p_n \Rightarrow A \rightarrow_i B} \ (\Rightarrow \rightarrow_i).$$

The sequent calculus $\mathsf{G}(\mathbf{C} + \mathbf{J})$ is sound and complete to the Kripke semantics described above, which was shown in [50].

This paper basically applies Restall's analysis to $\mathbf{C} + \mathbf{J}$ in terms of $\mathsf{G}(\mathbf{C}+\mathbf{J})$. However, two points of improvement and one open problem exist in Restall's analysis. The first point of improvement concerns the relationship between the admissibility of an inference rule and the corresponding satisfaction relation. The second point of improvement concerns the admissibility of the rule (Cut). These two points are overcome by employing the method provided by Takano [48] for fifteen modal logics. The open problem is the following one: is it possible to analyze the meaning of a formula in a combination of intuitionistic and classical propositional logic? This paper solves this open problem positively by showing that Restall's analysis, improved by Takano's method, is applicable to **C + J**.

It is also shown that an analysis based on unilateralism, which is the opposite position of bilateralism, is possible for **C + J**. Bilateralism is a position claiming that two linguistic acts are primitive when the meaning of a formula or a statement is considered, whereas unilateralism is a position claiming that only one linguistic act is primitive. Since Restall's analysis introduces the notions of assertion and denial as primitive, it is categorized as bilateralism, and the analysis improved by Takano's method may also be categorized as bilateralism. However, this paper shows that a unilateral approach is also possible for **C + J**.

The outline of this paper is as follows. Section 2 and Sect. 3 review Restall's analysis and **C + J**, respectively. Section 4 applies Takano's [48] method to **C + J**. Section 5 explains how the analysis in this paper is related to the bilateralism-unilateralism debate and shows that unilateral analysis is possible for **C + J**.

1.2 Motivation for Analyzing the Meaning of a Formula in a Combination of Intuitionistic and Classical Logic

Before proceeding to Sect. 2, let us see why an analysis of the meaning of a formula in a combination of intuitionistic and classical logic should be provided. Since Restall's analysis is possible for both intuitionistic and classical propositional logic separately, it may be thought that giving the meaning of a formula in a combination of both logics is not needed. This section provides an argument claiming that an analysis of the meaning of a formula in a combination of intuitionistic and classical logic is necessary.

By combining intuitionistic and classical logic, we can tackle the following question: how do advocates of intuitionistic/classical logic understand the meaning of a formula in the other logic?[1] As Quine [37] pointed out, intuitionistic and classical connectives can be regarded as denoting different subjects. By analyzing the meaning of a formula in a combination of intuitionistic and classical logic, in which connectives of both logics exist, we can codify how advocates of intuitionistic/classical logic understand the meaning of a formula in the other logic. For example, we can explain how an advocate of intuitionistic logic understands the meaning of a formula $\neg_c p \lor p$, where "$\neg_c$" denotes classical negation. Being an advocate of intuitionistic logic, he/she basically uses negation in the intuitionistic way. However, in order to give the analysis of the meaning of $\neg_c p \lor p$ as Restall did for classical and intuitionistic logic, the advocates of intuitionistic logic also need to appeal to the inference rules for the classical negation, since Restall's analysis is based on the inference rules for a connective. Therefore, in order to explain how the advocates of intuitionistic logic understand the meaning of $\neg_c p \lor p$, we should provide an analysis of the meaning of a formula in a combination of intuitionistic and classical logic whose proof theory contains the inference rules for both intuitionistic and classical connectives.[2]

---

[1] This question is not a new one. Similar questions were already mentioned in [26, 35].

[2] Some may consider ordinary intuitionistic logic itself to be a combination, since Kolmogorov-Gödel-Gentzen translation exists. A combination based on this view is studied in [31–33, 35]. However, such a view is criticized in [12].

Some may disagree with this argument claiming that there is no need to codify how advocates of intuitionistic/classical logic understand the meaning of a formula in the other logic, since they understand the meaning of a formula in the other logic by seeing a proof theory or semantics for it. For example, they may claim that advocates of classical logic understand the meaning of a formula in intuitionistic logic by seeing Kripke semantics for intuitionistic logic, and there is no need to appeal to a logic having both intuitionistic and classical connectives.

However, the codification is necessary. If we accept Quine's view that intuitionistic and classical connectives denote different subjects, it is admitted that the discussion between advocates of intuitionistic logic and those of classical logic is not about a valid logical law but about the use of connectives. For example, advocates of intuitionistic logic do not accept law of excluded middle. They do not accept $\neg_i A \vee A$ generally, where "$\neg_i$" denotes intuitionistic negation. On the other hand, advocates of classical logic accept law of excluded middle. They accept $\neg_c A \vee A$ generally. There is no disagreement about law of excluded middle between advocates of intuitionistic logic and those of classical logic, since it is possible that $\neg_c A \vee A$ is valid while $\neg_i A \vee A$ is not. Thus, the discussion between advocates of intuitionistic logic and those of classical logic is the following one: how should negation be used?, or what kind of meaning should be attached to negation? In this discussion, advocates of intuitionistic/classical logic should take a connective in the other logic into consideration. For example, if advocates of classical logic attempt to claim that negation should be used as in classical logic and that the use of law of excluded middle should be permitted, they must give an argument claiming that a formula containing intuitionistic implication, such as $\neg_c(p \rightarrow_i q) \vee (p \rightarrow_i q)$, is also to be admitted. The reason for this is that if an argument does not take such a formula into consideration, it is clearly begging the question. In order to formulate the discussion between advocates of intuitionistic and those of classical logic in this way, a formula such as $\neg_c(p \rightarrow_i q) \vee (p \rightarrow_i q)$ should be expressed and considered. Therefore, the explanation of the meaning of a formula consisting of intuitionistic and classical connectives is necessary.

Some may think that a combination does not contribute to such an argument, because since a combination of intuitionistic and classical logic is a conservative extension of both intuitionistic and classical logic, all the theorems in the ordinary intuitionistic and classical logics are also theorems in the combination. However, it is not guaranteed that all the theorems in the ordinary intuitionistic and classical logics are also theorems in a combination by the fact that it is a conservative extension of both logics. For example, $A \rightarrow_i (B \rightarrow_i A)$ is no longer a theorem in $\mathbf{C} + \mathbf{J}$, the combination dealt with in this paper, since $\neg_c p \rightarrow_i (q \rightarrow_i p)$ is not derivable. This may imply that advocates of intuitionistic logic cannot claim that all of the intuitionistic theorems should be admitted. This is because the addition of classical negation in the way of $\mathbf{C} + \mathbf{J}$ leads to an instance of this theorem that is not derivable in a proof theory of $\mathbf{C} + \mathbf{J}$.[3]

---

[3] It is noted that the results in $\mathbf{C} + \mathbf{J}$ may not be conclusive for deciding whether an intuitionistic or classical theorem should be admitted. The results in another combination also need to be considered.

2 Restall's Analysis, Two Points of Improvement, and One Open Problem

2.1 Restall's Analysis

This section reviews Restall's analysis proposed in [39]. As is noted in Sect. 1.1, the central idea of this analysis is to interpret inference rules in a sequent calculus by the notions of assertion and denial and to obtain the notion of a model from the admissibility of these inference rules. Restall regards inference rules in a sequent calculus as "normative constraints" on assertion and denial. Although this analysis is applied to classical propositional logic, intuitionistic propositional logic, and modal logic **S5**, only the case of classical propositional logic is described here.

We define the syntax of classical logic as consisting of a countably infinite set of propositional variables and the following logical connectives: falsum $\bot$, conjunction $\wedge$, disjunction $\vee$, and negation $\neg_c$.[4] As far as classical propositional logic is concerned, the subscript "c" for the negation is not necessary, but since intuitionistic negation is introduced in Sect. 3, we use this subscript from this section onward to avoid confusion. Classical implication $\rightarrow_c$ is not introduced as a primitive symbol, since it can be defined as follows: $A \rightarrow_c B := \neg_c A \vee B$. When classical propositional logic is analyzed, the propositional fragment of the sequent calculus **LK** is used. In the rest of this paper, the expression **LK** denotes only the propositional fragment. This calculus deals with an object called "a sequent," which has the following form: $\Gamma \Rightarrow \Delta$, where Γ and Δ are finite sets of formulas. The sequent calculus **LK** consists of the axioms and rules in Table 1.[5]

Table 1. Sequent Calculus **LK**

Axioms

$$\frac{}{A \Rightarrow A}\ (Id)\qquad \frac{}{\bot \Rightarrow}\ (\bot)$$

Structural Rules

$$\frac{\Gamma \Rightarrow \Delta}{\Gamma \Rightarrow \Delta, A}\ (\Rightarrow w)\qquad \frac{\Gamma \Rightarrow \Delta}{A, \Gamma \Rightarrow \Delta}\ (w \Rightarrow)\qquad \frac{\Gamma \Rightarrow \Delta, A \quad A, \Gamma \Rightarrow \Delta}{\Gamma \Rightarrow \Delta}\ (Cut)$$

Propositional Logical Rules

$$\frac{\Gamma \Rightarrow \Delta, A \quad \Gamma \Rightarrow \Delta, B}{\Gamma \Rightarrow \Delta, A \wedge B}\ (\Rightarrow \wedge)\qquad \frac{A, \Gamma \Rightarrow \Delta}{A \wedge B, \Gamma \Rightarrow \Delta}\ (\wedge \Rightarrow_1)\qquad \frac{B, \Gamma \Rightarrow \Delta}{A \wedge B, \Gamma \Rightarrow \Delta}\ (\wedge \Rightarrow_2)$$

$$\frac{\Gamma \Rightarrow \Delta, A}{\Gamma \Rightarrow \Delta, A \vee B}\ (\Rightarrow \vee_1)\qquad \frac{\Gamma \Rightarrow \Delta, B}{\Gamma \Rightarrow \Delta, A \vee B}\ (\Rightarrow \vee_2)\qquad \frac{A, \Gamma \Rightarrow \Delta \quad B, \Gamma \Rightarrow \Delta}{A \vee B, \Gamma \Rightarrow \Delta}\ (\vee \Rightarrow)$$

$$\frac{A, \Gamma \Rightarrow \Delta}{\Gamma \Rightarrow \Delta, \neg_c A}\ (\Rightarrow \neg_c)\qquad \frac{\Gamma \Rightarrow \Delta, A}{\neg_c A, \Gamma \Rightarrow \Delta}\ (\neg_c \Rightarrow)$$

---

[4] Note that $\bot$ is not considered in [39], because $\bot$ is definable by negation and conjunction. However, the addition of $\bot$ as a primitive symbol creates no problem.

[5] Since the antecedent and succedent of a sequent are defined as sets, contraction and exchange rules are not necessary. It is noted that although a sequent calculus that does not contain $(w \Rightarrow)$ or $(\Rightarrow w)$ is used in [39], this difference creates no problem.

The derivability of a sequent $\Gamma \Rightarrow \Delta$ in **LK** is defined by the existence of a finite tree consisting only of axioms and rules in **LK** whose root is the sequent. The derivability of $\Gamma \Rightarrow \Delta$ is usually interpreted as follows: if all of the formulas in Γ hold, then some of the formulas in Δ hold.

Restall starts his analysis by defining the notion of a "position."

Definition 1 (Position [39, Definition 1].) *A pair* $(\Gamma : \Delta)$ *of finite sets of formulas is a* position *if* $\Gamma \Rightarrow \Delta$ *is not derivable in* **LK**.

In the rest of this paper, $(\Gamma \cup \{A\} : \Delta \cup \{B\})$ is abbreviated as $(\Gamma, A : \Delta, B)$, for any finite sets $\Gamma \cup \{A\}, \Delta \cup \{B\}$ of formulas. The antecedent and succedent of a position are regarded as the set of asserted and denied formulas, respectively. A position expresses a coherent situation with respect to assertion and denial. Consider the pairs $(p : p \wedge q)$ and $(p : p \vee q)$. The former is a position, since $p \Rightarrow p \wedge q$ is not derivable in **LK**. This implies that to assert p and to deny $p \wedge q$ is coherent in classical logic. However, the latter is not a position, since $p \Rightarrow p \vee q$ is derivable in **LK**. This implies that to assert p and to deny $p \vee q$ is incoherent in classical logic. Accordingly, the derivability of $\Gamma \Rightarrow \Delta$ is interpreted by the notions of assertion and denial, as follows: it is incoherent to assert all the formulas in Γ and to deny all the formulas in Δ. An inference rule in **LK** is also interpreted by the notions of assertion and denial. For example, $(\wedge \Rightarrow_1)$ is interpreted by reading the rule from the lower sequent to the upper sequent, as follows: if it is coherent to assert $A \wedge B$ and all the formulas in Γ and to deny all the formulas in Δ, then it is also coherent to assert A and all the formulas in Γ and to deny all the formulas in Δ. The other rules in **LK** are interpreted in the same way. Since inference rules in **LK** govern assertion and denial, they are considered to be "normative constraints" on assertion and denial.

Based on the notion of a position, the notion of a "limit position" is defined.

Definition 2 (Limit Position [39, Definition 4]). *A pair* $(\Gamma : \Delta)$ *of sets of formulas is a* limit position *if it satisfies the following:*

- *For any finite sets* $\Gamma' \subseteq \Gamma$, $\Delta' \subseteq \Delta$ *of formulas, the pair* $(\Gamma' : \Delta')$ *is a position.*
- *The union of* Γ *and* Δ *contains all the formulas in classical logic,*

A limit position expresses an ideal situation with respect to assertion and denial, in which any formula in classical logic is either asserted or denied. Thus, a limit position does not express the actual linguistic situation, as was noted in [39, pp. 249-252]. Technically, the antecedent of a limit position corresponds to the notion of a maximal consistent set, the notion used to show the semantic completeness (cf. [5, Definition 4.15]).

Fact 1. [39, Fact 4] *For any position* $(\Gamma : \Delta)$, *there is a limit position* $(\Gamma^* : \Delta^*)$ *such that* $\Gamma \subseteq \Gamma^*$ *and* $\Delta \subseteq \Delta^*$.

This fact is shown by making use of (Cut). This rule ensures the following: if $(\Gamma : \Delta)$ is a position, then either $(\Gamma : \Delta, A)$ or $(A, \Gamma : \Delta)$ is also a position. The proof is almost the same as the one of extension lemma, the lemma used to show the semantic completeness (cf. [5, Lemma 4.17]).

Fact 2. **[39, Fact 5]** *For any limit position* $(\Gamma : \Delta)$, *all of the following hold:*

1. $A \wedge B \in \Gamma$ *iff* $A \in \Gamma$ *and* $B \in \Gamma$,
2. $A \wedge B \in \Delta$ *iff* $A \in \Delta$ *or* $B \in \Delta$,
3. $A \vee B \in \Gamma$ *iff* $A \in \Gamma$ *or* $B \in \Gamma$,
4. $A \vee B \in \Delta$ *iff* $A \in \Delta$ *and* $B \in \Delta$,

5. $\neg_c A \in \Gamma$ *iff* $A \in \Delta$,
6. $\neg_c A \in \Delta$ *iff* $A \in \Gamma$,
7. $\bot \in \Delta$.

This fact is shown by reading the rules in **LK** from the lower sequent to the upper sequent(s) and by appealing to the fact that the union of Γ and Δ is the set of all the formulas in classical logic. As is seen in Fact 2, if the formulas in the antecedent of a limit position are regarded as true, the truth conditions are obtained, while if the formulas in the succedent of a limit position are regarded as false, the false conditions are obtained. Therefore, starting from the admissibility of the inference rules in **LK**, the notion of a model for classical logic is obtained. Although the notion of a model is considered, it is not introduced as given but obtained by analyzing the rules in **LK**.[6] Thus, this analysis is proof-theoretic.

2.2   Two Points of Improvement and One Open Problem

Although Restall's analysis is very refined and explains the relationship between an inference rule in a sequent calculus and the corresponding satisfaction relation for a formula, two points of improvement and one open problem exist.

The first point of improvement concerns on the relationship between the admissibility of an inference rule and the corresponding satisfaction relation for a formula. Restall's analysis obtains the satisfaction relation for a formula from the admissibility of the corresponding inference rule. In other words, Restall's analysis explains the following: if an inference rule is admissible in a sequent calculus, then the corresponding satisfaction relation for a formula will be obtained. However, in addition to this, if it is possible to establish the other direction, the tighter relation between the admissibility of an inference rule and the corresponding satisfaction relation for a formula is obtained. The other direction tells us what kind of inference rule is admissible if we choose some satisfaction relation for a formula, which enables us to describe in detail the relation between the admissibility of an inference rule and the corresponding satisfaction relation for a formula.

The second point of improvement concerns the rule (Cut). Restall's analysis, especially Fact 1, depends on this rule. In terms of assertion and denial, (Cut) expresses the following normative constraint: if it is coherent to assert all the formulas in Γ and to deny all the formulas in Δ, then either the assertion of A or the denial of A is also coherent. However, it is far from trivial to accept this normative constraint, and some may refuse to accept this normative constraint.[7]

---

[6] Proof-theoretic semantics, the representative of the proof-theoretic analyses of meaning, explains the meaning of a formula by using purely syntactical objects, such as arguments or proofs directly (cf. [15,34,43]). On the other hand, Restall's analysis introduces the notion of a model. Thus, these two analyses are different on this point.

[7] For example, Ripley [40, Section 3.2] argues that there is no reason to postulate it. Even Restall [38, footnote 5] himself admits that the account of assertion and denial

If an analysis with no dependence on (Cut) is obtained, such an analysis will be acceptable for those who refuse to accept the normative constraint expressed by (Cut). Moreover, if the semantic condition corresponding to (Cut) is obtained, we can treat this rule in the same way as the rules for connectives, not as given.

The open problem is whether Restall's analysis is possible for a combination of intuitionistic and classical propositional logic. Although Restall's analysis is applicable to both of intuitionistic and classical propositional logic separately, this does not imply that it is applicable to a combination of both logics.

In Sect. 4, these two points of improvement are overcome by employing the method proposed by Takano [48]. Moreover, the open problem is solved positively by carrying out the analysis on a combination $\mathbf{C} + \mathbf{J}$ of intuitionistic and classical propositional logic. It should be noted that the analysis of this paper, which is based on Takano's method, does not appeal to König's infinite lemma or Zorn's lemma, the latter being appealed to in Restall's analysis. As noted in [1], it is controversial whether the axiom of choice is acceptable for advocates of intuitionistic logic. Since Zorn's lemma is equivalent to the axiom of choice and König's infinite lemma is weaker than Zorn's lemma, the fact that these lemmas are dispensable implies that our analysis does not presuppose any position about whether advocates of intuitionistic logic accept the axiom of choice. Thus, our analysis is acceptable for an advocate of intuitionistic logic, independently of whether he/she admits the axiom of choice.[8] Before proceeding to Takano's method, the combination $\mathbf{C} + \mathbf{J}$ is reviewed briefly in Sect. 3.

3   Combination of Intuitionistic and Classical Propositional Logic $\mathbf{C} + \mathbf{J}$

The combination $\mathbf{C} + \mathbf{J}$ is provided by Humberstone [18], and he proposed a natural deduction system. A Hilbert system for this logic was first proposed by del Cerro and Herzig [11], and De and Omori [10] proposed another Hilbert system by expanding a subintuitionistic logic. The single-succedent structured sequent calculus for this logic was proposed by Lucio [22]. The multi-succedent sequent calculus $\mathsf{G}(\mathbf{C} + \mathbf{J})$ was provided in [49,50]. A first-order expansion of $\mathbf{C} + \mathbf{J}$ was studied in [22,50]. Although many proof theories exist for $\mathbf{C} + \mathbf{J}$, we use the sequent calculus $\mathsf{G}(\mathbf{C} + \mathbf{J})$, because Restall's original analysis employs a sequent calculus.

The syntax of $\mathbf{C} + \mathbf{J}$ is obtained by adding intuitionistic implication to that of classical logic. Intuitionistic negation $\neg_i$ can be defined as follows: $\neg_i A := A \rightarrow_i \bot$. Since "$\rightarrow_c$" is definable, $\mathbf{C} + \mathbf{J}$ has two types of implication and negation.

---

recorded in (Cut) is a subtle one for advocates of intuitionistic logic. This paper does not discuss whether the normative constraint expressed by (Cut) is acceptable. Thus, this paper does not claim that it is unacceptable. What is shown in this paper is that it is not necessary to postulate the rule (Cut) in order to carry out a proof-theoretic analysis of the meaning of a formula.

[8] Clearly, this point holds only in the propositional setting. Therefore, if we try to expand the analysis in this paper to the first-order setting, we need to appeal to either König's infinite lemma or Zorn's lemma.

Let us proceed to the semantics for $\mathbf{C} + \mathbf{J}$. We introduce a Kripke semantics for $\mathbf{C} + \mathbf{J}$, provided in [11,18]. The Kripke semantics is obtained by adding the satisfaction relation for a formula whose main connective is classical negation to the Kripke semantics for intuitionistic propositional logic (cf. [7, Section 6.3]).

Definition 3 (Kripke Model [11]). *A Kripke model is a tuple $M = \langle W, R, V \rangle$, where*

- *W is a non-empty set of states,*
- *R is a preorder on W, i.e., R satisfies reflexivity and transitivity,[9]*
- *$V : \mathsf{Prop} \to \mathcal{P}(W)$ is a valuation function satisfying the following heredity condition: $w \in V(p)$ and wRv jointly imply $v \in V(p)$ for all states $w, v \in W$.*

Definition 4. [11] *Given a Kripke model $M = \langle W, R, V \rangle$, a state $w \in W$, and a formula A, the satisfaction relation $w \models_M A$ is defined inductively as follows:*

$w \models_M p$ iff $w \in V(p)$,
$w \not\models_M \perp$,
$w \models_M A \wedge B$ iff $w \models_M A$ and $w \models_M B$,
$w \models_M A \vee B$ iff $w \models_M A$ or $w \models_M B$,
$w \models_M \neg_c A$ iff $w \not\models_M A$,
$w \models_M A \to_i B$ iff for all $v \in W, wRv$ and $v \models_M A$ jointly imply $v \models_M B$.

The notion of a semantic consequence is defined by the truth preservation on an arbitrary state $w \in W$. A formula A is valid if A is a semantic consequence of $\emptyset$.

Let us proceed to the sequent calculus $\mathsf{G}(\mathbf{C} + \mathbf{J})$ for $\mathbf{C} + \mathbf{J}$.

Definition 5 (Sequent Calculus $\mathsf{G}(\mathbf{C}{+}\mathbf{J})$ [49]). *The sequent calculus $\mathsf{G}(\mathbf{C}{+}\mathbf{J})$ is obtained by adding to **LK**, consisting of the rules in Table 1, the right and left rules for intuitionistic implication, formulated as follows:*

$$\frac{A, C_1 \to_i D_1, \ldots, C_m \to_i D_m, p_1, \ldots, p_n \Rightarrow B}{C_1 \to_i D_1, \ldots, C_m \to_i D_m, p_1, \ldots, p_n \Rightarrow A \to_i B} \ (\Rightarrow \to_i)$$

$$\frac{\Gamma \Rightarrow \Delta, A \quad B, \Gamma \Rightarrow \Delta}{A \to_i B, \Gamma \Rightarrow \Delta} \ (\to_i \Rightarrow).$$

The left rule is the same as the one in the intuitionistic multi-succedent sequent calculus **mLJ**, proposed by Maehara [23]. However, the right rule should be restricted to the form described above. If this restriction were not imposed on the

---

[9] Although R is defined as a preorder on W in [11], it is defined as a partial order on W in the Kripke semantics provided in [18]. It is noted that both definitions are possible for a Kripke semantics for $\mathbf{C} + \mathbf{J}$ (cf. [5, Section 4.5]).

right rule for intuitionistic implication, intuitionistic implication would collapse into classical implication, as was pointed out in [4,17,38,52].[10]

Fact 3 (Soundness and Completeness [50, Theorems 1 and 3]). *The sequent calculus* G(C+J) *is sound and complete to the Kripke semantics, defined in Definitions 3 and 5.*

Fact 4 (Cut-Elimination and Subformula Property [50, Theorem 2]). *The sequent calculus* G(C + J) *is cut-free and satisfies the subformula property.*

4   Applying Takano's Method to C + J

This section applies the method proposed by Takano [48] to C + J and overcomes two points of improvement of Restall's original analysis. As a result, the open problem is solved positively.

Stipulation 1 (Sequent Calculus [48, Stipulation 1]). *A sequent calculus is a calculus having* $A \Rightarrow A$ *as an axiom for any A and having weakening rules.*

By Stipulation 1, a sequent calculus that has only some rules in C + J can be discussed. Note that the existence of (*Cut*) is not assumed in this stipulation. In the following, let **GL** be a sequent calculus in the sense of Stipulation 1.

Definition 6. *Let* Γ *be a finite set of formulas. Then, we define* $\mathsf{Sub}(\Gamma)$ *as the set of all subformulas of some formulas in* Γ. *A set* Γ *of formulas is* subformula-closed (sf-closed) *if* $\mathsf{Sub}(\Gamma) \subseteq \Gamma$ *and* $\bot \in \Gamma$.

In this paper, the definition of an sf-closed set of formulas is slightly different from the ordinary definition, since the condition $\bot \in \Gamma$ is required in Definition 6. This condition is necessary for dealing with the rule (I).

In the following, an sf-closed finite set Ξ of formulas is considered, while it is not considered in [48]. However, such a set is considered in [20,28,42,47], and a finite model will be obtained by considering it. The notion of derivability can be defined relative to Ξ.

Definition 7 (Ξ-derivability). *Let* Ξ *be an sf-closed finite set of formulas and* $\Gamma \cup \Delta \subseteq \Xi$. *A sequent* $\Gamma \Rightarrow \Delta$ *is* Ξ-derivable *in* **GL** *if it has a derivation in* **GL** *consisting solely of formulas in* Ξ.

In the following, when it is said that a sequent $\Gamma \Rightarrow \Delta$ is Ξ-derivable or Ξ-underivable, it is presupposed that $\Gamma \cup \Delta \subseteq \Xi$ holds.

---

[10] The reason why this restriction on the right rule for intuitionistic implication enables us to avoid collapsing is explained in [50]. Since the right rule for intuitionistic implication is restricted compared with the original rule in **mLJ**, some might wonder whether the semantic completeness of C + J fails. However, the semantic completeness holds, and the detailed proof is described in [50, Section 4]. Moreover, the rule ($\Rightarrow \rightarrow_i$) in G(C + J) can be regarded as the core of the ordinary right rule for implication in **mLJ**, as noted in [50, p.32].

Definition 8 (Ξ-underivable pair). *Let Ξ be an sf-closed finite set of formulas. A pair $(\Gamma : \Delta)$ of finite sets of formulas is a Ξ-underivable pair in a sequent calculus **GL** if $\Gamma \Rightarrow \Delta$ is not derivable in **GL**.*

The notion of a Ξ-underivable pair plays almost the same role as the notion of a position in Restall's analysis. It is noted that in Definition 8, the notion of derivability is defined relative to an sf-closed set Ξ and a sequent calculus **GL**. The antecedent and succedent of a Ξ-underivable pair can be regarded as the set of asserted and denied formulas, respectively, as is done in Restall's analysis. In the following, instead of the notion of a limit position, the notion of a Ξ-analytically saturated pair is introduced. This notion is obtained by modifying the notion of an *analytically saturated sequent*, defined in [48, Definition 1.1].

Definition 9 (Ξ-analytically saturated pair). *Let Ξ be an sf-closed finite set of formulas. A pair $(\Gamma : \Delta)$ of finite sets of formulas is Ξ-analytically saturated in a sequent calculus **GL** if it satisfies all of the following:*

*1. $\Gamma \Rightarrow \Delta$ is not Ξ-derivable in **GL**.*
2. For any formula $A \in \Xi$,
   *– $A \in \Gamma$ if $A, \Gamma \Rightarrow \Delta$ is not Ξ-derivable in **GL**,*
   *– $A \in \Delta$ if $\Gamma \Rightarrow \Delta, A$ is not Ξ-derivable in **GL**,*

The first condition of this definition is almost the same as the first condition of the definition of a limit position (Definition 2). The important difference from the notion of a limit position is contained in the second condition. In the second condition of the definition of a limit position (Definition 2), any formula A must be an element of either Γ or Δ. However, in the second condition of the definition of a Ξ-analytically saturated pair (Definition 9), this is not required.

Lemma 1. *Let Ξ be an sf-closed finite set of formulas and $(\Gamma : \Delta)$ be a Ξ-underivable pair in **GL**. Then, there exists a Ξ-analytically saturated pair $(\Gamma^* : \Delta^*)$ in **GL** such that $\Gamma \subseteq \Gamma^*$, $\Delta \subseteq \Delta^*$, and $\Gamma^* \cup \Delta^* \subseteq \Xi$.*

This lemma is shown in almost the same way as [48, Lemma 1.3]. Lemma 1 ensures that any Ξ-underivable pair of sets of formulas in **GL** can be extended to some Ξ-analytically saturated pairs in **GL**. This lemma corresponds to extension lemma of cut-free semantic completeness (cf. [27, Lemma 10]).

Definition 10. *For any sf-closed finite set Ξ of formulas, W^Ξ is defined as the set of all Ξ-analytically saturated pairs in **GL**.*

Definition 11. *For any $(\Gamma : \Delta), (\Pi : \Sigma) \in W^\Xi$, $(\Gamma : \Delta)R^\Xi(\Pi : \Sigma)$ if the following hold:*

– For any propositional variable $p \in \Xi$, if $p \in \Gamma$, then $p \in \Pi$,
– For any formulas $A \rightarrow_i B \in \Xi$, if $A \rightarrow_i B \in \Gamma$, then $A \rightarrow_i B \in \Pi$.

This definition of R^Ξ is imported from [50, Definition 11].

Definition 12. *A valuation V^Ξ is defined as follows for any propositional variable $p \in \Xi$ and any $(\Gamma : \Delta) \in W^\Xi$:*

$$(\Gamma : \Delta) \in V^\Xi(p) \text{ iff } p \in \Gamma.$$

The obtained tuple $\langle W^\Xi, R^\Xi, V^\Xi \rangle$ is a well-defined Kripke model described in Sect. 3. Since Ξ is finite, W^Ξ is finite. Thus, $\langle W^\Xi, R^\Xi, V^\Xi \rangle$ is a finite model.

Based on the notion of Ξ-derivability, we define the notion of Ξ-admissibility, the notion of admissibility relative to an sf-closed finite set Ξ of formulas.

Definition 13 (Ξ-admissibility). *An inference rule is Ξ-admissible in **GL** if whenever all of the upper sequents are Ξ-derivable in **GL**, then the lower sequent is also Ξ-derivable in **GL**.*

Definition 14. *If the side condition $A \in \mathsf{Sub}(\Gamma \cup \Delta)$ is imposed on (Cut), the restricted rule is defined as $(Cut)^a$.*

Theorem 1. *For any sf-closed finite set Ξ of formulas, all of the following hold:*

1. *The left rule for "$\wedge$" is Ξ-admissible in **GL** iff $A \wedge B \in \Gamma$ implies $A \in \Gamma$ and $B \in \Gamma$ for any $(\Gamma : \Delta) \in W^\Xi$,*
2. *The right rule for "$\wedge$" is Ξ-admissible in **GL** iff $A \wedge B \in \Delta$ implies $A \in \Delta$ or $B \in \Delta$ for any $(\Gamma : \Delta) \in W^\Xi$,*
3. *The left rule for "$\vee$" is Ξ-admissible in **GL** iff $A \vee B \in \Gamma$ implies $A \in \Gamma$ or $B \in \Gamma$ for any $(\Gamma : \Delta) \in W^\Xi$,*
4. *The right rule for "$\vee$" is Ξ-admissible in **GL** iff $A \vee B \in \Delta$ implies $A \in \Delta$ and $B \in \Delta$ for any $(\Gamma : \Delta) \in W^\Xi$,*
5. *The left rule for "$\neg_c$" is Ξ-admissible in **GL** iff $\neg_c A \in \Gamma$ implies $A \in \Delta$ for any $(\Gamma : \Delta) \in W^\Xi$,*
6. *The right rule for "$\neg_c$" is Ξ-admissible in **GL** iff $\neg_c A \in \Delta$ implies $A \subset \Gamma$ for any $(\Gamma : \Delta) \in W^\Xi$,*
7. *The left rule for "$\rightarrow_i$" is Ξ-admissible in **GL** iff for any $(\Gamma : \Delta) \in W^\Xi$, $A \rightarrow_i B \in \Gamma$ implies $A \in \Sigma$ or $B \in \Pi$ for any $(\Pi : \Sigma) \in W^\Xi$ such that $(\Gamma : \Delta)R^\Xi(\Pi : \Sigma)$,*
8. *The right rule for "$\rightarrow_i$" is Ξ-admissible in **GL** iff for any $(\Gamma : \Delta) \in W^\Xi$, $A \rightarrow_i B \in \Delta$ implies $A \in \Pi$ and $B \in \Sigma$ for some $(\Pi : \Sigma) \in W^\Xi$ such that $(\Gamma : \Delta)R^\Xi(\Pi : \Sigma)$,*
9. *The rule for "$\bot$" is Ξ-admissible in **GL** iff $\bot \notin \Gamma$ for any $(\Gamma : \Delta) \in W^\Xi$,*
10. *The rule (Cut) is Ξ-admissible in **GL** iff $A \in \Xi$ implies $A \in \Gamma$ or $A \in \Delta$ for any $(\Gamma : \Delta) \in W^\Xi$,*
11. *The rule $(Cut)^a$ is Ξ-admissible in **GL** iff $A \in \mathsf{Sub}(\Gamma \cup \Delta)$ implies $A \in \Gamma$ or $A \in \Delta$ for any $(\Gamma : \Delta) \in W^\Xi$.*

Proof. We show only (8) and (10) here. Fix any sf-closed finite set Ξ of formulas.

$(8)(\Rightarrow)$ Fix any $(\Gamma : \Delta) \in W^\Xi$ and suppose $A \rightarrow_i B \in \Delta$. Our goal is to show that there is some $(\Pi : \Sigma) \in W^\Xi$ such that $(\Gamma : \Delta)R^\Xi(\Pi : \Sigma)$, $A \in \Pi$ and $B \in \Sigma$. Let $\Theta = \{p \mid p \in \Gamma\} \cup \{C \rightarrow_i D \mid C \rightarrow_i D \in \Gamma\}$. By the first condition of the definition of a $\varXi$-analytically saturated pair (Definition 9), $\varGamma \Rightarrow \varDelta, A{\rightarrow}_i B$ is not $\varXi$-derivable in **GL**. Thus, $\varTheta \Rightarrow A{\rightarrow}_i B$ is also not $\varXi$-derivable in **GL**. By the $\varXi$-admissibility of $(\Rightarrow {\rightarrow}_i)$, $A, \varTheta \Rightarrow B$ is not $\varXi$-derivable in **GL**. By Lemma 1, there is $(\varPi : \varSigma) \in W^\varXi$ such that $\varTheta \cup \{A\} \subseteq \varPi$, $\{B\} \subseteq \varSigma$, and $\varPi \cup \varSigma \subseteq \varXi$. It suffices to show $(\varGamma : \varDelta)R^\varXi(\varPi : \varSigma)$, but this is ensured by $\varTheta \subseteq \varPi$, the construction of $\varTheta$, and the definition of $R^\varXi$ (Definition 11).

($\Leftarrow$) Let $\varTheta$ be a finite set of propositional variables and formulas whose main connective is "${\rightarrow}_i$". Suppose $\varTheta \Rightarrow A{\rightarrow}_i B$ is not $\varXi$-derivable in **GL**. Our goal is to show that $A, \varTheta \Rightarrow B$ is not $\varXi$-derivable in **GL**. By Lemma 1, there is $(\varGamma : \varDelta) \in W^\varXi$ such that $\varTheta \subseteq \varGamma$, $\{A{\rightarrow}_i B\} \subseteq \varDelta$, and $\varGamma \cup \varDelta \subseteq \varXi$. By the assumed semantic condition, there is $(\varPi : \varSigma) \in W^\varXi$ such that $(\varGamma : \varDelta)R^\varXi(\varPi : \varSigma)$, $A \in \varPi$, and $B \in \varSigma$. By the first condition of the definition of a $\varXi$-analytically saturated pair (Definition 9), $A, \varPi \Rightarrow B, \varSigma$ is not $\varXi$-derivable in **GL**. By $\varTheta \subseteq \varGamma$, $\varGamma R^\varXi \varPi$, and the definition of $R^\varXi$ (Definition 11), $\varTheta \subseteq \varPi$. Therefore, $A, \varTheta \Rightarrow B$ is not $\varXi$-derivable in **GL**.

(10)($\Rightarrow$) Fix any $(\varGamma : \varDelta) \in W^\varXi$ and any $A \in \varXi$. Our goal is to show $A \in \varGamma$ or $A \in \varDelta$. By the first condition of the definition of a $\varXi$-analytically saturated pair (Definition 9), $\varGamma \Rightarrow \varDelta$ is not $\varXi$-derivable in **GL**. By the $\varXi$-admissibility of (Cut), either $A, \varGamma \Rightarrow \varDelta$ or $\varGamma \Rightarrow \varDelta, A$ is not $\varXi$-derivable in **GL**. By the second condition of the definition of a $\varXi$-analytically saturated pair (Definition 9), $A \in \varGamma$ or $A \in \varDelta$, as desired.

($\Leftarrow$) Suppose $\varGamma \Rightarrow \varDelta$ is not $\varXi$-derivable in **GL**. Our goal is to show that either $\varGamma \Rightarrow \varDelta, A$ or $A, \varGamma \Rightarrow \varDelta$ is not $\varXi$-derivable in **GL**. By Lemma 1, there is $(\varGamma^* : \varDelta^*) \in W^\varXi$ such that $\varGamma \subseteq \varGamma^*$, $\varDelta \subseteq \varDelta^*$, and $\varGamma^* \cup \varDelta^* \subseteq \varXi$. By the assumed semantic condition, $A \in \varDelta^*$ or $A \in \varGamma^*$. By the first condition of the definition of a $\varXi$-analytically saturated pair (Definition 9), $\varGamma^* \Rightarrow \varDelta^*, A$ or $A, \varGamma^* \Rightarrow \varDelta^*$ is not $\varXi$-derivable in **GL**. Since $\varGamma \subseteq \varGamma^*$ and $\varDelta \subseteq \varDelta^*$, either $\varGamma \Rightarrow \varDelta, A$ or $A, \varGamma \Rightarrow \varDelta$ is not $\varXi$-derivable in **GL**.

This theorem shows that the two points of improvement of Restall's analysis are overcome. Firstly, in this theorem, the equivalence between the admissibility of an inference rule in **GL** and the corresponding satisfaction relation for a formula is shown. Secondly, the admissibility of (Cut) or $(Cut)^a$ is not presupposed in this analysis, and the semantic conditions corresponding to the admissibility of (Cut) and $(Cut)^a$ are identified.

Theorem 2. *Let $\varXi$ be an sf-closed finite set of formulas and $W^\varXi_{\mathbf{C+J}}$ be the set of all $\varXi$-analytically saturated pairs in $\mathrm{G}(\mathbf{C+J})$. Then, for any $(\varGamma : \varDelta) \in W^\varXi_{\mathbf{C+J}}$ and any formula $C \in \varXi$, the following holds:*

$$C \in \varGamma \text{ implies } (\varGamma : \varDelta) \models C \text{ and } C \in \varDelta \text{ implies } (\varGamma : \varDelta) \not\models C.$$

Theorem 2 is shown by induction on the construction of a formula C, as is done in [48]. This theorem corresponds to a lemma called "partial truth lemma" (cf. [27, Lemma 11]), which is established to show cut-free semantic completeness.

Theorem 2 ensures that Restall's analysis, improved by Takano's method, is carried out successfully for $\mathbf{C} + \mathbf{J}$. This is because the formulas in the antecedent and succedent of a $\varXi$-analytically saturated pair can be regarded as true and false in the state described by the pair. Thus, as is done in Sect. 2, the notion of a Kripke model is obtained from the admissibility of inference rules in $\mathsf{G}(\mathbf{C} + \mathbf{J})$. This means that the open problem of Restall's analysis is solved positively.

5   Analysis of C + J Based on Unilateralism

This section explains how the analysis presented in Sect. 4 is connected to the bilateralism-unilateralism debate and shows that a unilateral approach is also possible for $\mathbf{C} + \mathbf{J}$. As far as the author knows, the bilateralism-unilateralism debate occurs mainly in the field of philosophy of logic and philosophy of language. Bilateralism is the position claiming that two linguistic acts are primitive when the meaning of a formula or a statement is considered, whereas unilateralism is the position claiming that only one linguistic act is primitive. The representatives of unilateralism are Frege [16] and Dummett [13,14], while bilateralism is studied in [3,19,36,41,44].[11] Since the notions of assertion and denial are used, both Restall's analysis and the analysis presented in Sect. 4 are based on bilateralism.[12] In the following, it is argued that an analysis based on unilateralism is also possible for $\mathbf{C} + \mathbf{J}$. Classical negation plays a central role in this analysis.

The most straightforward way to choose unilateralism is to interpret the derivability of a sequent $\varGamma \Rightarrow \varDelta$ only by the notion of assertion, as follows: it is incoherent to assert all the formulas in $\varGamma$ but to assert no formulas in $\varDelta$. However, as was pointed out by Restall [38, pp. 4-5], this interpretation contains a too strong requirement.[13] Generally, we do not know every consequence of the assumptions. Therefore, if we assert some formulas, there is a possibility of not asserting a consequence of the formulas. Thus, when we interpret the derivability of a sequent in terms of linguistic acts, the notion of denial seems necessary.

---

[11] It is usually said that unilateralism fits intuitionistic logic (cf. [15]) and bilateralism fits classical logic (cf. [41]). The reason why unilateralism seems to fit intuitionistic logic but does not seem to fit classical logic lies in the fact that standard proof-theoretic semantics seems possible for the former but impossible for the latter. The reason why bilateralism seems to fit classical logic lies in the fact that by introducing the notion of denial, proof-theoretic semantics for classical logic seems possible, as Rumfitt [41] did.

[12] It is noted that Steinberger [45] claims that Restall's position is crucially different from the positions of Smiley [44] and Rumfitt [41].

[13] In [38], Restall argues against the following view: if A entails B, then it ought to be the case that if you accept A, then you accept B. If we consider an interpretation of the derivability of $\varGamma \Rightarrow \varDelta$ based on this view, we can obtain the following interpretation: it ought to be the case that if you accept all the formulas in $\varGamma$, then you accept some formulas in $\varDelta$. It is noted that if this interpretation is employed, the argument described here also works.

Another way of defending unilateralism is to claim that the notion of denial is not primitive, although it is necessary. In other words, it is claimed that the notion of denial is conceptually reduced to that of assertion. The most basic strategy of doing this is to define the denial of a formula as the assertion of the negation of the formula. However, this strategy does not work for every logic, since the denial of a formula and the assertion of the negation of a formula seem different in some logics, as was already pointed out in [38, pp. 2-3].

However, this strategy of defending unilateralism works for classical logic. The reason why this strategy works is the formulation of rules for classical negation in **LK** (cf. Table 1). The rules $(\Rightarrow \neg_c)$ and $(\neg_c \Rightarrow)$ imply that the denial and the assertion of $\neg_c A$ can be replaced with the assertion and the denial of A, respectively. By these rules, we can regard the denial of a formula as the assertion of the classical negation of the formula. This fact implies that advocates of classical logic who defend unilateralism can make use of the notion of denial, since it can be reduced to that of assertion.

On the other hand, this strategy does not work for intuitionistic logic. The reason for this is that the denial of A cannot be replaced with the assertion of $\neg_i A$, since the right rule for the intuitionistic multi-succedent sequent calculus **mLJ** is restricted to the following one:

$$\frac{A, \Gamma \Rightarrow}{\Gamma \Rightarrow \neg_i A} \ .$$

Thus, the notion of denial cannot be reduced to that of assertion by using only intuitionistic negation. This implies that advocates of intuitionistic logic who defend unilateralism, such as Dummett [13,14], face a difficulty. Since they cannot use the notion of denial, they have to interpret the derivability of a sequent $\Gamma \Rightarrow \Delta$ only by the notion of assertion, but the resulting interpretation contains a too strong requirement, as noted above.[14]

As noted above, advocates of classical logic who defend unilateralism do not fall into this problem, since they can use the strategy of reducing the notion of denial to that of assertion because of the existence of "$\neg_c$." However, this strategy is possible not only in classical logic but also in $\mathbf{C} + \mathbf{J}$. This implies that advocates of classical logic can view intuitionistic logic based on unilateralism. The rest of this section briefly sketches the unilateral analysis for $\mathbf{C} + \mathbf{J}$ based on this strategy.

Proposition 1. *For any formula A and any set $\Gamma \cup \Delta$ of formulas, $\Gamma \Rightarrow \Delta, A$ is derivable in $\mathsf{G}(\mathbf{C} + \mathbf{J})$ iff $\neg_c A, \Gamma \Rightarrow \Delta$ is derivable in $\mathsf{G}(\mathbf{C} + \mathbf{J})$.*

---

[14] This problem also holds when another proof theory is considered. For example, if a natural deduction system is considered, an interpretation of the derivability of a formula from a set of assumptions using only the notion of assertion should contain a too strong requirement. Thus, advocates of intuitionistic logic who defend unilateralism should propose an interpretation of the derivability that does not contain a too strong requirement, although it is usually said that unilateralism fits intuitionistic logic and bilateralism fits classical logic, as noted in footnote 11.

The direction from the left to the right of this proposition is shown by applying ($\neg_c \Rightarrow$). The other direction is shown by induction on the construction of a derivation, as is done in [24,51].[15] Note that this proposition no longer holds if classical negation is replaced with intuitionistic negation. Based on this equivalence, we can transform $G(\mathbf{C}+\mathbf{J})$ to a one-sided calculus by transmitting succedent to antecedent.[16] For example, (Id), (Cut), and $(\rightarrow_i \Rightarrow)$ are transformed to the following rules, respectively:

$$\frac{}{A, \neg_c A \Rightarrow} \qquad \frac{\Gamma, \neg_c A \Rightarrow \quad A, \Gamma \Rightarrow}{\Gamma \Rightarrow} \qquad \frac{\Gamma, \neg_c A \Rightarrow \quad B, \Gamma \Rightarrow}{A \rightarrow_i B, \Gamma \Rightarrow} \ .$$

A finite set Γ of formulas expresses a coherent situation with respect to assertion if $\Gamma \Rightarrow$ is not derivable in this one-sided calculus. Thus, the derivability of $\Gamma \Rightarrow$ is interpreted as follows: it is incoherent to assert all the formulas in Γ. The notion of denial does not exist in this interpretation. Accordingly, inference rules in the one-sided calculus are regarded as normative constraints on assertion. In the following, this one-sided calculus is called $\mathsf{GS}(\mathbf{C}+\mathbf{J})$. In order to carry out the analysis presented in Sect. 4, the notion of a subformula should be expanded to that of an *extended subformula*.

Definition 15. *The set* $\mathsf{Esub}(A)$ *of all* extended subformulas *of a formula A is defined inductively as follows:*

- $\mathsf{Esub}(p) := \{p\}$,
- $\mathsf{Esub}(\bot) := \{\bot\}$,
- $\mathsf{Esub}(A \Box B) := \{A \Box B\} \cup \mathsf{Esub}(A) \cup \mathsf{ESub}(B)(\Box \in \{\wedge, \vee\})$,
- $\mathsf{Esub}(A \rightarrow_i B) := \{A \rightarrow_i B\} \cup \mathsf{Esub}(\neg_c A) \cup \mathsf{Esub}(B)$,
- $\mathsf{Esub}(\neg_c p) := \{\neg_c p\}$,
- $\mathsf{Esub}(\neg_c \bot) := \{\neg_c \bot\}$,
- $\mathsf{Esub}(\neg_c(A \Box B)) := \{\neg_c(A \Box B)\} \cup \mathsf{Esub}(\neg_c A) \cup \mathsf{ESub}(\neg_c B)(\Box \in \{\wedge, \vee\})$,
- $\mathsf{Esub}(\neg_c(A \rightarrow_i B)) := \{\neg_c(A \rightarrow_i B)\} \cup \mathsf{Esub}(A) \cup \mathsf{Esub}(\neg_c B)$.

Definition 16. *Let Γ be a finite set of formulas. Then, we define* $\mathsf{ESub}(\Gamma)$ *as the set of all extended subformulas of some formulas in Γ. A set Γ of formulas is* extended subformula-closed (esf-closed) *if* $\mathsf{ESub}(\Gamma) \subseteq \Gamma$ *and* $\bot \in \Gamma$.

We can define the notion of Ξ-derivability in the one-sided calculus $G(\mathbf{C}+\mathbf{J})$ as in Definition 7. Based on this notion and the notion of an extended subformula, we can define the notion of a Ξ-analytically saturated set in the one-sided calculus $\mathsf{GS}(\mathbf{C}+\mathbf{J})$, which plays the same role as the notion of a Ξ-analytically saturated pair in the bilateral analysis provided in Sect. 4.

---

[15] The direction from the right to the left of Proposition 1 is the inversion of ($\neg_c \Rightarrow$). Inversion of rules for logical connectives is shown by induction on the construction of a derivation in [24, Theorem 3.1.1] and [51, Proposition 3.5.4]. Although rules for classical negation are not dealt with in [24,51], we can apply this induction to show this direction. Note that although the height-preserving inversion is shown in [24,51], the direction from the right to the left of Proposition 1 is not height-preserving.

[16] Similar transformations are carried out in [2,29,46,51], but one-sided calculi in [2, 29,46,51] are obtained by transmitting antecedent to succedent. Thus, the directions of transformation are different.

Definition 17 (Ξ-analytically saturated set). *Let Ξ be an esf-closed finite set of formulas. A finite set Γ of formulas is Ξ-analytically saturated in the one-sided calculus* $\mathsf{GS(C + J)}$ *if it satisfies all of the following:*

1. $\Gamma \Rightarrow$ is not Ξ-derivable in $\mathsf{GS(C + J)}$.
2. For any formula $A \in \Xi$, if $A, \Gamma \Rightarrow$ is not Ξ-derivable in $\mathsf{GS(C + J)}$, $A \in \Gamma$,

By this definition, the unilateral analysis becomes available by almost the same method as presented in Sect. 4, employing the one-sided calculus $\mathsf{GS(C + J)}$.

Once $\mathbf{C + J}$ is explained, this result may not be very surprising, because in $\mathsf{G(C + J)}$, the left and right rules for classical negation are formulated as in **LK**. However, it is far from trivial that this unilateral approach is possible not only for ordinary classical logic but also for a combination of intuitionistic and classical logic, since this approach is impossible for ordinary intuitionistic logic. This result implies that advocates of classical logic can obtain the meaning of not only formulas in classical logic but also formulas in intuitionistic logic, based on unilateralism. This is because, once classical negation is accepted, the analysis of $\mathbf{C + J}$ is possible independently of the choice between bilateralism and unilateralism. On the other hand, advocates of intuitionistic logic cannot carry out the analysis for $\mathbf{C + J}$ based on unilateralism. Thus, they have to accept classical negation in some way if they intend to give a unilateral analysis of the meaning of a formula. Finally, it should be noted that it is not ensured that this unilateral analysis is possible for another combination of intuitionistic and classical logic.

Acknowledgment. This paper is based on a discussion with Katsuhiko Sano (Hokkaido University), for which I thank him. I also thank an anonymous referee for giving very helpful comments. Shunsuke Yatabe (Kyoto University) asked very interesting questions and gave very helpful comments at LENLS19, and Koji Mineshima (Keio University) informed me about [52]. Moreover, Takuro Onishi (Kyoto University) asked very interesting questions and gave very helpful comments at the 55th Annual Meeting of Philosophy of Science Society, Japan. In spite of their help, I take full responsibility for the content of this paper. This research is partially supported by Grant-in-Aid for JSPS Fellows (Grant Number JP22J20341).

References

1. Aczel, P., Rathjen, M.: Notes on constructive set theory. Institut Mittag-Leffler: The Royal Swedish Academy of Science, Report No. 40 2000/2001 (2001). https://ncatlab.org/nlab/files/AczelRathjenCST.pdf
2. Arai, T.: Mathematical Logic: Expanded Revised Edition (in Japanese). University of Tokyo Press (2021)
3. Bendall, K.: Negation as a sign of negative judgement. Notre Dame J. Formal Logic **20**(1), 68–76 (1979). https://doi.org/10.1305/ndjfl/1093882402
4. Binder, D., Piecha, T., Schroeder-Heister, P.: On the theory of deduction, part II. The definitions of classical and intuitionist negation (written in 1948 by K. R. Popper). In Binder, D., Piecha, T., Schroeder-Heister, P. (eds.) The Logical Writings of Karl Popper, pp. 181–192. Springer, Cham (2022). https://doi.org/10.1007/978-3-030-94926-6_6

5. Blackburn, P., de Rijke, M., Venema, Y.: Modal Logic. Cambridge University Press (2001)
6. Caleiro, C., Ramos, J.: Combining classical and intuitionistic implications. In: Konev, B., Wolter, F. (eds.) Frontiers of Combining Systems. FroCoS 2007, LNCS, pp. 118–132. Springer, Cham (2007). https://doi.org/10.1007/978-3-540-74621-8_8
7. van Dalen, D.: Logic and Structure, 5th edn. Springer (2013)
8. De, M.: Empirical negation. Acta Analytica: International Periodical for Philosophy in the Analytical Tradition 28(1), 49–69 (2013). https://doi.org/10.1007/s12136-011-0138-9
9. De, M., Omori, H.: More on empirical negation. In: Goré, R., Kooi, B., Kurucz, A. (eds.) Advances in Modal Logic, vol. 10, pp. 114–133. College Publications (2014)
10. De, M., Omori, H.: Classical and empirical negation in subintuitionistic logic. In: Beklemishev, L., Demri, S., Máté, A. (eds.) Advances in Modal Logic, vol. 11, pp. 217–235. College Publications (2016)
11. del Cerro, L. F., Herzig, A.: Combining classical and intuitionistic logic or: Intuitionistic implication as a conditional. In: Badder, F., Schulz, K. U. (eds.) Frontiers of Combining Systems: FroCoS 1996, pp. 93–102. Springer, Cham (1996). https://doi.org/10.1007/978-94-009-0349-4_4
12. Dowek, G.: On the definition of the classical connectives and quantifiers. In: Haeusler, E.H., Campos Sanz W.d., Lopes, B. (eds.) Why is this a Proof?, pp. 228–238. College Publications (2015)
13. Dummett, M.: Truth. In: Truth and Other Enigmas, pp. 1–24. Harvard University Press (1959)
14. Dummett, M.: What is a theory of meaning? II. In: The Seas of Language (Reprinted Version), pp. 34–93. Oxford University Press (1976)
15. Dummett, M.: The Logical Basis of Metaphysics. Harvard University Press, Reprinted edition (1991)
16. Frege, G.: Logische Untersuchungen: Die Verneinung. In Beitr age zur Philosophie des deutschen Idealismus 1, 143–157 (1918)
17. Gabbay, D. M.: An overview of fibered semantics and the combination of logics. In Badder, F., Schulz, K. U. (eds.) Frontiers of Combining Systems: FroCoS 1996. Applied Logic Series (APLS), vol. 3, pp. 1–55. Springer (1996). https://doi.org/10.1007/978-94-009-0349-4_1
18. Humberstone, L.: Interval semantics for tense logic: Some remarks. J. Philos. Log. 8, 171–196 (1979). https://doi.org/10.1007/BF00258426
19. Humberstone, L.: The revival of rejective negation. J. Philos. Log. 29, 331–381 (2000). https://doi.org/10.1023/A:1004747920321
20. Kowalski, T., Ono, H.: Analytic cut and interpolation for bi-intuitionistic logic. Rev. Symbolic Logic 10(2), 259–283 (2017). https://doi.org/10.1017/S175502031600040X
21. Liang, C., Miller, D.: Kripke semantics and proof systems for combining intuitionistic logic and classical logic. Ann. Pure Appl. Logic 164(2), 86–111 (2013). https://doi.org/10.1016/j.apal.2012.09.005
22. Lucio, P.: Structured sequent calculi for combining intuitionistic and classical first-order logic. In: Kirchner, H., Ringeissen, C. (eds.) Frontiers of Combining Systems, FroCoS 2000, pp. 88–104. Springer, Cham (2000). https://doi.org/10.1007/10720084_7
23. Maehara, S.: Eine Darstellung der intuitionistischen Logik in der klassischen. Nagoya Math. J. 7, 45–64 (1954)
24. Negri, S., von Plato, J.: Structural Proof Theory. Cambridge University Press (2001)

25. Niki, S., Omori, H.: A note on Humberstone's constant Ω. Rep. Math. Logic **56**, 75–99 (2021). https://doi.org/10.4467/20842589RM.21.006.14376
26. Niki, S., Omori, H.: Another combination of classical and intuitionistic conditionals. In: Indrzejczak, A., Zawidzki, M. (eds.) Proceeding of the 10th International Conference on Non-Classical Logics. Theory and Applications, Electronic Proceedings in Theoretical Computer Science (EPTCS), vol. 358, pp. 174–188 (2022). https://doi.org/10.4204/EPTCS.358.13
27. Ono, H.: Semantical approach to cut elimination and subformula property in modal logic. In: Yang, S.C.M., Deng, D.M., Lin, H. (eds.) Structural Analysis of Non-Classical Logics: The Proceedings of the Second Taiwan Phiosophical Logic Colloquium, part of Logic in Asia: Studia Logica Library (LIAA), pp. 1–15. Springer, Heidelberg (2016). https://doi.org/10.1007/978-3-662-48357-2_1
28. Ono, H., Sano, K.: Analytic cut and Mints' symmetric interpolation method for bi-intuitionistic tense logic. In: Fernández-Duque, D., Palmigiano, A., Pinchinat, S. (eds.) Advances in Modal Logic, vol. 14, pp. 601–623 (2022)
29. Pattinson, D., Schröder, L.: Generic modal cut elimination applied to conditional logics. Logical Methods Comput. Sci. **7**(1), 1–28 (2011). https://doi.org/10.2168/LMCS-7%281%3A4%292011
30. Peregrin, J.: Meaning as an inferential role. Erkenntnis **64**, 1–35 (2006). https://doi.org/10.1007/s10670-005-4698-1
31. Pereira, L. C., Rodriguez, R. O.: Normalization, soundness and completeness for the propositional fragment of Prawitz' ecumenical system. Revista Portuguesa de Filosofia **73**(3/4), 1153–1168 (2017). http://www.jstor.org/stable/26291332
32. Pimentel, E., Pereira, L. C., de Paiva, V.: A proof theoretical view of ecumenical systems. In: Proceedings of the 13th Workshop on Logical and Semantic Framework with Applications, pp. 109–114 (2018)
33. Pimentel, E., Pereira, L.C., de Paiva, V.: An ecumenical notion of entailment. Synthese (2019). https://doi.org/10.1007/s11229-019-02226-5
34. Prawitz, D.: Meaning approached via proofs. Synthese **148**(3), 507–524 (2006). https://doi.org/10.1007/s11229-004-6295-2
35. Prawitz, D.: Classical versus intuitionistic logic. In: Haeusler, E.H., Campos Sanz, W.d., Lopes, B. (eds.) Why is this a Proof? pp. 15–32. College Publications (2015)
36. Price, H.: Why 'Not'? Mind **99**(394), 221–238 (1990). https://doi.org/10.1093/mind/xcix.394.221
37. Quine, W.V.O.: Philosophy of Logic, 2nd edn. Harvard University Press (1986)
38. Restall, G.: Multiple conclusions. In Hájek, P., Valdés-Villanueva, L., Westerståhl, D. (eds.) Logic, Methodology and Philosophy of Science Proceedings of the Twelfth International Congress, pp. 189–205. King's College Publications (2005). Page references to the pdf version: https://consequently.org/writing/multipleconclusions
39. Restall, G.: Truth values and proof theory. Stud. Logica. **92**, 241–264 (2009). https://doi.org/10.1007/s11225-009-9197-y
40. Ripley, D.: Anything goes. Topoi **34**(1), 25–36 (2015). https://doi.org/10.1007/s11245-014-9261-8
41. Rumfitt, I.: "Yes" and "no". Mind **109**(436), 781–823 (2000). https://doi.org/10.1093/mind/109.436.781
42. Sano, K., Yamasaki, S.: Subformula property and Craig interpolation theorem of sequent calculi for tense logics. In: Olivetti, N., Verbrugge, R. (eds.) Short Papers of Advances in Modal Logic (AiML 2020), pp. 97–101 (2020). https://doi.org/10.1007/978-981-10-6355-8_12
43. Schroeder-Heister, P.: Validity concepts in proof-theoretic semantics. Synthese **148**(3), 525–571 (2006). https://doi.org/10.1007/s11229-004-6296-1

44. Smiley, T.: Rejection. Analysis **56**(1), 1–9 (1996). http://www.jstor.org/stable/3328189

45. Steinberger, F.: Why conclusions should remain single. J. Philos. Log. **40**, 333–355 (2011). https://doi.org/10.1007/s10992-010-9153-3

46. Tait, W.W.: Lectures on Proof Theory. http://home.uchicago.edu/~wwtx/Proof.pdf

47. Takano, M.: A modified subformula property for the modal logics K5 and K5D. Bull. Sect. Logic **30**(2), 115–122 (2001)

48. Takano, M.: A semantical analysis of cut-free calculi for modal logics. Rep. Math. Logic **53**, 43–65 (2018). https://doi.org/10.4467/20842589RM.18.003.8836

49. Toyooka, M., Sano, K.: Analytic multi-succedent sequent calculus for combining intuitionistic and classical propositional logic. In Ghosh, S., Ramanujam, R (eds.) ICLA 2021 Proceedings: 9th Indian Conference on Logic and its Applications, pp. 128–133 (2021). https://www.isichennai.res.in/~sujata/icla2021/proceedings.pdf

50. Toyooka, M., Sano, K.: Combining first-order classical and intuitionistic logic. In: Indrzejczak, A., Zawidzki, M. (eds.) Proceeding of the 10th International Conference on Non-Classical Logics. Theory and Applications, volume 358 of Electronic Proceedings in Theoretical Computer Science (EPTCS), pp. 25–40 (2022). https://doi.org/10.4204/EPTCS.358.3

51. Troelstra, A.S., Schwichtenberg, H.: Basic Proof Theory, 2nd edn. Cambridge University Press (2012)

52. Williamson, T.: Equivocation and existence. Proc. Aristotelian Soc. **88**, 109–127 (1988). https://doi.org/10.1093/aristotelian/88.1.109

Constraining Parse Ambiguity
with Grammatical Codes

Alastair Butler[✉]

Faculty of Humanities and Social Sciences, Hirosaki University, Bunkyo-cho 1,
Hirosaki-shi 036-8560, Japan
`ajb129@hirosaki-u.ac.jp`

Abstract. This paper describes a wide coverage "toolkit" for producing syntactic parse and semantic dependency analysis for English sentence input, with a focus on the syntactic parser component. This is pursued from an overarching application aim of empowering students who are medium to advanced learners of English to experience techniques of language analysis that stem from their word analysis. The idea is to unite the strengths of both human provided word analysis and a rule-based automatic system that creates structure from disambiguated word information. The central concern is then with the word information that should be supported and the impacts of this information on subsequent depictions of derived analysis.

Keywords: wide coverage syntactic parsing · definite clause grammar · verb codes · English language teaching · semantic dependencies

1 Introduction

This paper describes a wide coverage "toolkit" for producing syntactic parse and semantic dependency analysis for English sentence input, with a focus on the syntactic parser component of the overall toolkit. The parser creates full syntactic parse analysis following the annotation scheme of a grammatically analysed corpus, the Treebank Semantics Parsed Corpus (TSPC; Butler 2022). The primary purpose for developing the toolkit has been to empower students who are medium to advanced learners of English to experience techniques of language analysis, and so acquire skills, e.g., relevant for exploiting the online TSPC resource with its forty thousand trees of analysed data.

Originally the syntactic component of the toolkit involved post-processing results from statistical and neural based parser systems (specifically the Stanford CoreNLP system (Manning et al. 2014) as detailed in Butler (2020) and the

---

This paper benefited from the comments of three anonymous reviewers who are gratefully acknowledged, especially for encouraging contextualising the approach from a language education resource stance. This research was supported by the Japan Society for the Promotion of Science (JSPS), Research Project Number: 19K00541.

D. Bekki et al. (Eds.): LENLS 2019, LNCS 14213, pp. 120–138, 2023.
https://doi.org/10.1007/978-3-031-43977-3_8

Berkeley Neural Parser (Kitaev, Cao and Klein (2019))). This gave wide coverage and a way to manage ambiguity: rely on a "best" guess from the parsing system. However, this also gave unpredictable parsing errors, requiring students to be sensitive to system miss-analysis.

Also, available statistical and neural based parser systems produce only a bare parse: There is no function information (e.g., subject, object, adverbial), and there are no zero elements (e.g., indications of displacement or relative clause traces). Such parse information is vital for resolving semantic dependency analysis that goes beyond internal clause relations, such as control relations seen in Sect. 7 below. Attempts to add this information with post-processing were error prone in non-obvious ways, leaving a new task that essentially requires a full parse to do better.

A further issue for the original toolkit was that it was too passive for the desired goal of having students learn about analysis: There were no opportunities for students to influence the parse result with their own ideas. This was unhelpful for student morale and limited opportunities for assessment.

These considerations motivated a re-orientation of the toolkit around a logic-based grammar approach: The underlying automatic parser is now a Definite Clause Grammar (DCG; Pereira and Warren 1980) of the XSB Tabling Prolog system (Swift and Warren 2022). DCGs are a mature parsing technology with a reputation for being limited to toy grammars. While early Prolog implementations were unable to support rules with left recursion, such as "xp --> xp, [and], xp." for coordination, this paper shows that DCGs are a viable choice as tools for extensive natural language analysis, particularly for educational purposes, which is the focus of this paper.

A DCG consists of a Prolog program for parsing content given with a difference list as input (Kowalski 1979). Prolog and DCGs are discussed in introductory textbooks by Clocksin and Mellish (1981), Pereira and Shieber (1986), Covington (1994), Matthews (1998), Blackburn, Bos and Striegnitz (2006), among others.

A DCG is written as phrase structure rules but enhanced with syntactic categories (Prolog terms) that can take extra logical parameters. The Prolog terms correspond to complex feature structures found in theories like GPSG and HPSG (see e.g., Shieber 1986 for discussion of how DCGs relate to other formalisms for encoding natural language grammars). The extra parameters can be used to accumulate structure from the parse or pass on other kinds of unifiable values such as selection criteria and records of long-distance dependencies.

The XSB implementation of DCGs is particularly notable for allowing phrase structure rules to include left recursion without infinite loops arising from rule evaluation. This is achieved by remembering what was already evaluated with a technique called tabling introduced by Swift and Warren (1994). Christiansen and Dahl (2018) discuss the evolution of natural language processing as it relates to Logic Programming, with particular focus on DCGs and tabling.

The availability of this parsing engine creates new challenges: to increase grammar coverage for unconstrained English input, and more crucially to deal with proliferations of parse ambiguity.

Classroom experience suggests creation of word analysis is something students can do well. In contrast, creation of full parse structure is a major challenge. Partly this is a matter of familiarity: Students are already well drilled into identifying nouns, verbs, adjectives, and adverbs. But familiarity aside, creation of a full parse can remain a hard task that depends on a comprehensive understanding of language grammar and word interactions. There are also practical issues of dealing with a format for parse representation.

The idea pursued is to unite the strengths of human created word analysis with the rule-based automatic system that a DCG provides. This leads to analysis structure from disambiguated word information input. The rest of the paper is organised as follows. The attempted parsing aims to reach full parse structure, and Sect. 2 is a cashing out of what this entails. Section 3 begins the description of the parser with a focus on how a sentence layer is built, which is the uppermost layer of a parse. Section 4 provides motivation for rich word analysis provided by humans. Section 5 sketches the role of word class together with grammar codes in providing the assumed word analysis for verbs linked to dictionary disambiguations of word sense. Section 6 focuses on the creation of parse analysis from verb word class and grammar code information. Section 7 looks at how the gained analysis can take us beyond the parse tree to a perspective of semantic dependency. Section 8 concludes the paper.

2 Full Parse Structure

This section notes what is intended in this paper by "full parse structure". This involves creating constituent structure with the tag labels of (1), possibly with the extension labels of (2) for marking grammatical function.

(1) ADJP=adjective phrase, ADVP=adverb phrase, CONJP=conjunction phrase, CP-QUE=top layer of interrogative clause (direct or indirect), CP-THT=*that* clause, FRAG=sentence fragment, IP-ADV=adverbial clause, IP-CLF=focus complement of cleft construction, IP-INF-CAT=layer with infinitive verb introduced by catenative verb, IP-INF=infinitival clause, IP-INF2=infinitival clause allowing only subject control, IP-INF-REL=infinitival relative clause, IP-IMP=imperative clause, IP-MAT=matrix clause, IP-PPL-CAT=layer with participle verb introduced by catenative verb, IP-PPL=participial clause, IP-PPL2=participial clause allowing only subject control, IP-REL=relative clause, IP-SUB=finite clause complement of CP, ILYR=clause intermediate level, NLYR=noun phrase intermediate level, NP-GENV=genitive noun phrase, NP=noun phrase, PP=preposition phrase, PP-SCON=subordinating conjunction

(2) -CLR=closely related (a verb sense selected function), -CSBJ=extension for cleft *it* noun phrase, -DOB1=derived object, -ESBJ=subject of a clause with existential there, -FOC=tag extension marking the focus of a cleft construction, -LGS=logical subject, -NIM=(not-important) non-selected adverbial function, -NSBJ=extraposed subject, -OB1=direct object, -OB2=indirect object, -PRD2=subject predicative, -PRD=object predicative, -SBJ=subject

The assumed full parse structure also includes zero elements with index-ing (*ICH*=interpret-constituent-here) to mark the place of interpretation for unbounded dependencies, and traces for relative clauses (*T*).

It is possible for syntactic information to be even richer in content. For exam-ple, the TSPC provides a finer-grained categorisation of the -NIM and -CLR exten-sion tags. Also, the TSPC parse annotation includes co-reference information for anaphoric elements, like pronouns and definite descriptions.

3 Sentence Layers

To give an idea of how grammar rules are written, let's consider the sentence layer, which is the topmost structural layer for the parse of a full sentence. Prolog code (3) defines a phrase structure rule that will create a structure with IP-MAT (declarative matrix clause) as the topmost node.

(3)

```
sentence([IP|L]-L) -->
  clause_top_layer(basic_clause,[],IPL-IPL1),
  punc(final,IPL1-[]),
  {
    IP =.. ['IP-MAT'|IPL]
  }.
```

To succeed, (3) needs content to parse from an input list of items where all but the last item satisfies a call of clause_top_layer with basic_clause (statement) word order and no inherited displaced items ([]), and where the last list item will be an instance of final punctuation (identified with punc).

In (4), two Prolog calls are made. The first call has tphrase_set_string to establish a list of items to parse. Let's call this the **parse list**. The second call has **parse** to question whether the established parse list has content to satisfy a sentence rule with the parameter for accumulating parse structure kept hidden internally to the parse call. If parse succeeds, then all parse results are pretty printed as bracketed tree output.

(4)

```
| ?- tphrase_set_string(['PRO'('He'),'VBP;~I'(smiles),'PUNC'('.')]),
parse(sentence).

(IP-MAT (NP-SBJ (PRO He))
        (VBP;~I smiles)
        (PUNC .))

yes
```

The pretty print from (4) shows the return of a structure with IP-MAT as the topmost node, from which it follows that rule (3) completed successfully.

124   A. Butler

As can be seen from rule (3), tree structure is built layer upon layer at parse time, with difference lists accumulating already built compound terms of the same layer. The difference list for a given layer is closed by the empty list (□) and has the layer name added as the head list item to then be converted to a compound term with the univ operator, as in (5).

(5)

```
| ?- IP =.. ['IP-MAT','NP-SBJ'('PRO'('He')),'VBP;~I'(smiles),'PUNC'('.')].

IP = IP-MAT(NP-SBJ(PRO(He)),VBP;~I(smiles),PUNC(.))

yes
```

4 Motivating Word Analysis and the Human Touch

A word can only occur in contexts that are compatible for its contribution, and this will in turn constrain the context available to other words of the same sentence and in this way much potential ambiguity is eliminated. Ambiguity surfaces when word analysis is not sufficiently sensitive to its context of occurrence and/or doesn't affect the contexts for other words.

Identifying word class significantly constrains potential ambiguity. Thus, a noun can be either (i) the head word of a noun phrase or (ii) the modifier of a same level head word of a noun phrase. Identifying a word as a finite verb leads to the projection of a clause layer. With this background and the parse list of (6) (where N=noun, VBP=present tense lexical verb, and PUNC=punctuation), we might therefore expect the parse results of either (7) or (8).

(6) ['N'('Word'),'N'('word'),'VBP'('word'),'PUNC'('.')]

```
(7)  (IP-MAT (NP-SBJ (N Word)         (8)  (IP-MAT (NP-109 (N Word))
                    (N word))                     (NP-SBJ (N word))
             (VBP word)                           (VBP word)
             (PUNC .))                            (NP-OB1 *ICH*-109)
                                                  (PUNC .))
```

For (7), the first noun is a modifier of the second noun which heads a single noun phrase that is the clause subject. For (8), each noun is the head of its own noun phrase, with the first noun phrase a displaced item that is indexed linked to take object function, while the second noun phrase is the clause subject. Which parse needs to apply hinges on the selection requirements of the verb: if the verb is intransitive, then (7) is valid structure; if the verb is mono-transitive taking a noun phrase object, then (8) is valid structure.

The extra selection information of the verb can be given as a student oriented task with grammatical codes: I=intransitive verb, and Tn=mono-transitive verb with noun phrase object, so that (9) will unambiguously lead to the parse of (7), while (10) will unambiguously lead to the parse of (8).

(9) ['N'('Cheese'),'N'('pizza'),'VBP;~I'('smells'),'PUNC'('.')]

(10) ['N'('Cheese'),'N'('people'),'VBP;~Tn'('smell'),'PUNC'('.')]

5   Word Class and Grammar Codes

The use of word class information and grammatical codes to feed parse analysis leads to the need for a system of word classes and a system of grammatical codes. The systems employed are both part of the annotation scheme for the TSPC, which in turn builds on word class analysis from BNC-Consortium (2005), and grammatical codes from Hornby (1975) and Cowie (1989).

The grammar code system is a cashing out of types of verb complementation found in English sentences, which are in turn associated with word sense definitions in Cowie (1989). For example, among its sense meanings, the verb *smell* can be an intransitive verb and so lack complements (code: I) with the word sense of (11), or it can be a transitive verb with selected noun phrase object (code: Tn) with the word sense of (12).

(11) [I] have an unpleasant smell: Your breath smells.

(12) [Tn] notice (sth/sb) by using the nose: Do you smell anything unusual?

Note how it is only word sense (11) that is compatible with (9) above, and it is only word sense (12) that is compatible with (10) above.

6   Verb Words

This section covers how verb words impose consequences for parse structure. The verb rule of (13) matches verb words from the parse list with labels created from two parameters: Tag and Code. The matched word information is added to the parse tree information accumulated from L.

(13)

```
verb(Tag,Code,[TagCodeWord|L]-L) -->
  [TagCodeWord],
  {
    atom_concat(Tag,Code,TagCode),
    TagCodeWord =.. [TagCode,Word]
  }.
```

Full integration of a verb word is realised by verb_with_complement_layer of (14). This combines a tag from verb_tag of (15) below consistent with the inflection information of the Infl parameter together with a compatible code from verb_code of (16), to then:

- find a verb word with matching word class information from the parse list by calling the `verb` rule of (13)

- establish the verb's complement selection requirements through a call of `verb_complement_layer` (from Sect. 6.2 below)

(14)

```
verb_with_complement_layer(Displaced,Sbj_type,Infl,Voice,L-L0) -->
  {
    verb_tag(Infl,Tag_list),
    member(Tag,Tag_list),
    sub_atom(Tag,0,1,_,C),
    verb_code(C,Infl,Code)
  },
  verb(Tag,Code,L-L1),
  (
    verb_complement_layer(Tag,Code,Displaced,Sbj_type,Voice,L1-L0)
  ;
    verb_complement_layer(Code,Displaced,Sbj_type,Voice,L1-L0)
  ).
```

In the remainder of this section: Subsect. 6.1 distinguishes different verb classes with tags that vary to mark form and inflection information. Subsection 6.2 illustrates some of the grammatical codes for verbs based on consequences for complement selection.

6.1   Verb Classes

Adapting word class analysis of the BNC-Consortium (2005) (C5 tagset) with tag names adapted from Santorini (2016), distinctions of verb words are made on the basis of form divided further to distinguish inflection, to give:

- lexical verbs with present tense form (VBP) (e.g., *forgets, sends, lives, forget, send, live*), past tense form (VBD) (e.g., *forgot, sent, lived*), infinitive or imperative form (VB) (e.g., *forget, send, live*), present participle (*-ing*) form (VAG) (e.g., *forgetting, sending, living*), and past or passive participle (*-en*) form (VVN) (e.g., *forgotten, sent, lived*)

- DO verbs with present tense form (DOP) (i.e., *do, does, 's*), past tense form (DOD) (i.e., *did*), infinitive or imperative form (DO) (i.e., *do*), present participle (*-ing*) form (DAG) (i.e., *doing*), and past or passive participle (*-en*) form (DON) (i.e., *done*)

- HAVE verbs with present tense form (HVP) (i.e., *have, 've, has, 's*), past tense form (HVD) (i.e., *had, 'd*), infinitive or imperative form (HV) (i.e., *have*), present participle (*-ing*) form (HAG) (i.e., *having*), and past participle (*-en*) form (HVN) (i.e., *had*)

- BE verbs with present tense form (BEP) (i.e., *is, am, are, 'm, 're, 's*), past tense form (BED) (i.e., *was, were*), infinitive or imperative form (BE) (i.e., *be*), present participle (*-ing*) form (BAG) (i.e., *being*), and past participle (*-en*) form (BEN) (i.e., *been*)

This verb tag information is accessed on the basis of inflection information with verb_tag of (15).

(15)

```
verb_tag(finite,['VBP','VBD','DOP','DOD','HVP','HVD','BEP','BED']).
verb_tag(imperative,['VB','DO','HV','BE']).
verb_tag(infinitive,['VB','DO','HV','BE']).
verb_tag(ing_participle,['VAG','DAG','HAG','BAG']).
verb_tag(en_participle,['VVN','DON','HVN','BEN']).
```

The verb_tag rules of (15) are called by verb_with_complement_layer of (14) above to obtain a tag compatible with the inflection of the Infl parameter when seeking to match a parse list with a verb and its complements.

6.2   Verb Codes

This section outlines verb codes as tag label extensions. The codes allow for a distinction of verbs to reflect the selection criteria each verb has for its complements.

For main verbs, there is an adoption of the verb code system from the fourth edition of the *Oxford Advanced Learner's Dictionary* (OALD4; Cowie 1989), where the codes are associated with word sense definitions. The system is a mnemonic based reworking of the earlier system of Hornby (1975). A code from the system has:

- a capital letter to signal the number and function of clause elements required by the main verb

- zero or more lower case letters, possibly separated by the dot ('.') character, to represent information about the form of the required elements

For example, the La code marks clause structure (L) with a linking verb + a subject predicative constituent that is an adjective phrase (a)).

In addition to the Cowie (1989) main clause codes, there are codes to distinguish:

- catenative verbs (prefixed cat_)

- existential verbs (prefixed ex_)

- equative verbs (prefixed equ_)

– cleft verbs (prefixed cleft_)

The different verb forms (lexical, DO, HAVE, or BE) allow for different verb codes. verb_code of (16) determines compatible verb codes, taking a capital letter as the value for its first parameter to identify the verb form: V for lexical verbs, D for DO verbs, H for HAVE verbs, or B for BE verbs. A verb_code call will then return through the Code parameter a code picked from the corresponding list for compatible codes.

(16)

```
verb_code('H',Infl,Code) :-
  (
    member(Infl,[imperative,ing_participle,en_participle]) ->
    member(Code,[';~Tn',';~cat_Vt'])
  ;
    member(Code,[';~Tn',';~cat_Vt',';~cat_Ve'])
  ).
verb_code('B',_,Code) :-
  member(Code,[
    ';~La',';~Ln',
    ';~I',';~Ip',';~Ipr',
    ';~cat_Vt',';~cat_Vg',';~cat_Ve',
    ';~ex_V',';~ex_Vp',';~ex_Vpr',';~ex_cat_Vt',';~ex_cat_Vg',';~ex_cat_Ve',
    ';~equ_Vf',';~equ_Vw',';~equ_Vt',';~equ_Vg',
    ';~cleft_Vn'
  ]).
verb_code('D',_,Code) :-
  member(Code,[';~I',';~Tn']).
verb_code('V',_,Code) :-
  member(Code,[
    ';~La',';~Ln',
    ';~I',';~Ip',';~Ipr',
    ';~Tn',';~Tn.p',';~Tn.pr',';~Tf',';~Tw',';~Tt',';~Tnt',';~Tni',
    ';~Tg',';~Tng',
    ';~Dn.n',';~Dpr.n',';~Dn.f',';~Dn.w',';~Dn.t',
    ';~Cn.a',';~Cn.n',';~Cn.t',';~Cn.i',';~Cn.g',
    ';~cat_Vt',';~cat_Vg',';~cat_Ve'
  ]).
```

In the case of HAVE verbs, the returned code will also depend on inflection information inherited with the Infl parameter, while all the other verbs have a code picked independently of inflection.

Having determined the verb class and the relevant verb code we are able to state the complement consequences that result. This is accomplished with verb_complement_layer rules, some rules of which are illustrated in Subsects. 6.2.1–6.2.5.

6.2.1 Linking Verbs

In addition to taking a filled subject, a linking verb requires a phrase with subject predicative function (-PRD2) as its complement. This subject predicative can be either an adjective phrase (code ;~La) or a noun phrase (code ;~Ln).

For (17) with code ;~La, there is selection of a subject predicative that is an adjective phrase, and so the parse list should have content for an adjective phrase (ADJP-PRD2).

(17)

```
verb_complement_layer(';~La',[],filled_subject,active,L) -->
  adjective_phrase('-PRD2',L).
```

As an example where (17) is called from verb_with_complement_layer of (14) because the ;~La code is encountered, consider (18).

(18)

```
| ?- tphrase_set_string(['VB;~La'('stay'),'ADJ'('happy')]),
parse(verb_with_complement_layer([],filled_subject,imperative,active)).

(verb_with_complement_layer (VB;~La stay)
                            (ADJP-PRD2 (ADJ happy)))

yes
```

For (19) with code ;~Ln, there is selection of a subject predicative that is a noun phrase, and so the parse list should have content for a noun phrase (NP-PRD2).

(19)

```
verb_complement_layer(';~Ln',[],filled_subject,active,L) -->
  noun_phrase('-PRD2',L).
verb_complement_layer(';~Ln',[np(ICH)],filled_subject,active,
['NP-PRD2'(ICH)|L]-L) -->
  [].
```

Note how there are two rules of (19) for the ;~Ln code. The first rule of (19) requires a parse list with content for a noun phrase to be integrated into the parse result as the subject predicative. The second rule captures the possibility of a displaced noun phrase having its index matched by np(ICH) to be the subject predicative. For this second rule to succeed, the parse list has to be empty.

As an example where the first rule of (19) for the ;~Ln code is called, consider (20).

(20)

```
| ?- tphrase_set_string(['VB;~Ln'('become'),'D'('the'),'N'('change')]),
parse(verb_with_complement_layer([],filled_subject,imperative,active)).

(verb_with_complement_layer (VB;~Ln become)
                            (NP-PRD2 (D the)
                                     (N change)))
```

yes

As an example where the second rule of (19) for the ;~Ln code is called, consider (21).

(21)

```
| ?- tphrase_set_string(['VB;~Ln'('become')]),
parse(verb_with_complement_layer([np('*ICH*-89')],filled_subject,
infinitive,active)).

(verb_with_complement_layer (VB;~Ln become)
                            (NP-PRD2 *ICH*-89))
```

yes

Here, the Displaced parameter has list item np('*ICH*-89') to provide the subject predicative content. Such a verb_with_complement_layer call is made when calculating the parse of (22).

(22)

```
| ?- tphrase_set_string(['WPRO'('What'),'DOP'('did'),'PRO'('he'),
'VB;~Ln'('become'),'PUNC'('?')]), parse(sentence).

(CP-QUE (IP-SUB (NP-89 (WPRO What))
               (DOP did)
               (NP-SBJ (PRO he))
               (VB;~Ln become)
               (NP-PRD2 *ICH*-89))
        (PUNC ?))
```

yes

6.2.2   Intransitive Verbs

For (23) with code ;~I there are no selected complement elements, and so the parse list should be empty.

(23)

```
verb_complement_layer(';~I',[],filled_subject,active,L-L) -->
  [].
```

6.2.3 Mono-Transitive Verbs

For (24) with code ;~Tn and active voice, there is selection of a noun phrase with object function (NP-OB1) which can occur: (the first rule) as content from the parse list, or (the second rule) as an ICH link to a displaced noun phrase. For passive voice, there are no selected complement elements and so the parse list should be empty (the third rule).

(24)

```
verb_complement_layer(';~Tn',[],filled_subject,active,L) -->
  noun_phrase('-OB1',L).
verb_complement_layer(';~Tn',[np(ICH)],filled_subject,active,
['NP-OB1'(ICH)|L]-L) -->
  [].
verb_complement_layer(';~Tn',[],filled_subject,passive,L-L) -->
  [].
```

For (25) with code ;~Tnt, there is selection of a noun phrase with derived object function (NP-DOB1) and a *to*-infinitive clause with object function (IP-INF-OB1).

(25)

```
verb_complement_layer_by_code(';~Tnt',[],filled_subject,active_voice,L-L0)
  --> noun_phrase('-DOB1',basic,L-L1),
  ip_to_inf_with_filled_subject('-OB1',[],L1-L0).
```

6.2.4 Catenative Verbs

For (26) with code ;~cat_Vg, there is selection of a present participle (*-ing*) clause with catenative complement function (IP-PPL-CAT) from the parse list.

(26)

```
verb_complement_layer(';~cat_Vg',Displaced,Sbj_type,active,L) -->
  ip_ppl('-CAT',Displaced,Sbj_type,ing_participle,L).
```

For (27) with code ;~cat_Ve, there is selection of a match from the parse list for either a past participle (*-en*) clause or a passive participle (*-en*) clause. These two choices both project intermediate clause structure with catenative complement function (`IP-PPL-CAT`). The choice that applies is selected as a consequence of the verb `Tag` information: word class information for a HAVE verb triggers matching a past participle (*-en*) clause, otherwise there should be content in the parse list for a passive participle (*-en*) clause.

(27)

```
verb_complement_layer(Tag,';~cat_Ve',Displaced,Sbj_type,active,L) -->
  {
    member(Tag,['HVP','HVD','HV','HAG','HVN'])
  },
  ip_ppl('-CAT',Displaced,Sbj_type,en_participle,L).
verb_complement_layer(Tag,';~cat_Ve',Displaced,Sbj_type,active,L) -->
  {
    \+ member(Tag,['HVP','HVD','HV','HAG','HVN'])
  },
  ip_ppl_passive('-CAT',Displaced,Sbj_type,L).
```

6.2.5   Equative Verbs

For (28) with code `;~equ_Vg` to mark an equative verb, there is selection of a present participle (*-ing*) clause with subject predicative function (`IP-PPL-PRD2`) from the parse list.

(28)

```
verb_complement_layer(';~equ_Vg',[],filled_subject,active,L) -->
  ip_ppl('-PRD2',[],filled_subject,ing_participle,L).
```

7   Insights Beyond the Parse Tree

While creating parse trees that conform to the TSPC annotation scheme is already revealing of language properties, there is opportunity to go further in regard to obtaining insight from analysis: The parse trees can be fed to the Treebank Semantics evaluation system (Butler 2021). This system can process (multiple) constituency tree annotations as input and return a logic-based meaning representation as output. As a recent development, it is now especially helpful to see created meaning representations as dependency graphs to make visually apparent connections that the design of the annotation captures in combination with the Treebank Semantics calculation.

As an example, consider word analysis for the minimal pair of (29) and (30), with differences hinging on the grammatical codes assigned to *was*.

(29) ['D'('The'),'N'('job'),'BED;~equ_Vg'('was'),'VAG;~Tn'('cleaning'),
     'D'('a'),'N'('dog'),'PUNC'('.')]

(30) ['D'('The'),'N'('boy'),'BED;~cat_Vg'('was'),'VAG;~Tn'('cleaning'),
     'D'('a'),'N'('dog'),'PUNC'('.')]

Differences are slightly magnified in terms of the labels of constituents resulting
from the creation of parse trees, seen in (31) and (32), but the differences are
hardly dramatic: Labels aside, the structural bracketing is identical.

(31)   (32)
```
(IP-MAT (NP-SBJ (D The)                 (IP-MAT (NP-SBJ (D The)
               (N job))                                (N boy))
        (BED;~equ_Vg was)                       (BED;~cat_Vg was)
        (IP-PPL-PRD2 (VAG;~Tn cleaning)          (IP-PPL-CAT (VAG;~Tn cleaning)
                     (NP-OB1 (D a)                            (NP-OB1 (D a)
                             (N dog)))                                (N dog)))
        (PUNC .))                               (PUNC .))
```

Yet differences are greatly magnified with the dependency analysis of (33)
and (34).

(33)

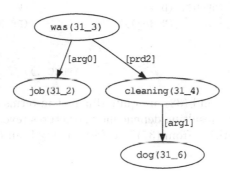

(34)

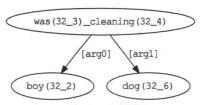

For (33), *was* as an equative verb (from code equ_Vg) is the main verb of the
matrix clause, establishing equivalence of the subject (arg0) with the subject
predicative (prd2) as the content from the present participle *cleaning* and its
object (arg1) argument *a dog*. For (34), *was* as a catenative verb (from code
cat_Vg) provides past progressive aspect for the main verb of the matrix clause
which is the present participle *cleaning* as seen from the subject (arg0) linking
to *The boy*.

134   A. Butler

Next, consider the contrast that arises between the parse lists of (35) and
(36).

(35) ['D'('The'),'N'('boy'),'HVD;~cat_Ve'('had'),'VVN;~Tn'('cleaned'),
     'D'('a'),'N'('dog'),'PUNC'('.')]

(36) ['D'('A'),'N'('dog'),'BED;~cat_Ve'('was'),'VVN;~Tn'('cleaned'),
     'P-ROLE'('by'),'D'('the'),'N'('boy'),'PUNC'('.')]

With the first rule of (27) applying from the match of HVD, parse list (35) leads
to the tree of (37), where *cleaned* is a past participle with object *a dog*. With
the second rule of (27) applied because of BED, parse list (36) leads to the tree of
(38), where *cleaned* is a passive participle marked by the same layer presence of
(NP-LGS *) (logical subject distinct from grammatical subject), and with *by the
boy* as a not-selected item (-NIM) of the parse.

(37)   (38)
(IP-MAT (NP-SBJ (D The)   (IP-MAT (NP-SBJ (D A)
            (N boy))   (N dog))
       (HVD;~cat_Ve had)   (BED;~cat_Ve was)
       (IP-PPL-CAT (VVN;~Tn cleaned) (IP-PPL-CAT (NP-LGS *)
                (NP-OB1 (D a)   (VVN;~Tn cleaned)
                        (N dog)))   (PP-NIM (P-ROLE by)
       (PUNC .))   (NP (D the)
                                                           (N boy))))
                                       (PUNC .))

While the trees of (37) and (38) are quite different in terms of the placement of
elements, a look at the resulting dependency structures reveals connections that
are alike, with (39) arising from (37) and (40) arising from (38).

(39)

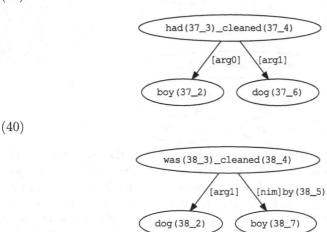

(40)

As a final example, consider the contrast between (41) and (42).

(41) ['PRO'('I'),'VBP;~Tnt'('need'),'N'('people'),'TO'('to'),
       'VB;~Tn'('understand'),'D;_nphd_'('this'),'PUNC'('.')]

(42) ['PRO'('You'),'VBP;~Tn'('need'),'N'('wisdom'),'P-CONN'('_'),
       'TO'('to'),'VB;~Tn'('understand'),'D;_nphd_'('this'),'PUNC'('.')]

With regards to word class information, the parse lists of (41) and (42) differ
in terms of the code for the first main verb: ;~Tnt for (41), and ;~Tn for (42).
Also, the parse list of (42) includes a subordinate conjunction as a postulated
word ('P-CONN'('_')) without which the parse list would fail to have a parse
result. Note that this postulated word could be made overt with the subordinate
conjunction word in_order. These differences lead to the parse results of (43) for
(41) and (44) for (42).

(43)   (44)
(IP-MAT (NP-SBJ (PRO I))   (IP-MAT (NP-SBJ (PRO You))
    (VBP;~Tnt need)   (VBP;~Tn need)
    (NP-DOB1 (N people))   (NP-OB1 (N wisdom))
    (IP-INF-OB1 (TO to)   (PP-SCON (P-CONN _)
            (VB;~Tn understand)   (IP-INF2 (TO to)
            (NP-OB1 (D;_nphd_ this)))   (VB;~Tn understand)
    (PUNC .))   (NP-OB1 (D;_nphd_
                                            this))))
                              (PUNC .))

During the creation of (43), rule (25) above is called so that the noun that follows
need is used to form a noun phrase with derived object function (NP-DOB1) and
the content for the *to*-infinitive clause that follows afterwards is used to form an
object (IP-INF-OB1). By contrast, with (42) the noun that follows *need* is used to
form a noun phrase with object function (NP-OB1) and subordinate conjunction is
needed to accommodate the *to*-infinitive clause content, which, with the selected
parse, is marked to accept only subject control (IP-INF2). Differences with the
integration of clause content are further magnified by looking at dependency
structures, with (45) derived from (43) and (46) derived from (44).

(45)

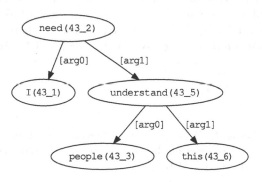

(46)

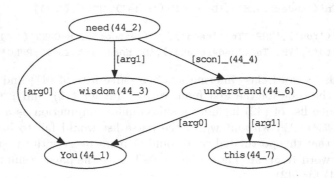

8   Conclusion

To sum up, this paper proposed an approach for wide coverage parsing of English that involves phrase structure rules for a DCG parsing engine to build up parse information from rich word information. The rich word information is made with markers of word class and grammatical codes. Grammatical codes given to verbs double as partial indicators of word sense.

The word information can be supplied by students who are learning about grammatical analysis. This takes away the mundane crunching tasks of reaching parse analysis while leaving the task of providing the essential information (word class and grammatical codes) to determine the directions a parse takes. These are the really hard decisions of parsing that computers are still not very good at making, but this is exactly the information that humans excel at giving and are representative of in-depth insight into language competency, so skills language learners need to master. Also, ambiguity is not eliminated from parse results by some "best" guess. In fact, all results are returned, only with tree structure where most spurious ambiguity is eliminated.

The use of human supplied codes gives similarity with discriminant-based treebanking (Oepen and Lonning 2006) or "bits of wisdom" (Basile et al. 2012) approaches that include human supplied constraints to guide wide coverage syntactic/semantic parsing. Arguably, the grammatical codes given to verbs considered in this paper are of special interest because they have an extra purpose too: They form information to disambiguate word sense linked to an existing dictionary resource. That is, the grammatical codes are themselves key insights into word sense that are independently of value for English language learners to know.

References

Basile, V., Bos, J., Evang, K., Venhuizen, N.J.: Developing a large semantically annotated corpus. In: Proceedings of the 8th Int. Conf. on Language Resources and Evaluation. Istanbul, Turkey (2012)

Blackburn, P., Bos, J., Striegnitz, K.: Learn Prolog Now! Texts in Computing, vol. 7. College Publications, London (2006)

Butler, A.: From discourse to logic with stanford CoreNLP and treebank semantics. In: Sakamoto, M., Okazaki, N., Mineshima, K., Satoh, K. (eds.) JSAI-isAI 2019. LNCS (LNAI), vol. 12331, pp. 182–196. Springer, Cham (2020). https://doi.org/10.1007/978-3-030-58790-1_12

Butler, Alastair. 2021. Meaning representations from treebanks. The Treebank Semantics Web Site. Available at: www.compling.jp/ajb129/ts.html

Butler, A.: The Treebank Semantics Parsed corpus (TSPC) Web Site. Hirosaki University. Available at: entrees.github.io (2022)

Christiansen, H., Dahl, V.: Natural language processing with (tabled and constraint) logic programming. In: Kifer, M., Liu, Y.A. (eds.) Declarative Logic Programming: Theory, Systems, and Applications, vol. 20. ACM Books, pp. 477–518. Association for Computing Machinery and Morgan & Claypool Publishers (2018)

Clocksin, W.F., Mellish, C.S.: Programming in Prolog. Springer, Heidelberg (1981)

Consortium, BNC. 2005. The BNC Sampler, XML version. Distributed by Oxford University Computing Services on behalf of the BNC Consortium. http://www.natcorp.ox.ac.uk

Covington, M.A.: Natural Language Processing for Prolog Programmers. Prentice-Hall, New Jersey (1994)

Cowie, A.P.: Oxford Advanced Learner's Dictionary, 4th edn. Oxford University Press, Oxford (1989)

Hornby, A.S.: Guide to Patterns and Usage in English, 2nd edn. Oxford University Press, Oxford (1975)

Kitaev, N., Cao, S., Klein, D.: Multilingual constituency parsing with self-attention and pre-training. In: Proceedings of the 57th Annual Meeting of the Association for Computational Linguistics (ACL 2019), pp. 3499–3505. Florence, Italy (2019)

Kowalski, R.: Logic for Problem Solving. Artificial Intelligence Series, vol. 7. New York and Oxford: Elsevier North Holland Inc. (1979)

Manning, C.D., Surdeanu, M., Bauer, J., Finkel, J., Bethard, S.J., McClosky, D.: The stanford CoreNLP natural language processing toolkit. In: Proceedings of the 52nd Annual Meeting of the Association for Computational Linguistics: System Demonstrations, pp. 55–60 (2014)

Matthews, C.: An Introduction to Natural Language Processing Through Prolog. Routledge, London (1998)

Oepen, S., Lønning, J.T.: Discriminant-based MRS banking. In Proceedings of the Fifth International Conference on Language Resources and Evaluation (LREC'06). Genoa, Italy: European Language Resources Association (ELRA) (2006)

Pereira, F.C.N., Shieber, S.M.: Prolog and Natural-Language Analysis. CSLI Lecture Notes, vol. 10. Stanford, California: CSLI Publications (1986)

Pereira, F.C.N., Warren, D.H.D.: Definite Clause Grammars for language analysis – a survey of the formalism and a comparison with Augmented Transition Networks. Artif. Intell. **13**(3), 231–278 (1980)

Santorini, B.: Annotation manual for the Penn Historical Corpora and the York-Helsinki Corpus of Early English Correspondence. Tech. rep., Department of Computer and Information Science, University of Pennsylvania, Philadelphia (2016). https://www.ling.upenn.edu/ppche/ppche-release-2016/annotation/

Shieber, S.M.: An Introduction to Unification-based Approaches to Grammar. CSLI Lecture Notes, vol. 4. Stanford, California: CSLI Publications (1986)

138   A. Butler

Swift, T., Warren, D.S.: An abstract machine for SLG resolution: definite programs. In: Bruynooghe, M. (ed.) Logic Programming, Proceedings of the 1994 International Symposium, pp. 633–652. Ithaca, New York, USA (1994)

Swift, T., Warren, D.S.: The XSB System, Version 5, Volume 1: Programmer's Manual. Tech. rep., Stony Brook University (2022). http://xsb.sourceforge.net/manual1/manual1.pdf

Detecting Modality and Evidentiality

Against Purely Temporal-Aspectual Analyses of the German Semi-Modal *Drohen*

Shinya Okano[1,2]([✉])

[1] Chiba University, Chiba, Japan
saare272@hotmail.com

[2] Japan Women's University, Tokyo, Japan

Abstract. This paper argues that the semi-modal use of *drohen* 'threaten' in German, which roughly means that something undesirable is going to happen, has a modal as well as an evidential component. To this end, we first provide an argument against the purely temporal-aspectual analysis proposed by Reis (2005, 2007) [27,28], and more generally, against a reductionist attempt to apply an analysis of prospective aspect (e.g. [4,5]) to *drohen*. The crucial observation for establishing modality in the semantics of *drohen* is that when used in the present tense, it is incompatible with propositions entailing the negation of its prejacent, as is the case with epistemic modals. Evidence for evidentiality in *drohen* comes from its infelicity in contexts in which the prejacent is regarded as possible, but no concrete evidence is available. To capture these observations, we provide a semantics of *drohen* that contains both modal and evidential components in a framework that is an extension of Mandelkern's (2019) [16] work, which draws on the notion of local context in the sense of Schlenker (2009) [30]. More specifically, we make local contexts time-sensitive to address different behaviors of *drohen* in the present and past tenses. The analysis is presented in a compositional setting based on Rullman & Matthewson's (2018) [29] framework for tense-aspect-modality interactions.

Keywords: Modality · Evidentiality · German semi-modals · Local contexts

I am grateful to two anonymous reviewers of the abstract, the participants in LENLS19, and one anonymous reviewer of this paper for their helpful comments and suggestions. For judgments of the constructed examples and comments on them, I am deeply indebted to Ingrid Kaufmann and Christian Klink. I am also grateful to Daniel Gutzmann, Klaus von Heusinger, Łukasz Jędrzejowski, Yoshiki Mori, Carla Umbach, and the other participants at Germanistik zwischen Köln und Tokio (GAKT) 6, where I presented a related talk on *drohen*, for their insightful comments and discussions. All errors are my own.

D. Bekki et al. (Eds.): LENLS 2019, LNCS 14213, pp. 139–156, 2023.
https://doi.org/10.1007/978-3-031-43977-3_9

1   Introduction

This paper discusses the semantics of the so-called semi-modal use of *drohen*, which can be translated as 'threaten' in English, as illustrated in (1a). This use does not describe someone's act of threatening, as in (1b), but conveys that something undesirable is going to happen. For example, (1a) roughly conveys that the weather is going to become worse and that such an event is undesirable.

(1)   a.   The semi-modal use
           Das Wetter droht   schlechter zu werden.
           the weather DROH.PRES.3SG worse   to become.INF
           'The weather threatens to become worse.'
      b.   The speech-act describing use
           Paul droht   dem   Nachbarn, den   Baum zu fällen.
           Paul DROH.PRES.3SG the.DAT neighbor the.ACC tree   to cut/down.INF
           'Paul threatens the neighbor to cut down the tree.'

                                                        [Adapted from p. 8, [28]]

As the paraphrase indicates, this use has a future orientation in the sense of [7]: The prejacent[1] eventuality of *drohen* must be temporally located after the evaluation time of the entire clause. In (1a), for example, the prejacent event, i.e., the weather's becoming worse, must take place after the evaluation time of the entire sentence, which is set to the utterance time due to the present tense of *drohen*. By contrast, when the prejacent eventuality overlaps with the utterance time, the use of *drohen* causes infelicity. This is shown by the infelicity of (2), which is intended to convey a conjecture about some present situation; in this case, the current residence of Nicole.

(2)   [I had expected that Nicole still lives in Amsterdam.]

      #Aber nun droht   sie auf einmal in Berlin zu wohnen.
      but   now DROH.PRES.3SG she suddenly   in Berlin to live.INF

      '#But now she suddenly threatens to live in Berlin.'

                                                       [Adapted from p. 239, [6]]

This basic observation has led many researchers to assume that the semantics of *drohen* involves a temporal-aspectual component (e.g. [6,12,27,28]). Among them, Reis (2005, 2007) [27,28] goes so far as to argue that *drohen* is a purely temporal-aspectual expression that should be distinguished from other modals and evidentials in German. In Reis' analysis, *drohen* has an aspectual component that refers to the initial state or to the preparatory states of the prejacent event.

---

[1] By the *prejacent* of *drohen*, we mean what is denoted by the remainder of the sentence excluding *drohen*(i.e., the infinitival complement together with *drohen*'s subject). In other words, we assume that *drohen* takes semantic scope over the rest of the sentence. A more precise compositional setting is shown in Sect. 5.

[6], partly based on [27,28], proposes further that the future component can be derived from this aspectual component. Assuming the reduction of the temporal component to the aspectual one, we will call the type of analysis that Reis proposes a *purely prospective analysis (PPA)*. One of the goals in this paper is to argue against PPAs based on a novel observation. Instead, we argue for an analysis of *drohen* that assumes a modal as well as an evidential component in its semantics.

This paper is structured as follows. First, we formulate a PPA of *drohen* more precisely that is based on recent analyses of prospective aspect as an existential quantification over pre-states of the prejacent eventuality, and present a data point that poses a problem for this formulation of PPAs (Sect. 2). In Sect. 3, we argue for a modal component in the semantics of *drohen*, based on *drohen*'s behavior in the present tense that is similar to that of epistemic modals such as *might*, i.e., its incompatibility with propositions that entail the negation of its prejacent, regardless of whether they are embedded or unembedded. We also consider data that indicate that *drohen* can be used when the likelihood of the prejacent holding true is extremely small, and conclude that *drohen* has an epistemic modal component whose modal force is that of possibility. In Sect. 4, we argue that *drohen* also has an evidential component by presenting data that show that epistemic possibility alone is not sufficient: Even if the prejacent is entertained as a possibility, the use of *drohen* is infelicitous when no concrete evidence is present. In Sect. 5, in order to capture these observations, we apply Mandelkern's (2019) [16] local context analysis of epistemic modals to the semantics of *drohen*, and formulate it in a compositional setting that is proposed by Rullman & Matthewson (2018) [29]. Section 6 discusses further issues and concludes the paper.

2   Against Purely Prospective Analyses of *Drohen*

Let us first formulate what we are against, namely, PPAs of the semi-modal *drohen*. The most prominent among such accounts is that proposed by Reis (2005, 2007) [27,28], who calls her analysis a "purely temporal-aspectual" one. However, when we examine her formulation, which is shown in (3), whether what she endorses is actually a "purely temporal-aspectual" analysis is unclear. We have two comments in this regard.

(3)   *Drohen* denotes a proposition p' that is defined by features $f_1, \ldots, f_n$ indicative of the (imminent) coming about of p.
  -   $f_1, \ldots, f_n$ correspond either to features unambiguously **indicating** the initial state of p or a [the?] phase preceding it such that, in the normal course of events, the realization of p follows.
  -   p is nonstative, an "event" proper.

[p. 18, [28], slightly adapted, emphasis added]

First, it appears to have an evidential flavor: According to Reis, the denotation of *drohen* involves features $f_1, ..., f_n$, which indicate the initial state of the prejacent p or a phase preceding it. Furthermore, Reis claims elsewhere that *drohen* "asserts that the reported situation [...] contains clear signs for p to be imminent or to unfold" (p. 18, [28]). Thus, taken at face value, the analysis appears to involve an evidential component because *sign* is a notion closely related to evidence (cf. [1]).

Second, the analysis does not involve an explicit reference to temporal conditions: It only refers to the phases of the prejacent eventuality, and not its temporal location with respect to the evaluation time. In fact, [6], partly based on Reis' work, proposes that *drohen*'s temporal component, i.e., futurity, can be derived from its aspectuality: *drohen* describes a situation that involves pre- or initial states of the prejacent event, which implies that the prejacent event has not yet been realized.

Based on these two considerations, we regard Reis' analysis either as evidential or as purely aspectual. In the former interpretation, we agree with Reis (as does [6]): *drohen*'s semantics does refer to the existence of some signs of the prejacent, as we will argue in Sect. 4. It is the second interpretation that we are against: We claim that *drohen* is not a purely aspectual marker or, more precisely, it should not be analyzed as a purely prospective marker.

The crucial data point is (4). In this example, the subordinate clause introduced by *obwohl* 'although' involves an occurrence of *drohen* that is negated by the negative frequency adverb *nie* 'never.' *Drohen*'s prejacent that 'such a thing happens,' when resolved anaphorically, corresponds to the proposition that a packet explodes. The argument can be summarized as follows: If *drohen* is a purely prospective expression, it should signal the existence of pre-states for the prejacent eventualities. The negation of the *drohen*-clause should then imply the non-existence of pre-states for the prejacent eventuality.[2] This, in turn, should lead to incompatibility with a sentence that entails the realization of that eventuality. However, the felicity of (4) contradicts this prediction: Despite the negated *drohen*, the first clause does, in fact, imply the realization of its prejacent. Hence, *drohen* is not a purely prospective expression.

(4)   Um 12:30 Uhr   ist   auf dem Marktplatz   plötzlich   ein
       at   12:30 o'clock PERF.PRES on the   market.place suddenly a
       Paket   explodiert, obwohl bis zu diesem Zeitpunkt so   etwas
       packet explode.PP though till to this   time   such something
       nie   zu passieren gedroht   hatte.
       never to happen   DROH.PP PERF.PST

---

[2] Strictly speaking, since [27, 28]'s original analysis makes reference to the initial state, as well as to the pre-states of the prejacent, it is not completely equivalent to our purely prospective reconstruction of the analysis. However, the original analysis should also predict that negated *drohen*-sentences imply the non-existence of pre-states of the prejacent due to the disjunctive reference to phases of the prejacent eventuality (the initial states *or* pre-states).

'At 12:30 a package suddenly exploded in the marketplace, although until this time such a thing had never threatened to happen.'

In order for this argument to work, we make two assumptions that we regard as being plausible. The first assumption is that the non-existence of pre-states implies the non-existence of the eventualities that follow them. To defend this claim, we need a more precise notion of "pre-states." One of the outstanding accounts that suggest such a notion is Moens & Steedman (1988) [21]. To analyze the functions of various aspectual and temporal operators in natural language, the authors assume and exploit a tripartite structure of events (Fig. 1). In their ontology, an event, which they call a *nucleus*, consists of a preparatory process, a culmination, and a consequent state. These three components are associated with each other via what the authors call the *contingent relation* between events. While we follow [5] in calling the preparatory process a *pre-state* and regarding the three components as distinct eventualities, we assume, in line with [5, 21], that the relation holding between events and their pre-states is that of contingency. Crucially, the contingent relation subsumes the causal relation.[3] Thus, if the existence of pre-states for some event is denied, the existence of any causes of that event is also denied. As long as events are conceived of as having causes, the absence of pre-states implies the absence of causes, which, in turn, implies the absence of the event in question.

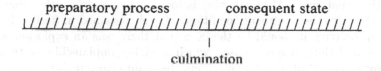

preparatory process   consequent state

culmination

Fig. 1. Moens & Steedman's (1988) tripartite event structure.

The second assumption is that prospective aspect contributes an existential quantifier over pre-states. We simply endorse this because it is shared by recent proposals dedicated to the semantics of aspectual operators such as [4, 5], and [17], of which we illustrate the former two in (5) and (6).[4] What these analyses have in common is that prejacent eventualities and their pre-states are existentially quantified. When applied to a predicate of eventualities of type $\langle l, t \rangle$ (the type for functions from eventualities to truth values), the operators amount to saying that there exist a prejacent eventuality e and a pre-state s of e such that s stands in a certain relation to e and the given time or the topic time is included in the runtime of s. Although the relation between e and s is differently conceived, in both analyses, the relation subsumes a causal one. Thus, if such prospective operators are negated, the existence of such pre-states is denied.

---

[3] The contingent relation covers not only causal links between events but also links based on agencies' planning, prediction, intention, etc. (p. 16, [21]).

[4] [17]'s analysis is based on [4].

(5) Bohnemeyer's (2014) [4] analysis of prospective aspect
$\lambda P.\exists e \exists s(s \gg e \wedge t_{topic} \subseteq \tau(s) \wedge P(e))$

[p. 949, [4], notation slightly adapted; $\gg$ denotes a causal relation.]

(6) Bowler's (2018) [5] analysis of the prospective marker -(y)AçAk in Tatar
$\lambda P.\lambda i.\exists e \exists s(s$ is a suitable pre-state for $e \wedge s \gg e \wedge i \subseteq \tau(s) \wedge P(e))$

[p. 180, [5], notation slightly adapted; $\gg$ denotes a contingent relation in the sense of [21].]

Returning to (4), the prejacent eventuality of *drohen* is a 'happening of such a thing,' which amounts to 'an explosion of a packet' when resolved anaphorically, which, in turn, gives rise to the logical form of the subordinate clause in (4), as shown in (7a). Since *drohen* is used in the pluperfect construction and it has most plausibly the past-in-the-past interpretation in this sentence, we introduce a relative past semantics for the perfect component, as in (7b), following [4] and [29], among others, and the referential past tense (7c), following [24] and many others. Given a PPA of *drohen* in (7d), its truth condition can be stated as in (7e), which entails (7f). This means that, for any time t before the given past time t_{past} (the time of the explosion in this case), any explosion event e and its pre-state s, s is not temporally included in t. However, this condition is not fulfilled under the plausible assumption that there is a pre-state for the explosion event and the assumption (7g) (shared by [5]) that the time of the pre-state s abuts[5] the event time: Although $\tau(s)$ is located before t_{past} (the time of the explosion) due to the abutment condition, $\tau(s)$ is contained in itself. Therefore, for (7e) to be true, it should be the case that there was an explosion without pre-states, and thus without causes, which is highly implausible, or that there was no explosion at all, which contradicts the main clause in (4).

(7) a. [...] so etwas nie zu passieren gedroht hatte
('such a thing had never threatened to happen') [from (4)]
$\rightsquigarrow \neg(\text{PERFECT}(\text{DROH}_{prosp}(\text{explosion-of-a-packet})))(\text{PAST})$

b. $[\![\text{PERFECT}]\!] = \lambda\phi.\lambda t.\exists t'(t' < t \wedge \phi(t'))$

c. $[\![\text{PAST}]\!] = t_{past}$

d. $[\![\text{DROH}_{prosp}]\!] = \lambda P.\lambda i.\exists e \exists s(s \gg e \wedge i \subseteq \tau(s) \wedge P(e))$

e. $\neg\exists t(t < t_{past} \wedge \exists e \exists s(s \gg e \wedge \textit{explosion-of-a-packet}(e) \wedge \tau(s) \subseteq t))$

f. $\forall t(t < t_{past} \rightarrow$
$\forall e \forall s((s \gg e \wedge \textit{explosion-of-a-packet}(e)) \rightarrow \tau(s) \not\subseteq t))$

g. $\forall e \forall s(s \gg e \rightarrow \tau(s) \asymp \tau(e))$

Given this difficulty with the negation data, we refute PPAs of *drohen*. In Sect. 5, we propose an alternative analysis that involves quantification over future times (relative to the evaluation time) but does not posit a prospective component, i.e., quantification over pre-states.

---

[5] A time t_1 abuts a time t_2 ($t_1 \asymp t_2$) iff t_1 precedes t_2 ($t_1 < t_2$) and there is no t_3 such that $t_1 < t_3 < t_2$.

3 Detecting Epistemic Modality

In this section, we argue for the existence of a modal component in the semantics of *drohen*. This is accomplished by pointing out that *drohen* in the present tense demonstrates epistemic-modal-like behavior: *drohen* is incompatible with propositions that entail the negation of its prejacent, as (8) illustrates. In this example, the prejacent of *drohen* is that the dam bursts under the floods; however, the second sentence, which states that the dam will hold, implies the negation of this, which causes infelicity.

(8)   #Der Damm droht   unter den Fluten zu brechen, aber er
       the   dam   DROH.PRES.3SG under the floods to break   but   it
       hält   stand.
       holds stand

       '#The dam threatens to burst under the floods, but it will hold.'

                                                           [p. 241, [6]]

This observation is reminiscent of the infelicity of epistemic modals in conjunction with sentences implying the negation of their prejacent. For example, sentences of the form *might p but not p*, which [16] calls *Wittgenstein sentences*, are known to be infelicitous, as illustrated in (9).

(9)   # It might be raining, but it's not raining. [p. 3, [16]]

However, this parallel is not sufficient *per se* to establish an epistemic modal component in the semantics of *drohen*, since attitudes such as *believe* or *know* also cause infelicity in a similar environment; this phenomenon is known as Moore's paradox.[6]

(10)   a. #I went to the pictures last Tuesday but I don't believe that I did.
                                              [Adapted from p. 543, [22]]
       b. #It is raining and I do not know that it is raining.
                                              [Adapted from p. 984, [31]]

One of the important findings in the recent literature (e.g. [16,31]) is that the infelicity of Wittgenstein sentences persists in embedding environments, as illustrated in (11a). Crucially, this property is not shared by attitude verbs such as *know* or *belief*: While Moore-paradoxical sentences are infelicitous in the matrix clause, they can be used felicitously in embedded environments, as (11b) shows:

(11)   a. #If it might not be raining and it is, then we should still bring an
           umbrella.

---

[6] As (10a) illustrates, Moore's own example in [22] is of the form *p, but I don't believe p*, but sentences of the form *p, but I don't know p* are often treated analogously (e.g. [13]). We follow [31] in calling both types of sentences *Moore-paradoxical*.

[p. 24, [16]]

    b. If it is not raining and I do not know it, then there is something I do not know.

[p. 987, [31]]

Furthermore, the impossibility of embedding Wittgenstein sentences extends to other environments, such as embedding under attitudes (12a, b):

(12)   a. #Suppose it might not be raining but it is.

[p. 26, [16]]

    b. #John believes that it might be raining and that it's not.

[Adapted from p. 27, [16]]

Crucially, *drohen* in the present tense also shows the same effect in embedded environments: As (13) illustrates, clauses of the form *drohen p but not p* cause infelicity even when they are embedded in conditional antecedents (13a) and under the attitude verb *glauben* 'believe' (13b, c).

(13)   a. #Wenn es bald zu regnen   droht   aber nicht bald
          if   it soon to rain.INF DROH.PRES.3SG but   not   soon
          regnen wird,   brauchst du den   Regenschirm nicht
          rain.INF FUT.3SG need   you the.ACC umbrella   not
          mitzunehmen.
          bring.to.INF
          '#If it threatens to rain soon but won't rain soon, you don't need to take the umbrella.'

    b. #Hans glaubt, dass es bald zu regnen   droht,   aber nicht
          Hans   believes that it soon to rain.INF DROH.PRES.3SG but not
          bald regnen   wird.
          soon rain.INF FUT.3SG
          '#Hans believes that it threatens to rain soon but won't rain soon.'

    c. #Hans glaubt, dass es bald zu regnen   droht,   und dass
          Hans   believes that it soon to rain.INF DROH.PRES.3SG and that
          es nicht bald regnen   wird.
          it not   soon rain.INF FUT.3SG
          '#Hans believes that it threatens to rain soon and that it won't rain soon.'

These data suggest that we should, in fact, consider *drohen* to involve an epistemic modal component like *might*.

Moreover, based on recent arguments [16,31] for capturing the infelicity of clauses of the form *might p, but not p* in semantic terms rather than purely pragmatically, we claim that *drohen*'s epistemic modal component should also be captured semantically.

More precisely, the contrast between (11a) and (11b) poses difficulties for applying pragmatic accounts of Moore-paradoxical sentences to the infelicity of *might p, but not p*. Such accounts attribute the infelicity to the inconsistency between the content of the attitudinal conjunct *I don't believe/know p* and the implication of the assertion of the non-attitudinal conjunct *p* that the speaker believes/knows that p.[7] However, since there is no such implication of assertions in the embedded environments that we observed, pragmatic accounts have difficulty explaining the infelicity of (11a) and (12) with epistemic modals, as well as of (13) with *drohen*.

Thus, our analysis of *drohen* adopts a semantic apparatus to capture the infelicity of *drohen p, but not p*, rather than explaining the infelicity in (13) in pragmatic terms (Sect. 5).

Now that we regard *drohen* as a kind of epistemic modal, the question that arises pertains to which modal force it has. (14) shows that it must be that of possibility: *drohen* can be used even when the context makes it explicit that the likelihood of the prejacent holding true is extremely small. In this case, the prejacent event is a collision of an asteroid named *Bennu* with the earth. Although the likelihood of such an event is calculated as being 0.037 percent by NASA, *drohen* can take the corresponding proposition as its prejacent.

(14) [Bennu is an asteroid which might collide with the earth in 2182. The probability of impact is calculated to be 0.037 percent.]

Bennu droht   auf die Erde zu stürzen.
Bennu DROH.PRES.3SG onto the earth to crash.INF

'Bennu threatens to crash into the earth.'[8]

In summary, all the data in this section point toward the conclusion that *drohen* has an epistemic modal component whose modal force is that of possibility.

4 Detecting Evidentiality

Given the data thus far, it might appear that *drohen* is an epistemic possibility modal with future orientation. However, a further observation supports the existence of another component in the semantics of *drohen*: Even if there is a salient agent with an epistemic state that is compatible with the prejacent being realized in the future, this alone is insufficient for the speaker to assert a *drohen*-claim. This is illustrated by the infelicity of (15), in which it is contextually established that Max entertains the possibility[9] that the prejacent eventuality, namely rainfall on a mountain, might happen but that there is no concrete evidence for this.

---

[7] See [10] for an overview and discussions of this topic.

[8] Retrieved from https://www.berliner-zeitung.de/news/studie-so-koennte-eine-atombombe-den-asteroiden-einschlag-verhindern-li.188246.

[9] Note that the context makes Max's awareness of the question of whether it will rain soon explicit. As [32] points out, the use of epistemic modals requires the relevant

(15) [Max is on the top of a mountain. Knowing that the weather in the mountains can change quickly, he entertains the possibility that it might rain soon, even though it is now completely cloudless and windless. He describes the situation as follows:]

#Es droht   bald zu regnen.
it   DROH.PRES.3SG soon to rain.INF

'#It threatens to rain soon.'

By contrast, in another context (16), differing from (15) only in that sufficient evidence for rainfall is established (i.e., dark clouds are gathering quickly above Max and the wind is increasing), the same sentence becomes felicitous. This can be explained if the semantics of *drohen* requires the existence of some concrete evidence for the prejacent.

(16) [Max is on the top of a mountain. Knowing that the weather in the mountains can change quickly, he considers the possibility that it might rain soon. In fact, dark clouds are gathering quickly above him and the wind is increasing. He describes the situation as follows:]

Es droht   bald zu regnen.
it DROH.PRES.3SG soon to rain.INF

'It threatens to rain soon.'

Note that the infelicity of (15) is unlikely to be due to a low degree of probability being assigned to the raining event.[10] As we saw in (14), the prejacent of *drohen* can be highly unlikely. The minimal difference between (15) and (16) is whether concrete evidence was available to Max. Alternatively, one could argue that (15) is infelicitous because it is evaluated from the perspective of the hearer of this sentence, as relativists about epistemic modals (e.g. [8,15]) would say: If the hearer (unlike Max) does not regard rainfall in the given context as being sufficiently likely, this could account for the infelicity. We argue that such an account is also unsuccessful, because one cannot be entirely certain about a change in weather in the future. Again, if *drohen* can tolerate a very low possibility for its prejacent, why should the hearer exclude its use? For these reasons, we take this observation to be evidence of evidentiality in the semantics of *drohen*.

Furthermore, Reis (2005, 2007) [27,28] point out that there is a restriction on the type of evidence that is compatible with the use of *drohen*. According to

---

agent's belief to be sensitive to a question for which the prejacent is an answer or a partial answer (p. 316). For example, it is inappropriate to assert "Hank thinks it might be raining in Topeka" in a context in which the question of rain in Topeka never occurs to Hank while his belief is compatible with it raining there. However, the treatment of this belief-sensitivity of epistemic modals is beyond the scope of this paper.

[10] I thank one of the reviewers for pointing out this possibility.

Reis, perceptual evidence is acceptable, while quotative evidence is not, as (17) illustrates. This suggests the evidential nature of *drohen* because, in general, it is quite normal for evidentials to have their own evidential restrictions: Languages with morphological evidential paradigms typically have at least two different evidential markings, distinguishing (at least) between direct and indirect evidence, or between quotative and non-quotative evidence [25]. Even in languages that do not have such paradigms, individual evidential expressions often specify their own evidential "flavor." For example, the evidential use of the German *sollen* is restricted to reportative evidence [18]. Similarly, the data in question can be taken as indicating that *drohen* is an evidential expression that is dedicated to inferential evidentiality.

(17)   Paul droht   wieder krank zu werden.
       Pauls DROH.PRES.3SG again   sick   to be.INF

       'Paul threatens to become sick again.'

    a. "perceptual" evidence
       ... er hustet so furchtbar. '... he coughs so terribly.'

    b. "quotative" evidence
       ... $^{??}$seine Frau hat mich schluchzend angerufen.
       '... his wife called me, totally in tears.'

[Adapted from p. 15, [28]]

In summary, this section has shown that *drohen* is sensitive to the existence of a certain type of concrete evidence; thus, it is concluded that its semantics has an evidential component.

5   Analysis

In our analysis, the modal and evidential components in the semantics of *drohen* are captured as in (18).

(18)   a. κ is a function from times to information states (sets of worlds).

    b. For any world w, time t, and tenseless propositions P (a set of world-time pairs), $[\![\text{drohen}_k]\!]^{g,\kappa}(w)(t)(P)$ is defined only if for any $w' \in \kappa(t) : g(k)(w')(t) \subseteq \kappa(t)$.
      If defined, $[\![\text{drohen}_k]\!]^{g,\kappa}(w)(t)(P) = 1$ iff

      i. [Modal Condition] there is some $w' \in g(k)(w)(t)$ such that for some $t' > t$, $P(w')(t') = 1$ and

      ii. [Evidential Condition] there is some concrete evidence at w, t for P's holding true at some $t' > t$.

With regard to modality, in order to predict the incompatibility of *drohen* in the present tense (henceforth *droh*.PRES) with propositions implying the negation of its prejacent, we adapt Mandelkern's (2019) [16] analysis of epistemic modals, which makes use of the notion of *local context* proposed in [30]. The local context is represented as a parameter κ of the evaluation index. However, unlike the original formulation, it is relativized to a time (see (18a)) to capture the fact that *drohen* can be semantically tensed. *Drohen*'s modality (18b-i) amounts to existential quantification over a set of worlds representing some salient individual's (typically, the speaker's) epistemic state at the evaluation time and world. To obtain this set, the subscript on *drohen* (k in (18b)) is mapped to a function from times to epistemic accessibility relations by an assignment function.

Crucially, *drohen*'s definedness condition requires that any epistemic state that is obtained by applying $g(k)$ to a world in the local context at the given time t ($\kappa(t)$) be a subset of this very local context at t. Together with the following truth conditions of conjunction (19a), negation (19b), and attitudes such as *glaub-(en)* '(to) believe' (19c), *droh*.PRES p *but not* p is predicted to be a contradiction, regardless of whether it is embedded or unembedded:

(19)   For any local context function κ, assignment g, times t_0, t_c, world w, tensed clause p, and clause P whose tense is abstracted over:

    a. $[\![\text{p und/aber q}]\!]^{g,t_c,t_0,\kappa}(w) = 1$
       iff $[\![\text{p}]\!]^{g,t_c,t_0,\kappa^q_{g,t_0}} = 1$ and $[\![\text{q}]\!]^{g,t_c,t_0,\kappa^p_{g,t_0}} = 1$.

    b. $[\![\text{nicht p}]\!]^{g,t_c,t_0,\kappa}(w) = 1$ iff $[\![\text{p}]\!]^{g,t_c,t_0,\kappa}(w) = 0$.

    c. $[\![\text{a glaub- P}]\!]^{g,t_c,t_0,\kappa}(w)(t) = 1$ iff for any world w' in $B_{a,w}(t)$ (the set of worlds compatible with $[\![\text{a}]\!]^{g,t_c,t_0,\kappa}$'s belief at w and t), and any 'subjective now' t_1 of $[\![\text{a}]\!]^{g,t_c,t_0,\kappa}$ at w and t: $[\![\text{P}]\!]^{g,t_c,t_1,B_{a,w}}(w')(t_1) = 1$.

(20)   For any local context function κ, assignment g, times t_0, t, world w and tensed clause ϕ:

$$\kappa^\phi_{g,t_0}(t) = \begin{cases} \kappa(t_0) \cap \{w' : [\![\phi]\!]^{g,t_c,t_0,\kappa}(w') = 1\} & \text{if } t = t_0 \\ \kappa(t) & \text{otherwise} \end{cases}$$

More specifically, the conjunction (19a) requires that each conjunct be interpreted with respect to a new information state function, defined in (20); it is almost identical to the original function (κ in (19a)), with the only difference being that it maps a designated time in the index (t_0 in (19–20), which, by default, is identified with the time of context t_c) to a set of worlds in which the other conjunct is true. Conforming to the default, let us assume that this designated time t_0 is identical to t_c, and is thus used to evaluate *droh*.PRES p *but not* p.[11] Then, the local context function for the first conjunct with *drohen* is $\kappa^{\neg p}_{g,t_0}$ and is applied to $t_c (= t_0)$. Since $\kappa^{\neg p}_{g,t_0}(t_c) = \kappa(t_0) \cap \{w' : [\![\neg p]\!]^{g,t_c,t_0,\kappa}(w') = 1\} = \kappa(t_0) \cap \{w' : [\![\text{p}]\!]^{g,t_c,t_0,\kappa}(w') = 0\}$, the resulting information state supports the negation of the second conjunct. On the other hand, for the first conjunct *droh*.PRES p to be defined, it must be the case that for any

---

[11] More precisely, t_c is used as a temporal argument of *drohen* due to its present tense. How semantic composition proceeds between *drohen* and the other elements in a sentence is illustrated below.

$w' \in \kappa_{g,t_0}^{\neg p}(t_c) : g(\mathrm{k})(w')(t_c) \subseteq \kappa_{g,t_0}^{\neg p}(t_c)$. Letting w be the evaluation world for the entire clause, it holds that either $w \in \kappa_{g,t_0}^{\neg p}(t_c)$ or $w \notin \kappa_{g,t_0}^{\neg p}(t_c)$. If $w \notin \kappa_{g,t_0}^{\neg p}(t_c)$, this amounts to $[\![\neg p]\!]^{g,t_c,t_0,\kappa}(w) \neq 1$ given $w \in \kappa(t_c)$ (veridicality of the information state), falsifying the second conjunct. If $w \in \kappa_{g,t_0}^{\neg p}(t_c)$, it follows that $g(\mathrm{k})(w)(t_c) \subseteq \kappa_{g,t_0}^{\neg p}(t_c)$ due to *drohen*'s definedness condition, which means that $g(\mathrm{k})(w)(t_c)$ contains only non-p worlds. However, this contradicts the modal part of the truth condition of *drohen p* (18b-i) which requires that $g(\mathrm{k})(w)(t_c)$ contain some p-world. Either way, one conjunct or the other is false, which results in the falsity of the entire conjunction.

For the embedded cases seen in (13), too, essentially the same explanation holds: Although a relevant local context function might be set to a different one from the matrix clause (e.g., the subject referent's belief in the case of belief predicates as in (19c)) and a relevant designated time might be shifted (e.g., the subject referent's "subjective now" for the belief predicate case),[12] in order to evaluate *droh*.PRES *p*, a modified local context function is used which, given the designated time, returns a state "informed about" the other conjunct *q*; if *q* entails $\neg p$, infelicity arises, as in the matrix cases.

While the above prediction could be made without making local contexts temporally sensitive (cf. [16]), we adopt temporalized ones to capture a further observation that *drohen* in the past tense (*droh*.PAST), in contrast to *droh*.PRES, is compatible with the negation of its prejacent, as illustrated by (21): The second conjunct implies the negation of the prejacent of *droh*.PAST in the first conjunct (i.e., 'The child did not drown.'). Crucially, in the case of the past tense, some time other than the designated time in the index serves as an argument of the modified information state function. As defined in (20), the result of applying the function to that temporal argument is exactly the same as the result of applying the original function to it; thus, the information about the other conjunct is not utilized, unlike in the present cases. Therefore, no infelicity arises.

(21)   Ein zweijähriges Kind drohte   zu ertrinken, wurde   aber
       a   two-year-old child DROH.PST.3SG to drown   PASS.PST.3SG but
       von Badegästen gerettet.
       by bathers   rescued

       'A two-year-old child threatened to drown but was rescued by bathers.'[13]

Drohen's evidentiality is reflected in the metalanguage expression 'there is some concrete evidence' in the truth condition (18b-ii), which is left vague in this study.[14] The felicity of the negated *drohen* in (4) can be captured due to

---

[12] Whether or how to shift the designated time for conditional antecedents is beyond the scope of this paper and is left for future research.

[13] Retrieved from https://www.westfalen-blatt.de/owl/kreis-herford/herford/herford-badegaste-retten-kind-2-im-freibad-vor-dem-ertrinken-2588193.

[14] Unlike [23], which also posits a primitive evidence relation in the semantics of evidentials, no explicit evidence holder is represented in the present analysis. This is in order to deal with cases in which no evidence holder can be considered to be present. In the following example, the prejacent pertains to the concentration of oxygen a few

the conjunctive semantics of the modal and the evidential components: Since negated *drohen*-sentences are true as long as the evidential part does not hold, the negated *drohen* does not entail the negation of the modal part, which, in turn, would imply the negation of the prejacent.[15]

---

million years ago, when no intellectual being that would have had some evidence of this eventuality could be assumed to have existed. In this case, we need an objective notion of evidence that is independent of the existence of evidence holders (cf. [1] for several objective notions regarding evidence).

(i)   Vor   einigen Millionen Jahren drohte   der wachsende
      before a.few   millions   years   DROH.PST.3SG the growing
      Sauerstoffgehalt   in der Atmosphäre alles Leben auf der Erde
      oxygen.concentration in the atmosphere all   life   on the earth
      auszulöschen.
      to.wipe.out.INF
      'A few million years ago, the growing concentration of oxygen in the atmosphere
      threatened to wipe out all life on Earth.' [Retrieved from https://dict.leo.org/
      forum/viewGeneraldiscussion.php?idForum=12&idThread=1215882].

[15] An anonymous reviewer raises a concern regarding whether the evidential component of *drohen* is an at-issue content, which can be the target of negation (cf. [23] for the non-at-issueness of evidential expressions in English and Cheyenne; but see also [20] and [9] for the at-issue behaviors of Japanese inferential evidentials and the German reportative *sollen*, respectively). The felicity of the following discourse shows that *drohen*'s evidential meaning can, in fact, be negated and should thus be located in the at-issue dimension:

(i)   [An economist answers the question of whether a bubble threatens to burst.]

      Die Blase   droht   nicht zu platzen. Solch eine Möglichkeit
      the bubble DROH.PRES.3SG not   to burst.INF such a   possibility
      kann   man zwar   nicht völlig   ausschließen, aber es
      can.PRES.3SG one admittedly not   completely exclude.INF   but   it
      gibt   zurzeit   kein Anzeichen dafür.
      give.PRES.3SG at.present no   sign   for.it

      'The bubble does not threaten to burst. Such a possibility cannot be ruled out
      entirely, but there is no sign of it at present.'

The last two sentences in this discourse describe a situation in which the possibility of the prejacent becoming true is admitted, although there is no evidence for the prejacent. In other words, in this context, the modal condition is satisfied while the evidential condition is not. If *drohen*'s evidential meaning were in a non-at-issue dimension, the modal condition would be the only meaning that the negation (contributed by *nicht*) could target, so that the negated *drohen*-sentence would be incompatible with the following sentence. By contrast, our analysis predicts the felicity of (i) since the non-satisfaction of the evidential condition is sufficient for the truth of the negated *drohen*-claim.

Finally, we present a compositional setting in which *drohen* composes with other elements. In this paper, we use Rullman & Matthewson's (2018) [29] framework for tense-aspect-modality interactions. According to the authors, the hierarchical structure of these grammatical elements is as follows: tense > modal > ordering aspect (e.g., perfect, progressive) > inclusion aspect (e.g., imperfective, perfective) > VP. The overall type structure is shown in (22), where e, t, s, i, and l are types for individuals, truth values, possible worlds, times, and events, respectively.

(22)

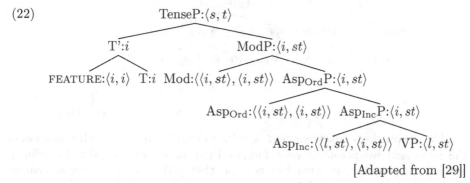

[Adapted from [29]]

In this setting, we assume that *drohen* is an amalgam of a modal and an ordering aspectual head.[16] That *drohen* involves a modal head is an assumption based on considerations of semantic composition and *drohen*'s epistemic modal meaning that was illustrated in Sect. 3.[17] On the other hand, that *drohen* incorporates an ordering aspectual component can be motivated by the non-embeddability of perfect infinitives under *drohen*, as shown in (23), based on the assumption that such infinitives themselves involve an ordering aspectual structure.[18]

(23)   *Es droht   geregnet zu haben.
        it   DROH.PRES.3SG rain.PP   to PERF
        'It threatened to have rained.'

[Adapted from p. 62, [12]]

---

[16] Such a sublexical treatment is also assumed in [29] for English modals.

[17] Simon Goldstein (p.c.) pointed out that if *drohen* did not tolerate embedding under other epistemic modals, that would provide evidence for its epistemic modal nature. Although his point seems to be correct, it doesn't imply its inverse, at least in terms of type-driven semantic composition: Since modals are of type $\langle\langle i, \langle st\rangle, \langle i, \langle st\rangle\rangle$, they return objects of type $\langle i, \langle st\rangle\rangle$ when applied to their prejacents of type $\langle i, \langle st\rangle\rangle$; thus, it is predicted that they can scope under another modal element. In fact, occasional examples in which *drohen* occurs under epistemic modals can be found in the Deutsche Referenzkorpus (p. 263, [6]). What such sentences mean and how to capture them in a formal analysis is beyond the scope of this paper.

[18] Similarly, [14] argues that the semi-modal use of *versprechen* 'promise,' which is close to the semi-modal *drohen* in meaning and syntax, occupies the Asp_prospective head, which corresponds to our Asp_{Ord}. Investigation into *drohen*'s precise syntactic position must be left for future research, however.

Below, it is shown how the sentence *Es droht zu regnen* 'It threatens to rain' is translated into its logical form (24a) and how *drohen* composes with the other elements, such as the perfective aspect (PFV) and the present tense (PRES) in the given structure (24b).

(24) a. Es droht zu regnen. 'It threatens to rain.'
      $\rightsquigarrow$ (drohen$_k$(PFV(es$_j$ zu regnen)))(PRES(t$_i$))

  b.

The denotation of each element is given in (25),[19] and the truth condition of the entire sentence is calculated as follows. First, in order for (24a) to be defined, given g, t_c, t_0 and κ, it must be the case that $g(i) = t_c$ (the presupposition of the present tense[20]) and for any $w' \in \kappa(t_c), g(k)(w')(t_c) \subseteq \kappa(t_c)$ (*drohen*'s definedness condition). If defined, it is true at w iff (a) for some $w' \in g(k)(w)(t_c)$ and some $t' > t_c$, there is a raining event in w' whose runtime is included t' and (b) there is some concrete evidence at w, t_c for a raining event that is temporally included in some $t' > t_c$.

(25) a. $[\![\text{droh}_k]\!]^{g,t_c,t_0,\kappa} = \lambda P.\lambda w.\lambda t : \forall w' \in \kappa(t)(g(k)(w')(t) \subseteq \kappa(t)).$
         $\exists w' \in g(k)(w)(t)\exists t'(t < t' \wedge P(t')(w')) \wedge$
         $evid(w, t, \lambda w'.\exists t'(P(t')(w')))$

      b. $[\![\text{es}_j]\!]^{g,t_c,t_0,\kappa} = g(j)$

      c. $[\![\text{zu regnen}]\!]^{g,t_c,t_0,\kappa} = \lambda x.\lambda e.\lambda w.rain(e)(w)$

      d. $[\![\text{PFV}]\!]^{g,t_c,t_0,\kappa} = \lambda P.\lambda i.\lambda w.\exists e(\tau(e) \subseteq i \wedge P(e)(w))$

      e. $[\![\text{PRES}(t_i)]\!]^{g,t_c,t_0,\kappa} = \begin{cases} g(i) & \text{if } g(i) = t_c \\ undefined & \text{otherwise.} \end{cases}$

6   Conclusion and Further Issues

This paper argued that the semi-modal use of *drohen* in German is not a purely prospective operator, but is a future-oriented epistemic possibility modal as well as an evidential and that the incompatibility of *drohen* in the present tense with the negation of the prejacent can be captured by extending (temporalizing) the notion of local contexts proposed in [30] and endorsed by [16]. In this section, we briefly discuss two remaining issues.

---

[19] *evid* is short for *there is some concrete evidence*.

[20] Here, we follow [29] in adopting a presuppositional treatment of tenses.

First, the present analysis does not address the malefactive meaning of *drohen* that its prejacent is undesirable for some evaluator. Although we cannot provide details about this meaning aspect due to space constraints, we suggest that it has the characteristics of CIs in [26]'s sense: the independence of truth values (i.e., the at-issue content is defined even if the malefactive meaning does not reflect the utterance situation), projection from under other at-issue operators such as negation, and non-cancellation by conditional antecedents. Given that *drohen*'s prejacent is "used" twice, once for the truth condition given in this paper and once for the malefactive meaning ('the prejacent is undesirable'), it seems desirable to treat *drohen* as what [11] calls a *functional mixed U[se]C[onditional]I[tem]*, which requires a framework such as [19]'s $\mathcal{L}_{CI}^+$ or [11]'s $\mathcal{L}_{TU}$. Capturing *drohen*'s multidimensional meaning more precisely is left for future work.

Second, our notion of local contexts is stipulative in nature in that they are made sensitive to a designated time in the index (cf. (20)). This is at odds with [30]'s original conception adopted in [16], according to which a local context is "whatever is redundant at that point in the sentence, *given everything else in the sentence*" (p. 18, [16]), and is calculated using a general algorithm. However, as [16] admits (p. 34), his framework does not predict the felicity of *might have p, but not p* and thus cannot capture the felicity of *droh*.PAST *p, but not p* in its original form. Therefore, our departure from the original conception is empirically motivated – to capture the different behaviors of *drohen* in the present and the past tenses. In this regard, some researchers argue for stipulative local contexts: [2] argues that local contexts of determiners must contain the information carried by their restrictor and that this is only possible via stipulation. While [3] proposes a continuation-based account that can calculate the local contexts of determiners without stipulations, it remains to be seen if such a non-stipulative account can be provided for our observations about *drohen*.

References

1. Achinstein, P.: The Book of Evidence. Oxford University Press, New York (2001)
2. Anvari, A., Blumberg, K.: Subclausal local contexts. J. Semant. **38**(3), 393–414 (2021)
3. Barker, C.: Composing local contexts. J. Semant. **39**(2), 385–407 (2022)
4. Bohnemeyer, J.: Aspect vs. relative tense: the case reopened. Nat. Lang. Semant. **32**(3), 917–954 (2014)
5. Bowler, M.L.: Aspect and evidentiality. Ph.D. thesis, University of California Los Angeles (2018)
6. Colomo, K.: Modalität im Verbalkomplex. Ph.D. thesis, Ruhr-Universität Bochum (2011)
7. Condoravdi, C.: Temporal interpretation of modals: modals for the present and the past. In: Beaver, D., Martinez, L.C., Clark, B., Kaufmann, S. (eds.) The Construction of Meaning, pp. 59–88. CSLI Publications, Stanford (2002)
8. Egan, A., Hawthorne, J., Weatherson, B.: Epistemic modals in context. In: Preyer, G., Peter, G. (eds.) Contextualism in Philosophy: Knowledge, Meaning, and Truth, pp. 131–169. Oxford University Press, Oxford and New York (2005)

9. Faller, M.: Evidentiality below and above speech acts (2006). https:// personalpages.manchester.ac.uk/staff/martina.t.faller/documents/Evidentiality. Above.Below.pdf
10. Green, M., Williams, J.N.: Moore's Pradox: New Essays on Belief, Rationality, and the First Person. Clarendon Press, Oxford (2007)
11. Gutzmann, D.: Use-Conditional Meaning: Studies in Multidimensional Semantics. Oxford University Press, Oxford (2015)
12. Heine, B., Miyashita, H.: Accounting for a functional category: German drohen 'to threaten'. Lang. Sci. **30**(1), 53–101 (2008)
13. Hintikka, J.: Knowledge and Belief. Cornell University Press, Ithaca (1962)
14. Jędrzejowski, L.: On the grammaticalization of temporal-aspectual heads: the case of German versprechen 'promise'. In: Truswell, R., Mathieu, É. (eds.) Micro-change and Macro-change in Diachronic Syntax, pp. 307–336. Oxford University Press, Oxford (2017)
15. MacFarlane, J.: Assessment Sensitivity. Oxford University Press, Oxford (2014)
16. Mandelkern, M.: Bounded modality. Philos. Rev. **128**(1), 1–61 (2019)
17. Matthewson, L., Todorović, N., Schwan, M.D.: Future time reference and view point aspect: evidence from Gitksan. Glossa: J. Gener. Linguist. **7**(1), 1–37 (2022)
18. Matthewson, L., Truckenbrodt, H.: Modal flavour/modal force interactions in German: soll, sollte, muss and müsste. Linguist. Berichte **255**, 3–48 (2018)
19. McCready, E.: Varieties of conventional implicatures. Semant. Pragmat. **3**, 1–57 (2010)
20. McCready, E., Ogata, N.: Evidentiality, modality and probability. Linguist. Philos. **30**(2), 147–206 (2007)
21. Moens, M., Steedman, M.: Temporal ontology and temporal reference. Comput. Linguist. **14**(2), 15–28 (1988)
22. Moore, G.E.: A reply to my critics. In: Schilpp, P.A. (ed.) The Philosophy of G. E. Moore, pp. 535–677. Open Court, La Salle (1942)
23. Murray, S.E.: The Semantics of Evidentials, Oxford Studies in Semantics and Pragmatics, vol. 9. Oxford University Press, Oxford (2017)
24. Partee, B.H.: Some structural analogies between tenses and pronouns in English. J. Philos. **70**(18), 601–609 (1973)
25. Plungian, V.A.: The place of evidentiality within the universal grammatical space. J. Pragmat. **33**(3), 349–357 (2001)
26. Potts, C.: The Logic of Conventional Implicatures. Oxford University Press, Oxford (2005)
27. Reis, M.: Zur Grammatik der sog. Halbmodale drohen/versprechen + Infinitiv. In: d'Avis, F. (ed.) Deutsche Syntax: Empirie und Theorie, pp. 125–145. Acta Universitatis Gothoburgensis, Göteborg (2005)
28. Reis, M.: Modals, so-called semi-modals, and grammaticalization in German. Interdisc. J. Germanic Linguist. Semiotic Anal. **12**, 1–57 (2007)
29. Rullmann, H., Matthewson, L.: Towards a theory of modal-temporal interaction. Language **94**(2), 281–331 (2018)
30. Schlenker, P.: Local contexts. Semant. Pragmat. **2**(3), 1–78 (2009)
31. Yalcin, S.: Epistemic modals. Mind **116**(464), 983–1026 (2007)
32. Yalcin, S.: Nonfactualism about epistemic modality. In: Egan, A., Weatherson, B. (eds.) Epistemic Modality, pp. 144–178. Oxford University Press, Oxford (2011)

Deriving Formal Semantic Representations from Dependency Structures

Philippe de Groote[✉]

LORIA, UMR 7503, Université de Lorraine, CNRS, Inria, 54000 Nancy, France
Philippe.de.Groote@loria.fr

Abstract. We outline the essentials of a formal semantic theory for dependency grammars. This theory, which derives from Montague's semantics, is fully compositional, allows for a treatment of quantification, and is robust in the sense that it supports the interpretation of partial dependency structures.

1 Introduction

Dependency grammars provide an interesting alternative to phrase structure grammars. They derive from a long linguistic tradition [9,16], and are gaining more and more interest in the computational linguistic international community, mainly due to the Universal Dependencies initiative [12].

One of their advantages is that dependency parsing appears to be more robust than constituency parsing. Indeed, while parsing an agrammatical sentence with a phrase structure grammar usually leads to a failure, parsing it with a dependency grammar can result in an incomplete dependency structure that nevertheless carries some semantic information.

Dependency grammars, however, do not seem suitable for a formal semantic treatment, in the tradition of Montague [11]. Formal semantics [5,6,14,17], being compositional, relies heavily on the notion of constituent, a notion that does not appear explicitly within dependency structures. A possible remedy to this situation is to normalize the dependency structures in order to recover a (possibly implicit) notion of constituent. There are indeed procedures that can be used to this end[1] (see [7,18], for instance). This approach, however, is not robust in the sense that it does not allow for the interpretation of partial dependency structures. Moreover it does not shed any light on the fundamental question of what should be a proper semantics of dependency structures (see [4] for a discussion and an interesting proposal).

The goal of this paper is to remedy this problem by laying the grounds for a new formal theory of dependency semantics, in the spirit of Montague. We expect the resulting theory to satisfy the following requirements:

---

[1] This migth seem a little bit ironic for several dependency parsers are derived from constituency parsers [8].

D. Bekki et al. (Eds.): LENLS 2019, LNCS 14213, pp. 157–172, 2023.
https://doi.org/10.1007/978-3-031-43977-3_10

1. It should be robust in the sense that it should allow partial or incomplete dependency structures to be interpreted.
2. It should be fully compositional.
3. It should allow for a treatment of quantification and be amenable (in principle) to advanced linguistics constructs.
4. It should take the notion of dependency seriously and not rely on any explicit or implicit notion of constituent.

This is not the first attempt at providing dependency structures with a formal semantics. Among the several proposals existing in the literature, the one by Reddy et al. [15] is the closest in spirit to our work. The solution they propose, however, remains partial. In particular, it does not meet requirement 3 nor does it fully meet requirement 4.

The paper is organized as follows. In the next section, we provide a brief review of Montague semantics with the goal of discussing the problems to be solved when trying to adapt Montague approach to dependency grammars. In Sect. 3, we address the issue of encoding a dependency structure as a λ term. Such an encoding is indeed mandatory in order to define a proper syntactic-semantic interface for dependency grammars. In Sect. 4, we state a coherence principle according to which the semantics of a dependency structure should be independent of the evaluation strategy. This makes us adopt a neo-Davidsonian event semantics. In Sect. 5, we explore the consequences of the coherence principle by addressing the question of the semantic treatment of noun phrases. In Sect. 6, the principle of coherence leads us to revisit the semantics of subject and object dependencies. Section 7 illustrates the robustness of our proposal with a few examples. Section 8 adresses the problem of scope ambiguities and shows how this phenomenon can be handled as an exception to the coherence principle. Finally, we conclude in Sect. 9.

2   Montague Semantics

As we intend to lay possible foundations for a Montague-like compositional semantics for dependency structures, let us brievly review some features of Montague grammar. This will allow us to stress the apparent incompatibilities between a classical Montagovian approach and dependency parsing, incompatibilities that we will have to circumvent.

Let us explain the basic concepts of Montague semantics by means of an example. Consider the following fragment of a possible phrase structure grammar:

$$S \rightarrow NP\ VP$$
$$VP \rightarrow TV\ NP$$
$$NP \rightarrow DET\ N$$
$$N \rightarrow ADJ\ N$$
$$TV \rightarrow praises$$
$$NP \rightarrow Michael$$
$$N \rightarrow man$$
$$ADJ \rightarrow wise$$
$$DET \rightarrow a$$

This grammar allows the sentence:

(1)   *Michael praises a wise man*

to be parsed as follows.

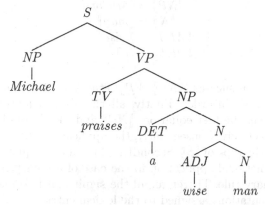

One may take advantage of this parse tree in order to derive the truth-conditional meaning of Sentence (1). To this end, we need to provide the above grammar with a Montagovian semantics.

In a Montague grammar, the semantics of syntactic constituents are expressed as terms of higher-order (intensional) logic. The first step in doing so is to associate to each syntactic category a semantic category expressed as a type of Church's simple theory of types [3]. Let us write s for the semantic type corresponding to the syntactic category S, and similarly for the other categories. Following Montague [10], one considers two basic types, e (the type of *entities*) and t (the type of *truth values*), and one posits:

$$
\begin{aligned}
\text{s} &= \mathbf{t} \\
\text{VP} &= \mathbf{e} \rightarrow \mathbf{t} \\
\text{N} &= \mathbf{e} \rightarrow \mathbf{t} \\
\text{NP} &= \text{VP} \rightarrow \text{s} = (\mathbf{e} \rightarrow \mathbf{t}) \rightarrow \mathbf{t} \\
\text{TV} &= \text{NP} \rightarrow \text{VP} = ((\mathbf{e} \rightarrow \mathbf{t}) \rightarrow \mathbf{t}) \rightarrow \mathbf{e} \rightarrow \mathbf{t} \\
\text{ADJ} &= \text{N} \rightarrow \text{N} = (\mathbf{e} \rightarrow \mathbf{t}) \rightarrow \mathbf{e} \rightarrow \mathbf{t} \\
\text{DET} &= \text{N} \rightarrow \text{NP} = (\mathbf{e} \rightarrow \mathbf{t}) \rightarrow (\mathbf{e} \rightarrow \mathbf{t}) \rightarrow \mathbf{t}
\end{aligned}
$$

The next step is to associate to each production rule of the grammar a seman-tic equation expressed in the language of higher-order logic, i.e., the language of the simply typed λ-calculus. These equations specify how to compute the seman-tics of the constituents related to lefthand sides of the production rules from the semantics of the constituents related to the non-terminal symbols occurring in the righthand sides. Writing $[\![S]\!]$ for the semantics of the constituent related to symbol S (and similarly for the other symbols), the semantic equations associ-ated to the production rules of our toy grammar are as follows:

$$[\![S]\!] = ([\![NP]\!]\,[\![VP]\!])$$
$$[\![VP]\!] = ([\![TV]\!]\,[\![NP]\!])$$
$$[\![NP]\!] = ([\![DET]\!]\,[\![N]\!])$$
$$[\![N]\!] = ([\![ADJ]\!]\,[\![N]\!])$$
$$[\![TV]\!] = [\![praises]\!]$$
$$[\![NP]\!] = [\![Michael]\!]$$
$$[\![N]\!] = [\![man]\!]$$
$$[\![ADJ]\!] = [\![wise]\!]$$
$$[\![DET]\!] = [\![a]\!]$$

where an expression such as $([\![NP]\!]\,[\![VP]\!])$ stands for functional application.

Two remarks are in order. Firstly, all the above equations are well-typed. Take, for instance, the first equation. $[\![NP]\!]$ and $[\![VP]\!]$ are of type $(e \to t) \to t$ and $e \to t$, respectively. Consequently, the application $([\![NP]\!]\,[\![VP]\!])$ is of type t, which is indeed the type of $[\![S]\!]$. Secondly, all the above equations are very simple and uniform: functional application in the case of a binary rule, and identity in the case of a unary rule. Therefore, all the significant information resides in the semantic representations assigned to the lexical entries.

Let us write MICHAEL for $[\![Michael]\!]$, and similarly for the other lexical items. The semantic λ-terms assigned to the different lexical entries are as follows:

$$\text{PRAISES} = \lambda px.\, p\,(\lambda y.\, \textbf{praise}\, x\, y) : ((e \to t) \to t) \to e \to t$$
$$\text{MICHAEL} = \lambda p.\, p\,\textbf{m} \qquad\qquad\quad : (e \to t) \to t$$
$$\text{MAN} = \lambda x.\, \textbf{man}\, x \qquad\qquad\quad\;\; : e \to t$$
$$\text{WISE} = \lambda px.\, (p\,x) \wedge (\textbf{wise}\, x) \;\; : (e \to t) \to e \to t$$
$$\text{A} = \lambda pq.\, \exists x.\, (p\,x) \wedge (q\,x) \;\; : (e \to t) \to (e \to t) \to t$$

where **praise**, **m**, **man**, and **wise** are functional or relational symbols of the following types:

$$\textbf{praise} : e \to e \to t$$
$$\textbf{m} : e$$
$$\textbf{man} : e \to t$$
$$\textbf{wise} : e \to t$$

The reader may then check that the Montague grammar we have sketched allows Sentence (1) to be assigned the following semantic λ-term:

(2) $(\text{MICHAEL}\,(\text{PRAISES}\,(\text{A}\,(\text{WISE MAN}))))$

and that this λ-term β-reduces to the following first-order formula:

$$(\text{MICHAEL}\,(\text{PRAISES}\,(\text{A}\,(\text{WISE MAN})))) \twoheadrightarrow_\beta (\exists x.\, (\textbf{man}\, x) \wedge (\textbf{wise}\, x) \wedge ((\textbf{praise}\,\textbf{m})\, x))$$

Now, what are the difficulties one faces when trying to adapt the Montagovian approach to the case of dependency structures? As we mentioned in the introduction, the compositional aspects of Montague semantics rely on the notion of constituent, and a λ-term such as (2) reflects indeed the constituency structure of

Sentence (1). By contrast, dependency structures are not based on constituents but on head-subordinate relations. For instance, dependency parsing Sentence (1) yields the following structure[2]:

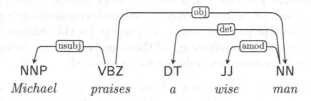

In this structure, *man* is the head of the noun phrase, *a wise man*, while both the determiner, *a*, and the adjective, *wise*, are considered as subordinates of that head.

Interestingly enough, lambda-terms provide a relation similar to the head-subordinate relation. This relation is the functor-argument relation. Consider a functional application such as $f\,a_1\,a_2\,\ldots\,a_n$, and define the operator f to be the head, and the operands a_1, a_2, ..., a_n to be the subordinates. Applying this idea to λ-term (2) leads to the following dependency-like structure:

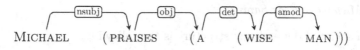

This structure immediately highlights the mismatch that exists between syntactic heads and what we may call *semantic heads*. Indeed, from a semantic point of view, the head of the noun phrase, *a wise man*, is the determiner *a*. Similarly, the semantic head of the nominal group, *wise man* is the adnominal modifier *wise*. This mismatch is quite known and its reasons and consequences have been adressed in the literature (see [4] for an interesting related discussion). Nevertheless, the structural similarity that exists between the head-subordinate relation, on the one hand, and the functor-argument relation, on the other hand, remains a source of inspiration when trying to lay the foundations of a formal semantic theory of dependency structures.

It is time to take stock and draw a few conclusions from the above discussion:

1. In a Montague grammar all the relevant semantic information resides in the so-called semantic recipes attached to the lexical items. The constituency structure is just needed in order to know how to compose these lexical semantic recipes. Consequently, the task we face is to devise a way of composing the semantics of lexical items using a dependency structure.
2. The structural information which is needed to compose the semantics of the lexical items occurring in a sentence may be encoded in a λ-term akin to Term (2). This is the keystone of a modern view of the syntax-semantics

---

[2] All the dependency structures occurring in this paper have been obtained using the online Stanford parser: https://corenlp.run/. In the resulting structures, labels such as NNP, VBZ or DT are not syntactic categories but part-of-speech tags.

interface [1]. In order to follow a similar approach, we therefore need a way of representing a dependency structure as a λ-term.

3. There is a mismatch between the notion of syntactic head on which dependency grammars are based and the notion of semantic head derived from Montague semantics. Since we expect a semantic composition based on dependency structures to be head-driven, we need to fix this mismatch. A possible way to do this is to take advantage of the operation of *type raising* [13], which allows the functor-argument relation to be reversed.

The question raised by point 1 is a reformulation and refinement of the central problem that we address in this paper. Answering the question related to point 2, the question of encoding a dependency structure by means of a λ-term, is the aim of the next section. Finally, question 3, that of repairing the mismatch between syntactic and semantic heads, is addressed in Sects. 4, 5 and 6.

3   Representing Dependency Structures as Functional Terms

Consider the following simple sentence:

(3)   *Michael praises Samuel*

Its associated dependency structure is the following:

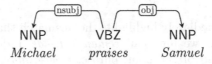

Encoding this structure using the functor-argument relation would yield a λ-term akin to the following one:

(4)   PRAISES MICHAEL SAMUEL

This possible solution, however, is not satisfactory because we have lost the grammatical functions of the subordinates. We may of course state the convention that the first argument is the *subject* and the second one the *object* but such a convention would be arbitrary or possibly based on an implicit notion of constituent. Another, even more serious problem is that the number of possible subordinates of a given head is not fixed. For instance, consider the following variant of Sentence (3):

(5)   *Michael warmly praises Samuel*

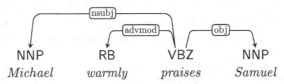

It would give rise to the following λ-term:

(6)   PRAISES MICHAEL SAMUEL WARMLY

Now, there is no simple way of assigning a type to PRAISES so that both terms (4) and (6) are well-typed.

We therefore develop an alternative solution that takes the dependency relations seriously and assign them semantic roles. This solution, which is similar to the one adopted by [15], consists in representing dependency relations as binary functions that take the head and the subordinate as arguments. Accordingly, the dependency structure associated to Sentence (3) is encoded by the following term:

(7)   nsubj (obj PRAISES SAMUEL) MICHAEL

where obj and nsubj should be assigned appropriate types.

To conclude this section, let us work out a possible interpretation of obj and nsubj in such a way that term (7) allows one to assign an appropriate semantics to Sentence (3). We consider that the proper names receive their standard Montagovian interpretation:

$$\text{MICHAEL} = \lambda p.\, p\, \mathbf{m} : (\mathbf{e} \to \mathbf{t}) \to \mathbf{t}$$
$$\text{SAMUEL} = \lambda p.\, p\, \mathbf{s}\ : (\mathbf{e} \to \mathbf{t}) \to \mathbf{t}$$

As for the transitive verb, we simply interpret it as a binary relation:

$$\text{PRAISES} = \lambda xy.\, \mathbf{praise}\, x\, y : \mathbf{e} \to \mathbf{e} \to \mathbf{t}$$

We may then provide the dependencies with the following semantic interpretations:

$$\text{obj} = \lambda vox.\, o\, (\lambda y.\, v\, x\, y) : (\mathbf{e} \to \mathbf{e} \to \mathbf{t}) \to ((\mathbf{e} \to \mathbf{t}) \to \mathbf{t}) \to \mathbf{e} \to \mathbf{t}$$
$$\text{nsubj} = \lambda vs.\, s\, v \qquad\quad : (\mathbf{e} \to \mathbf{t}) \to ((\mathbf{e} \to \mathbf{t}) \to \mathbf{t}) \to \mathbf{t}$$

Using the above interpretations, the reader can check that:

$$\text{obj PRAISES SAMUEL} \twoheadrightarrow_\beta \lambda x.\, \mathbf{praise}\, x\, \mathbf{s}$$

and

$$\text{nsubj (obj PRAISES SAMUEL) MICHAEL} \twoheadrightarrow_\beta \mathbf{praise}\, \mathbf{m}\, \mathbf{s}$$

So far, so good. The fact that we were able to work out apparently appropriate interpretations of nsubj and obj demonstrates the feasibility of the approach. The proposed solution, however, is too simple and not yet satisfactory. This will be explained in the next section.

4   The Coherence Principle

Trying to built on the ideas we have discussed in the previous section, we soon run into an obstacle. There is indeed no canonical way of representing a dependency structure as a term. Consider, again Sentence (3) (repeated here as (8)) together with its dependency structure:

(8)   *Michael praises Samuel*

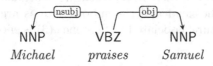

There is in fact two ways of encoding the above dependency structure as a term:

(9)   a.   nsubj (obj PRAISES SAMUEL) MICHAEL
       b.   obj (nsubj PRAISES MICHAEL) SAMUEL

One could try to circumvent this difficulty by preferring one of these representations to the other. But again, such a choice would be arbitrary. Moreover, the resulting solution would not be robust in the sense that it would not allow for the interpretation of partial dependency structures. Consequently, we require the coherence condition that both terms (9-a) and (9-b) must yield the same semantic interpretation.

One way of satisfying this coherence condition (at the level of the sentences) is to adopt a neo-Davidsonian semantics. This is the solution adopted by [15], where sentences are interpreted as sets of events, i.e., terms of type $(\mathbf{v} \to \mathbf{t})$, with $\mathbf{v}$ being the type of events. Let us review this solution. Verbs are now interpreted as sets of events:

$$\text{PRAISES} = \lambda e.\, \mathbf{praise}\, e : \mathbf{v} \to \mathbf{t}$$

where **praise** is a relational symbol of type $\mathbf{v} \to \mathbf{t}$. In words, the semantic interpretation of *praises* is the set of "praising events". We then keep the standard interpretation of the proper names:

$$\text{MICHAEL} = \lambda p.\, p\, \mathbf{m} : (\mathbf{e} \to \mathbf{t}) \to \mathbf{t}$$
$$\text{SAMUEL} = \lambda p.\, p\, \mathbf{s} \; : (\mathbf{e} \to \mathbf{t}) \to \mathbf{t}$$

and interpret the subject and object dependencies as follows:

$$\text{obj} = \lambda vne.\, (v\, e) \wedge (n\, (\lambda x.\, \mathbf{th}\, x\, e)) : (\mathbf{v} \to \mathbf{t}) \to ((\mathbf{e} \to \mathbf{t}) \to \mathbf{t}) \to \mathbf{v} \to \mathbf{t}$$
$$\text{nsubj} = \lambda vne.\, (v\, e) \wedge (n\, (\lambda x.\, \mathbf{ag}\, x\, e)) : (\mathbf{v} \to \mathbf{t}) \to ((\mathbf{e} \to \mathbf{t}) \to \mathbf{t}) \to \mathbf{v} \to \mathbf{t}$$

where **ag** and **th** are relational symbols of type $\mathbf{e} \to \mathbf{v} \to \mathbf{t}$ wich stands for the thematic relations *agent* and *theme*, respectively.

The above solution certainly meets the coherence requirement. In particular, it is completely symmetric with respect to the nsubj and obj dependencies. Both are interpreted by similar λ-terms. The only difference is the thematic relation they introduce: **ag** in the case of nsubj, and **th** in the case of obj.

Interpreting verbs as sets of events, however, is known to badly interact with quantification and scope[3]. As a result, the above solution is not amenable to a proper treatment of quantification. A way out of this difficulty has been proposed by Champolion [2]. It consists in interpreting a sentence as a family of sets of events, i.e., as a term of type $(\mathbf{v} \rightarrow \mathbf{t}) \rightarrow \mathbf{t}$. In this setting, a verb such as *praises* is interpreted as the family of all the sets of events that contain at least one "praising event".

The adaptation of our current solution to Champolion's proposal consists essentially in applying type shifting operations where needed, and leads to the following semantic interpretation:

$$\text{GS} = (\mathbf{v} \rightarrow \mathbf{t}) \rightarrow \mathbf{t}$$

$$\text{MICHAEL} = \lambda p. \, p \, \mathbf{m} : \text{NP}$$
$$\text{SAMUEL} = \lambda p. \, p \, \mathbf{s} : \text{NP}$$
$$\text{PRAISES} = \lambda p. \, \exists e. \, (\mathbf{praise} \, e) \wedge (p \, e) : \text{GS}$$

$$\text{nsubj} = \lambda v n. \, \lambda p. \, n \, (\lambda x. \, v \, (\lambda e. \, (\mathbf{ag} \, e \, x) \wedge (p \, e))) : \text{GS} \rightarrow \text{NP} \rightarrow \text{GS}$$
$$\text{obj} = \lambda v n. \, \lambda p. \, n \, (\lambda x. \, v \, (\lambda e. \, (\mathbf{th} \, e \, x) \wedge (p \, e))) : \text{GS} \rightarrow \text{NP} \rightarrow \text{GS}$$

We now invite the reader to check that:

nsubj (obj PRAISES SAMUEL) MICHAEL $\twoheadrightarrow_\beta$

$$\lambda f. \, \exists e. \, (\mathbf{praise} \, e) \wedge (\mathbf{th} \, e \, \mathbf{s}) \wedge (\mathbf{ag} \, e \, \mathbf{m}) \wedge (f \, e)$$

and that:

obj (nsubj PRAISES MICHAEL) SAMUEL $\twoheadrightarrow_\beta$

$$\lambda f. \, \exists e. \, (\mathbf{praise} \, e) \wedge (\mathbf{ag} \, e \, \mathbf{m}) \wedge (\mathbf{th} \, e \, \mathbf{s}) \wedge (f \, e)$$

These two forms are clearly logically equivalent.

5   Interpreting the Noun Phrases

As we have seen in Sect. 1, Montagovian semantics assigns to the (common) nouns the semantic type $\text{N} = \mathbf{e} \rightarrow \mathbf{t}$. It assigns to the adnominal modifiers, such as the adjectives, the category $\text{ADJ} = \text{N} \rightarrow \text{N}$, and to the determiners, the category $\text{DET} = \text{N} \rightarrow \text{NP}$. This approach is not directly transferable to the case of dependency structures. Consider indeed the following noun phrase and its associated dependency structure:

---

[3] The problem is that when applying an existential closure operator to a set of events, one cannot guarantee that it will take the narrowest scope. This results in paradoxical interpretations. For instance, *John does not walk* would be interpreted as *there is a walking event of which John is not the agent* instead of *there is no walking event of which John is the agent*.

(10)   *a wise man*

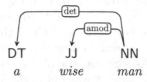

DT   JJ   NN
a   *wise*   *man*

As a consequence of the coherence condition, all the following expressions must be assigned the same semantic type:

(11)   a.   MAN
         b.   amod MAN WISE
         c.   det MAN A
         d.   det (amod MAN WISE) A
         e.   amod (det MAN A) WISE

More generally, consider a head with two subordinates:

$$\text{dep}_1 \qquad \text{dep}_2$$

a   b   c

Let dep_1 and dep_2 be the semantic recipes corresponding to the dependencies, and without loss of generality, consider that they have the following types:

$$\text{dep}_1 : \alpha_1 \to \beta_1 \to \gamma_1$$
$$\text{dep}_2 : \alpha_2 \to \beta_2 \to \gamma_2$$

Since both $(\text{dep}_1 \, B \, A)$ and $(\text{dep}_2 \, B \, C)$ are typable, we must have $\alpha_1 = \alpha_2$. In addition, since $(\text{dep}_2 \, (\text{dep}_1 \, B \, A) \, C)$ is also typable, we must have $\gamma_1 = \alpha_2$. By symmetry, we must also have $\gamma_2 = \alpha_1$. In consequence, every semantic recipe associated to a dependency must obey the following type scheme:

$$\alpha \to \beta \to \alpha$$

where α is the semantic type assigned to the source of the dependency edge, and β, the semantic type assigned to its target.

A way of satisfying both the coherence condition and the above requirement is to parametrize the type assigned to the head of a dependency relation with the types assigned to all its possible subordinates. In the case of the expressions listed in (11), this type is then the following one:

$$\text{GNP} = \text{DET} \to \text{ADJ} \to \text{NP}$$

Accordingly, the semantic recipes associated to the lexical items and dependency relations are as follows:

$$A = \lambda pq. \exists x. (p\,x) \wedge (q\,x) : \text{DET}$$
$$\text{WISE} = \lambda nx. (n\,x) \wedge (\mathbf{wise}\,x) : \text{ADJ}$$
$$\text{MAN} = \lambda da. d\,(a\,\mathbf{man}) : \text{GNP}$$

$$\mathsf{amod} = \lambda na. \lambda db. n\,d\,(\lambda z. b\,(a\,z)) : \text{GNP} \rightarrow \text{ADJ} \rightarrow \text{GNP}$$
$$\mathsf{det} = \lambda nd. \lambda ea. n\,d\,a : \text{GNP} \rightarrow \text{DET} \rightarrow \text{GNP}$$

Let us comment the above interpretation. The first two entries (the one assigned to the determiner and the one assigned to the adjective) are the standard Montagovian interpretations. This is because we have made the simplifying assumption that a determiner or an adjective cannot be the head of a phrase (an assumption that could be relaxed without difficulty). In the third entry, the variables d and a correspond to the possible subordinates of the head, namely, a determiner (d) or an adnominal modifier (a). Then, the entries corresponding to the dependency relations amod and det take a first argument of type GNP (roughly speaking a noun phrase) and pass it their second argument (an adnominal modifier in the case of amod, and a determiner in the case of det). In both cases, it should result in a term of type GNP. Therefore, the bodies of the two terms start with a double abstraction with variables of type DET and ADJ. In the case of amod, the abstracted variable of type ADJ (b) occurs in the term. This corresponds to the fact that adnominal modification can be iterated. By contrast, in the case of det, the abstracted variable of type DET (e) does not appear in the term. This corresponds to the fact that a noun expects at most one determiner.

6   Revisiting the Subject and Object Dependencies

The typing principle we posited in the previous section must be propagated throughout the grammar. Therefore, the type assigned to nsubj and obj should no longer be GS → NP → GS but GS → GNP → GS. Similarly, the semantic type assigned to a proper name should be GNP rather than NP. Let us illustrate this by coming back to Sentence (1), repeated here as (12):

(12)   *Michael praises a wise man*

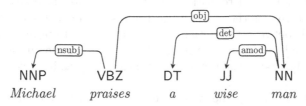

Putting together the principles we have discussed in this paper, this example can be handled using the following semantic recipes:

$$\text{A} = \text{SOME} = \lambda pq. \exists x. (p\,x) \wedge (q\,x) : \text{DET}$$
$$\text{WISE} = \lambda nx. (n\,x) \wedge (\mathbf{wise}\,x) : \text{ADJ}$$
$$\text{MAN} = \lambda da. d\,(a\,\mathbf{man}) : \text{GNP}$$
$$\text{MICHEL} = \lambda dap. p\,\mathbf{m} : \text{GNP}$$
$$\text{PRAISE} = \lambda p. \exists e. (\mathbf{praise}\,e) \wedge (p\,e) : \text{GS}$$

$$\text{amod} = \lambda na. \lambda db. n\,d\,(\lambda z. b\,(a\,z)) : \text{GNP} \to \text{ADJ} \to \text{GNP}$$
$$\text{det} = \lambda nd. \lambda ea. n\,d\,a : \text{GNP} \to \text{DET} \to \text{GNP}$$
$$\text{nsubj} = \lambda vn. \lambda p. n\,\text{SOME}\,(\lambda x. x)\,(\lambda x. v\,(\lambda e. (\mathbf{ag}\,e)\,x) \wedge (p\,e))) : \text{GS} \to \text{GNP} \to \text{GS}$$
$$\text{obj} = \lambda vn. \lambda p. n\,\text{SOME}\,(\lambda x. x)\,(\lambda x. v\,(\lambda e. (\mathbf{th}\,e)\,x) \wedge (p\,e))) : \text{GS} \to \text{GNP} \to \text{GS}$$

The main difference with respect to the interpretations we have developed in the previous sections resides in the definitions of nsubj and obj. In both cases, their second parameter (n) is of type GNP, i.e., DET $\to$ ADJ $\to$ NP. Therefore, in the bodies of nsubj and obj, the variable n must be given two additional arguments: one determiner, and one adnominal modifier. For the second argument, we naturally give the neutral modifier, i.e., $\lambda x.x$. For the first argument, we give a determiner by default. Now, if the term instantiating variable n already carries a determiner (or does not need any, as in the case of a proper name), the default determiner will be discarded because of a dummy abstraction.

The reader may then check that the four possible expressions that encode the above dependency structure, namely:

$$\text{nsubj}\,(\text{obj}\,\text{PRAISES}\,(\text{det}\,(\text{amod}\,\text{MAN}\,\text{WISE})\,\text{A}))\,\text{MICHAEL}$$
$$\text{nsubj}\,(\text{obj}\,\text{PRAISES}\,(\text{amod}\,(\text{det}\,\text{MAN}\,\text{A})\,\text{WISE}))\,\text{MICHAEL}$$
$$\text{obj}(\text{nsubj}\,\text{PRAISES}\,\text{MICHAEL})(\text{det}\,(\text{amod}\,\text{MAN}\,\text{WISE})\text{A})$$
$$\text{obj}\,(\text{nsubj}\,\text{PRAISES}\,\text{MICHAEL})\,(\text{amod}\,(\text{det}\,\text{MAN}\,\text{A})\,\text{WISE})$$

yield all the same semantic interpretation[4] of Sentence (12):

$$\lambda f. \exists x(\mathbf{man}\,x) \wedge (\mathbf{wise}\,x) \wedge (\exists e. (\mathbf{praise}\,e) \wedge (\mathbf{ag}\,e\,\mathbf{m}) \wedge (\mathbf{th}\,e\,x) \wedge (f\,e))$$

7 Robustness

There are two sources of robustness in the system we have advocated. At the sentential level, that is the use of a neo-Davidsonian event semantics that does not distinguish between the notions of mandatory and optional arguments. At the subsentential level (i.e., the noun phrase level in the simple examples we have developed), that is the use of default argument (as in nsubj and obj, in our example).

In order to illustrate the first kind of robustness, consider the following (incomplete) dependency structures.

---

[4] up to conjunction commutativity.

The fact that these dependency structures may correspond to ungrammatical sentences, and are therefore incomplete, does not prevent them from being encoded by the following terms:

nsubj PRAISES MICHAEL   obj PRAISES SAMUEL

Then, using the semantic interpretations we have developed, we obtain:

$$\text{nsubj PRAISES MICHAEL} \twoheadrightarrow_\beta \lambda f.\, \exists e.\, (\mathbf{praise}\, e) \wedge (\mathbf{ag}\, e\, \mathbf{m}) \wedge (f\, e)$$
$$\text{obj PRAISES SAMUEL} \twoheadrightarrow_\beta \lambda f.\, \exists e.\, (\mathbf{praise}\, e) \wedge (\mathbf{th}\, e\, \mathbf{s}) \wedge (f\, e)$$

In order to illustrate the second source of robustness, let us consider another incomplete dependency structure:

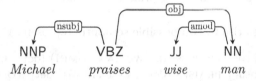

Again, the fact that this dependency structure is incomplete does not prevent it from being encoded as a λ-term:

nsubj (obj PRAISES (amod MAN WISE)) MICHAEL

Then, evaluating this term yields the following semantic interpretation:

$$\lambda f.\exists x.(\mathbf{man}\ x) \wedge (\mathbf{wise}\ x) \wedge (\exists e.(\mathbf{praise}\ e) \wedge (\mathbf{th}\ e x) \wedge (\mathbf{ag}\ \mathbf{m}\ x) \wedge (f\ e))$$

where the first quantifier $(\exists x)$ results from the default determiner provided by obj.

Of course, the two sources of robustness may interact, allowing a dependency structure such as the following one to be interpreted.

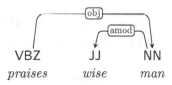

8   Scope Ambiguities

We have seen how determiners are assigned their standard Montagovian interpretation:

$$\text{SOME} = \lambda pq. \exists x. (p\,x) \wedge (q\,x) : \text{DET}$$
$$\text{EVERY} = \lambda pq. \forall x. (p\,x) \rightarrow (q\,x) : \text{DET}$$

We have also seen how to treat common nouns as terms of type GNP:

$$\text{MAN} = \lambda da. d\,(a\,\mathbf{man}) : \text{GNP}$$
$$\text{WOMAN} = \lambda da. d\,(a\,\mathbf{woman}) : \text{GNP}$$

We are therefore in a position of analysing sentences that present sope ambiguities.

(13)   *every man praises some woman*

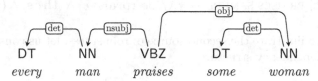

DT	NN	VBZ	DT	NN
every	*man*	*praises*	*some*	*woman*

Sentence (13) gives rise to two possible semantic representations:

(14)   a.   nsubj (obj PRAISES (det WOMAN SOME)) (det MAN EVERY)
         b.   obj (nsubj PRAISES (det MAN EVERY)) (det WOMAN SOME)

The difference between these two terms is mainly operational: they differ in their evaluation strategy. According to the coherence principle, these two terms should yield the same result. However, the present case appears as an exception to the coherence principle, exception that provides an account of scope ambiguity. We have indeed the following reductions:

obj PRAISES (det WOMAN SOME) $\twoheadrightarrow_\beta$
$$\lambda f. \exists y. (\mathbf{woman}\,y) \wedge (\exists e. (\mathbf{praise}\,e) \wedge (\mathbf{th}\,e\,y) \wedge (f\,e))$$
nsubj PRAISES (det MAN EVERY) $\twoheadrightarrow_\beta$
$$\lambda f. \forall x. (\mathbf{man}\,x) \rightarrow (\exists e. (\mathbf{praise}\,e) \wedge (\mathbf{ag}\,e\,x) \wedge (f\,e))$$

Hence:

nsubj (obj PRAISES (det WOMAN SOME)) (det MAN EVERY) $\twoheadrightarrow_\beta$
$$\lambda f. \forall x. (\mathbf{man}\,x) \rightarrow$$
$$(\exists y. (\mathbf{woman}\,y) \wedge (\exists e. (\mathbf{praise}\,e) \wedge (\mathbf{th}\,e\,y) \wedge (\mathbf{ag}\,e\,x) \wedge (f\,e)))$$
obj (nsubj PRAISES (det MAN EVERY)) (det WOMAN SOME) $\twoheadrightarrow_\beta$
$$\lambda f. \exists y. (\mathbf{woman}\,y) \wedge$$
$$(\forall x. (\mathbf{man}\,x) \rightarrow (\exists e. (\mathbf{praise}\,e) \wedge (\mathbf{ag}\,e\,x) \wedge (\mathbf{th}\,e\,y) \wedge (f\,e)))$$

9 Conclusions

We have investigated the way dependency grammars may be provided with a formal compositional semantics. In particular, we have addressed the problem of representing a dependency structure as a lambda-term in order to define a syntax-semantic interface suitable for dependency grammars. This led us to state a coherence principle, the consequences of which enabled us to lay the foundations of a formal theory of dependency semantics. We have then shown, using simple examples, how the resulting system satisfies several interesting properties: it is robust, it allows for a treatment of quantification, and provides an account of scope ambiguities.

The next step of this work will consist in conducting a real size experiment in order to study the feasibility of our approach. To this end, we will take advantage of the existence of numerous corpora annotated with dependencies. We do not expect our approach to fully scale up without any difficulty but hope that the experiment will allow our semantic theory to be refined and improved. We also expect that the difficulties and failures that we will encounter will serve to discuss some possible limitations of dependency parsing and contribute to its improvement.

References

1. van Benthem, J.: Essays in Logical Semantics. Reidel, Dordrecht (1986)
2. Champollion, L.: The interaction of compositional semantics and event semantics. Linguist. Philos. **38**(1), 31–66 (2015)
3. Church, A.: A formulation of the simple theory of types. J. Symb. Log. **5**, 56–68 (1940)
4. Dikovsky, A.: What should be a proper semantics for dependency structures. In: Apresjan, J., et al. (eds.) Meanings, Texts and Other Exciting Things. A Festschrift to Commemorate the 80th Anniversary of Professor Igor Alexandrovich Mel'cuk, pp. 112–123. Languages of Slavic Culture, Moscou (2012)
5. Dowty, D., Wall, R., Peters, S.: Introduction to Montague Semantics, Studies in Linguistics and Philosophy, vol. 11. D. Reidel Publishing Company (1981)
6. Heim, I., Kratzer, A.: Semantics in Generative Grammar. Blackwell Publishing (1998)
7. Kong, L., Rush, A.M., Smith, N.A.: Transforming dependencies into phrase structures. In: Proceedings of the 2015 Conference of the North American Chapter of the Association for Computational Linguistics: Human Language Technologies, pp. 788–798. Association for Computational Linguistics (2015)
8. de Marneffe, M.C., MacCartney, B., Manning, C.D.: Generating typed dependency parses from phrase structure parses. In: Proceedings of the Fifth International Conference on Language Resources and Evaluation (LREC'06), pp. 449–454. European Language Resources Association (ELRA) (2006)
9. Mel'čuk, I.: Dependency Syntax: Theory and Practice. State University of New York Press (1988)
10. Montague, R.: The proper treatment of quantification in ordinary English. In: Hintikka, J., Moravcsik, J., Suppes, P. (eds.) Approaches to natural language: proceedings of the 1970 Stanford workshop on Grammar and Semantics. Reidel, Dordrecht (1973), reprinted: [11, pages 247–270]

11. Montague, R.: Formal Philosophy: selected papers of Richard Montague, edited and with an introduction by Richmond Thomason. Yale University Press (1974)
12. Nivre, J., et al.: Universal Dependencies v1: a multilingual treebank collection. In: Proceedings of the Tenth International Conference on Language Resources and Evaluation (LREC'16), pp. 1659–1666. European Language Resources Association (ELRA), Portorož, Slovenia, May 2016
13. Partee, B.: Noun phrase interpretation and type shifting principles. In: Groenendijk, J., de Jong, D., Stokhof, M. (eds.) Studies in Discourse Representation Theories and the Theory of Generalized Quantifiers. Foris, Dordrecht (1987)
14. Portner, P.H.: What is Meaning? Blackwell. Fundamentals of Formal Semantics, Fundamentals of Linguistics (2005)
15. Reddy, S., et al.: Transforming dependency structures to logical forms for semantic parsing. Trans. Assoc. Comput. Linguistics **4**, 127–140 (2016)
16. Tesnière, L.: Eléments de syntaxe structurale. Klincksieck, Paris (1959)
17. Winter, Y.: Elements of Formal Semantics: An Introduction to the Mathematical Theory of Meaning in Natural Language. Edinburgh Advanced Textbooks in Linguistics, Edinburgh University Press (2018)
18. Xia, F., Rambow, O., Bhatt, R., Palmer, M., Sharma, D.M.: Towards a multi-representational treebank. In: Eynde, F.V., Frank, A., Smedt, K.D., van Noord, G. (eds.) Proceedings of the Seventh International Workshop on Treebanks and Linguistic Theories (TLT 7), pp. 159–170. LOT Occasional series, LOT (2009)

Logic Operators and Quantifiers in Type-Theory of Algorithms

Roussanka Loukanova[✉]

Institute of Mathematics and Informatics, Bulgarian Academy of Sciences,
Acad. G. Bonchev Street, Block 8, 1113 Sofia, Bulgaria
rloukanova@gmail.com

Abstract. In this work, I introduce the Type-Theory of Algorithms (TTA), which is an extension of Moschovakis Type-Theory of Algorithms and its reduction calculus, by adding logic operators and quantifiers. The formal language has two kinds of terms of formulae, for designating state-independent and state-dependent propositions and predications. The logic operators include conjunction, disjunction, conditional implication, and negation. I add state-dependent quantifiers, for enhancing the standard quantifiers of predicate logic. I provide an extended reduction calculus of the Type-Theory of Acyclic Algorithms, for reductions of terms to their canonical forms. The canonical forms of the terms provide the algorithmic semantics for computing the denotations.

Keywords: recursion · type-theory · acyclic algorithms · denotational semantics · algorithmic semantics · reduction calculus · logic operators · quantifiers

1   Introduction

This paper is part of the author's work on development of a new type-theory of the mathematical notion of algorithms, its concepts, and potentials for applications to advanced, computational technologies, with a focus on Computational Semantics and Syntax-Semantics-Semantics Interfaces for formal and natural languages.

For the initiation of this approach to mathematics of algorithms, see the original work on the formal languages of recursion (FLR) by Moschovakis [15–17]. The formal languages of recursion FLR are untyped systems. The typed version of this approach to algorithmic, acyclic computations was introduced, for the first time, by Moschovakis [18], with the type theory L_{ar}^λ. Type theory L_r^λ covers full recursion and is an extension of type theory of acyclic recursion L_{ar}^λ.

For more recent developments of the language and theory of acyclic algorithms L_{ar}^λ, see, e.g., [6 8]. The work in [11] presents an algorithmic η-rule with the induced η-reduction acting on canonical terms in L_{ar}^λ, as a special case of (γ^*). The algorithmic expressiveness of L_{ar}^λ has been demonstrated by its applications to computational semantics of natural language. Algorithmic semantics of quantifier scope ambiguities and underspecification is presented in [3]. Computational grammar of natural language that covers syntax-semantics interfaces

D. Bekki et al. (Eds.): LENLS 2019, LNCS 14213, pp. 173–198, 2023.
https://doi.org/10.1007/978-3-031-43977-3_11

is presented in [5]. The work in [8] is on fundamental notions of algorithmic binding of argument slots of relations and functions, across assignments in recursion terms. It models functional capacities of neural receptors for neuroscience of language. A generalised restrictor operator is introduced in L_{ar}^{λ} for restricted, parametric algorithms, e.g., in semantics of definite descriptors, by [9], which is extended in a forthcoming publication. Currying order and limited, restricted algorithmic β-conversion in L_{ar}^{λ} are presented by [10].

In this paper, I extend the formal language, reduction calculus, and semantics of L_{ar}^{λ} and L_{r}^{λ}, by adding logic operators and logic quantifiers, with two versions of truth values: pure truth values and state-dependent ones. I introduce the logic operators of conjunction, disjunction, implication, and negation in the formal languages of L_{ar}^{λ} and L_{r}^{λ} by categorematic, logic constants, which have the benefits of sharing various properties and reduction rules with non-logic constants, while maintaining their logical characteristics.

In Sect. 2, I introduce the extended type-theory L_{ar}^{λ} and L_{r}^{λ} of acyclic algorithms, by its syntax and denotational semantics. The focus of the rest of the paper is on the acyclic type-theory L_{ar}^{λ}. In Sect. 3, I present the extended system of reduction rules and the induced γ^{*}-reduction calculus of L_{ar}^{λ}. The additional reduction rule (γ^{*}) greatly reduces the complexity of the terms, without affecting the denotational and algorithmic semantics of L_{ar}^{λ}, in any significant way. I provide the full, formal definition of the congruence relation between terms, which is part of the reduction system of both L_{ar}^{λ} and L_{r}^{λ}. The reduction calculus of L_{ar}^{λ} reduces each L_{ar}^{λ} term to its canonical form. For every term A, its canonical form is unique modulo congruence. The canonical form of every proper L_{ar}^{λ} term determines the algorithm for computing its denotation and saving the component values, including functions, in memory slots for reuse. Section 4 is on the algorithmic expressiveness of L_{ar}^{λ}. Theorem 2 proves that L_{ar}^{λ} is a proper extension of Gallin TY_2, see Gallin [1]. There are L_{ar}^{λ} recursion terms that are not algorithmically equivalent to any explicit, λ-calculus, i.e., TY_2 terms. In addition, such L_{ar}^{λ} recursion terms, provide subtle semantic distinctions for expressions of natural language. The focus of Sect. 5 is on the semantic and algorithmic distinctions between coordinated predication and sentential conjunction. In Sect. 6, I overview some relations between let-expressions for λ-calculus and L_{ar}^{λ} recursion terms. I give an explanation why the L_{ar}^{λ} recursion terms are not algorithmically equivalent to λ-terms in L_{ar}^{λ} representing let-expressions. I demonstrate the extended reduction calculus with reductions of terms to their canonical forms, which offer distinctive, algorithmic semantics of natural language expressions.

2   Introduction to Type-Theory of Acyclic Algorithms

Type-theory of algorithms (TTA), in each of its variants of full and acyclic recursion, L_{r}^{λ} and L_{ar}^{λ}, respectively, is a computational system, which extends the standart, simply-typed λ-calculus in its syntax and semantics.

The basis for the formal languages of L_{r}^{λ} and L_{ar}^{λ}, and their denotational and algorithmic semantics is a tuple $B_{r}^{\lambda} = \langle \mathsf{TypeR}, \mathsf{K}, \mathsf{Vars}, \mathsf{TermR}, \mathsf{RedR} \rangle$, where:

(1) TypeR is the set of the rules that defines the set Types
(2) K = Consts is a set of constants (2a)
(3) Vars is a set of variables (2f) of two kinds, pure and recursion (2d)–(2e)
(4) TermR is the set of the rules for the terms of L_r^λ and L_{ar}^λ, given in Definition 1
(5) RedR is the set of the reduction rules given in Sect. 3.2

The focus of this work is on the type-theory L_{ar}^λ of acyclic algorithms (TTAA).

Notation 1. *We shall use the following meta-symbols (1)–(2):*

(1) "≡" is used for notational abbreviations and definitions, i.e., for literal, syntactic identities between expressions. The equality sign "=" is for the identity relation between objects of L_{ar}^λ (L_r^λ)
(2) ":≡" is for the replacement, i.e., substitution operation, in syntactic constructions, and sometimes for definitional constructions

2.1 Syntax

The set Types of L_{ar}^λ is defined recursively, e.g., in Backus-Naur Form (BNF):

$$\tau ::= e \mid t \mid s \mid (\tau \to \tau) \qquad \text{(Types)}$$

The type e is for basic entities and L_{ar}^λ terms denoting such entities, e.g., for animals, people, etc., animate or inanimate objects. The type s is for states that carry context information, e.g., possible worlds, time and space locations, speakers, listeners, etc. The denotations of some expressions of natural language, e.g., proper names and other noun phrases (NPs), can be rendered (translated) to L_{ar}^λ terms of type (s → e). The type t is for truth values. For any $\tau_1, \tau_2 \in$ Types, the type $(\tau_1 \to \tau_2)$ is for functions from objects of type τ_1 to objects of type τ_2, and for L_{ar}^λ terms denoting such functions. We shall use the following abbreviations:

$$\tilde{\sigma} \equiv (s \to \sigma), \quad \text{for state-dependent objects of type } \tilde{\sigma} \qquad (1a)$$

$$\tilde{e} \equiv (s \to e), \quad \text{for state-dependent entities} \qquad (1b)$$

$$\tilde{t} \equiv (s \to t), \quad \text{for state-dependent truth values} \qquad (1c)$$

$$(\vec{\tau} \to \sigma) \equiv (\tau_1 \to \cdots \to (\tau_n \to \sigma)) \in \text{Types} \,(n \geq 1)$$
$$\text{currying coding, for } \sigma, \tau_i \in \text{Types}, \ i = 1, \ldots, n \qquad (1d)$$

Typed Vocabulary of L_{ar}^λ: For every $\sigma \in$ Types, L_{ar}^λ has denumerable sets of *constants*, and two kinds of infinite, denumerable sets of pure and recursion variables, all in pairwise different sets:

$$\mathsf{K}_\sigma = \mathsf{Consts}_\sigma = \{c_0^\sigma, c_1^\sigma, \dots\}; \qquad\qquad \mathsf{K} = \mathsf{Consts} = \bigcup_{\tau \in \mathsf{Types}} K_\tau \qquad\qquad (2a)$$

$$\wedge, \vee, \rightarrow\ \in \mathsf{Consts}_{(\tau \rightarrow (\tau \rightarrow \tau))},\ \tau \in \{\mathsf{t}, \tilde{\mathsf{t}}\} \qquad\qquad (\textit{logical constants}) \quad (2b)$$

$$\neg \in \mathsf{Consts}_{(\tau \rightarrow \tau)},\ \tau \in \{\mathsf{t}, \tilde{\mathsf{t}}\} \qquad\qquad (\textit{logical constant for negation}) \quad (2c)$$

$$\mathsf{PureV}_\sigma = \{v_0^\sigma, v_1^\sigma, \dots\}; \qquad\qquad \mathsf{PureV} = \bigcup_{\tau \in \mathsf{Types}} \mathsf{PureV}_\tau \qquad\qquad (2d)$$

$$\mathsf{RecV}_\sigma = \mathsf{MemoryV}_\sigma = \{p_0^\sigma, p_1^\sigma, \dots\}; \quad \mathsf{RecV} = \bigcup_{\tau \in \mathsf{Types}} \mathsf{RecV}_\tau \qquad\qquad (2e)$$

$$\mathsf{PureV}_\sigma \cap \mathsf{RecV}_\sigma = \varnothing; \quad \mathsf{Vars}_\sigma = \mathsf{PureV}_\sigma \cup \mathsf{RecV}_\sigma; \quad \mathsf{Vars} = \bigcup_{\tau \in \mathsf{Types}} \mathsf{Vars}_\sigma \ (2f)$$

Pure variables PureV are used for λ-abstraction and quantification. On the other hand, the recursion variables, which are called also *memory variables, memory locations (slots, cells)*, or *location variables*, play a special role in algorithmic computations, for saving information. Values, which can be obtained either directly by immediate, variable valuations, or by algorithmic computations, via recursion or iteration, can be saved, i.e., memorised, in typed memory locations, i.e., in memory variables, of the set RecV, by assignments. Sets of assignments can determine mutually recursive or iterative computations.

I shall use mixed notations for type assignments, $A : \tau$ and A^τ, to express that a term A or an object A is of type τ.

In Definition 1, I introduce the logical constants as categorematic constants for conjunction, disjunction, implication, $\wedge, \vee, \rightarrow\ \in \mathsf{Consts}_{(\tau \rightarrow (\tau \rightarrow \tau))}$, and negation, $\neg \in \mathsf{Consts}_{(\tau \rightarrow \tau)}$, in two variants of truth values $\tau \in \{\mathsf{t}, \tilde{\mathsf{t}}\}$.

Definition 1. $\mathsf{Terms} = \mathsf{Terms}(L_{ar}^\lambda) = \bigcup_{\tau \in \mathsf{Types}} \mathsf{Terms}_\tau$ *is the set of the terms of L_{ar}^λ, where, for each $\tau \in \mathsf{Types}$, Terms_τ is the set of the terms of type τ, which are defined recursively by the rules* TermR *in (3a)–(3g), in a typed style of Backus-Naur Form (TBNF):*

$$A :\equiv \mathsf{c}^\tau : \tau \mid x^\tau : \tau \qquad\qquad (\textit{constants and variables}) \quad (3a)$$

$$\mid B^{(\sigma \rightarrow \tau)}(C^\sigma) : \tau \qquad\qquad (\textit{application terms}) \quad (3b)$$

$$\mid \lambda(v^\sigma)(B^\tau) : (\sigma \rightarrow \tau) \qquad\qquad (\lambda\textit{-abstraction terms}) \quad (3c)$$

$$\mid A_0^{\sigma_0} \text{ where } \{p_1^{\sigma_1} := A_1^{\sigma_1}, \dots, p_n^{\sigma_n} := A_n^{\sigma_n}\} : \sigma_0 \quad (\textit{recursion terms}) \quad (3d)$$

$$\mid \wedge(A_2^\tau)(A_1^\tau) : \tau \mid \vee(A_2^\tau)(A_1^\tau) : \tau \mid \rightarrow (A_2^\tau)(A_1^\tau) : \tau$$
$$(\textit{conjunction} \ / \ \textit{disjunction} \ / \ \textit{implication terms}) \tag{3e}$$

$$\mid \neg(B^\tau) : \tau \qquad\qquad (\textit{negation terms}) \quad (3f)$$

$$\mid \forall(v^\sigma)(B^\tau) : \tau \mid \exists(v^\sigma)(B^\tau) : \tau \qquad (\textit{pure, logic quantifier terms}) \quad (3g)$$

given that

(1) $\mathsf{c} \in K_\tau = \mathsf{Consts}_\tau$
(2) $x^\tau \in \mathsf{PureV}_\tau \cup \mathsf{RecV}_\tau$ *is a pure or memory (recursion) variable,*
      $v^\sigma \in \mathsf{PureV}_\sigma$ *is a pure variable*
(3) $A_1^\tau, A_2^\tau, B, A_i^{\sigma_i} \in \mathsf{Terms}$ $(i = 0, \dots, n)$ *are terms of the respective types*
(4) *In* (3d), *for* $i = 1, \dots, n$, $p_i \in \mathsf{RecV}_{\sigma_i}$ *are pairwise different recursion (memory) variables;* $A_i^{\sigma_i} \in \mathsf{Terms}_{\sigma_i}$ *assigned to* p_i *is of the same corresponding*

type; and the sequence of assignments $\{ p_1^{\sigma_1} :- A_1^{\sigma_1}, \ldots, p_n^{\sigma_n} := A_n^{\sigma_n} \}$ *is acyclic, by satisfying the Acyclicity Constraint (AC) in Definition 2.*

(5) *In* (3e)–(3g), $\tau \in \{ \mathsf{t}, \tilde{\mathsf{t}} \}$ *are for state-independent and state-dependent truth values, respectively*

Definition 2 (Acyclicity Constraint (AC)). *For any* $A_i \in \mathsf{Terms}_{\sigma_i}$ *and pairwise different memory (recursion) variables* $p_i \in \mathsf{RecV}_{\sigma_i}$, $i \in \{ 1, \ldots, n \}$, *the sequence* (4):

$$\{ p_1^{\sigma_1} := A_1^{\sigma_1}, \ldots, p_n^{\sigma_n} := A_n^{\sigma_n} \} \quad (n \geq 0) \tag{4}$$

is an acyclic system of assignments *iff there is a function* rank

$$\begin{aligned} &\mathsf{rank} : \{ p_1, \ldots, p_n \} \to \mathbb{N}, \text{ such that, for all } p_i, p_j \in \{ p_1, \ldots, p_n \}, \\ &\text{if } p_j \text{ occurs freely in } A_i, \text{ then } \mathsf{rank}(p_j) < \mathsf{rank}(p_i) \end{aligned} \tag{AC}$$

Free and Bound Variables. The sets $\mathsf{FreeVars}(A)$ and $\mathsf{BoundVars}(A)$ of the free and bound variables of every term A are defined by structural induction on A, in the usual way, with the exception of the recursion terms. For the full definition, see [8]. For any given recursion term A of the form (3d), the constant where designates a binding operator, which binds all occurrences of $p_1, \ldots, p_n$ in A:

$$\text{For } A \equiv A_0 \text{ where } \{ p_1 := A_1, \ldots, p_n := A_n \} \in \mathsf{Terms} \tag{5a}$$

$$\mathsf{FreeV}(A) = \cup_{i=0}^{n}(\mathsf{FreeV}(A_i)) - \{ p_1, \ldots, p_n \} \tag{5b}$$

$$\mathsf{BoundV}(A) = \cup_{i=0}^{n}(\mathsf{BoundV}(A_i)) \cup \{ p_1, \ldots, p_n \} \tag{5c}$$

The formal language of full recursion L_r^{λ} is by Definition 1 without the Acyclicity Constraint (AC),

(A) The terms A of the form (3d) are called *recursion terms*. The constant where designates a binding operator, which binds the recursion variables $p_1, \ldots, p_n$ in A. Its entire scope is A called where-scope or its local recursion scope. The sub-terms A_i, $i = 0, \ldots, n$, are the parts of A and A_0 is its *head* part

(B) We say that a term A is *explicit* iff the constant where does not occur in it

(C) A is a *λ-calculus term*, i.e., a term of Gallin TY_2, iff it is explicit and no recursion variable occurs in it

Definition 3 (Free Occurrences and Replacement Operation). *Assume that* $A, C \in \mathsf{Terms}$, $X \in \mathsf{PureV} \cup \mathsf{RecV}$ *are such that, for some type* $\tau \in \mathsf{Types}$, $X, C : \tau$.

(1) *An occurrence of* X *in* A *is* free *(in* A*) if and only if it is not in the scope of any binding operator (e.g.,* $\xi \in \{ \lambda, \exists, \forall \}$ *and* where*) that binds* X

(2) *The result of the* simultaneous replacement *of all free (unless otherwise stated) occurrences of* X *with* C *in* A *is denoted by* $A\{ X :\equiv C \}$

(3) *The replacement* $A\{X := C\}$ *of* X *with* C *in* A *is free if and only if no free occurrence of* X *in* A *is in the scope of any operator that binds some variable having free occurrences in* C: *i.e., no variable that is free in* C *becomes bound in* $A\{X := C\}$. *We also say that* C *is free for (replacing)* X *in* A.

Notation 2. *Often, we do not write the type assignments in the term expressions.*

Sometimes, we shall use different kinds of or extra parentheses, or omit such. Application is associative to the left, λ-abstraction and quantifiers to the right.

In addition, we shall use abbreviations for sequences, e.g. $(n \geq 0)$:

$$\overrightarrow{p} := \overrightarrow{A} \equiv p_1 := A_1, \ \ldots, \ p_n := A_n \quad (n \geq 0) \tag{6a}$$

$$H(\overrightarrow{A}) \equiv H(A_1)\ldots(A_n) \equiv (\ldots H(A_1)\ldots)(A_n) \quad \text{(left-association)} \tag{6b}$$

$$\begin{array}{l} \xi(\overrightarrow{v})(A) \equiv \xi(v_1)\ldots\xi(v_n)(A) \equiv \xi(v_1)\big[\ldots[\xi(v_n)(A)]\big] \quad \text{(right-association)} \\ \xi \in \{\lambda, \exists, \forall\} \quad (n \geq 0) \end{array} \tag{6c}$$

$$\begin{array}{l} \overrightarrow{\xi(v)}(A) \equiv \xi_1(v_1)\ldots\xi_n(v_n)(A) \equiv \xi_1(v_1)\big[\ldots[\xi_n(v_n)(A)]\big], \\ \xi_i \in \{\lambda, \exists, \forall\}, \ i \in \{1, \ldots, n\} \quad (n \geq 0) \end{array} \tag{6d}$$

$$\mathsf{lgh}(\overrightarrow{X}) = \mathsf{lgh}((X_1)\ldots(X_n)) = n, \quad \mathsf{lgh}(\xi(\overrightarrow{v})) = n, \quad \mathsf{lgh}(\overrightarrow{\xi(v)}) = n \tag{6e}$$

2.2   Overview of Algorithmic Semantics in $\mathrm{L}_{\mathrm{ar}}^{\lambda}$ (L_r^{λ})

The syntax-semantics interface in $\mathrm{L}_{\mathrm{ar}}^{\lambda}$ (L_r^{λ}) provides the interrelations between denotational and algorithmic semantics.

Definition 4 (Immediate and Pure Terms). *The set of the* immediate terms *consists of all terms of the form* (7), *for* $p \in$ RecVars, $u_i, v_j, \in$ PureVars $(i = 1, \ldots, n, \ j = 1, \ldots, m, \ m, n \geq 0)$, $V \in$ Vars:

$$T :\equiv V \mid p(v_1)\ldots(v_m) \mid \lambda(u_1)\ldots\lambda(u_n)p(v_1)\ldots(v_m), \quad \text{for } m, n \geq 0 \tag{7}$$

Every term A *that is not immediate is* proper.

The immediate terms $T \equiv \lambda(\overrightarrow{u})p(\overrightarrow{v})$ have no algorithmic meanings. Their denotational value $\mathsf{den}(T)(g)$ is given immediately, by the valuation functions g for $g(v_i)$, and abstracting away from the values u_j, for λ-bound pure variables $\lambda(\overrightarrow{u})p(\overrightarrow{v})$.

For every proper, i.e., non-immediate, term A, there is an algorithm $\mathsf{alg}(A)$ for computing $\mathsf{den}(A)(g)$. The canonical form $\mathsf{cf}_{\gamma^*}(A)$ of a proper term A determines the algorithm for computing its denotational value $\mathsf{den}(A)(g) = \mathsf{den}(\mathsf{cf}_{\gamma^*}(A))(g)$ from the components $\mathsf{den}(A_i)(g)$ of $\mathsf{cf}_{\gamma^*}(A)$. See γ^*-Canonical Form Theorem 1, and [6–8,18].

– The type theories $\mathrm{L}_{\mathrm{ar}}^{\lambda}$ have *effective reduction calculi*, see Sect. 3:
  For every $A \in$ Terms, there is a unique, up to congruence, canonical form $\mathsf{cf}_{\gamma^*}(A)$, which can be obtained from A, by a finite number of reductions:

$$A \Rightarrow_{\gamma^*}^* \mathsf{cf}_{\gamma^*}(A) \tag{8}$$

For a given, fixed semantic structure $\mathfrak{A}$ and valuations G, for every *algorithmically meaningful*, i.e., proper, $A \in \mathsf{Terms}_\sigma$, the algorithm $\mathsf{alg}(A)$ for computing $\mathsf{den}(A)$ is determined by $\mathsf{cf}(A)$, so that:

$$\mathsf{den}(A)(g) = \mathsf{den}(\mathsf{cf}(A))(g), \text{ for } g \in G \tag{9}$$

Figure 1 depicts of the syntax-semantics relations between the syntax of Natural Language, their rendering to the terms L_{ar}^λ and the corresponding algorithmic and denotational semantics.

Syntax: NL / L_{ar}^λ $\Longrightarrow$ Algorithms for Iterative Computations: $\mathsf{cf}_{\gamma^*}(A)$ $\Longleftrightarrow$ Denotations

Canonical Computations

Computational Syn-Sem: Algorithmic and Denotational Semantics of NL via NL $\xrightarrow{\text{render}}$ L_{ar}^λ

Fig. 1. Computational Syntax-Semantics Interface for Algorithmic Semantics of Natural Language via Compositional Rendering to L_{ar}^λ.

2.3 Denotational Semantics of L_{ar}^λ

Definition 5. *A standard semantic structure of the formal language $\mathrm{L}_{ar}^\lambda(K)$ is a tuple $\mathfrak{A}(K) = \langle \mathbb{T}, \mathcal{I}(K) \rangle$, where $\mathbb{T}$ is a frame of sets (or classes) $\mathbb{T} = \{ \mathbb{T}_\sigma \mid \sigma \in \mathsf{Types} \}$, and the following conditions (S1)–(S3) are satisfied:*

(S1) sets of basic, typed semantic objects:
  - $\mathbb{T}_e \neq \varnothing$ *is a nonempty set (class) of entities called* individuals
  - $\mathbb{T}_t = \{ 0, 1, er \} \subseteq \mathbb{T}_e$, $\mathbb{T}_t$ *is called the set of the* truth values
  - $\mathbb{T}_s \neq \varnothing$ *is a nonempty set of objects called* states

(S2) $\mathbb{T}_{(\tau_1 \to \tau_2)} = \{ f \mid f : \mathbb{T}_{\tau_1} \to \mathbb{T}_{\tau_2} \}$

(S3) The interpretation function $\mathcal{I}$, $\mathcal{I} : K \to \bigcup \mathbb{T}$, *is such that for every constant* $\mathsf{c} \in K_\tau$, $\mathcal{I}(\mathsf{c}) = c$, *for some* $c \in \mathbb{T}_\tau$

Definition 6. *Assume a given semantic structure $\mathfrak{A}$. The set $G^{\mathfrak{A}}$ of all variable valuations (assignments) in $\mathfrak{A}$ is (10a)–(10b):*

$$G^{\mathfrak{A}} = \{ g \mid g : (\mathsf{PureV} \cup \mathsf{RecV}) \to \bigcup \mathbb{T}, \tag{10a}$$

$$\text{and } g(x) \in \mathbb{T}_\tau, \text{ for all } \tau \in \mathsf{Type} \text{ and } x \in \mathsf{PureV}_\tau \cup \mathsf{RecV}_\tau \} \tag{10b}$$

Definition 7 (Denotation Function). *A denotation function $\mathsf{den}^{\mathfrak{A}}$ of the semantic structure $\mathrm{L}_{ar}^\lambda(K)$, $\mathsf{den}^{\mathfrak{A}} : \mathsf{Terms} \to (G \to \bigcup \mathbb{T})$, is defined by structural recursion, for all $g \in G$:*

(D1) Variables and constants:

$$\mathsf{den}^{\mathfrak{A}}(x)(g) = g(x), \text{ for } x \in \mathsf{Vars}; \quad \mathsf{den}^{\mathfrak{A}}(\mathsf{c})(g) = \mathcal{I}(\mathsf{c}), \text{ for } c \in K \tag{11}$$

(D2) Application:

$$\text{den}^{\mathfrak{A}}(A(B))(g) = \text{den}^{\mathfrak{A}}(A)(g)(\text{den}^{\mathfrak{A}}(B)(g)) \tag{12}$$

(D3) λ-abstraction: *for all* $x : \tau$, $B : \sigma$, $\text{den}^{\mathfrak{A}}(\lambda(x)(B))(g) : \mathbb{T}_\tau \to \mathbb{T}_\sigma$ *is the function such that, for every* $t \in \mathbb{T}_\tau$,

$$[\text{den}^{\mathfrak{A}}(\lambda(x)(B))(g)](t) = \text{den}^{\mathfrak{A}}(B)(g\{x := t\}) \tag{13}$$

(D4) Recursion:

$$\text{den}^{\mathfrak{A}}(A_0 \text{ where } \{ \overrightarrow{p} := \overrightarrow{A} \})(g) = \text{den}^{\mathfrak{A}}(A_0)(g\{ \overrightarrow{p_i} := \overrightarrow{\overline{p}_i} \}) \tag{14}$$

where $\overline{p}_i \in \mathbb{T}_{\tau_i}$ *are computed by recursion on* $\text{rank}(p_i)$, *i.e., by* (15):

$$\overline{p}_i = \text{den}^{\mathfrak{A}}(A_i)(g\{ p_{i,1} := \overline{p}_{i,1}, \ldots, p_{i,k_i} := \overline{p}_{i,k_i} \}) \tag{15}$$
$$\textit{for all } p_{i,1}, \ldots, p_{i,k_i}, \textit{ such that } \text{rank}(p_{i,k}) < \text{rank}(p_i)$$

The denotation $\text{den}(A_i)(g)$ *may depend essentially on the values stored in* p_j, *for* $\text{rank}(p_j) < \text{rank}(p_i)$.

(D5) *Here, for the denotations of the constants of the logic operators, we shall present the state dependent cases, including the erroneous truth values. The state-independent cases are simpler and straightforwardly similar.*

(D5a) $\text{den}^{\mathfrak{A}}(A_1 \wedge A_2)(g) : \mathbb{T}_{\mathsf{s}} \to \mathbb{T}_{\mathsf{t}}$ *is the function such that, for every state* $s \in \mathbb{T}_{\mathsf{s}}$:

$$[\text{den}^{\mathfrak{A}}(A_1 \wedge A_2)(g)](s) = V \in \mathbb{T}_{\mathsf{t}}, \textit{ where } V \textit{ is as in } (17a) - (17c) \tag{16}$$

$$V = \begin{cases} 1, & \textit{if } [\text{den}^{\mathfrak{A}}(A_i)(g)](s) = 1, \textit{ for } i = 1, 2 & (17a) \\ 0, & \textit{if } [\text{den}^{\mathfrak{A}}(A_i)(g)](s) = 0, \textit{ for at least one } i = 1, 2 & (17b) \\ & \textit{and } [\text{den}^{\mathfrak{A}}(A_i)(g)](s) \neq er, \textit{ for } i = 1, 2 \\ er, & \textit{otherwise, i.e.,} & (17c) \\ & \textit{if } [\text{den}^{\mathfrak{A}}(A_i)(g)](s) = er, \textit{ for at least one } i = 1, 2 \end{cases}$$

(D5b) $\text{den}^{\mathfrak{A}}(A_1 \vee A_2)(g) : \mathbb{T}_{\mathsf{s}} \to \mathbb{T}_{\mathsf{t}}$ *is the function such that, for every state* $s \in \mathbb{T}_{\mathsf{s}}$:

$$[\text{den}^{\mathfrak{A}}(A_1 \vee A_2)(g)](s) = V \in \mathbb{T}_{\mathsf{t}}, \textit{ where } V \textit{ is as in } (19a) - (19c) \tag{18}$$

$$V = \begin{cases} 1, & \textit{if } [\text{den}^{\mathfrak{A}}(A_i)(g)](s) = 1, \textit{ for at least one } i = 1, 2 & (19a) \\ & \textit{and } [\text{den}^{\mathfrak{A}}(A_i)(g)](s) \neq er, \textit{ for } i = 1, 2 \\ 0, & \textit{if } [\text{den}^{\mathfrak{A}}(A_i)(g)](s) = 0, \textit{ for } i = 1, 2 & (19b) \\ er, & \textit{otherwise, i.e.,} & (19c) \\ & \textit{if } [\text{den}^{\mathfrak{A}}(A_i)(g)](s) = er, \textit{ for at least one } i = 1, 2 \end{cases}$$

The definition of $\mathsf{den}^{\mathfrak{A}}(A_1 \to A_2)(g)$ *is in a similar mode.*

(D6) $\mathsf{den}^{\mathfrak{A}}\big(\neg(A)\big)(g) : \mathbb{T}_\mathsf{s} \to \mathbb{T}_\mathsf{t}$ *is such that, for every state* $s \in \mathbb{T}_\mathsf{s}$:

$$[\mathsf{den}^{\mathfrak{A}}(\neg(A))(g)](s) = \begin{cases} 1, & \textit{if } [\mathsf{den}^{\mathfrak{A}}(A)(g)](s) = 0 & (20a) \\ 0, & \textit{if } [\mathsf{den}^{\mathfrak{A}}(A)(g)](s) = 1 & (20b) \\ er, & \textit{otherwise, i.e., if } [\mathsf{den}^{\mathfrak{A}}(A)(g)](s) = er & (20c) \end{cases}$$

(D7) Pure Universal Quantifier $\forall$:[1]

  (D7a) For the state-independent quantifier $\forall$ *(* $\tau = \mathsf{t}$*), the definition is similar to the state dependent one, and we do not present its details*

  (D7b) For the state-dependent quantifier $\forall$ *(* $\tau = \tilde{\mathsf{t}}$*), for every state* $s \in \mathbb{T}_\mathsf{s}$:

$$\big[\mathsf{den}^{\mathfrak{A}}\big(\forall(v^\sigma)(B^\tau)\big)(g)\big](s) = V, \textit{ where:}$$

$$V = \begin{cases} 1, & \textit{if } [\mathsf{den}^{\mathfrak{A}}(B^\tau)(g\{v := a\})](s) = 1, \textit{ for all } a \in \mathbb{T}_\sigma & (21a) \\ 0, & \textit{if } [\mathsf{den}^{\mathfrak{A}}(B^\tau)(g\{v := a\})](s) = 0, \textit{ for some } a \in \mathbb{T}_\sigma & (21b) \\ & \textit{and } [\mathsf{den}^{\mathfrak{A}}(B^\tau)(g\{v := b\})](s) \neq er, \textit{ for all } b \in \mathbb{T}_\sigma \\ er, & \textit{otherwise} & (21c) \end{cases}$$

(D8) Pure Existential Quantifier $\exists$:

  (D8a) For the state-independent quantifier $\exists$*, with* $\tau = \mathsf{t}$*, the definition is similar to the state dependent one, and we do not present it here*

  (D8b) For the state-dependent quantifier $\exists$*, (* $\tau = \tilde{\mathsf{t}}$*), for every state* $s \in \mathbb{T}_\mathsf{s}$:

$$\big[\mathsf{den}^{\mathfrak{A}}\big(\exists(v^\sigma)(B^\tau)\big)(g)\big](s) = V, \textit{ where:}$$

$$V = \begin{cases} 1, & \textit{if } [\mathsf{den}^{\mathfrak{A}}(B^\tau)(g\{v := a\})](s) = 1, \textit{ for some } a \in \mathbb{T}_\sigma & (22a) \\ & \textit{and } [\mathsf{den}^{\mathfrak{A}}(B^\tau)(g\{v := b\})](s) \neq er, \textit{ for all } b \in \mathbb{T}_\sigma \\ 0, & \textit{if } [\mathsf{den}^{\mathfrak{A}}(B^\tau)(g\{v := a\})](s) = 0, \textit{ for all } a \in \mathbb{T}_\sigma & (22b) \\ er, & \textit{otherwise} & (22c) \end{cases}$$

Often, we shall skip the superscript in $G^{\mathfrak{A}}$ and $\mathsf{den}^{\mathfrak{A}}$, by writing G and den.

3   Gamma-Star Reduction Calculus of $\mathsf{L}^\lambda_{\mathsf{ar}}$

I designate the logic operators as a set of specialised, logic constants. In this way, I classify the reduction rules for the terms formed by (3e)–(3f) as special cases of the reduction rule for application terms.

   In this section, I extend the set of the $\mathsf{L}^\lambda_{\mathsf{ar}}$-reduction rules introduced in [18], by adding:

(1) the reduction rules (ξ) for the quantifier terms (3g) together with the λ-abstract terms, $\xi \in \{\lambda, \exists, \forall\}$
(2) an additional reduction rule, the (γ^*) rule, (30a)–(30b), which extends the corresponding rule in [7]

---

[1] There are other possibilities for the truth values of the erroneous truth value *er* for the quantifiers, which we do not consider in this paper.

3.1   Congruence Relation Between Terms

Definition 8. *The* congruence *relation is the smallest equivalence relation (i.e., reflexive, symmetric, transitive) between terms* $\equiv_c$ $\subseteq$ Terms $\times$ Terms, *that is closed under:*

(1) operators of term-formation:
  - *application, which includes logic constants because we introduced them as categorematic constants*
  - *λ-abstraction and pure, logic quantifiers*
  - *acyclic recursion*

$$\text{If } A \equiv_c A' \text{ and } B \equiv_c B', \text{ then } A(B) \equiv_c A'(B') \qquad \text{(ap-congr)}$$

$$\text{If } A \equiv_c B, \text{ and } \xi \in \{\lambda, \exists, \forall\}, \text{ then } \xi(u)(A) \equiv_c \xi(u)(B) \qquad \text{(lq-congr)}$$

$$\text{If } A_i \equiv_c B_i, \text{ for } i = 0, \ldots, n, \text{ then:}$$
$$A_0 \text{ where } \{\, p_1 := A_1, \ldots, p_n := A_n \,\} \qquad \text{(rec-congr)}$$
$$\equiv_c B_0 \text{ where } \{\, p_1 := B_1, \ldots, p_n := B_n \,\}$$

(2) renaming bound pure and recursion variables without variable collisions, by free replacements, see Definition 3
  (a) renaming pure variables bound by λ-abstraction and pure, logic quantifiers

$$\xi(x)(A) \equiv_c \xi(y)(A\{x := y\}), \quad \text{for } x, y \in \mathsf{PureV}_\tau, \xi \in \{\lambda, \exists, \forall\}$$
$$\text{assuming } y \in \mathsf{FreeV}(A) \text{ and } y \text{ is free for (replacing) } x \text{ in } A \qquad (24a)$$

  (b) renaming memory location (variables) bound by the recursion operator where, *in assignments*

$$A \equiv A_0 \text{ where } \{\, p_1 := A_1, \ldots, p_n := A_n \,\}$$
$$\equiv_c A'_0 \text{ where } \{\, p'_1 := A'_1, \ldots, p'_n := A'_n \,\} \qquad (25a)$$
$$\text{assuming } p'_i \in \mathsf{FreeV}(A) \text{ and } p'_i \text{ is free for (replacing) } p_i \text{ in } A_j$$

$$A'_j \equiv A_j\{p_1 := p'_1, \ldots, p_n := p'_n\} \equiv A_j\{\overrightarrow{p} := \overrightarrow{p'}\},$$
$$i \in \{1, \ldots, n\}, \ j \in \{0, \ldots, n\} \qquad (25b)$$

(3) re-ordering of the assignments within the recursion terms

$$\text{for every permutation } \pi : \{1, \ldots, n\} \xrightarrow[\text{onto}]{1-\text{to}-1} \{1, \ldots, n\}$$
$$A_0 \text{ where } \{\, p_1 := A_1, \ldots, p_n := A_n \,\} \qquad (26)$$
$$\equiv_c A_0 \text{ where } \{\, p_{\pi(1)} := A_{\pi(1)}, \ldots, p_{\pi(n)} := A_{\pi(n)} \,\}$$

3.2   Reduction Rules of Extended L^{λ}_{ar}

In this section, we define the set RedR of the reduction rules of TTA, which are the same for its variants of full and acyclic recursion L^{λ}_r and L^{λ}_{ar}, respectively.

Congruence	If $A \equiv_c B$, then $A \Rightarrow B$	(cong)
Transitivity	If $A \Rightarrow B$ and $B \Rightarrow C$, then $A \Rightarrow C$	(trans)

Compositionality Replacement of sub-terms with correspondingly reduced ones respects the term structure by the definition of the term syntax:

$$\text{If } A \Rightarrow A' \text{ and } B \Rightarrow B', \text{ then } A(B) \Rightarrow A'(B') \qquad \text{(ap-comp)}$$

$$\text{If } A \Rightarrow B, \text{ and } \xi \in \{\lambda, \exists, \forall\}, \text{ then } \xi(u)(A) \Rightarrow \xi(u)(B) \qquad \text{(lq-comp)}$$

If $A_i \Rightarrow B_i$, for $i = 0, \ldots, n$, then

$$A_0 \text{ where } \{p_1 := A_1, \ldots, p_n := A_n\} \qquad \text{(rec-comp)}$$
$$\Rightarrow B_0 \text{ where } \{p_1 := B_1, \ldots, p_n := B_n\}$$

Head Rule Given that, for all $i = 1, \ldots, n$, $j = 1, \ldots, m$, $p_i \neq q_j$ and p_i does not occur freely in B_j:

$$\left(A_0 \text{ where } \{\overrightarrow{p} := \overrightarrow{A}\}\right) \text{ where } \{\overrightarrow{q} := \overrightarrow{B}\}$$
$$\Rightarrow A_0 \text{ where } \{\overrightarrow{p} := \overrightarrow{A}, \; \overrightarrow{q} := \overrightarrow{B}\} \qquad \text{(head)}$$

Bekič-Scott Rule Given that, for all $i = 1, \ldots, n$, $j = 1, \ldots, m$, $p_i \neq q_j$ and q_j does not occur freely in A_i

$$A_0 \text{ where } \{p := (B_0 \text{ where } \{\overrightarrow{q} := \overrightarrow{B}\}), \overrightarrow{p} := \overrightarrow{A}\} \qquad \text{(B-S)}$$
$$\Rightarrow A_0 \text{ where } \{p := B_0, \overrightarrow{q} := \overrightarrow{B}, \overrightarrow{p} := \overrightarrow{A}\}$$

Recursion-Application Rule Given that, for all $i = 1, \ldots, n$, p_i does not occur freely in B

$$\left(A_0 \text{ where } \{\overrightarrow{p} := \overrightarrow{A}\}\right)(B) \Rightarrow A_0(B) \text{ where } \{\overrightarrow{p} := \overrightarrow{A}\} \qquad \text{(recap)}$$

Application Rule Given that $B \in$ Terms is proper and $b \in$ RecV is fresh, i.e., $b \in \left[\text{RecV} - (\text{FreeV}(A(B)) \cup \text{BoundV}(A(B)))\right]$,

$$A(B) \Rightarrow A(b) \text{ where } \{b := B\} \qquad \text{(ab)}$$

λ and Quantifier Rules Let $\xi \in \{\lambda, \exists, \forall\}$

$$\xi(u)\,(A_0 \text{ where } \{p_1 := A_1, \ldots, p_n := A_n\})$$
$$\Rightarrow \xi(u)\,A'_0 \text{ where } \{p'_1 := \lambda(u)\,A'_1, \ldots, p'_n := \lambda(u)\,A'_n\} \qquad (\xi)$$

given that, for every $i = 1, \ldots, n$ $(n \geq 0)$, $p'_i \in$ RecV is a fresh recursion (memory) variable, and A'_i $(0 \leq i \leq n)$ is the result of the replacement of all the free occurrences of $p_1, \ldots, p_n$ in A_i with $p'_1(u), \ldots, p'_n(u)$, respectively, i.e.:

$$A'_i \equiv A_i\{p_1 :\equiv p'_1(u), \ldots, p_n :\equiv p'_n(u)\} \equiv A_i\{\overrightarrow{p} :\equiv \overrightarrow{p'(u)}\} \; (0 \leq i \leq n) \quad (29)$$

γ^*-Rule

$$A \equiv_c A_0 \text{ where } \{ \overrightarrow{a} := \overrightarrow{A}, p := \lambda(\overrightarrow{u})\lambda(v)P, \overrightarrow{b} := \overrightarrow{B} \} \tag{30a}$$

$$\Rightarrow_{\gamma^*} A_0' \text{ where } \{ \overrightarrow{a} := \overrightarrow{A}', p' := \lambda(\overrightarrow{u})P, \overrightarrow{b} := \overrightarrow{B}' \} \tag{γ^*}$$

$$\equiv A_0\{ p(\overrightarrow{u})(v) :\equiv p'(\overrightarrow{u}) \} \text{ where } \{$$
$$\overrightarrow{a} := \overrightarrow{A}\{ p(\overrightarrow{u})(v) :\equiv p'(\overrightarrow{u}) \},$$
$$p' := \lambda(\overrightarrow{u})P, \tag{30b}$$
$$\overrightarrow{b} := \overrightarrow{B}\{ p(\overrightarrow{u})(v) :\equiv p'(\overrightarrow{u}) \} \}$$

given that:

- the term $A \in$ Terms satisfies the γ^*-condition (given in Definition 9) for the assignment $p := \lambda(\overrightarrow{u})\lambda(v)P : (\overrightarrow{\vartheta} \rightarrow (\vartheta \rightarrow \tau))$
- $p' \in \mathsf{RecV}_{(\overrightarrow{\vartheta} \rightarrow \tau)}$ is a fresh recursion variable
- for each part X_i of $\overrightarrow{X}$ in (γ^*) and (30b) (i.e., for each $X_i \equiv A_i$ in $\overrightarrow{X} \equiv \overrightarrow{A}$, and each $X_i \equiv B_i$ in $\overrightarrow{X} \equiv \overrightarrow{B}$), X_i' is the result of the free replacements $X_i' \equiv X_i\{ p(\overrightarrow{u})(v) :\equiv p'(\overrightarrow{u}) \}$ of all occurrences of $p(\overrightarrow{u})(v)$ by $p'(\overrightarrow{u})$ (in the free occurrences of p), modulo renaming the variables $\overrightarrow{u}, v$, for $i \in \{0, \dots, n_X\}$, i.e.:

$$\overrightarrow{X'} \equiv \overrightarrow{X}\{ p(\overrightarrow{u})(v) :\equiv p'(\overrightarrow{u}) \} \tag{31}$$

Definition 9 (γ^*-Condition). *Assume that $i = 1, \dots, n$ ($n \geq 0$), $\tau, \vartheta, \vartheta_i \in$ Types, $u, u_i \in$ PureV, $p \in$ RecV, $P \in$ Terms, are such that $u : \vartheta$, $u_i : \vartheta_i$, $p : (\overrightarrow{\vartheta} \rightarrow (\vartheta \rightarrow \tau))$, $P : \tau$, and thus, $\lambda(\overrightarrow{u \vartheta})\lambda(v^\vartheta)(P^\tau) : (\overrightarrow{\vartheta} \rightarrow (\vartheta \rightarrow \tau))$.*

A recursion term $A \in$ Terms satisfies the γ^*-condition for an assignment $p := \lambda(\overrightarrow{u^\vartheta})\lambda(v^\vartheta)(P^\tau) : (\overrightarrow{\vartheta} \rightarrow (\vartheta \rightarrow \tau))$, with respect to $\lambda(v)$, if and only if A is of the form (32)

$$A \equiv A_0 \text{ where } \{ \overrightarrow{a} := \overrightarrow{A}, p := \lambda(\overrightarrow{u})\lambda(v)P, \overrightarrow{b} := \overrightarrow{B} \} \tag{32}$$

with the sub-terms of appropriate types, such that the following holds:

(1) $P \in$ Terms$_\tau$ does not have any free occurrences of v, i.e., $v \notin$ FreeVars(P)

(2) All occurrences of p in A_0, $\overrightarrow{A}$, and $\overrightarrow{B}$ are free with respect to p (by renaming bound occurrences of recursion variables) and are occurrences in sub-terms $p(\overrightarrow{u})(v)$, which are in binding scope of $\xi_1(u_1), \dots, \xi_n(u_n), \xi(v)$, for $\xi_i, \xi \in \{ \lambda, \exists, \forall \}$, modulo renaming the bound variables $\overrightarrow{u}, v$, $i = 1, \dots, n$ ($n \geq 0$)

Note: If we take away the second part of (2), which requires $p(\overrightarrow{u})(v)$ to be within the binding scopes of $\overrightarrow{\xi(u)}$, $\xi(v)$, the (γ^*) rule may remove free occurrences of pure variables, e.g., v in $p(\overrightarrow{u})(v)$, from some of the parts of the terms. This (strong) form of the γ^*-condition is introduced in [7].

When a recursion term A of the form (32) satisfies the γ^*-condition, given in Definition 9, we also say that *the assignment* $p := \lambda(\overrightarrow{u})\lambda(v)P$ *satisfies the* γ^*-*condition, for any term* A' *such that* $A' \equiv_c A$, *i.e., modulo congruence.*

Definition 10 (γ^*-Rules). *We shall call the set* RedR *of the reduction rules* (cong)–(ξ), (γ^*), γ^*-*reduction rules and also, simply* L_{ar}^{λ}-*reduction rules.*

3.3   Reduction Relation

The extended set of reduction rules of L_{ar}^{λ}, (cong)–(ξ), (γ^*), given in Sect. 3.2, defines the extended reduction relation $\Rightarrow_{\gamma^*}^*$ between L_{ar}^{λ}-terms, $A \Rightarrow_{\gamma^*}^* B$, by the alternatively expressed, equivalent Definition 11 and Definition 12.

Definition 11. *The* γ^*-*reduction relation* $\Rightarrow_{\gamma^*}^*$ *between terms is the smallest relation* $\Rightarrow_{\gamma^*}^* \subseteq$ Terms $\times$ Terms, *which is the reflexive and transitive closure of the immediate reductions by any of the reduction rules* (cong)–(ξ), (γ^*).

Definition 12 (γ^*-Reduction). *For all* $A, B \in$ Terms, $A \Rightarrow_{\gamma^*}^* B$ *iff there is a sequence of consecutive, immediate reductions by* (cong)–(γ^*), *i.e.:*

$$A \Rightarrow_{\gamma^*}^* B \iff \text{ there exist } A_i \in \text{Terms}, 0 \leq i < n, \text{ such that:}$$

$$A \equiv A_0, \ A_n \equiv B, \text{ and} \tag{33}$$

$$A_i \Rightarrow A_{i+1}, \text{ for some of the rules (cong)} - (\gamma^*)$$

$$\iff (\text{abbreviated}) \ A \equiv A_0 \Rightarrow \ldots \Rightarrow A_n \equiv B \ (n \geq 0) \tag{34}$$

Often, we shall write $A \Rightarrow B$ instead of $A \Rightarrow_{\gamma^*}^* B$, including when applying none or more than one rule.

Lemma 1 (γ^*-Reducing Multiple, Innessential λ-Abstractions in an Assignment). *Assume that* $A \in$ Terms *is of the form* (35a)–(35b):

$$A \equiv A_0 \text{ where } \{ \ \overrightarrow{a} := \overrightarrow{A}, \ b := \lambda(\overrightarrow{u_1})\lambda(v_1)\ldots\lambda(\overrightarrow{u_k})\lambda(v_k)\lambda(\overrightarrow{u_{k+1}})B, \tag{35a}$$

$$\overrightarrow{c} := \overrightarrow{C} \ \} \tag{35b}$$

such that A *satisfies the* γ^*-*condition in Definition 9 for the assignment for* b *in* (35a), *with respect to all* λ-*abstractions* $\lambda(v_j)$, *for* $1 \leq j \leq k$, $k \in \mathbb{N}$, $k \geq 1$.
   Then, the following reductions (36a)–(36b) *can be done:*

$$A \Rightarrow_{\gamma^*}^* A_0^k \text{ where } \{ \ \overrightarrow{a} := \overrightarrow{A^k}, \ b^k := \lambda(\overrightarrow{u_1})\ldots\lambda(\overrightarrow{u_k})\lambda(\overrightarrow{u_{k+1}})B, \tag{36a}$$

$$\overrightarrow{c} := \overrightarrow{C^k} \ \} \tag{36b}$$

where for each part X_i *of* $\overrightarrow{X}$ *in* (35a)–(35b) *(i.e., for* $X_i \equiv A_i$ *in* $\overrightarrow{X} \equiv \overrightarrow{A}$ *or* $X_i \equiv C_i$ *in* $\overrightarrow{X} \equiv \overrightarrow{C}$*)* X_i^k *in* $\overrightarrow{X^k}$ *is the result of the replacements* (37a)–(37b), *modulo renaming the bound variables* $\overrightarrow{u_l}, v_j$, *for* $i \in \{0, \ldots, n_X\}$:

$$X_i^k \equiv X_i\{ \ b(\overrightarrow{u_1})(v_1)\ldots(\overrightarrow{u_k})(v_k)(\overrightarrow{u_{k+1}}) := b^k(\overrightarrow{u_1})\ldots(\overrightarrow{u_k})(\overrightarrow{u_{k+1}}) \}$$
$$\text{for } i \in \{0, \ldots, n_X\} \tag{37a}$$

$$\overrightarrow{X^k} \equiv \overrightarrow{X^k}\{ \ b(\overrightarrow{u_1})(v_1)\ldots(\overrightarrow{u_k})(v_k)(\overrightarrow{u_{k+1}}) := b^k(\overrightarrow{u_1})\ldots(\overrightarrow{u_k})(\overrightarrow{u_{k+1}}) \} \tag{37b}$$

Proof. The proof is by induction on $k \in \mathbb{N}$, for L_{ar}^{λ} extended by (ξ) and (γ^*) rules, for $\xi \in \{\lambda, \exists, \forall\}$. We do not provide it here, because it is long. For such a lemma about the L_{ar}^{λ}, without logic operators and pure quantifiers, see [4,7]. $\square$

Lemma 2 (γ^*-Reduction of the Assignments of a Recursion Term).
For every recursion term $P \equiv P_0$ where $\{ \overrightarrow{p} := \overrightarrow{P} \}$, (38a), there is a term Q of the form in (38b), such that Q does not satisfy the γ^*-condition in Definition 9, for any of its assignments $q_i := Q_i$ ($i = 1, \ldots, n$) in (38b), and $P \Rightarrow_{\gamma^*}^* Q$, abbreviated by $P \Rightarrow Q$.

$$P \equiv P_0 \text{ where } \{ p_1 := P_1, \ldots, p_n := P_n \} \equiv P_0 \text{ where } \{ \overrightarrow{p} := \overrightarrow{P} \} \quad (38a)$$

$$\Rightarrow_{\gamma^*}^* Q \equiv Q_0 \text{ where } \{ q_1 := Q_1, \ldots, q_n := Q_n \} \equiv Q_0 \text{ where } \{ \overrightarrow{q} := \overrightarrow{Q} \} \quad (38b)$$

Proof. See [4] extended by (ξ) and (γ^*) rules, for $\xi \in \{\lambda, \exists, \forall\}$. $\square$

Definition 13 (γ^*-Irreducible Terms). *We say that a term $A \in$ Terms is γ^*-irreducible if and only if (39) holds:*

$$\text{for all } B \in \text{Terms}, \quad A \Rightarrow_{\gamma^*}^* B \implies A \equiv_c B \quad (39)$$

3.4   Canonical Forms and γ^*-Reduction

Theorem 1 (γ^*-Canonical Form: Existence and Uniqueness of Canonical Forms). *See [6–8, 18]. For every term $A \in$ Terms, the following hold:*

(1) *(Existence of a γ^*-canonical form of A) There exist explicit, γ^*-irreducible $A_0, \ldots, A_n \in$ Terms ($n \geq 0$), such that the term $cf_{\gamma^*}(A)$ that is of the form (40) is γ^*-irreducible, i.e., irreducible and does not satisfy the γ-condition:*

$$cf_{\gamma^*}(A) \equiv A_0 \text{ where } \{ p_1 := A_1, \ldots, p_n := A_n \} \quad (40)$$

Thus, $cf_{\gamma^*}(A)$ is γ^*-irreducible.

(2) *A and $cf_{\gamma^*}(A)$ have the same constants and free variables:*

$$\text{Consts}(A) = \text{Consts}(cf_{\gamma^*}(A)) \quad (41a)$$
$$\text{FreeV}(A) = \text{FreeV}(cf_{\gamma^*}(A)) \quad (41b)$$

(3) *$A \Rightarrow_{\gamma^*}^* cf_{\gamma^*}(A)$*
(4) *If A is γ^*-irreducible, then $A \equiv_c cf_{\gamma^*}(A)$*
(5) *If $A \Rightarrow_{\gamma^*}^* B$, then $cf_{\gamma^*}(A) \equiv_c cf_{\gamma^*}(B)$*
(6) *(Uniqueness of $cf_{\gamma^*}(A)$ with respect to congruence) For every $B \in$ Terms, such that $A \Rightarrow_{\gamma^*}^* B$ and B is γ^*-irreducible, it holds that $B \equiv_c cf_{\gamma^*}(A)$, i.e., $cf_{\gamma^*}(A)$ is unique, up to congruence. We write:*

$$A \Rightarrow_{cf_{\gamma^*}} B \iff B \equiv_c cf_{\gamma}(A) \quad (42)$$

Proof. The proof is by induction on term structure of A, in Definition 1, i.e., (3a)–(3g), using reduction rules, and properties of the extended γ^*-reduction relation.

Note: the reduction rules don't remove or add any constants and free variables. $\square$

Algorithmic Semantics. The *algorithmic meaning* of a proper $A \in$ Terms, i.e., a non-immediate, algorithmically meaningful term, is designated by $\mathsf{alg}(A)$ and is determined by its canonical form $\mathsf{cf}(A)$.

Informally, for each proper $A \in$ Terms, the *algorithm* $\mathsf{alg}(A)$ for computing its denotation $\mathsf{den}(A)$ consists of computations provided by the basic parts A_i of its canonical form $\mathsf{cf}(A) \equiv A_0$ where $\{p_1 := A_1, \ldots, p_n := A_n\}$, according to their structural rank, by recursive iteration.

For every $A \in$ Terms, $\mathsf{cf}(A)$, i.e., $\mathsf{cf}_{\gamma^*}(A)$, is obtained from A by the reduction calculus of $\mathrm{L}_{\mathrm{ar}}^{\lambda}$, introduced in Sect. 3.2.

Definition 14 (Algorithmic Equivalence). *Assume a given semantic structure* $\mathfrak{A}$. *For all* $A, B \in$ Terms, A *and* B *are* γ^*-*algorithmically equivalent (i.e., synonymous) in* $\mathfrak{A}$, $A \approx_{\gamma^*} B$ *iff*

- *A and B are both immediate, or*
- *A and B are both proper*

and, in each of these cases, there are explicit, γ^*-*irreducible terms (of appropriate types),* $A_0, \ldots, A_n, B_0, \ldots, B_n, n \geq 0$, *such that:*

(1) $A \Rightarrow_{\gamma^*}^* A_0$ *where* $\{ p_1 := A_1, \ldots, p_n := A_n \} \equiv \mathsf{cf}_{\gamma^*}(A)$
(2) $B \Rightarrow_{\gamma^*}^* B_0$ *where* $\{ q_1 := B_1, \ldots, q_n := B_n \} \equiv \mathsf{cf}_{\gamma^*}(B)$
(3) for all $i \in \{0, \ldots, n\}$:

$$\mathsf{den}^{\mathfrak{A}}(A_i)(g) = \mathsf{den}^{\mathfrak{A}}(B_i)(g), \text{ for every variable valuation } g \in G \qquad (43a)$$
$$\mathsf{den}^{\mathfrak{A}}(A_i) = \mathsf{den}^{\mathfrak{A}}(B_i) \qquad (43b)$$

When $A \approx_{\gamma^*} B$, we say that A and B are algorithmically γ^*-equivalent, alternatively, that A and B are γ^*-synonymous. Sometimes, we skip the label γ^*.

4 Algorithmic Expressiveness of $\mathrm{L}_{\mathrm{ar}}^{\lambda}$

Moschovakis [18], via Theorem §3.24, proves that $\mathrm{L}_{\mathrm{ar}}^{\lambda}$ is a proper extension of Gallin TY_2, see Gallin [1]. Gallin [1], via his Theorem 8.2, can provide an interpretation of Montague IL [14] into TY_2. Suitable interpretation can be given in $\mathrm{L}_{\mathrm{ar}}^{\lambda}$ (L_r^{λ}), too. That is not our purpose in this paper.

Theorem 2, has the same formulation as Theorem §3.24 in [18]. The difference is that Theorem 2 covers the extended $\mathrm{L}_{\mathrm{ar}}^{\lambda}$ and its $\Rightarrow_{\gamma^*}^*$ reduction.

Theorem 2 (Conditions for Explicit and Non-Explicit Terms). *See Theorem §3.24, Moschovakis [18].*

(1) Necessary Condition for Explicit Terms: *For any explicit* $A \in$ Terms, *there is no memory (recursion) location that occurs in more than one part* A_i *($0 \leq i \leq n$) of* $\mathsf{cf}_{\gamma^*}(A)$

(2) Sufficient Condition for Non-Explicit Terms: *Assume that $A \in$ Terms is such that a location $p \in$ RecV occurs in (at least) two parts of* cf(A)*, and respectively, of* cf$_{\gamma^*}(A)$*, and the denotations of those parts depend essentially on p:*

$$A \Rightarrow_{\gamma^*}^* \mathsf{cf}_{\gamma^*}(A) \equiv A_0 \text{ where } \{ p_1 := A_1, \ldots, p_n := A_n \} \tag{44a}$$

$$p \in \mathsf{FreeV}(A_k), \quad p \in \mathsf{FreeV}(A_l) \ (k \neq l) \tag{44b}$$

$$\mathsf{den}(A_k)(g\{p :\equiv r\}) \neq \mathsf{den}(A_k)(g\{p :\equiv r'\}), \text{ for some } r, r' \in \mathbb{T}_\sigma \tag{44c}$$

$$\mathsf{den}(A_l)(g\{p :\equiv r\}) \neq \mathsf{den}(A_l)(g\{p :\equiv r'\}), \text{ for some } r, r' \in \mathbb{T}_\sigma \tag{44d}$$

Then, there is no explicit term to which A is algorithmically equivalent.

The proof of Theorem §3.24, Moschovakis [18] is extended for the logic operators, pure quantifiers and the γ^*-reduction. □

The extended, algorithmic expressiveness of $\mathrm{L}_{\mathrm{ar}}^\lambda$ is demonstrated by the terms in the following examples, which provide specific instantiations of algorithmic patterns of large classes and subtle semantic distinctions.

Logic Quantifiers and Reductions with Quantifier Rules: Assume that $\mathrm{L}_{\mathrm{ar}}^\lambda$ has $cube, large_0 \in \mathsf{Consts}_{(\tilde{e}\to\tilde{t})}$, and $large \in \mathsf{Consts}_{((\tilde{e}\to\tilde{t})\to(\tilde{e}\to\tilde{t}))}$ as a modifier.

$$\text{Some cube is large} \xrightarrow{\text{render}} B \equiv \exists x (cube(x) \wedge large_0(x)) \tag{45a}$$

$$B \Rightarrow \exists x ((c \wedge l) \text{ where } \{ c := cube(x), \ l := large_0(x) \}) \tag{45b}$$

$$2\mathrm{x(ab) \ to \ } \wedge; (\text{lq-comp})$$

$$\Rightarrow \underbrace{\exists x (c'(x) \wedge l'(x))}_{B_0 \text{ algorithmic pattern}} \text{ where } \{ \tag{45c}$$

$$\underbrace{c' := \lambda(x)(cube(x)), \ l' := \lambda(x)(large_0(x))}_{\text{instantiations of memory slots } c', l'} \} \tag{45d}$$

$$\equiv \mathsf{cf}(B) \quad \text{from (45b), by } (\xi) \text{ to } \exists$$

$$\approx \underbrace{\exists x (c'(x) \wedge l'(x))}_{B_0 \text{ algorithmic pattern}} \text{ where } \{ \quad \underbrace{c' := cube, \ l' := large_0}_{\text{instantiations of memory slots } c', l'} \quad \} \equiv B' \tag{45e}$$

$$\text{by Definition 14 from (45c)} - \text{(45d)}, \mathsf{den}(\lambda(x)(cube(x))) = \mathsf{den}(cube), \\ \mathsf{den}(\lambda(x)(large_0(x))) = \mathsf{den}(large_0) \tag{45f}$$

Repeated Calculations:

Some cube is large $\xrightarrow{\text{render}} T$, $\quad large \in \mathsf{Consts}_{((\tilde{e}\to\tilde{t})\to(\tilde{e}\to\tilde{t}))}$ (46a)

$T \equiv \exists x \big[cube(x) \wedge \underbrace{large(cube)(x)} \big] \Rightarrow \dots$ (46b)

$\qquad\qquad\qquad\qquad$ by predicate modification

$\Rightarrow \exists x \big[(c_1 \wedge l) \text{ where } \{ c_1 := cube(x),\, l := large(c_2)(x),\, c_2 := cube \} \big]$ (46c)

$\qquad\qquad\qquad$ (ab) to $\wedge$; (lq-comp), (B-S)

$\Rightarrow \exists x \underbrace{(c_1'(x) \wedge l'(x))}_{T_0} \text{ where } \{ c_1' := \lambda(x)(cube(x)),$ (46d)

$\qquad l' := \lambda(x)(large(c_2'(x))(x)),\, c_2' := \lambda(x)cube \}$ (46e)

$\qquad\qquad$ (46d) $-$ (46e) is by (ξ) on (46c) for $\exists$

$\Rightarrow_{\gamma^*} \exists x(c_1'(x) \wedge l'(x)) \text{ where } \{ c_1' := \lambda(x)(cube(x)),$ (46f)

$\qquad l' := \lambda(x)(large(c_2)(x)),\, c_2 := cube \}$ (46g)

$\equiv \mathsf{cf}_{\gamma^*}(T) \qquad\qquad$ by (γ^*) rule to $c_2'(x)$ for $c_2' := \lambda(x)cube$

$\approx \exists x(c_1'(x) \wedge l'(x)) \text{ where } \{ c_1' := cube,$ (46h)

$\qquad l' := \lambda(x)(large(c_2)(x)),\, c_2 := cube \}$ (46i)

Proposition 1. *The L_{ar}^{λ}-terms $C \approx \mathsf{cf}(C)$ in (47a)–(47e), similarly to many other L_{ar}^{λ}-terms, are not algorithmically equivalent to any explicit term. Therefore, L_{ar}^{λ} (L_r^{λ}) is a strict, proper extension of Gallin TY_2.*

Proof. It follows from (47a)–(47e), by Theorem 2, (2), since c' occurs in two parts of $\mathsf{cf}(C)$ in (47e):

Some cube is large $\xrightarrow{\text{render}} C$ (47a)

$C \equiv \underbrace{\exists x \big[c'(x) \wedge large(c')(x) \big]}_{E_0} \text{ where } \{ c' := cube \}$ (47b)

$\Rightarrow \underbrace{\exists x \big[(c'(x) \wedge l) \text{ where } \{ l := large(c')(x) \} \big]}_{E_1} \text{ where } \{ c' := cube \}$ (47c)

$\qquad$ from (47b), by (ab) to $\wedge$ of E_0; (lq-comp) of $\exists$; (rec-comp)

$\Rightarrow \underbrace{\big[\exists x(c'(x) \wedge l'(x)) \text{ where } \{ l' := \lambda(x)(large(c')(x)) \} \big]}_{E_2} \text{ where } \{$ (47d)

$\qquad c' := cube \} \qquad\qquad$ from (47c), by (ξ) to $\exists$

$\Rightarrow \underbrace{\exists x(c'(x) \wedge l'(x))}_{C_0:\text{ an algorithmic pattern}} \text{ where } \{ \underbrace{c' := cube,\, l' := \lambda(x)(large(c')(x))}_{\text{instantiations of memory } c',l'} \}$ (47e)

$\equiv \mathsf{cf}(C) \quad$ from (47d), by (head); (cong) of reordering assignments

5   Expressiveness of L_{ar}^λ for Coordination in Natural Language Phrases

5.1   Coordinated Predication Versus Sentential Conjunction

In this paper, we have extended the algorithmic expressiveness of L_{ar}^λ.

We demonstrate it by comparing natural language sentences and their renderings into L_{ar}^λ recursion terms, which express their algorithmic meanings, e.g., (49c)–(49d) and (50j)–(50k). The canonical forms $\mathsf{cf}(A)$ in (49c)–(49d) and (50j)–(50k) are denotationally and algorithmically equivalent to the λ-calculus term A in (49b) and (50a).

In addition, there are L_{ar}^λ recursion terms that are not algorithmically equivalent to any λ-calculi terms, see (A)–(C), Proposition 2, and also Sect. 6.

Coordinated Predication: a class of sentences with coordinated VPs

$$[\Phi_j]_{\mathrm{NP}}\,\big[[\Theta_L \text{ and } \Psi_H]\,[W_w]_{\mathrm{NP}}\big]_{\mathrm{VP}} \xrightarrow{\text{render}} A_0 \tag{48a}$$

$$A_0 \equiv \underbrace{\lambda x_j\big[\lambda y_w\,(L(x_j)(y_w) \wedge H(x_j)(y_w))(w)\big](j)}_{\text{algorithmic pattern with memory parameters } L,H,w,j} \tag{48b}$$

Specific Instantiations of Parametric Algorithms, e.g., (48a)–(48b) and (49c), by (49d):

$$[\text{John}]_j \text{ loves and honors } [\text{his}]_j \text{ wife.} \xrightarrow{\text{render}} A \tag{49a}$$

$$A \equiv \lambda x_j\big[\lambda y_w\,(loves(y_w)(x_j) \wedge honors(y_w)(x_j))(wife(x_j))\big](john) \tag{49b}$$

$$\Rightarrow \dots \Rightarrow \mathsf{cf}(A) \equiv \underbrace{\lambda x_j\big[\lambda y_w\,(L''(x_j)(y_w) \wedge H''(x_j)(y_w))(w'(x_j))\big](j)}_{\text{algorithmic pattern with memory parameters } L'',H'',w',j} \tag{49c}$$

$$\begin{aligned} \text{where } \{\, & L'' := \lambda x_j \lambda y_w\, loves(y_w)(x_j), \\ & H'' := \lambda x_j \lambda y_w\, honors(y_w)(x_j), \\ & \underbrace{w' := \lambda x_j\, wife(x_j),\ j := john}_{\text{instantiations of memory } L'',H'',w',j} \,\} \end{aligned} \tag{49d}$$

The predication by the sentence (49a) is expressed denotationally by the rendering term A in (49b). The algorithm for computing its denotation $\mathsf{den}(A)$ in L_{ar}^λ, is determined by its canonical form $\mathsf{cf}(A)$ (49c)–(49d).

Reduction of Coordinated Relation to Canonical Form. A reduction of the predication term A in (49b) to its canonical form $\mathsf{cf}(A)$ (49c)–(49d) is provided by (50a)–(50j):

$$A \equiv \lambda x_j \Big[\lambda y_w \big[love(y_w)(x_j) \wedge honors(y_w)(x_j)\big](wife(x_j))\Big](john) \tag{50a}$$

$$\Rightarrow \lambda x_j \Big[\lambda y_w \big[(L \wedge H) \text{ where } \{\, L := love(y_w)(x_j),$$
$$H := honors(y_w)(x_j)\,\}\big](wife(x_j))\Big](john) \tag{50b}$$

(50b) is by: 2x(ab) to $\wedge$, 2x(lq-comp), (ap-comp), from (50a)

$$\Rightarrow \lambda x_j \Big[\big[\lambda y_w\,(L'(y_w) \wedge H'(y_w))\text{ where }\{\, L' := \lambda y_w\, love(y_w)(x_j),$$
$$H' := \lambda y_w\, honors(y_w)(x_j)\,\}\big](wife(x_j))\Big](john) \tag{50c}$$

(50c) is by (ξ) for λy_w, (ap-comp), (lq-comp), (ap-comp), from (50b)

$$\Rightarrow \lambda x_j \Big[\big[\lambda y_w\,(L'(y_w) \wedge H'(y_w))\big](wife(x_j))\big]$$
$$\text{where } \{\, L' := \lambda y_w\, love(y_w)(x_j), \tag{50d}$$
$$H' := \lambda y_w\, honors(y_w)(x_j)\,\}\big](john)$$

(50d) is by (recap), (lq-comp), (ap-comp), from (50c)

$$\Rightarrow \lambda x_j \Big[\big[\lambda y_w\,(L'(y_w) \wedge H'(y_w))\big](w)\text{ where }\{\, w := wife(x_j)\,\}\big]$$
$$\text{where } \{\, L' := \lambda y_w\, love(y_w)(x_j), \tag{50e}$$
$$H' := \lambda y_w\, honors(y_w)(x_j)\,\}\big](john)$$

(50e) is by (ab), (rec-comp), (lq-comp), (ap-comp), from (50d)

$$\rightsquigarrow \lambda x_j \big[[\lambda y_w\,(L'(y_w) \wedge H'(y_w))](w)\big]$$
$$\text{where } \{\, L' := \lambda y_w\, love(y_w)(x_j),$$
$$H' := \lambda y_w\, honors(y_w)(x_j), \tag{50f}$$
$$w := wife(x_j)\,\}\big](john)$$

(50f) is by (head), (cong), (lq-comp), (ap-comp), from (50e)

$$\Rightarrow \Big[\lambda x_j[\lambda y_w\,(L''(x_j)(y_w) \wedge H''(x_j)(y_w))(w'(x_j))]$$
$$\text{where } \{\, L'' := \lambda x_j \lambda y_w\, love(y_w)(x_j),$$
$$H'' := \lambda x_j \lambda y_w\, honors(y_w)(x_j), \tag{50g}$$
$$w' := \lambda x_j\, wife(x_j)\,\}\big](john)$$

(50g) is by (ξ) to λx_j, (ap-comp) from (50f)

$$\Rightarrow \Big[[\lambda x_j[\lambda y_w\,(L''(x_j)(y_w) \wedge H''(x_j)(y_w))(w'(x_j))]]\big](john)$$
$$\text{where } \{\, L'' := \lambda x_j \lambda y_w\, love(y_w)(x_j),$$
$$H'' := \lambda x_j \lambda y_w\, honors(y_w)(x_j), \tag{50h}$$
$$w' := \lambda x_j\, wife(x_j)\,\}\Big]$$

(50h) is by (recap), from (50g)

$$\Rightarrow \Big[[[\lambda x_j [\lambda y_w \, (L''(x_j)(y_w) \wedge H''(x_j)(y_w))(w'(x_j))]](j)$$

$$\text{where } \{\, j := john \,\}\Big]$$

$$\text{where } \{\, L'' := \lambda x_j \lambda y_w \, love(y_w)(x_j), \tag{50i}$$

$$H'' := \lambda x_j \lambda y_w \, honors(y_w)(x_j),$$

$$w' := \lambda x_j \, wife(x_j) \,\}\Big]$$

(50i) is by (ab), (rec-comp), from (50h)

$$\Rightarrow \big[\lambda x_j [\lambda y_w \, (L''(x_j)(y_w) \wedge H''(x_j)(y_w))(w'(x_j))](j) \text{ where } \{$$

$$L'' := \lambda x_j \lambda y_w \, love(y_w)(x_j), \tag{50j}$$

$$H'' := \lambda x_j \lambda y_w \, honors(y_w)(x_j), \; w' := \lambda x_j \, wife(x_j), \; j := john \,\}\big]$$

(50j) is by (head), (cong), from (50i)

$$\approx \big[\lambda x_j [\lambda y_w \, (L''(x_j)(y_w) \wedge H''(x_j)(y_w))(w'(x_j))](j) \text{ where } \{$$

$$L'' := \lambda x_j \lambda y_w \, love(y_w)(x_j), \tag{50k}$$

$$H'' := \lambda x_j \lambda y_w \, honors(y_w)(x_j), \; w' := wife, \; j := john \,\}\big]$$

(50k) is by Definition 14 and $\mathsf{den}(\lambda x_j \, wife(x_j)) = \mathsf{den}(wife)$, from (50j)

In contrast to (49a)–(49b), the propositional content of the sentence in (51a), which is a predicative conjunction, can be represented by the following recursion terms (51b)–(51c) of $\mathrm{L}^{\lambda}_{ar}$. The terms in (51b)–(51c) are algorithmically equivalent (synonymous), by the reduction calculus of $\mathrm{L}^{\lambda}_{ar}$, and their head parts are conjunction propositions, which is expressed by the sentence (51a) too:

$$[John]_j \text{ loves } [[his]_j \, wife]_w \text{ and } [he]_j \text{ honors } [her]_w \tag{51a}$$

$$\xrightarrow{\text{render}}_{\text{co-index}_{ar}} \big[love(w)(j) \wedge honors(w)(j) \big] \text{ where } \{$$

$$j := john, \; w := wife(j) \,\} \tag{51b}$$

$$\Rightarrow_{\mathsf{cf}_{\gamma^*}} \big[L \wedge H \big] \text{ where } \{ L := love(w)(j), \; H := honors(w)(j),$$

$$j := john, \; w := wife(j) \,\} \tag{51c}$$

Proposition 2. *(1) The terms in the reduction sequence (50a)–(50j) are all algorithmically equivalent with each other and with (50k)*

(2) The terms in (50a)–(50j), (50k) are not algorithmically equivalent with the ones in (51b)–(51c)

(3) The terms (51b)–(51c) are not algorithmically equivalent to any explicit $\mathrm{L}^{\lambda}_{ar}$, which are λ-calculus, i.e., Gallin TY_2 terms (see (A)–(C) on page 5)

(4) The terms (51b)–(51c) are not algorithmically equivalent to any λ-calculus terms that are interpreted IL terms into TY_2

Proof. (1)–(2) follow directly from Definition 14 and (43a)–(43b). (3)–(4) follow from Theorem 2, and also from Theorem §3.24 in [18]. This is because there is a recursion variable (i.e., two, j and w) occurring in more than one part of the γ^*-canonical form (51c). $\qquad\square$

6 Some Relations Between Let-Expressions and Recursion Terms

Scott [21] introduced the let-expressions by the LCF language of λ-calculus, which has been implemented by the functional programming languages, e.g., ML, see e.g., Milner [13], Scheme,[2] Haskell,[3] e.g., see Marlow [12], OCaml, etc. Classic imperative languages, e.g., ALGOL and Pascal, implement let-expressions for the scope of functions in their definitions.

A lambda calculus with a formal language that includes terms of let-binding is presented by Nishizaki [19]. A constant where is used in the formation of terms in Landin [2], which are similar to let-expressions.

The formal language of full recursion L_r^λ, see Definition 1, (3a)–(3d), without the acyclicity (AC), is an extension of the language LCF introduced by Plotkin [20]. The λ-calculus of LCF has been having a grounding significance in Computer Science, for the distinctions between denotational and operational semantics.

Details of possible similarities and differences between let-expressions in λ-calculus, and the recursion L_{ar}^λ terms of the form (3d) ($n \geq 1$), in Definition. 1, need carefull representation, which is not in the scope of the work.

In this section, we show that, in general, the recursion L_{ar}^λ terms diverge from the standard let-expressions, in the sense that the reduction calculi of L_{ar}^λ provide algorithmic meanings of the L_{ar}^λ terms via their canonical forms $\mathsf{cf}(A)$ and $\mathsf{cf}_{\gamma^*}(A)$, and the γ^*-Canonical Form Theorem 1.

The algorithmic semantics by L_{ar}^λ and L_r^λ is provided by the reduction system, which includes, very importantly, division of the variables into two kinds, proper and recursion, and also of terms as either immediate or proper. Recursion variables $p \in \mathsf{RecV}$ are for assignments in the scope of the where operator. They can not be used for λ-abstraction, which uses pure variables. To have a correspondence of a recursion term A, e.g. as in (53a), with a let-expression via a sequence of characteristic λ-abstractions, as in (52a), we can use one-to-one, bijective replacements with fresh pure variables, as in (54a).

The λ-terms of the form in (52a) are characteristic for the values of the corresponding let-expressions, and can be used as a defining representation of let-expressions:

$$\text{let } x_1 = D_1, \ldots, x_n = D_n \text{ in } D_0 \equiv \lambda(x_1)\big(\ldots[\lambda(x_n)(D_0)](D_n)\ldots\big)(D_1) \quad (52a)$$

$$\text{if } x_j \in \mathsf{FreeV}(D_i), \text{ then } j < i, \text{ i.e., } \mathsf{den}(D_i) \text{ may depend on } \mathsf{den}(x_j) \quad (52b)$$

Assume that $A \in \mathsf{Terms}$ is a L_{ar}^λ term of the form (53a), for some $A_j \in \mathsf{Terms}$, $j \in \{0, \ldots, n\}$, such that:

(1) A_j has no occurrences of recursion (memory) variables that are different from $p_i \in \mathsf{RecV}$, $i \in \{1, \ldots, n\}$

---

[2] https://www.scheme.com/tspl4/start.html#./start:h4,.
[3] https://www.haskell.org.

(2) rank is such that (53b) holds

$$A \equiv \mathsf{cf}_{\gamma^*}(A) \equiv A_0 \text{ where } \{p_1 := A_1, \ldots, p_n := A_n\} \tag{53a}$$
$$\mathsf{rank}(p_i) = i, \text{ for } i \in \{1, \ldots, n\} \tag{53b}$$

Note: It can be proved that, for each $\mathrm{L}_{\mathrm{ar}}^{\lambda}$ term (3d), Definition 1, there is at least one such rank, see [6]. For any i, j, such that $j < i$, it is not required that $p_j \in \mathsf{FreeV}(A_i)$, but this is possible, even for more than one i, see Theorem 2, sentences like (51a) and terms (51b)–(51c).

For the purpose of the demonstration in this section, we introduce specific let-expressions, by the abbreviations (54a)–(54b). We focus on the special case of $n = 1$, (56), in the rest of this section.

$$\mathsf{let} \ x_1 = D_1, \ldots, x_n = D_n \ \mathsf{in} \ D_0 \tag{54a}$$
$$\equiv \lambda(x_1)(\ldots [\lambda(x_n)(D_0)](D_n) \ldots)(D_1) \tag{54b}$$
$$x_i \in \mathsf{PureV}_{\tau_i}, x_i \notin \mathsf{Vars}(A), n \geq 1, \text{ for } i \in \{1, \ldots, n\}$$
$$D_j \equiv A_j\{p_1 := x_1, \ldots, p_n := x_n\}, \text{ for } j \in \{0, \ldots, n\}$$

In the special case of $n = 1$, with just one assignment::

$$A \equiv \mathsf{cf}_{\gamma^*}(A) \equiv A_0 \text{ where } \{p_1 := A_1\}, \quad p_1 \notin \mathsf{Vars}(A_1) \text{ for acyclicity} \tag{55}$$
$$\mathsf{let} \ x_1 = A_1 \ \mathsf{in} \ A_0\{p_1 := x_1\} \equiv \lambda(x_1)(A_0\{p_1 := x_1\})(A_1) \tag{56}$$

When replacing a memory variable $p \in \mathsf{RecV}$ with a pure variable $x \in \mathsf{PureV}$, in an explicit, irreducible term A, the result can be reducible term, by (ab). When an immediate term of the form $\lambda(\overrightarrow{u})p(\overrightarrow{v})$, for $(\mathsf{lgh}(\overrightarrow{u}) + \mathsf{lgh}(\overrightarrow{v})) \geq 1$, e.g., $p(u)$, $\lambda(v)p$, $\lambda(v)p(u)$, etc., occurs in an argument position of A. After replacement, $\lambda(\overrightarrow{u})x(\overrightarrow{v})$ is not an immediate term, by Definition 4.

Lemma 3. *Assume that $C \in$ Terms is explicit, irreducible, such that (1)–(2):*

(1) $p_1 \in \mathsf{RecV}_{\tau_1}$, $\overrightarrow{u}, \overrightarrow{v}, z \in \mathsf{PureV}$, such that $(\mathsf{lgh}(\overrightarrow{u}) + \mathsf{lgh}(\overrightarrow{v})) \geq 1$
(2) $p_1 \notin \mathsf{FreeV}(C)$

Let $A_0 \equiv \lambda(z)[C(\lambda(\overrightarrow{u})p_1(\overrightarrow{v}))]$. Let $x_1 \in \mathsf{PureV}_{\tau_1}$ and x_1 be fresh for A_0, i.e., $x_1 \notin \mathsf{Vars}(A_0)$. Then:

$$C(\lambda(\overrightarrow{u})p_1(\overrightarrow{v})) \text{ and } A_0 \equiv \lambda(z)[C(\lambda(\overrightarrow{u})p_1(\overrightarrow{v}))] \text{ are explicit, irreducible} \tag{57a}$$
$$[C(\lambda(\overrightarrow{u})p_1(\overrightarrow{v}))]\{p_1 := x_1\} \text{ and } A_0 \text{ are reducible} \tag{57b}$$

Proof. By (2), $C\{p_1 := x_1\} \equiv C$. The following reductions can be done:

$$[C(\lambda(\overrightarrow{u})p_1(\overrightarrow{v}))]\{p_1 := x_1\} \equiv C(\lambda(\overrightarrow{u})x_1(\overrightarrow{v})) \tag{58a}$$
$$\Rightarrow C(r_1) \text{ where } \{r_1 := \lambda(\overrightarrow{u})x_1(\overrightarrow{v})\} \qquad \text{by (ab) from (58a)} \tag{58b}$$

Then:

$$A_0\{p_1 :\equiv x_1\} \equiv \lambda(z)\big[C\big(\lambda(\overrightarrow{u})p_1(\overrightarrow{v})\big)\big]\{p_1 :\equiv x_1\}$$
$$\equiv \lambda(z)\big[C\big(\lambda(\overrightarrow{u})x_1(\overrightarrow{v})\big)\big] \tag{59a}$$

$$\Rightarrow \lambda(z)\big[C(r_1) \text{ where } \{\, r_1 := \lambda(\overrightarrow{u})x_1(\overrightarrow{v})\,\}\big] \qquad\qquad \text{by (ab), (lq-comp)} \tag{59b}$$

$$\Rightarrow \lambda(z)\big[C(r_1'(z))\big] \text{ where } \{\, r_1' := \lambda(z)\lambda(\overrightarrow{u})x_1(\overrightarrow{v})\,\} \equiv A_0' \ \text{ by } (\xi) \text{ for } \lambda(z) \tag{59c}$$

There are two cases:
  Case 1 $z \in \mathsf{FreeV}(\lambda(\overrightarrow{u})p_1(\overrightarrow{v}))$. Then $A_0\{p_1 :\equiv x_1\} \Rightarrow A_0' \equiv \mathsf{cf}_{\gamma^*}(A_0')$.
  Case 2 $z \notin \mathsf{FreeV}(\lambda(\overrightarrow{u})x_1(\overrightarrow{v}))$. Then:

$$A_0' \Rightarrow_{(\gamma^*)} \lambda(z)\big[C(r_1)\big] \text{ where } \{\, r_1 := \lambda(\overrightarrow{u})x_1(\overrightarrow{v})\,\} \equiv \mathsf{cf}_{\gamma^*}(A_0') \quad \text{by } (\gamma^*) \tag{60a}$$
$$A_0\{p_1 :\equiv x_1\} \Rightarrow A_0' \Rightarrow_{\gamma^*} \mathsf{cf}_{\gamma^*}(A_0') \tag{60b}$$

□

Lemma 4. *Assume that $A \in \mathsf{Terms}$ is as in* (61), *with the variables as in Lemma 3, Case 2, i.e., $p_1 \in \mathsf{RecV}_{\tau_1}$, $\overrightarrow{u}, \overrightarrow{v}, z \in \mathsf{PureV}$, for explicit, irreducible $C, A_1 \in \mathsf{Terms}$, such that A_1 is proper, and $p_1 \notin \mathsf{FreeV}(C)$ ($p_1 \notin \mathsf{FreeV}(A_1)$ by acyclicity), $x_1 \in \mathsf{PureV}_{\tau_1}$, $x_1 \notin \mathsf{Vars}(A)$, and $z \notin \mathsf{FreeV}(\lambda(\overrightarrow{u})x_1(\overrightarrow{v}))$:*

$$A \equiv \mathsf{cf}_{\gamma^*}(A) \equiv \underbrace{\lambda(z)\big[C\big(\lambda(\overrightarrow{u})p_1(\overrightarrow{v})\big)\big]}_{A_0} \text{ where } \{\, p_1 := A_1\,\} \tag{61}$$

Then, the conversion of the assignment in A into a λ-abstract over A_0, applied to A_1, results in a term, which is not algorithmically equivalent to A (similarly, for Case 1):

$$A \not\approx_{\gamma^*} A' \equiv \big[\lambda(x_1)\big(A_0\{p_1 :\equiv x_1\}\big)\big](A_1) \tag{62}$$

Proof.

$$A' \equiv \big[\lambda(x_1)\big(A_0\{p_1 :\equiv x_1\}\big)\big](A_1) \tag{63a}$$

$$\equiv \lambda(x_1)\Big[\underbrace{\big[\lambda(z)\big[C\big(\lambda(\overrightarrow{u})p_1(\overrightarrow{v})\big)\big]\big]}_{A_0}\{p_1 :\equiv x_1\}\Big](A_1) \tag{63b}$$

$$\Rightarrow \lambda(x_1)\Big[\lambda(z)\big[C(r_1)\big] \text{ where } \{\, r_1 := \lambda(\overrightarrow{u})x_1(\overrightarrow{v})\,\}\Big](A_1) \tag{63c}$$
$$\qquad \text{by (60a), (lq-comp), (ap-comp)}$$

$$\Rightarrow \Big[\lambda(x_1)\big[\lambda(z)\big[C(r_1^1(x_1))\big]\big] \text{where } \{\, r_1^1 := \lambda(x_1)\lambda(\overrightarrow{u})x_1(\overrightarrow{v})\,\}\Big](A_1) \tag{63d}$$
$$\qquad \text{by } (\xi) \text{ for } \lambda(x_1), \text{ (ap-comp)}$$

$$\Rightarrow \lambda(x_1)\big[\lambda(z)\big[C(r_1^1(x_1))\big]\big](A_1) \text{ where } \{\, r_1^1 := \lambda(x_1)\lambda(\overrightarrow{u})x_1(\overrightarrow{v})\,\} \tag{63e}$$
$$\qquad \text{by (recap)}$$

$$\Rightarrow \Big[\lambda(x_1)\big[\lambda(z)\big[C(r_1^1(x_1))\big]\big](p_1) \text{ where } \{\, p_1 := A_1\,\}\Big] \tag{63f}$$
$$\qquad\qquad \text{where } \{\, r_1^1 := \lambda(x_1)\lambda(\overrightarrow{u})x_1(\overrightarrow{v})\,\}$$

by (ab), (rec-comp)

$$\Rightarrow \lambda(x_1)[\lambda(z)[C(r_1^1(x_1))]](p_1) \text{ where}$$
$$\{p_1 := A_1, \ r_1^1 := \lambda(x_1)\lambda(\overrightarrow{u})x_1(\overrightarrow{v})\} \equiv \mathsf{cf}_{\gamma^*}(A') \qquad \text{by (head)} \quad (63g)$$

Thus, (62) holds: A and A' are not algorithmically equivalent, $A \not\approx_{\gamma^*} A'$, which follows, by Definition 14, from (61) and (63g). (Similarly, for *Case 1*.)   □

Proposition 3. *In general, the algorithmic equivalence does not hold between the L_{ar}^{λ} recursion terms of the form (53a) and the λ-calculus terms (54a)–(54b), which are characteristic for the corresponding let-expressions in λ-calculus.*

Proof. By Lemma 4, the special set of terms in it provide counterexamples to alleged algorithmic equality between all terms in (53a) and (54a)–(54b).   □

The let-expressions, represented by the specific, characteristic λ-terms (54a)–(54b) in L_{ar}^{λ}, are only denotationally equivalent to the corresponding recursion terms, but not algorithmically in the most significant cases. The full proofs are the subject of forthcoming papers.

7   Conclusion and Outlook for Future Work

In this paper, I have presented some of the major characteristics of L_{ar}^{λ}, by also developing it for enhancing its mathematical capacities for logic, theoretically, by targeting applications.

Algorithmic Semantics: The essential theoretic features of L_{ar}^{λ} provide algorithmic semantics of formal and natural languages. Computational semantics by L_{ar}^{λ} has the fundamental distinction between algorithmic and denotational semantics. The algorithms determined by terms in canonical forms compute their denotations, see Fig. 1.

While the theory has already been quite well developed, with eyes towards versatile applications, it is an open subject with many open and ongoing tasks and perspectives. The greater semantic distinctions of the formal language and calculi of L_{ar}^{λ} enhance type-theoretic semantics by traditional λ-calculi. I have demonstrated that, by being a strict extension of Gallin TY_2 [1], L_{ar}^{λ} exceeds also the facilities of Montague [14] IL, e.g., see Sect. 4, Propositions 1–2.

Algorithmic Patterns for Computational Semantics: Memory locations, i.e., recursion variables in L_{ar}^{λ} terms represent parameters that can be instantiated by corresponding canonical forms, depending on context, the specific areas of applications, and domain specific texts, e.g., as in (45c) and (47d); and (48a)–(48b), as in (50k).

Logical Constants and Quantifiers in L_{ar}^{λ}: Canonical forms can be used for reasoning and inferences of semantic information by automatic provers and proof assistants. This is a subject of future work.

References

1. Gallin, D.: Intensional and Higher-Order Modal Logic: With Applications to Montague Semantics. North-Holland Publishing Company, Amsterdam and Oxford, and American Elsevier Publishing Company (1975). https://doi.org/10.2307/2271880
2. Landin, P.J.: The mechanical evaluation of expressions. Comput. J. **6**(4), 308–320 (1964). https://doi.org/10.1093/comjnl/6.4.308
3. Loukanova, R.: Relationships between specified and underspecified quantification by the theory of acyclic recursion. ADCAIJ Adv. Distrib. Comput. Artif. Intell. J. **5**(4), 19–42 (2016). https://doi.org/10.14201/ADCAIJ2016541942
4. Loukanova, R.: Gamma-star reduction in the type-theory of acyclic algorithms. In: Rocha, A.P., van den Herik, J. (eds.) Proceedings of the 10th International Conference on Agents and Artificial Intelligence (ICAART 2018). vol. 2, pp. 231–242. INSTICC, SciTePress – Science and Technology Publications, Lda. (2018). https://doi.org/10.5220/0006662802310242
5. Loukanova, R.: Computational syntax-semantics interface with type-theory of acyclic recursion for underspecified semantics. In: Osswald, R., Retoré, C., Sutton, P. (eds.) IWCS 2019 Workshop on Computing Semantics with Types, Frames and Related Structures. Proceedings of the Workshop, Gothenburg, Sweden, pp. 37–48. The Association for Computational Linguistics (ACL) (2019). https://www.aclweb.org/anthology/W19-1005
6. Loukanova, R.: Gamma-reduction in type theory of acyclic recursion. Fund. Inform. **170**(4), 367–411 (2019). https://doi.org/10.3233/FI-2019-1867
7. Loukanova, R.: Gamma-star canonical forms in the type-theory of acyclic algorithms. In: van den Herik, J., Rocha, A.P. (eds.) ICAART 2018. LNCS (LNAI), vol. 11352, pp. 383–407. Springer, Cham (2019). https://doi.org/10.1007/978-3-030-05453-3_18
8. Loukanova, R.: Type-theory of acyclic algorithms for models of consecutive binding of functional neuro-receptors. In: Grabowski, A., Loukanova, R., Schwarzweller, C. (eds.) AI Aspects in Reasoning, Languages, and Computation. SCI, vol. 889, pp. 1–48. Springer, Cham (2020). https://doi.org/10.1007/978-3-030-41425-2_1
9. Loukanova, R.: Type-theory of parametric algorithms with restricted computations. In: Dong, Y., Herrera-Viedma, E., Matsui, K., Omatsu, S., González Briones, A., Rodríguez González, S. (eds.) DCAI 2020. AISC, vol. 1237, pp. 321–331. Springer, Cham (2021). https://doi.org/10.1007/978-3-030-53036-5_35
10. Loukanova, R.: Currying order and restricted algorithmic beta-conversion in type theory of acyclic recursion. In: Materna, P., Jespersen, B. (eds.) Logically Speaking. A Festschrift for Marie Duží. Book Tribute, vol. 49, pp. 285–310. College Publications (2022). https://doi.org/10.13140/RG.2.2.34553.75365
11. Loukanova, R.: Eta-reduction in type-theory of acyclic recursion. ADCAIJ: Adv. Distrib. Comput. Artif. Intell. J. **12**(1), 1–22 (2023). Ediciones Universidad de Salamanca. https://doi.org/10.14201/adcaij.29199
12. Marlow, S.: Haskell 2010, language report. Technical report (2010). https://www.haskell.org, https://www.haskell.org/onlinereport/haskell2010/
13. Milner, R.: A theory of type polymorphism in programming. J. Comput. Syst. Sci. **17**(3), 348–375 (1978). https://doi.org/10.1016/0022-0000(78)90014-4
14. Montague, R.: The proper treatment of quantification in ordinary English. In: Hintikka, J., Moravcsik, J., Suppes, P. (eds.) Approaches to Natural Language, vol. 49, pp. 221–242. Synthese Library. Springer, Dordrecht (1973), https://doi.org/10.1007/978-94-010-2506-5_10

15. Moschovakis, Y.N.: The formal language of recursion. J. Symb. Log. **54**(4), 1216–1252 (1989). https://doi.org/10.1017/S0022481200041086

16. Moschovakis, Y.N.: Sense and denotation as algorithm and value. In: Oikkonen, J., Väänänen, J. (eds.) Logic Colloquium 1990: ASL Summer Meeting in Helsinki, Lecture Notes in Logic, vol. 2, pp. 210–249. Springer-Verlag, Berlin (1993). https://projecteuclid.org/euclid.lnl/1235423715

17. Moschovakis, Y.N.: The logic of functional recursion. In: Dalla Chiara, M.L., Doets, K., Mundici, D., van Benthem, J. (eds.) Logic and Scientific Methods, vol. 259, pp. 179–207. Springer, Dordrecht (1997). https://doi.org/10.1007/978-94-017-0487-8_10

18. Moschovakis, Y.N.: A logical calculus of meaning and synonymy. Linguist. Philos. **29**(1), 27–89 (2006). https://doi.org/10.1007/s10988-005-6920-7

19. Nishizaki, S.: Let-binding in a linear lambda calculus with first-class continuations. IOP Conf. Ser. Earth Environ. Sci. **252**(4), 042011 (2019). https://doi.org/10.1088/1755-1315/252/4/042011

20. Plotkin, G.D.: LCF considered as a programming language. Theoret. Comput. Sci. **5**(3), 223–255 (1977). https://doi.org/10.1016/0304-3975(77)90044-5

21. Scott, D.S.: A type-theoretical alternative to ISWIM, CUCH, OWHY. Theoret. Comput. Sci. **121**(1), 411–440 (1993). https://doi.org/10.1016/0304-3975(93)90095-B

Slurs' Variability, Emotional Dimensions, and Game-Theoretic Pragmatics

Víctor Carranza-Pinedo[1,2]([✉]) [iD]

[1] École Normale Supérieure de Paris, Paris, France
[2] Università degli Studi di Milano, Milan, Italy
victor.carranza@uni-muenster.de

Abstract. Slurs' meaning is highly unstable. A slurring utterance like 'Hey, F, where have you been?' (where F is a slur) may receive a wide array of interpretations depending on various contextual factors such as the speaker's social identity, their relationship to the target group, tone of voice, and more. Standard semantic, pragmatic, and non-content theories of slurs have proposed different mechanisms to account for some or all types of variability observed, but without providing a unified framework that allows us to understand how different contextual factors simultaneously influence slurs' interpretation. To address this issue, I argue that slurs convey dimensional qualities such as, e.g., 'negative valence, neutral arousal, high dominance' instead of discrete emotional categories such as 'contempt'. Then, I translate this hypothesis into a game-theoretic model of slurs' interpretation inspired by Heather Burnett's pioneering work on identity construction. This new model, called 'Affective Meaning Games' (AMG), captures the variability of slurs and integrates pragmatic reasoning within an independently motivated psychological understanding of emotional states.

Keywords: Slurs · PAD Model of Emotions · Signaling Games · Expressivity

1 Introduction

Slurs are pejorative expressions employed to disparage individuals based on their association with social categories such as ethnicity (e.g., 'spic'), religion (e.g., 'kike'), gender (e.g., 'faggot'), etc. Even though slurs are typically used to express (and elicit) negative affective states such as contempt, hostility, or rage, it has been observed that their interpretation is not constant across different speech-act situations [12, 16, 17, 24, 32]. An utterance including a slur F like 'Hey, F, where have you been?' can receive a multitude of interpretations contingent upon various contextual factors including the speaker's social identity (e.g., their membership status in the group denoted by the slur), their relationship to the target group (e.g., whether they are close acquaintances), the intonation used (e.g., whether F is uttered with contempt or in a friendly tone), etc.

  Semantic, pragmatic, and non-content theories of slurs have proposed diverse mechanisms to account for the phenomenon of variability. Firstly, theories that semantically associate slurs with injurious attitudes explain slurs' variability by suggesting that some

D. Bekki et al. (Eds.): LENLS 2019, LNCS 14213, pp. 199–212, 2023.
https://doi.org/10.1007/978-3-031-43977-3_12

slurs are polysemous [16], or that perlocutionary mechanisms can influence the conventional expression of these attitudes [17]. Secondly, theories that view slurs as conversationally associated with clusters of negative stereotypes explain this variability by appealing to the role of speakers' communicative intentions and the varying degrees of severity of the associated stereotypes [7]. Lastly, theories that link slurs to prohibitions explain variability by claiming that these prohibitions can be enforced with varying degrees of severity or even 'suspended' in certain situations [1].

However, it is increasingly recognized that people infer agents' underlying emotional states by simultaneously integrating multiple contextual factors [15, 28, 29]. For instance, empirical evidence suggest that observers not only rely on facial expressions when inferring an agent's emotions but also consider other contextual cues such as body posture [3], background scenery [4], cultural norms [22], and so on, when these are available. Thus, in addition to evaluating the various mechanisms proposed to account for slurs' variability (i.e., meaning change, speaker's intentions, stereotypes, prohibitions, etc.), we also need a unified framework that allows us to understand both (i) how slurs' offensiveness arise and (ii) how different contextual factors interact with one another during the interpretation process, thereby giving rise to the attested variability.

To address (i), I characterize slurs as expressing values derived from continuous emotional dimensions (i.e., pleasure, arousal, and dominance) rather than discrete emotional categories (e.g., 'contempt'). Then, I argue that slurs' distinctive offensive profile is rooted in the high level of dominance they typically convey toward their target. To address (ii), I translate this hypothesis into a game-theoretic model of slurs' interpretation, drawing inspiration from Heather Burnett's pioneering work on identity construction [8, 9]. Under this new approach, called 'Affective Meaning Games' (AMG), a slur is indexically linked with a set of affective attributes (e.g., 'negative pleasure, neutral arousal, high dominance'), any one of which can emerge depending on prior assumptions about the speaker's emotional stance towards the target group. These assumptions are, in turn, influenced by different contextual factors (e.g., the speaker's identity, their relationship to the target, etc.), thereby providing a compact framework to analyze slurs' instability.

The paper is structured as follows. In Sect. 2, I distinguish two types of variability in slurs: first, variation in terms of the emotional states they express, and second, variation in terms of the offense they may provoke in others. Section 3 introduces the PAD model of emotions and proposes to characterize slurs' affective meaning in terms of negative pleasure and high dominance. Section 4 introduces Affective Meaning Games, and Sect. 5 explores some of their possible applications. Section 6 discusses further aspects of slurring speech acts and Sect. 7 concludes.

2 Two Types of Variation

The variation of slurs is Janus-faced. On the one hand, speakers use slurs to *express* a diverse spectrum of emotions. Typically, speakers display negative emotions such as contempt (i.e., 'Fs are not allowed here') or fear (i.e., 'Those Fs are invading us'). However, in different circumstances, such as when the slur is used among members of the target group, the speaker is typically characterized as expressing positive emotions like solidarity (e.g., 'Hey, my F, I have missed you') or pride (e.g., 'We should be proud of being Fs'). It is also noteworthy that the intensity of the emotion expressed can also vary, ranging from, e.g., mild condescension (e.g., 'I don't even see you as a F') to intense hatred (e.g., 'All Fs are greedy').

On the other hand, speakers typically *elicit* different degrees of offense among listeners by using slurs. This variation may occur in two ways: (i) across the lexical items employed or (ii) across the contexts in which slurs are uttered. With respect to (i), variation may occur across lexical items that target a single social group (e.g., 'beaner' may be considered more offensive than 'greaser') or different groups (e.g., 'chink' may be considered more offensive than 'guido'). With respect to (ii), variation may occur across different uses of the same expression, depending on who uses it (e.g., uses of 'faggot' within members of the LGTB community are considered less offensive than those performed by outsiders), the manner in which it is used (e.g., with a contemptuous or friendly intonation), etc.

Importantly, it has been observed that the offense a slur elicits is often orthogonal to the valence of the emotion it expresses. For example, although some members of the hippie subculture used the term 'spade' to express admiration or fondness for African Americans, the expression was still deemed offensive by the latter [27]. Conversely, certain insults that express extreme contempt or loathing are nonetheless perceived as inoffensive [32]. This occurs with insults directed at dominant groups (e.g., 'limey', 'toff', etc.) or that refer to an individual's personal traits (e.g., 'bastard', 'wimp', etc.). In contrast to these expressions, slurs distinctive scornful denigration is designed to manifest that the target is inferior [19].

These observations appear to undermine the idea that the offensiveness of slurs is related to the affective or any psychological states that the speaker is expressing through their use. For instance, Jeshion's [17] influential theory of slurs, which posits that all slurs are conventionally linked to the expression of contempt, has been criticized on the grounds that the expression of contempt is not sufficient nor necessary to explain the distinct scornful denigration that slurs inflict upon their targets [10]. An expression can be highly contemptuous without thereby being a slur, and a slur can express other emotions (e.g., fear, disgust, disdain or even amusement) and still be highly offensive.

Should we conclude that slurs' offensiveness is altogether independent of the emotions they convey? In what follows, I argue that this is not the case. To wit, emotions are not only analyzed as discrete emotional categories (e.g., 'contempt', 'joy', 'surprise', etc.), but also as states that we can characterize using basic affective dimensions (i.e., pleasure, arousal, and dominance). Thus, although the valence expressed by slurs may not be correlated to the offense they elicit, emotions have other basic components that can assist in understanding this phenomenon. In the following section, I argue that slurs (i) tend to express affective states that qualify as negatively valenced but highly dominant, and (ii) that it is this latter dimension, dominance, that lies at the root of the offensiveness of slurs.

3 Slurs and the PAD Model of Emotions

What characteristics define an affective episode? Mehrabian and Russell [26] propose to describe affective episodes using a psychometric approach that employs three continuous, bipolar, and orthogonal dimensions: pleasure, arousal, and dominance. This approach, known as the 'PAD' model of emotions, was first introduced by Wundt [37] and is widely used for analyzing affective episodes in a continuous, rather than discrete, framework [25, 33, 34]. The three dimensions are defined as follows:

- PLEASURE: corresponds to a continuum that ranges from negatively valenced affective states (e.g., sadness) to positively valenced ones (e.g., joy) with respect to the stimulus. It is the evaluative component.
- AROUSAL: corresponds to the continuum ranging from low mental alertness (e.g., boredom) to high mental alertness (e.g., excitement). It is the physiological component.
- DOMINANCE: corresponds to the continuum ranging from the sensation of feeling controlled or submissive (e.g., frustration) to the sensation of feeling in control or powerful (e.g., anger) with respect to the stimulus. It is the relational component.

Dominance pertains to the degree to which an agent feels behaviorally constrained with respect to a stimulus (e.g., individuals, objects, events, etc.), on the basis of perceived qualities like physical strength, social status, hostility, etc. [26, 30]. Note that the level of dominance experienced is inversely proportional to the level of dominance perceived in the stimulus. For example, when provoked by stimuli perceived to be less dominant (e.g., an individual considered to be of 'lower status'), offenses are more likely to elicit anger than frustration (and vice-versa). With this being said, how can the content of slurs be characterized using the PAD dimensions?

1. Slurs typically express the speaker's negative appraisal of a specific group. For example, when the speaker utters 'That building is full of Fs', the listener is likely to infer that the speaker experiences DISPLEASURE with respect to F's target group or, similarly, that 'Fs are bad for being Fs'.
2. Interestingly, slurs do not seem to be significantly associated with a particular degree of AROUSAL. In contrast to other highly colloquial expressions such as 'fucking' or 'shitty', slurs don't come as infelicitous in situations where the speaker is only experiencing mild emotions. Slurs belong to the bigot's idiolect, rather than being reserved for extreme situations.
3. Lastly, slurs typically express that the speaker regards himself as superior to the target group. By uttering slurring sentences like 'Fs are not allowed here', the speaker communicates that the members of the target group rank as low in worth, thereby attempting to establish a DOMINANCE hierarchy.

Why do slurs signal high dominance across different groups? One reason is that slurs are labels that arise as straightforward impositions to the target groups, and thus undermine their ability to build their own identity in an autonomous way [1]. Moreover, the act of slurring is 'action-engendering', that is, it grants permission for other forms of unjust treatment, such as physical or structural violence [21]. Therefore, slurs are uttered not only for the purposes of expressing a negative assessment, but also seek to establish or strengthen an unjust hierarchy between the speaker and the target through the expression of dominance (and, by extension, between the broader social groups to which they belong). I call this the 'valence-dominance' hypothesis.

It could be argued, however, that the expression of high dominance, which involves deeming individual targets as inferior, necessarily presupposes the expression of a negative evaluation. For example, in Jeshion's view [18, p. 133], slurs (i) express contempt towards a target group G, i.e., where contempt 'involves ranking another person as low in worth along the moral domain on a certain basis', and (ii) aim at specifying what members of G fundamentally are, based on the idea that belonging to G is a 'fundamental negative characteristic-defining feature of the targets'. In this theory, negatively evaluating G serves as the basis for treating its members as low in worth along the moral domain.

However, despite the fact that the aspects of high dominance and low pleasure often co-occur in slurring utterances, they are dissociated in many contexts. Indeed, it is possible to evaluate an individual negatively without expressing that they are inferior (e.g., when one qualifies someone as uninteresting or lethargic). Conversely, it is possible to express that an individual is lesser as a person without evaluating them negatively (e.g., racist ideologies about Chinese people are built on positive evaluations, such as that they are intelligent or hardworking). Being evaluated as good in some aspect doesn't preclude being simultaneously judged as inferior, and vice-versa.

How can the valence-dominance hypothesis explain slurs' offensiveness? As noted earlier, slurs can express emotions of opposite valence and still be regarded as offensive (e.g., contempt towards the target group or amusement at their expense). Nevertheless, in both cases, slurs invariably seek to dehumanize individuals by placing them beneath others within a dominance hierarchy. Hence, the valence-dominance hypothesis provides a straightforward account of slurs' offense: because slurs are linked with high-dominance states, their utterance warrants offense to those who find oppression detrimental to society. That is, their utterance provides moral justification for those who reject unjust forms of group-based hierarchy to take offense.

In this section, I have used the PAD model to characterize a subset of the vast array of affective states that can be potentially expressed by slurs in a particular utterance context. In the following, I will translate the valence-dominance hypothesis into a probabilistic model of slurs' interpretation, in order to understand how slurs' variation emerges from the integration of multiple contextual cues.[1]

---

[1] In Sect. 2, I mentioned that slurs can express fear, despite fear being associated with low dominance behaviors such as freezing or fleeing. However, an alternative way to understand slurs is to view them as expressions of phobias, such as homophobia or xenophobia, which are affective dispositions based on the misrepresentation of the target as a threat to the agent's social privilege. Since phobias can trigger dominant behaviors, such as hostility or aggression, they warrant offense. Thanks to Isidora Stojanovic for drawing my attention to the non-dominant character of fear.

4 Affective Meaning Games

How can we operationalize emotions in a theory of meaning? Following Burnett's research on identity construction [8, 9], I postulate a structure $\langle Q, > \rangle$, where 'Q' denotes a set of relevant affective qualities (e.g., high dominance or '[D+]') and '>' encodes relations of mutual exclusivity between them (e.g., individuals cannot experience a [P−] and [P+] state at the same time). As noted earlier, slurs don't correlate with a specific degree of arousal, so this dimension is omitted:

$$Q = \{[P+], [P−], [D−], [D+]\}.$$

a. $[P+] > [P−]$ (1)

b. $[D−] > [D+]$

Based on $\langle Q, > \rangle$, we can derive four distinct types of affective states α, such as the [P+, D−] state, labeled AFFILIATION, or the [P−, D+] state, labeled CONTEMPT. Importantly, these labels assemble different discrete emotional categories together. For example, CONTEMPT represents [P−, D+] states in general (e.g., rage, hostility, etc.), and not only contempt:

Table 1. Affective states $\alpha \in$ AFF

AFF	AFFILIATION	AMUSEMENT	ANXIETY	CONTEMPT
α	[P+, D−]	[P+, D+]	[P−, D−]	[P−, D+]

Then, I posit that for a given slurring term F, there is a non-slurring alternative F* that derogates the same social group G. For example, we assume that 'Spic' and 'Hispanic' are such alternatives, as the former probably emerged as a hypocoristic variant of the latter. Note, however, that we don't need to assume that F and F* are fully co-referential or etymologically related, but merely that they are salient lexical choices within the conversational interaction.

How can we characterize the link between the alternatives F/F* and the affective states $\alpha \in$ AFF that they have the potential to express? Since it is not possible to assign a stable interpretation to slurs across different contexts, I assume that the link between F/F* and affective states is *indexical*, that is, grounded on the statistical correlation between the use of F/F* and a variety of affective qualities, any of which may be activated within a particular context [13, 35].

Specifically, I posit that slurs exhibit a stronger correlation with [D+] states, such as CONTEMPT, as opposed to [D−] states, such as AFFILIATION. To capture these regularities, I assign to F a probability distribution $\Pr(F|\alpha)$, which represents the likelihood of uttering F given an affective state α [14]. Notably, as Table 2 illustrates, the non-slurring alternative F* is associated with the distribution $\Pr(F*|\alpha) = 1 - \Pr(F|\alpha)$.

Then, I assume that slurs are interpreted based on the listeners' L prior beliefs regarding the speaker's affective stance toward the group being targeted by the insult. Inspired by [8, 9], I represent L's prior beliefs as a probability distribution $\Pr(\alpha)$, which

Table 2. Affective-indexical meaning of F and F*

AFF	AFFILIATION	AMUSEMENT	ANXIETY	CONTEMPT
$\Pr(F|\alpha)$	0.3	0.6	0.4	0.7
$\Pr(F^*|\alpha)$	0.7	0.4	0.6	0.3

denotes the probability distribution that the speaker S feels an affective state α towards target group G. In situations where L has no prior expectations about S's emotional stance towards G, we can represent $\Pr(\alpha)$ as a uniform distribution over affective states. See Table 3:

Table 3. L's prior beliefs about S's affective stance α

AFF	AFFILIATION	AMUSEMENT	ANXIETY	CONTEMPT
$\Pr(\alpha)$	0.25	0.25	0.25	0.25

In other contexts, L's prior beliefs will be influenced by multiple factors, such as the speaker's identity, her relationship with the addressee, her previous actions, etc. For example, we can consider identities as social markers that we use to group each other and, more importantly, to shape our perception of their behavioral dispositions [2]. If someone is Catholic, we may assume that they experience [P+] states towards the Catholic church and endorse its teachings. If someone is Latino, we expect that they don't experience [D+] states toward Latinos, etc. While these assumptions may be proven incorrect, identities nevertheless guide our expectations regarding how others feel and behave.

Finally, once the speaker S utters a slur F directed at a social group G, L updates her prior beliefs by conditioning $\Pr(\alpha)$ on F's affective meaning, $\Pr(F|\alpha)$. In other terms, the interpretation process involves (i) combining the likelihood of F's signaling an affective state α with the L's prior beliefs about S's affective stance toward G, and then (ii) readjusting the outcome measure with a normalizing constant, i.e., the sum of these terms calculated for all affective states $\alpha \in$ AFF:

$$\Pr(\alpha|F) = \frac{\Pr(\alpha) \times \Pr(F|\alpha)}{\sum_{\alpha \in \text{aff}} \Pr(\alpha) \times \Pr(F|\alpha)} \tag{2}$$

After introducing the fundamental elements of Affective Meaning Games, we can state its key conjecture: the affective information expressed by the use of a slur, perceived by a member of the audience, is constrained by the perceived affective relationship — according to that particular audience member — between the speaker and the social group G that is the target of the slur. In other terms, reasoning about S's potential emotions towards the target group G can alter the weighting of the various affective states $\alpha \in$ AFF in a particular context, thus giving rise to the variation observed in Sect. 2. In the following section, we will put this model into work by examining how it accounts for the Janus-faced variability of slurs' content.[2]

5 Explaining Slurs' Variability

In Sect. 2, it was observed that the impact of slurs varies across lexical items and different uses of the same lexical item. In this section, I explore how AMGs elucidate these phenomena and other aspects related to the usage and nature of slurs.

5.1 Variation Across Lexical Items

The offensiveness of slurs varies across terms directed at the same group (e.g., 'beaner' vs. 'greaser') or different social groups (e.g., 'chink' vs. 'guido'). Our model explains this phenomenon as a result of the indexical character of the link between a given slur and values on the PAD dimensions. In contrast to conventional or conversational inferences, indexical associations are grounded in the co-occurrence of a particular sign and state, emerging from co-presence, causality, or other mechanisms [5, 31]. As a result, through repeated use and circulation, slurs gradually come to be associated with different indexical meanings that reflect the PAD values they regularly co-occur with. Thus, a term like 'chink' is more offensive than 'guido', or a term like 'beaner' more offensive than 'greaser', due to the higher intensity of the [D+] states or outcomes normally accompanying its use (e.g., hostile behaviors).

Indexicality also offers insight into how slurs' meaning shifts over time, for example during processes of appropriation [6]. Terms initially conveying a positive evaluation may be later reinterpreted as expressing dominance (e.g., 'redskin' or 'spade'), while terms expressing dominance are later linked to a positive evaluation (e.g., 'queer' or 'gay'). Our model attributes this phenomenon to the 'multilayered' character of indexical associations, which constantly acquire new meanings [36]. For example, using '-in' instead of '-ing' (e.g., 'fishin'' rather than 'fishing') was seen as signaling 'casualness', but then it was also linked to an insincere or condescending persona [11]. As new indexical associations coexist with the old ones, interpreters must be attentive to contextual factors during the inferential process, as we will see in the next subsection.

Finally, it is worth noting that indexicality can also account for the projective behavior of slurs, that is, the fact that slurs' content can survive entailment-canceling operators such as negations or disjunctions (e.g., the slur F in 'It is false that the building is full of F' elicits offense despite occurring under the syntactic scope of a negation). To wit, indexical associations are not restricted to lexical items, but rather apply to the phenomenon of variation between alternatives more generally. Any instance of human behavior, like clothing, habits, or activities, can index social (or affective) qualities, as long as they evoke a contrast between alternatives [13]. Therefore, since indexicality is

---

[2] From this point on, we may introduce further elaborations to the model. For instance, we could assume that speakers do not merely express their actual emotions through slurs, but also make strategic decisions about whether to employ them based on factors such as the social costs that result from their use, or whether the addressee is likely to approve their use [14]. I leave the exploration of these extensions to future research.

not exclusively a linguistic phenomenon, entailment-canceling operators are ineffective in blocking slurs' expression of high dominance.

5.2 Variation Across Context of Utterance

Slurs' offense varies with respect to multiple contextual factors such as the social identity of the speaker, their relationship with the addressee, their intonation, etc. We can illustrate how AMGs integrates these factors by describing four prototypical scenarios. In the first one, speaker S is not Latino and utters the sentence in (3), so we expect the slur to be interpreted as offensive by listener L.

(3) There will be a lot of spics at Mary's party.

To derive this interpretation, we assume that L lacks any preconception regarding S's emotional disposition towards Latinos. Hence, we plug the uniform distribution in Table 3 and the affective meaning of 'spic' (as outlined in Table 2) into the formula in (2). As a result, we derive that L is likely to interpret (3) as expressing the speaker's CONTEMPT (cf. the fourth row in Table 4). Then, following the valence-dominance hypothesis, we explain why this utterance elicits offense (Table 4):

Table 4. Neutral scenario

AFF	AFFILIATION	AMUSEMENT	ANXIETY	CONTEMPT
$Pr(\alpha)$	0.25	0.25	0.25	0.25
$Pr(spic|\alpha)$	0.3	0.6	0.4	0.7
$Pr(\alpha) \cdot Pr(spic|\alpha)$	0.075	0.150	0.100	0.175
$Pr(\alpha|spic)$	0.15	0.30	0.20	0.35

Note that, regardless of whether S is perceived as evaluating Latinos positively or negatively by uttering (3), L's posterior beliefs will invariably tend to favor [D+] states. That is, if S is perceived as experiencing [P+] states (e.g., as uttering (3) in a friendly manner), he will be interpreted as expressing amusement at the expense of Latinos, implying that this social group is worthy of discriminatory practices such as racist jokes

Secondly, in a scenario where S, despite not being Latino, possesses a certain 'insider' status within that community (e.g., S migrated to Latin America at a young age), we may expect (3) to express positive or negative emotions, but not necessarily to elicit offense. To account for this situation, we plug a distribution that favors [D−] states, and the affective meaning of the slur, in the formula in (2). As a result, as Table 5 illustrates, we obtain that S is interpreted as expressing ANXIETY or AFFILIATION, which are inoffensive states.

Table 5. Insider scenario

AFF	AFFILIATION	AMUSEMENT	ANXIETY	CONTEMPT
Pr(α)	0.40	0.10	0.40	0.10
Pr(spic|α)	0.3	0.6	0.4	0.7
Pr(α)·Pr(spic|α)	0.12	0.06	0.16	0.07
Pr(α|spic)	0.29	0.15	0.39	0.17

In a third scenario, where S is Latino and utters (3), the slur will be even more clearly interpreted as inoffensive by L. The reason is that L will expect S to feel [P+] and [D–] states towards Latinos, as it is unlikely to feel members of one's groups as bad or worthy of contempt. As a result, as Table 6 illustrates, L will interpret S as expressing AFFILIATION (e.g., affection, friendship, pride, etc.) towards members of the Latino community.

Table 6. Friendly scenario

AFF	AFFILIATION	AMUSEMENT	ANXIETY	CONTEMPT
Pr(α)	0.60	0.15	0.15	0.10
Pr(spic|α)	0.3	0.6	0.4	0.7
Pr(α)·Pr(spic|α)	0.18	0.09	0.06	0.07
Pr(α|spic)	0.450	0.225	0.150	0.175

Finally, what occurs when a speaker S uses a slur to dehumanize someone despite belonging to the group that is derogated? In a fourth scenario (which we may call 'alienated'), a Latino utters (3) with a contemptuous tone of voice, or use 'spic' in reference to one of their Latino employees, which many would interpret as offensive. In such a case, L may presume that S is trying to accommodate the presupposition that he doesn't identify as a Latino, as this appears necessary to interpret their utterance as an expression of contempt. However, if L rejects that presupposition, they may see S as experiencing ANXIETY instead, that is, as feeling unease at the mismatch between their culture of origin and the one they aspire to belong to.

In this section, we have examined how Affective Meaning Games explain the two types of variation discussed in Sect. 2. The first type is explained by the indexical nature of the association between slurs and affective dimensions. The second is explained by how such indexical associations are weighted against multiple background assumptions about the speaker's affective stance towards the target. We presented four scenarios to see the interplay between these assumptions. The first scenario depicted typical instances of slurs being used as weapons. The second and third demonstrate how the harmful effects of slurs are diluted when the speaker belongs to, or is perceived as belonging to, the target group. Finally, the fourth scenario illustrates that in-group uses of slurs are not necessarily 'innocent', that is, don't always express positive emotions like pride or affiliation.

6 Comparison

In this section, I will compare Affective Meaning Games to two other models of slurs' interpretation that share a common interest in accounting for the unstable nature of slurs.

The first model, proposed by McCready and Davis [24] (based on [23]), uses different axiom schemas that interact with one another in order to infer the speaker's attitude towards the targeted group. These schemas represent our folk beliefs about the typical interpretation of an agents' emotions given certain assumptions (e.g., normative facts about the world, the agent's relationship to the target, etc.). The main feature of this model is its nonmonotonic quality, i.e., the possibility to override conclusions by adding more specific information to the set of premises [24, p. 265]. During the inference of slur's emotional/offensive impact, certain cues are thus considered more prevalent than others due to their specificity. For example, if the speaker uses a slur F, we will typically infer that he feels contempt towards members of the target group. However, if we also know that the speaker is a member of the target group, we will cancel the former inference and think instead that the speaker is expressing affiliation.

Hence, like our proposal, McCready examines the interpretation of slurs as part of a broader process of reasoning about the speakers' emotions from various contextual factors. In fact, McCready [23] notes that this proposal can also be modeled in terms of Bayesian reasoning, where we obtain various conclusions held with different probabilities instead of a single defeasible one [23, p. 259]. However, it is worth noting that interpreters typically weigh contextual factors (e.g., posture, social identity, facial expressions, etc.) based on their perceived reliability rather than their specificity [20, 38]. Indeed, co-occurring cues that are equally specific can be in conflict with each other (e.g., a positive facial expression can accompany a contemptuous tone of voice). As a result, interpreters are sometimes required to assess the cues' relative degree of reliability independently of how specific they are (cf. The fourth scenario in Sect. 5.2).

In the second model, proposed by Popa-Wyatt and Wyatt [32], slurs are conversational moves that subordinate individuals by assigning them a lower discursive role within a conversation game. Moreover, the discursive roles of the participants draw upon and reinforce long-standing social roles, thus creating or reinforcing an unjust power imbalance. As a result, this theory explains slurs' offensiveness by appealing (i) to the allocation of a dominant/submissive discursive role to the speaker and target, respectively, and (ii) to the social roles they evoke in the history of oppression. Importantly, for the offense to occur, the speaker must 'fit' the oppressor's role; if the speaker cannot fit that role (e.g., because they belong to the oppressed group), then the assignment won't be felicitous and the offense can't take place.

Popa-Wyatt and Wyatt's theory accounts for many instances of slur's variation. For example, it predicts that 'chink' is more offensive than 'guido' due to the greater degree of oppression experienced by people of Chinese descent. Similarly, it explains that 'spic' is not offensive when uttered by a Latino because such person doesn't fit the oppressor role.

However, the authors acknowledge that some cases cannot be explained by appealing to group-membership alone, and that 'other flags, such as tone, familiarity between the participants, appropriateness of context, will all modulate whether the felicity condition is met.' [32], p. 22]. The authors suggest that these conditions are additive, meaning that if enough of them are present, offense arises. Nevertheless, as mentioned before, contextual cues are not always in harmony with each other, such as when a member of the group derogated utters a slur with a contemptuous tone of voice. Therefore, adding these cues up may not be always adequate to interpret the slur. While group membership is usually a reliable cue, it interacts with other factors that have the potential to become more reliable during the interpretation process.

7 Conclusion

In this paper, I have put forward a novel account on the affective meaning of slurs, which highlights the role of the valence and dominance dimensions of emotions. By focusing on the dominance dimension as the key factor driving slurs' offensive nature, this paper opens a new avenue for exploring the intricate relationship between emotions, communication, and power dynamics. Indeed, the game-theoretic model proposed offers a unified framework for analyzing the variability of slurs' affective impact, and its flexibility holds promise for extending the analysis to other forms of injurious expressions, including pejorative nicknames and particularistic insults. While empirical testing is needed to confirm the model's predictions, it demonstrates the potential of psychological models of affect to inform the modelling of affective meaning. By bridging the gap between continuous models of emotions and formal pragmatic analysis, this paper contributes to the exploration of the wider psychological implications of slurs within social interactions.

Acknowledgements. I would like to express my gratitude to Elin McCready, Heather Burnett, Michael Franke, Filippo Domaneschi, Daniel Gutzmann, and particularly to Elisa Paganini, Márta Abrusán and Isidora Stojanovic for their valuable feedback and suggestions on earlier versions of this paper. All errors or omissions that remain are mine.

References

1. Anderson, L., Lepore, E.: Slurring words. Noûs **47**, 25–48 (2013). https://doi.org/10.1111/j.1468-0068.2010.00820.x
2. Appiah, K.A.: The Ethics of Identity. Princeton University Press, Princeton (2010). https://doi.org/10.1515/9781400826193
3. Aviezer, H., Trope, Y., Todorov, A.: Body cues, not facial expressions, discriminate between intense positive and negative emotions. Science **338**(6111), 1225–1229 (2012). https://doi.org/10.1126/science.1224313
4. Barrett, L.F., Kensinger, E.A.: Context is routinely encoded during emotion perception. Psychol. Sci. **21**(4), 595–599 (2010). https://doi.org/10.1177/0956797610363547
5. Beltrama, A.: Social meaning in semantics and pragmatics. Lang. Linguistics Compass **14**(9), e12398 (2020). https://doi.org/10.1111/lnc3.12398

6. Bianchi, C.: Slurs and appropriation: an echoic account. J. Pragmat. **66**, 35–44 (2014). https://doi.org/10.1016/j.pragma.2014.02.009
7. Bolinger, R.J.: The pragmatics of slurs. Nous **51**(3), 439–462 (2015). https://doi.org/10.1111/nous.12090
8. Burnett, H.: Sociolinguistic interaction and identity construction: the view from game-theoretic pragmatics. J. Socioling. **21**(2), 238–271 (2017). https://doi.org/10.1111/josl.12229
9. Burnett, H.: Signalling games, sociolinguistic variation and the construction of style. Linguist. Philos. **42**(5), 419–450 (2019). https://doi.org/10.1007/s10988-018-9254-y
10. Camp, E.: Slurring perspectives. Analytic. Philosophy **54**(3), 330–349 (2013). https://doi.org/10.1111/phib.12022
11. Campbell-Kibler, K.: Listener perceptions of sociolinguistic variables: The case of (ING). Ph.D. thesis, Stanford University, Stanford CA (2005)
12. Davis, C., McCready, E.: The instability of slurs. Grazer Philosophische Studien **97**(1), 63–85 (2020). https://doi.org/10.1163/18756735-09701005
13. Eckert, P.: Variation and the indexical field. J. Socioling. **12**(4), 453–476 (2008). https://doi.org/10.1111/j.1467-9841.2008.00374.x
14. Henderson, R., McCready, E.: Dogwhistles and the at-issue/non-at-issue distinction. In: Gutzmann, D., Turgay, K. (eds.) Secondary Content, pp. 222–245. Brill (2019). https://doi.org/10.1163/9789004393127_010
15. Hess, U., Hareli, S.: The role of social context for the interpretation of emotional facial expressions. In: Mandal, M.K., Awasthi, A. (eds.) Under-Standing Facial Expressions in Communication, pp. 119–141. Springer (2015). https://doi.org/10.1007/978-81-322-1934-7_7
16. Hom, C.: The semantics of racial epithets. J. Philosophy **105**(8), 416–440 (2008). https://doi.org/10.5840/jphil2008105834
17. Jeshion, R.: Expressivism and the offensiveness of slurs. Philos. Perspect. **27**(1), 231–259 (2013). https://doi.org/10.1111/phpe.12027
18. Jeshion, R.: Slur creation, bigotry formation: the power of expressivism. Phenomenology Mind (11), 130–139 (2016). https://doi.org/10.13128/Phe_Mi-20113
19. Jeshion, R.: Varieties of pejoratives. In: Khoo, J., Sterkin, R. (eds.) Rout-ledge Handbook of Social and Political Philosophy of Language (2020). https://doi.org/10.4324/9781003164869
20. Kayyal, M., Widen, S., Russell, J.A.: Context is more powerful than we think: contextual cues override facial cues even for valence. Emotion **15**(3), 287 (2015). https://doi.org/10.1037/emo0000032
21. Lynne, T.: Genocidal language games. In: Ishani Maitra, M.K.M. (ed.) Speech and Harm, pp. 174–221. Oxford University Press (2012). https://doi.org/10.1093/acprof:oso/9780199236282.003.0008
22. Masuda, T., Ellsworth, P.C., Mesquita, B., Leu, J., Tanida, S., Van de Veerdonk, E.: Placing the face in context: cultural differences in the perception of facial emotion. J. Pers. Soc. Psychol. **94**(3), 365 (2008). https://doi.org/10.1037/0022-3514.94.3.365
23. McCready, E.: Emotive equilibria. Linguist. Philos. **35**(3), 243–283 (2012). https://doi.org/10.1007/s10988-012-9118-9
24. McCready, E., Davis, C.: An invocational theory of slurs. Proceedings of LENLS 14 (2017)
25. Mehrabian, A.: Pleasure-arousal-dominance: a general framework for describing and measuring individual differences in temperament. Curr. Psychol. **14**(4), 261–292 (1996). https://doi.org/10.1007/BF02686918
26. Mehrabian, A., Russell, J.A.: An approach to environmental psychology. MIT Press (1974)
27. Nunberg, G.: The social life of slurs. In: Fogal, D., Harris, D.W., M.M. (ed.) New Work on Speech Acts, pp. 237–295. Oxford University Press (2018). https://doi.org/10.1093/oso/9780198738831.001.0001

28. Ong, D.C., Zaki, J., Goodman, N.D.: Affective cognition: Exploring lay theories of emotion. Cognition **143**, 141–162 (2015). https://doi.org/10.1016/j.cognition.2015.06.010
29. Ong, D.C., Zaki, J., Goodman, N.D.: Computational models of emotion inference in theory of mind: a review and roadmap. Top. Cogn. Sci. **11**(2), 338–357 (2019). https://doi.org/10.1111/tops.12371
30. Oosterhof, N.N., Todorov, A.: The functional basis of face evaluation. Proc. Natl. Acad. Sci. **105**(32), 11087–11092 (2008). https://doi.org/10.1073/pnas.0805664105
31. Peirce, C.S.: Philosophical writings of Peirce, vol. 217. Courier Corporation (1955)
32. Popa-Wyatt, M., Wyatt, J.L.: Slurs, roles and power. Philos. Stud. **175**(11), 2879–2906 (2017). https://doi.org/10.1007/s11098-017-0986-2
33. Reisenzein, R.: Pleasure-arousal theory and the intensity of emotions. J. Pers. Soc. Psychol. **67**(3), 525 (1994). https://doi.org/10.1037/0022-3514.67.3.525
34. Russell, J.A.: A circumplex model of affect. J. Pers. Soc. Psychol. **39**(6), 1161 (1980). https://doi.org/10.1017/S0954579405050340
35. Silverstein, M.: Shifters, linguistic categories, and cultural description. Meaning in anthropology, pp. 11–55 (1976)
36. Silverstein, M.: Indexical order and the dialectics of sociolinguistic life. Lang. Commun. **23**(3–4), 193–229 (2003). https://doi.org/10.1016/S0271-5309(03)00013-2
37. Wundt, W.: Compendio de psicología. La España Moderna (1896)
38. Zaki, J.: Cue integration: a common framework for social cognition and physical perception. Perspect. Psychol. Sci. **8**(3), 296–312 (2013). https://doi.org/10.1177/1745691613475454

Measurement Theory Meets Mereology in Multidimensionality in Resemblance Nominalism

Satoru Suzuki[✉]

Faculty of Arts and Sciences, Komazawa University,
1-23-1, Komazawa, Setagaya-ku, Tokyo 154-8525, Japan
bxs05253@nifty.com

Abstract. The problem of particulars and universals is one of the most essential problems in the formal philosophy of language in the sense that it consists in a crossroads of ontology and semantics. According to Resemblance Nominalism, resemblance relations are primitive and the properties of a thing are defined by them. We (2020) proposed, in terms of measurement theory, a first-order modal resemblance logic MRL that can furnish solutions to the problems with which Resemblance Nominalism is confronted. Yi (2014) raises a new version of degree of resemblance problem with Resemblance Nominalism of Rodriguez-Pereyra (2002). We think this problem to be a problem of multidimensionality. When we considered this problem, we realized that the model of MRL was not able to deal appropriately with the multidimensionality of this type of problem. The aim of this paper is to revise MRL so that the revised first-order modal resemblance logic RMRL can solve Rodriguez-Pereyra-Yi Problem in terms of measurement-theoretic multidimensional representation. Measurement theory makes it possible that qualitative resemblance relations can represent quantitative (numerical) functions, whereas it is not designed to explicate the parthood between a particular and its parts referred to for determining the raking on a resemblance relation. So, in the construction of the multidimensional model of RMRL, we connect measurement-theory with mereology that can explicate the parthood between a particular and its parts referred to for determining the raking on a resemblance relation. The punch line of Resemblance Nominalism is the reducibility of universals into resemblance relations. The point of formalizing Resemblance Nominalism in RMRL is to avoid the circularity in this reduction into which it tends to slide.

Keywords: first-order logic · formal philosophy of language · measurement theory · mereology · model theory · multidimensionality · nominalism · ontology · particulars · Platonism · realism · resemblance relation · resemblance nominalism · universals

D. Bekki et al. (Eds.): LENLS 2019, LNCS 14213, pp. 213–232, 2023.
https://doi.org/10.1007/978-3-031-43977-3_13

1   Motivation

The *problem of particulars and universals* is one of the most essential problems in the *formal philosophy of language* in the sense that it consists in a crossroads of *ontology* and *semantics*: When we translate a natural language into a first-order (modal) language, (though it is a problem which formal language we should adopt in this translation), the *semantic problem* as to which entity we should choose as the semantic value of a symbol in the *model* of first-order modal logic depends crucially on the *ontological problem* as to which ontology we should adopt. According to Rodriguez-Pereyra [5], there are at least two kinds of *Nominalism*: one that maintains that there are no *universals* and the other that maintains that there are no *abstract objects* like classes, functions, numbers and possible worlds. On the other hand, *Realism* about universals is the doctrine that there are universals, and *Platonism* about abstract objects is the doctrine that there are abstract objects. The doctrines about universals and the doctrines about abstract objects are *independent*. Nominalisms about universals can be classified into at least eight types: Trope Theory, Predicate Nominalism, Concept Nominalism, Ostrich Nominalism, Mereological Nominalism, Class Nominalism, Resemblance Nominalism, and Causal Nominalism.[1] In this paper we focus on Resemblance Nominalism. Rodriguez-Pereyra [4] is the most frequently mentioned work in the field of Resemblance Nominalism. As Rodriguez-Pereyra [5] argues, according to Resemblance Nominalism, it is not because things are scarlet that they resemble one another, but what makes them scarlet is that they resemble one another. Resemblance relations are *primitive* and the *properties* of a thing are *defined* by resemblance relations. Resemblance Nominalism reifies neither resemblance relations nor accessibility relations in themselves. Resemblance Nominalism in general is confronted with at least seven problems: Imperfect Community Problem, Companionship Problem, Mere Intersections Problem, Contingent Coextension Problem, Necessary Coextension Problem, Infinite Regress Problem, and Degree of Resemblance Problem.[2] We [8] proposed, in terms of *measurement theory*, a first-order modal resemblance logic MRL that can furnish solutions to all of these problems. Yi [10] raises a version of degree of resemblance problem. Yi [10, pp.622-625] argues as follows:

(1)   Carmine resembles vermillion more than it resembles triangularity.

(2) is a resemblance-nominalistic formulation that expresses what makes (1) true:

(2)   Some carmine particular resembles some vermillion particular more closely than any carmine particular resembles any triangular particular.

Rodriguez-Pereyra [4, p.65] defines the *degree of resemblance* as follows :

Definition 1 (Degree of Resemblance). *The particulars resemble to the degree n iff they share n properties.*

---

[1] Refer to Rodriguez-Pereyra [5] for details of these eight types.
[2] Refer to Rodriguez-Pereyra [4] for details of these seven problems.

By "properties", Rodriguez-Pereyra means *sparse* properties. Rodriguez-Pereyra [4, p.20,pp.50-52] adopts the following Lewis [2]'s distinction between abundant and sparse properties:

[The *abundant* properties] pay no heed to the qualitative joints, but carve things up every which way. Sharing them has nothing to do with *similarity* [(*resemblance*)] ... There is one of them for any condition we could write down, even if we could write at infinite length and even if we could name all those things that must remain nameless because they fall outside our acquaintance. [They] are as abundant as the sets themselves, because for any whatever, there is the property of belonging to that set ... The *sparse* properties are another story. Sharing of them makes for qualitative *similarity* [(*resemblance*)], they carve at the joints, they are intrinsic, they are highly specific, the sets of their instances are *ipso facto* not miscellaneous, they are only just enough of them to characterise things completely sand without redundancy.[2, pp. 59-60]

In this paper, we use "properties" in this sense of sparse properties as well as Rodriguez-Pereyra. Under Definition 1, (2) compares the *maximum* degrees of resemblance. But (2) is false because a possible carmine particular completely resembles a possible triangular particular. For the same particular might be both carmine and triangular. Rodriguez-Pereyra [6] responses to Yi by replacing (2) by (3):

(3) Some carmine particular resembles some triangular particular less closely than any carmine particular resembles any vermillion particular.

Again under Definition 1, (3) compares the *minimum* degrees of resemblance. Rodriguez-Pereyra [6, p.225] argues that (3) is true because the minimum degree to which a carmine particular can resemble a triangular particular (degree 0) is smaller than the minimum degree to which a carmine particular can resemble a vermillion particular (a degree greater than 0). Yi [11, p.796] criticizes this Rodriguez-Pereyra's response by arguing that it rests on a false assumption: the minimum degree to which a carmine particular can resemble a vermillion particular is greater than 0. For, on Rodriguez-Pereyra's notion of resemblance, a carmine particular cannot resemble a vermillion particular unless they share a sparse property, but they might not share any such property. A carmine particular and a vermillion particular might share no non-color sparse property, and two such particulars share also no color sparse property because they have different determinate color properties (i.e., carminity and vermillionity). Although they share *determinable* color properties (e.g., red), this does not help because, in Rodriguez-Pereyra's view, determinable properties are not sparse properties. So the minimum degree to which a carmine particular can resemble a vermillion particular might be 0. No doubt this argument by Yi needs examining in detail, but we can safely say that the main culprit of this Rodriguez-Pereyra-Yi Problem is Definition 1 on which both (2) and (3) are based. We consider this problem to be a problem of multidimensionality (such three dimensionality as carminity, vermillionity and triangularity) that requires *quantitative (numerical)* representations because we cannot have computational method of *aggregation* only in terms of qualitative resemblance relations. When we considered this problem, we realized that the model of MRL was not able to deal appropriately with the multidimensionality of this type of problem. The *aim* of this paper is to revise MRL so that the *revised first-order modal resemblance logic* RMRL can solve Rodriguez-Pereyra-Yi Problem in terms of measurement-theoretic multidimensional representation.[3] Measurement theory makes it possible that qualitative resemblance relations can represent quantitative (numerical) functions, whereas it is not designed to explicate the *parthood between a particular and its parts* (referred to for determining the raking on a resemblance relation). So, in the construction of the *multidimensional model* of RMRL, we would like to connect measurement-theory with *mereology*[4] that can explicate the *parthood between a particular and its parts* referred to for determining the raking on a resemblance relation. The punch line of Resemblance Nominalism is the *reducibility* of universals into resemblance relations. The point of *formalizing* Resemblance Nominalism in RMRL is to avoid the *circularity* in this reduction into which it tends to slide. In this paper, we try to give a solution to Rodriguez-Pereyra-Yi Problem by *defining* in RMRL the *degree of unresemblance* (*Definition 20*), instead of using Definition 1 (on which both (2) and (3) are based) that is the main culprit of this problem so that, in the multidimensional comparison of unresemblance of (1),

> the *weighted sum* of the degrees of unresemblance of carmine particulars to triangular particulars may be greater than that of carmine particulars to vermillion particulars.

In so doing, RMRL obtains the capacity to deal with multidimensionality in general beyond Rodriguez-Pereyra-Yi Problem. In the semantics of RMRL, a resemblance relation is *primitive* and the degree of unresemblance is *defined* in Definition 20 by it via Representation Theorem (Theorem 3) and Uniqueness Theorem (Theorem 4).

The structure of this paper is as follows. In Subsect. 2.1, we define the language $\mathscr{L}$ of RMRL. In Subsubsect. 2.2.1, we define three measurement-theoretic concepts. In Subsubsect. 2.2.2, we prepare the seven steps to a mereological additive difference factorial proximity structured model $\mathfrak{M}$ of RMRL. In Subsubsect. 2.2.3, we provide RMRL with a satisfaction definition relative to $\mathfrak{M}$, define the truth at $w \in W$ in $\mathfrak{M}$, define validity. In Subsubsect. 2.2.4, we show the representation and uniqueness theorems for (multidimensional) resemblance predicates. In Sect. 3, we conclude by giving a solution to Rodriguez-Pereyra-Yi Problem by RMRL.

---

[3] About measurement-theoretic multidimensional representation, refer to Suppes et al. [7].

[4] About mereology, refer to Varzi [9].

2   Measurement Theory Meets Meleology in RMRL

2.1   Language

In this paper, we focus only on the ontology of *properties* that are the sematic values of one-place predicate symbols. So we do not introduce n-place predicate symbols ($n \geq 2$) in general into the language of RMRL the semantic values of which are n-ary relations, though we introduce *four-place resemblance predicate symbols* indexed by one-place predicate symbols. We define the language $\mathscr{L}$ of revised first-order modal resemblance logic RMRL:

Definition 2 (Language).

- *Let $\mathscr{V}$ denote a class of individual variables, $\mathscr{C}$ a class of individual constants, and $\mathscr{P}$ a class of* one-place *predicate symbols.*
- *Let $\leqslant_F$ denote a four-place resemblance predicate symbol indexed by F.*
- *When $n \geq 2$, let $\leqslant_{F_1 \times \cdots \times F_n}$ denote a four-place resemblance predicate symbol indexed by $F_1, \ldots, F_n$.*
- *The language $\mathscr{L}$ of RMRL is given by the following BNF grammar:*

$$t ::= x \mid a$$
$$\varphi ::= F(t) \mid t_1 = t_2 \mid \bot \mid \neg\varphi \mid \varphi \wedge \psi \mid$$
$$(t_1, t_2) \leqslant_F (t_3, t_4) \mid (t_1, t_2) \leqslant_{F_1 \times \cdots \times F_n} (t_3, t_4) \mid \Box\varphi \mid \forall x\varphi,$$

  where $x \in \mathscr{V}$, $a \in \mathscr{C}$, and $F_1, \ldots, F_n \in \mathscr{P}$.
- *$\top$, $\vee$, $\rightarrow$, $\leftrightarrow$, $<_F$, $<_{F_1 \times \cdots \times F_n}$, $\Diamond$ and $\exists$ are introduced by the standard definitions.*
- *$(t_1, t_2) \leqslant_F (t_3, t_4)$ means that t_3 does not resemble t_4 more than t_1 resembles t_2 with respect to F-ness.*
- *When $n \geq 2$, $(t_1, t_2) \leqslant_{F_1 \times \cdots \times F_n} (t_3, t_4)$ means that t_3 does not resemble t_4 more than t_1 resembles t_2 with respect to F_1-ness and $\ldots$ and F_n-ness.*
- *The set of all well-formed formulae of $\mathscr{L}$ is denoted by $\Phi_{\mathscr{L}}$.*

Remark 1 (Modal Part of RMRL). *In this paper, we do not deal with Contingent Coextension and Necessary Coextension Problems above neither of which relates to multidimensionality that is the main topic of this paper, though we did in [8]. The motivation to introduce a modality $\Box$ into $\mathscr{L}$ is only to solve Contingent Coextension and Necessary Coextension Problems.*

2.2   Semantics

2.2.1   Three Measurement-Theoretic Concepts   Here we would like to define such measurement-theoretic concepts as

1. *scale types,*
2. *representation* and *uniqueness theorems,* and
3. *measurement types*

on which the argument of this paper is based: *First*, according to Roberts [3, pp. 64-69], we classify *scale types* in terms of the class of *admissible transformations* φ:

Definition 3 (Scale Types).

- *A scale is a triple* $(\mathfrak{U}, \mathfrak{V}, f)$ *where* $\mathfrak{U}$ *is an observed relational structure that is qualitative,* $\mathfrak{V}$ *is a numerical relational structure that is quantitative, and* f *is a homomorphism from* $\mathfrak{U}$ *into* $\mathfrak{V}$.
- *Sometimes we sloppily refer to* f *alone as a scale.*
- *Suppose that* $\mathscr{D}$ *is the domain of* $\mathfrak{U}$ *and that* $\mathscr{D}'$ *is the domain of* $\mathfrak{V}$. *Suppose that* φ *is a function that maps the range of* f, *the set* $f(\mathscr{D}) := \{f(\mathfrak{d}) : \mathfrak{d} \in \mathscr{D}\}$, *into* $\mathscr{D}'$. *Then the composition* $\varphi \circ f$ *is a function from* $\mathscr{D}$ *into* $\mathscr{D}'$. *If* $\varphi \circ f$ *is a homomorphism from* $\mathfrak{U}$ *into* $\mathfrak{V}$, *we call* φ *an* admissible transformation *of scale.*
- *When the admissible transformations are all the functions* φ *of the form* $\varphi(x) := \alpha x; \alpha > 0$. φ *is called a* similarity transformation, *and a scale with the similarity transformations as its class of admissible transformations is called a* ratio scale.
- *When the admissible transformations are all the functions* φ *of the form* $\varphi(x) := \alpha x + \beta; \alpha > 0$, φ *is called a* positive affine transformation, *and a corresponding scale is called an* interval scale.
- *When the admissible transformations are all the functions* φ *of the form* $\varphi(x) := \alpha x + \beta; \alpha \neq 0$, φ *is called an* affine transformation, *and a corresponding scale is called a* quasi-interval scale.
- *When a scale is unique up to* order, *the admissible transformations are monotone increasing functions* $\varphi(x)$, *that is, functions* $\varphi(x)$ *satisfying the condition that* $x \precsim y$ *iff* $\varphi(x) \leq \varphi(y)$, *where* $\precsim$ *is a binary relation on* $\mathscr{D}$. *Such a scale is called an* ordinal scale.

Example 1 (Mass and Temperature).

- *The measurement of mass is the assignment of a homomorphism* f *from the observed relational structure* $(A, H, \bigcirc)$ *(where we judge* $\mathfrak{d}_1$ *to be heavier than* $\mathfrak{d}_2$ *and the binary operation satisfies* $f(\mathfrak{d}_1 \bigcirc \mathfrak{d}_2) = f(\mathfrak{d}_1) + f(\mathfrak{d}_2)$ *for any* $\mathfrak{d}_1, \mathfrak{d}_2 \in A$) *to the numerical relational structure* $(\mathbb{R}, >, +)$. *Mass is an example of a ratio scale.*
- *The measurement of temperature is the assignment of a homomorphism* f *from the observed relational structure* (A, W) *(where* A *is a set of objects and the binary relation* $\mathfrak{d}_1 W \mathfrak{d}_2$ *holds iff we judge* $\mathfrak{d}_1$ *to be warmer than* $\mathfrak{d}_2$) *to the numerical relational structure* $(\mathbb{R}, >)$. *Temperature is an example of an interval scale.*

Second, according to Roberts [3, pp. 54-56], we define *representation* and *uniqueness theorems*:

Definition 4 (Representation Theorem and Uniqueness Theorem).

- *The first basic problem of measurement theory is the* representation prob-lem: *Given a numerical relational structure* $\mathfrak{V}$, *find conditions on an observed relational structure* $\mathfrak{U}$ *(necessary and) sufficient for the* existence *of a homo-morphism* f *from* $\mathfrak{U}$ *to* $\mathfrak{V}$ *that preserves all the relations and operations in* $\mathfrak{U}$.
- *The theorem stating conditions on* $\mathfrak{U}$ *are (necessary and) sufficient for the existence of* f *is called a* representation theorem.
- *The second basic problem of measurement theory is the* uniqueness problem: *Find the transformation of the homomorphism* f *under which all the relations and operations in* $\mathfrak{U}$ *are preserved.*
- *The theorem stating the type of transformation up to which* f *is unique is called a* uniqueness theorem.

Third, according to Roberts [3, pp. 122-131, pp. 134-142] and Krantz et al., [1, pp. 136-157], we classify *measurement types*:

Definition 5 (Measurement Types).

- *Suppose* $\mathcal{D}$ *is a set,* $\precsim'$ *is a binary relation on* $\mathcal{D}$, $\bigcirc$ *is a binary operation on* $\mathcal{D}$, $\precsim$ *is a quaternary relation on* $\mathcal{D}$, *and* f *is a real-valued function.*
- *Then we call the representation* $\mathfrak{d}_1 \precsim' \mathfrak{d}_2$ *iff* $f(\mathfrak{d}_1) \leq f(\mathfrak{d}_2)$, *for any* $\mathfrak{d}_1, \mathfrak{d}_2 \in \mathcal{D}$, *and* $f(\mathfrak{d}_1 \bigcirc \mathfrak{d}_2) = f(\mathfrak{d}_1) + f(\mathfrak{d}_2)$, *for any* $\mathfrak{d}_1, \mathfrak{d}_2 \in \mathcal{D}$, *extensive measurement.*
- *We call the representation* $(\mathfrak{d}_1, \mathfrak{d}_2) \precsim (\mathfrak{d}_3, \mathfrak{d}_4)$ *iff* $f(\mathfrak{d}_1) - f(\mathfrak{d}_2) \leq f(\mathfrak{d}_3) - f(\mathfrak{d}_4)$, *for any* $\mathfrak{d}_1, \mathfrak{d}_2, \mathfrak{d}_3, \mathfrak{d}_4 \in \mathcal{D}$, *when the direction of differences is taken into con-sideration,* positive-difference measurement, *when the direction of differences is not taken into consideration,* algebraic-difference measurement.
- *We call the representation* $(\mathfrak{d}_1, \mathfrak{d}_2) \precsim (\mathfrak{d}_3, \mathfrak{d}_4)$ *iff* $|f(\mathfrak{d}_1) - f(\mathfrak{d}_2)| \leq |f(\mathfrak{d}_3) f(\mathfrak{d}_4)|$ *for any* $\mathfrak{d}_1, \mathfrak{d}_2, \mathfrak{d}_3, \mathfrak{d}_4 \in \mathcal{D}$, *absolute-difference measurement.*

2.2.2 Seven Steps to Construct Model $\mathfrak{M}$ of RMRL By using some measurement-theoretic concepts of Krantz et al. [1] and Suppes et al. [7], we prepare the following *seven steps* to construct a model $\mathfrak{M}$ of RMRL:

2.2.2.1 First Step
The first step is a step to prepare an *absolute difference* structure for the seman-tics of $\leqslant_F$ and $\leqslant_{F_1 \times \cdots \times F_n}$. We resort to an *absolute difference structure* in order to solve the problems of Resemblance Nominalism. Krantz et al. [1, pp.172-173] define an absolute difference structure:

Definition 6 (Absolute Difference Structure). *Suppose* $\mathcal{D}$ *is a nonempty set and* $\precsim$ *a quaternary relation on* $\mathcal{D}$ *(binary relation on* $\mathcal{D} \times \mathcal{D}$*).* $(\mathcal{D}, \precsim)$ *is an* absolute difference structure *iff, for any* $\mathfrak{d}_1, \mathfrak{d}_2, \mathfrak{d}_3, \mathfrak{d}_4, \mathfrak{d}'_1, \mathfrak{d}'_2, \mathfrak{d}'_3 \in \mathcal{D}$, *the following* six *conditions are satisfied:*

Condition 1 (Weak Order) $\precsim$ *is a weak order (*Connected *and* Transitive*).*
Condition 2 (Absoluteness) *If* $\mathfrak{d}_1 \neq \mathfrak{d}_2$, *then* $(\mathfrak{d}_1, \mathfrak{d}_1) \sim (\mathfrak{d}_2, \mathfrak{d}_2) \prec (\mathfrak{d}_1, \mathfrak{d}_2) \sim (\mathfrak{d}_2, \mathfrak{d}_1)$, *where* $(\mathfrak{d}_1, \mathfrak{d}_2) \sim (\mathfrak{d}_3, \mathfrak{d}_4) := (\mathfrak{d}_1, \mathfrak{d}_2) \precsim (\mathfrak{d}_3, \mathfrak{d}_4)$ *and* $(\mathfrak{d}_3, \mathfrak{d}_4) \precsim (\mathfrak{d}_1, \mathfrak{d}_2)$, *and* $(\mathfrak{d}_1, \mathfrak{d}_2) \prec (\mathfrak{d}_3, \mathfrak{d}_4) := (\mathfrak{d}_3, \mathfrak{d}_4) \not\precsim (\mathfrak{d}_1, \mathfrak{d}_2)$.

Condition 3 (Betweenness)

 1. If $\eth_2 \neq \eth_3$, $(\eth_1, \eth_2), (\eth_2, \eth_3) \precsim (\eth_1, \eth_3)$, and $(\eth_2, \eth_3), (\eth_3, \eth_4) \precsim (\eth_2, \eth_4)$,
  then $(\eth_1, \eth_3), (\eth_2, \eth_4) \precsim (\eth_1, \eth_4)$.

 2. If $(\eth_1, \eth_2), (\eth_2, \eth_3) \precsim (\eth_1, \eth_3)$ and $(\eth_1, \eth_3), (\eth_3, \eth_4) \precsim (\eth_1, \eth_4)$, then
  $(\eth_1, \eth_3) \precsim (\eth_1, \eth_4)$.

Condition 4 (Weak Monotonicity) *Suppose that* $(\eth_1, \eth_2), (\eth_2, \eth_3) \precsim (\eth_1, \eth_3)$.
If $(\eth_1, \eth_2) \precsim (\eth_1', \eth_2')$ *and* $(\eth_2, \eth_3) \precsim (\eth_2', \eth_3')$, *then* $(\eth_1, \eth_3) \precsim (\eth_1', \eth_3')$. *Moreover*
if either $(\eth_1, \eth_2) \prec (\eth_1', \eth_2')$ *or* $(\eth_2, \eth_3) \prec (\eth_2', \eth_3')$, *then* $(\eth_1, \eth_3) \prec (\eth_1', \eth_3')$.

Condition 5 (Solvability) *If* $(\eth_3, \eth_4) \precsim (\eth_1, \eth_2)$, *then there exists* $\eth_4' \in \mathscr{D}$ *such*
that $(\eth_4', \eth_2) \precsim (\eth_1, \eth_2)$ *and* $(\eth_1, \eth_4') \sim (\eth_3, \eth_4)$.

Condition 6 (Archimedean Property) *If* $\eth_1^{(1)}, \eth_1^{(2)}, \ldots, \eth_1^{(i)}, \ldots$ *is a strictly*
bounded standard sequence (i.e., there exist $\eth_2, \eth_3 \in \mathscr{D}$ *such that for any* $i =$
$1, 2, \ldots$, $(\eth_1^{(i)}, \eth_1^{(1)}) \precsim (\eth_1^{(i+1)}, \eth_1^{(1)}) \prec (\eth_2, \eth_3)$ *and* $(\eth_1^{(1)}, \eth_1^{(1)}) \prec (\eth_1^{(2)}, \eth_1^{(1)}) \sim$
$(\eth_1^{(i+1)}, \eth_1^{(i)}))$, *then the sequence is finite.*

The following definition [1, p.172] makes Conditions 3-6 easy to understand.

Definition 7 (Betweenness). *Suppose* $(\mathscr{D}, \precsim)$ *satisfies Conditions 1 and 2 of*
Definition 6. We say that $\eth_2$ *is between* $\eth_1$ *and* $\eth_3$ *(in symbols,* $\eth_1|\eth_2|\eth_3$) *iff*
$(\eth_1, \eth_2), (\eth_2, \eth_3) \precsim (\eth_1, \eth_3)$.

We can replace Conditions 3-6 by the following Conditions 3'-6':

Condition 3' (Betweenness)

 1. If $\eth_2 \neq \eth_3$, $\eth_1|\eth_2|\eth_3$, and $\eth_2|\eth_3|\eth_4$, then both $\eth_1|\eth_2|\eth_4$ and $\eth_1|\eth_3|\eth_4$.

 2. If $\eth_1|\eth_2|\eth_3$ and $\eth_1|\eth_3|\eth_4$, then $\eth_1|\eth_2|\eth_4$.

Condition 4' (Weak Monotonicity) *If* $\eth_1|\eth_2|\eth_3$, $\eth_1'|\eth_2'|\eth_3'$, *and* $(\eth_1, \eth_2) \sim$
$(\eth_1', \eth_2')$, *then* $(\eth_2, \eth_3) \precsim (\eth_2', \eth_3')$ *iff* $(\eth_1, \eth_3) \precsim (\eth_1', \eth_3')$.

Condition 5' (Solvability) *If* $(\eth_3, \eth_4) \precsim (\eth_1, \eth_2)$ *then there exists* $\eth_4' \in \mathscr{D}$ *with*
$\eth_1|\eth_4'|\eth_2$ *and* $(\eth_1, \eth_4') \sim (\eth_3, \eth_4)$.

Condition 6' (Archimedean Property) *If* $\eth_1^{(i+1)}|\eth_1^{(i)}|\eth_1^{(1)}$ *for any* $i = 1, 2, \ldots$,
successive intervals are equal and nonnull, and $(\eth_1^{(i)}, \eth_1^{(1)})$ *is strictly bounded,*
then the sequence is finite.

Krantz et al. [1, pp.173-177] prove the following theorems:

Fact 1 (Representation). *If* $(\mathscr{D}, \precsim)$ *is an* absolute difference structure, *then*
there exists a real-valued function f *on* $\mathscr{D}$ *such that, for any* $\eth_1, \eth_2, \eth_3, \eth_4 \in \mathscr{D}$,
$(\eth_1, \eth_2) \precsim (\eth_3, \eth_4)$ *iff* $|f(\eth_1) - f(\eth_2)| \leq |f(\eth_3) - f(\eth_4)|$.

Fact 2 (Uniqueness). *The above function* f *is a* quasi-interval scale.

2.2.2.2 Second Step

The second step is a step to prepare a basic *multidimensional* structure for
$\leqslant_{F_1 \times \cdots \times F_n}$. Suppes et al. [7, pp. 160-161] define a basic multidimensional comparison structure, called a *factorial proximity structure*:

Definition 8 (Factorial Proximity Structure).

- $(\mathscr{D}, \precsim)$ *is a proximity structure iff the following conditions are satisfied for any* $\mathfrak{d}_1, \mathfrak{d}_2 \in \mathscr{D}$:
  - $\precsim$ *is a weak order.*
  - $(\mathfrak{d}_1, \mathfrak{d}_1) \prec (\mathfrak{d}_1, \mathfrak{d}_2)$ *whenever* $\mathfrak{d}_1 \neq \mathfrak{d}_2$.
  - $(\mathfrak{d}_1, \mathfrak{d}_1) \sim (\mathfrak{d}_2, \mathfrak{d}_2)$ *(Minimality).*
  - $(\mathfrak{d}_1, \mathfrak{d}_2) \sim (\mathfrak{d}_2, \mathfrak{d}_1)$ *(Symmetricity).*

- *The structure is called* n-*factorial iff* $\mathscr{D} := \prod_{i=1}^{n} \mathscr{D}_i$.
- *We use the expression* "$\mathfrak{d}_1 \cdots \mathfrak{d}_n (\in \mathscr{D})$" *for the* n-*tuple of* $\mathfrak{d}_i \in \mathscr{D}_i$ *(*$1 \leq i \leq n$*).*

Remark 2 (Motivation to Introduce Mereology into Model of RMRL**).**
The motivation to introduce mereology into the model $\mathfrak{M}$ *of* RMRL *is that the ontological status of this* n-*tuple* $\mathfrak{d}_1 \cdots \mathfrak{d}_n$ *is not clear.*

2.2.2.3 Third Step

In order to make each dimensional factor the *absolute* value of a scale *difference*, we first establish decomposability of a factorial proximity structure $(\mathscr{D}, \precsim)$ into each factor $(\mathscr{D}_i, \precsim_i)$ where $\precsim_i$ is an induced weak order of Definition 10 below. To achieve it, $(\mathscr{D}, \precsim)$ must satisfy *Betweenness, Restricted Solvability*, and the *Archimedean Property*. In order to define Betweenness, we need *One-Factor Independence*. Suppes et al. [7, pp.178-181] define these concepts as follows:

Definition 9 (One-Factor Independence). *A factorial proximity structure* $(\mathscr{D}, \precsim)$ *satisfies* One-Factor Independence *iff the following holds for any* $\mathfrak{d}_1, \mathfrak{d}_1', \mathfrak{d}_2, \mathfrak{d}_2', \mathfrak{d}_3, \mathfrak{d}_3', \mathfrak{d}_4, \mathfrak{d}_4' \in \mathscr{D}$: *If the two elements in each of the pairs* $(\mathfrak{d}_1, \mathfrak{d}_1'), (\mathfrak{d}_2, \mathfrak{d}_2'), (\mathfrak{d}_3, \mathfrak{d}_3'), (\mathfrak{d}_4, \mathfrak{d}_4')$ *have identical components on all but one factor, and two elements in each of the pairs* $(\mathfrak{d}_1, \mathfrak{d}_3), (\mathfrak{d}_1', \mathfrak{d}_3'), (\mathfrak{d}_2, \mathfrak{d}_4), (\mathfrak{d}_2', \mathfrak{d}_4')$ *have identical components on the remaining factor, then*

$$(\mathfrak{d}_1, \mathfrak{d}_2) \precsim (\mathfrak{d}_1', \mathfrak{d}_2') \quad \text{iff} \quad (\mathfrak{d}_3, \mathfrak{d}_4) \precsim (\mathfrak{d}_3', \mathfrak{d}_4').$$

If we consider all pairs whose elements differ with respect to the i th factor only, then one-factor independence asserts that for any $i(1 \leq i \leq n)$ the induced weak order $\precsim_i$ on $\mathscr{D}_i \times \mathscr{D}_i$ of Definition 10 below is independent of the fixed components of the remaining $\mathscr{D}_i \times \mathscr{D}_i$ for $j \neq i$.

Definition 10 (Betweenness).

- *Let* $(\mathscr{D} := \prod_{i=1}^{n} \mathscr{D}_i, \precsim)$ *be a factorial proximity structure that satisfies One-Factor Independence.*
- *Let* $\precsim_i$ *denote an induced weak order on* $\mathscr{D}_i \times \mathscr{D}_i$.
- *We say that* $\mathfrak{d}_2$ *is between* $\mathfrak{d}_1$ *and* $\mathfrak{d}_3$, *denoted by* $\mathfrak{d}_1 | \mathfrak{d}_2 | \mathfrak{d}_3$, *iff*

$$(\mathfrak{d}_1^{(i)}, \mathfrak{d}_2^{(i)}), (\mathfrak{d}_2^{(i)}, \mathfrak{d}_3^{(i)}) \precsim_i (\mathfrak{d}_1^{(i)}, \mathfrak{d}_3^{(i)}) \quad \text{for any } i.$$

- *A factorial proximity structure* $(\mathscr{D}, \precsim)$ *satisfies* Betweenness *iff the following hold for any* $\mathfrak{d}_1, \mathfrak{d}_2, \mathfrak{d}_3, \mathfrak{d}_4, \mathfrak{d}_1', \mathfrak{d}_2', \mathfrak{d}_3' \in \mathscr{D}$:

1. Suppose that $\mathfrak{d}_1, \mathfrak{d}_2, \mathfrak{d}_3, \mathfrak{d}_4$ differ on at most one factor, and $\mathfrak{d}_2 \neq \mathfrak{d}_3$, then
   (a) if $\mathfrak{d}_1|\mathfrak{d}_2|\mathfrak{d}_3$ and $\mathfrak{d}_2|\mathfrak{d}_3|\mathfrak{d}_4$, then $\mathfrak{d}_1|\mathfrak{d}_2|\mathfrak{d}_4$ and $\mathfrak{d}_1|\mathfrak{d}_3|\mathfrak{d}_4$, and
   (b) if $\mathfrak{d}_1|\mathfrak{d}_2|\mathfrak{d}_3$ and $\mathfrak{d}_1|\mathfrak{d}_3|\mathfrak{d}_4$, then $\mathfrak{d}_1|\mathfrak{d}_2|\mathfrak{d}_4$ and $\mathfrak{d}_2|\mathfrak{d}_3|\mathfrak{d}_4$.
2. Suppose that $\mathfrak{d}_1, \mathfrak{d}_2, \mathfrak{d}_3, \mathfrak{d}'_1, \mathfrak{d}'_2, \mathfrak{d}'_3$ differ on at most one factor, $\mathfrak{d}_1|\mathfrak{d}_2|\mathfrak{d}_3$, $\mathfrak{d}'_1|\mathfrak{d}'_2|\mathfrak{d}'_3$, and $(\mathfrak{d}_2, \mathfrak{d}_3) \sim (\mathfrak{d}'_2, \mathfrak{d}'_3)$, then

$$(\mathfrak{d}_1, \mathfrak{d}_2) \precsim (\mathfrak{d}'_1, \mathfrak{d}'_2) \quad \text{iff} \quad (\mathfrak{d}_1, \mathfrak{d}_3) \precsim (\mathfrak{d}'_1, \mathfrak{d}'_3).$$

Betweenness (Definition 10) is an extension of the one-dimensional concept of Betweenness (Condition 3) of Definition 6 above. Betweenness (Definition 10) is a one-dimensional property that each induced weak order $\precsim_i$ must satisfy.

Definition 11 (Restricted Solvability). *A factorial proximity structure* $(\mathscr{D}, \precsim)$ *satisfies* Restricted Solvability *iff, for any* $\mathfrak{d}_1, \mathfrak{d}_3, \mathfrak{d}_4, \mathfrak{d}_5, \mathfrak{d}_6 \in \mathscr{D}$, *if* $(\mathfrak{d}_4, \mathfrak{d}_3) \precsim (\mathfrak{d}_5, \mathfrak{d}_6) \precsim (\mathfrak{d}_4, \mathfrak{d}_1)$, *then there exists* $\mathfrak{d}_2 \in \mathscr{D}$ *such that* $\mathfrak{d}_1|\mathfrak{d}_2|\mathfrak{d}_3$ *and* $(\mathfrak{d}_4, \mathfrak{d}_2) \sim (\mathfrak{d}_5, \mathfrak{d}_6)$.

Just as the role of Solvability (Condition 5) of Definition 6 above is to determine a class of absolute difference structures of Definition 6 on the basis of which Fact 1 (Representation) above can be proved, so the role of Restricted Solvability is to determine a class of additive difference factorial proximity structures of Definition 15 below on the basis of which Theorem 1 (Representation) below can be proved.

Definition 12 (Archimedean Property). *A factorial proximity structure* $(\mathscr{D}, \precsim)$ *satisfies the* Archimedean Property *iff, for any* $\mathfrak{d}_1, \mathfrak{d}_2, \mathfrak{d}_3, \mathfrak{d}_4 \in \mathscr{D}$ *with* $\mathfrak{d}_1 \neq \mathfrak{d}_2$, *any sequence* $\{\mathfrak{d}_5^{(i)} : \mathfrak{d}_5^{(i)} \in \mathscr{D}, i = 0, 1, \ldots\}$ *that varies on at most one factor, such that*

$$\mathfrak{d}_5^{(0)} = \mathfrak{d}_3,$$

$$(\mathfrak{d}_1, \mathfrak{d}_2) \prec (\mathfrak{d}_5^{(i)}, \mathfrak{d}_5^{(i+1)}) \text{ and } (\mathfrak{d}_3, \mathfrak{d}_5^{(i)}) \prec (\mathfrak{d}_3, \mathfrak{d}_5^{(i+1)}) \prec (\mathfrak{d}_3, \mathfrak{d}_4) \text{ for any } i,$$

is finite.

Just as the Archimedean Property (Condition 6) of Definition 6 above is a technically necessary condition to prove Fact 1 (Representation) above and Fact 5 (Representation) below, so the Archimedean Property (Definition 12) is a technically necessary condition to prove Fact 3 (Representation) below. Suppes et al. [7, p. 181] prove the following theorems:

Fact 3 (Representation). *Suppose* $(\mathscr{D}, \precsim)$ *is a factorial proximity structure that satisfies One-Factor Independence (Definition 9), Betweenness (Definition 10), Restrict Solvability (Definition 11), and the Archimedean Property (Definition 12). Then there exist real-valued functions* f_i *defined on* $\mathscr{D}_i$ $(1 \leq i \leq n)$ *and real-valued function* g *that increases in each of* n *real arguments such that*

$$\delta(\mathfrak{d}_1, \mathfrak{d}_2) := g(|f_1(\mathfrak{d}_1^{(1)}) - f_1(\mathfrak{d}_2^{(1)})|, \ldots, |f_n(\mathfrak{d}_1^{(n)})) - f_n(\mathfrak{d}_2^{(1)})|)$$

and

$$(\mathfrak{d}_1, \mathfrak{d}_2) \precsim (\mathfrak{d}_3, \mathfrak{d}_4) \quad \text{iff} \quad \delta(\mathfrak{d}_1, \mathfrak{d}_2) \leq \delta(\mathfrak{d}_3, \mathfrak{d}_4).$$

Fact 4 (Uniqueness). *The above functions f_i are interval scales, and the above function g is an ordinal scale.*

2.2.2.4 Fourth Step

In order to represent the *sum* of dimensional factors, a factorial proximity structure $(\mathscr{D}, \precsim)$ should satisfy *Independence* and the *Thomsen Condition* only for the dimensionality $n = 2$. Suppes et al. [7, p. 182] define these concepts as follows:

Definition 13 (Independence). *A factorial proximity structure $(\mathscr{D}, \precsim)$ satisfies Independence iff the following holds for any $\mathfrak{d}_1, \mathfrak{d}'_1, \mathfrak{d}_2, \mathfrak{d}'_2, \mathfrak{d}_3, \mathfrak{d}'_3, \mathfrak{d}_4, \mathfrak{d}'_4 \in \mathscr{D}$: If the two elements in each of $(\mathfrak{d}_1, \mathfrak{d}'_1), (\mathfrak{d}_2, \mathfrak{d}'_2), (\mathfrak{d}_3, \mathfrak{d}'_3), (\mathfrak{d}_4, \mathfrak{d}'_4)$ have identical components on one factor, and the two elements in each of $(\mathfrak{d}_1, \mathfrak{d}_3), (\mathfrak{d}'_1, \mathfrak{d}'_3), (\mathfrak{d}_2, \mathfrak{d}_4), (\mathfrak{d}'_2, \mathfrak{d}'_4)$ have identical components on all the remaining factors, then*

$$(\mathfrak{d}_1, \mathfrak{d}_2) \precsim (\mathfrak{d}'_1, \mathfrak{d}'_2) \quad \text{iff} \quad (\mathfrak{d}_3, \mathfrak{d}_4) \precsim (\mathfrak{d}'_3, \mathfrak{d}'_4).$$

Remark 3 (One-Factor Independence and Independence) Independence *(Definition 13) implies* One-Factor Independence *(Definition 9).*

Just as One-Factor Independence (Definition 9) above is a necessary condition to prove Fact 3 (Representation) above, so Independence (Definition 13) is a necessary condition to prove Fact 5 (Representation) below.

Definition 14 (Thomsen Condition). *A factorial proximity structure $(\mathscr{D}, \precsim)$ with $\mathscr{D} := \mathscr{D}_1 \times \mathscr{D}_2$ satisfies the Thomsen Condition iff, for any $\mathfrak{d}_1^{(i)}, \mathfrak{d}_2^{(i)}, \mathfrak{d}_3^{(i)}, \mathfrak{d}_4^{(i)}, \mathfrak{d}_5^{(i)}, \mathfrak{d}_6^{(i)} \in \mathscr{D}_i \ (i = 1, 2),$*

$$(\mathfrak{d}_1^{(1)}\mathfrak{d}_5^{(2)}, \mathfrak{d}_2^{(1)}\mathfrak{d}_6^{(2)}) \sim (\mathfrak{d}_5^{(1)}\mathfrak{d}_3^{(2)}, \mathfrak{d}_6^{(1)}\mathfrak{d}_4^{(2)})$$

and

$$(\mathfrak{d}_5^{(1)}\mathfrak{d}_1^{(2)}, \mathfrak{d}_6^{(1)}\mathfrak{d}_2^{(2)}) \sim (\mathfrak{d}_3^{(1)}\mathfrak{d}_5^{(2)}, \mathfrak{d}_4^{(1)}\mathfrak{d}_6^{(2)})$$

imply

$$(\mathfrak{d}_1^{(1)}\mathfrak{d}_1^{(2)}, \mathfrak{d}_2^{(1)}\mathfrak{d}_2^{(2)}) \sim (\mathfrak{d}_3^{(1)}\mathfrak{d}_3^{(2)}, \mathfrak{d}_4^{(1)}\mathfrak{d}_4^{(2)}).$$

Remark 4 (Thomsen Condition Only for Two Dimensionality). *The Thomsen Condition must be assumed only when the dimensionality $n = 2$.*

Suppes et al. [7, p. 183] prove the following theorems:

Fact 5 (Representation). *Suppose that $(\mathscr{D}, \precsim)$ is a factorial proximity structure that satisfies Restrict Solvability (Definition 11) and Independence (Definition 13), and that each structure $(\mathscr{D}_i, \precsim_i)$, where $\precsim_i$ is an induced weak order on $\mathscr{D}_i \times \mathscr{D}_i$, satisfies the Archimedean Property (Condition 6 of Definition 6). If $n \geq 3$, then there exist real-valued functions f_i defined on $\mathscr{D}_i \times \mathscr{D}_i \ (1 \leq i \leq n)$ such that for any $\mathfrak{d}_1, \mathfrak{d}_2, \mathfrak{d}_3, \mathfrak{d}_4 \in \mathscr{D}$,*

$$(\mathfrak{d}_1^{(1)} \cdots \mathfrak{d}_1^{(n)}, \mathfrak{d}_2^{(1)} \cdots \mathfrak{d}_2^{(n)}) \precsim (\mathfrak{d}_3^{(1)} \cdots \mathfrak{d}_3^{(n)}, \mathfrak{d}_4^{(1)} \cdots \mathfrak{d}_4^{(n)})$$

iff

$$\sum_{i=1}^{n} f_i(\mathfrak{d}_1^{(i)}, \mathfrak{d}_2^{(i)}) \geq \sum_{i=1}^{n} f_i(\mathfrak{d}_3^{(i)}, \mathfrak{d}_4^{(i)}).$$

If $n = 2$, then the above assertions hold provided the Thomsen Condition (Definition 14) is also satisfied.

Fact 6 (Uniqueness). *The above functions f_i are interval scales.*

2.2.2.5 *Fifth Step*

The fifth step is a step to combine the third and fourth steps. Suppes et al. [7, p. 184] define an *additive difference factorial proximity structure* as follows:

Definition 15 (Additive Difference Factorial Proximity Structure).

When $n \geq 2$ and the factorial proximity structure $(\mathscr{D}(:= \prod_{i=1}^{n} \mathscr{D}_i), \precsim)$ *satisfies* Betweenness, Restricted Solvability, *the* Archimedean Property, Independence, *and the* Thomsen Condition, *we call it an* additive difference factorial proximity structure.

By combining Facts 3–6, Suppes et al. [7, p. 185] prove the following theorems:

Fact 7 (Representation). *If $(\mathscr{D}, \precsim)$ is an additive difference factorial proximity structure (Definition 15), there exist real-valued functions f_i defined on $\mathscr{D}_i$ $(1 \leq i \leq n)$ such that for any $\mathfrak{d}_1, \mathfrak{d}_2, \mathfrak{d}_3, \mathfrak{d}_4 \in \mathscr{D}$,*

$$(\mathfrak{d}_1^{(1)} \cdots \mathfrak{d}_1^{(n)}, \mathfrak{d}_2^{(1)} \cdots \mathfrak{d}_2^{(n)}) \precsim (\mathfrak{d}_3^{(1)} \cdots \mathfrak{d}_3^{(n)}, \mathfrak{d}_4^{(1)} \cdots \mathfrak{d}_4^{(n)})$$

iff

$$\sum_{i=1}^{n} g_i(|f_i(\mathfrak{d}_1^{(i)}) - f_i(\mathfrak{d}_2^{(i)})|) \leq \sum_{i=1}^{n} g_i(|f_i(\mathfrak{d}_3^{(i)}) - f_i(\mathfrak{d}_4^{(i)})|)$$

Fact 8 (Uniqueness). *The above functions f_i are interval scales and the above functions g_i are interval scales with a common unit.*

2.2.2.6 *Sixth Step*

The *ontological status* of an n-tuple $\mathfrak{d}_1 \cdots \mathfrak{d}_n$ in Definition 8 is not clear. So in order to describe the *parthood between a particular and its parts* referred to for determining the raking on a resemblance relation, we would like to introduce *mereology*:

Definition 16 (Mereology).

– *A mereological parthood relation P (Varzi [9, p.14]) is a binary relation on $\mathscr{D}$ satisfying the following properties:*
  - *For any $\mathfrak{d} \in \mathscr{D}$, $P(\mathfrak{d}, \mathfrak{d})$ (Reflexivity).*
  - *For any $\mathfrak{d}_1, \mathfrak{d}_2, \mathfrak{d}_3 \in \mathscr{D}$, if $P(\mathfrak{d}_1, \mathfrak{d}_2)$ and $P(\mathfrak{d}_2, \mathfrak{d}_3)$, then $P(\mathfrak{d}_1, \mathfrak{d}_3)$ (Transitivity).*

- For any $\eth_1, \eth_2 \in \mathscr{D}$, if $P(\eth_1, \eth_2)$ and $P(\eth_2, \eth_1)$, then $\eth_1$ equals $\eth_2$ (Antisymmetry).
- For any $\eth_1, \eth_2 \in \mathscr{D}$, a mereological proper parthood relation $PP(\eth_1, \eth_2)$ is such a binary relation on $\mathscr{D}$ that $P(\eth_1, \eth_2)$ and $\eth_1$ does not equal $\eth_2$.
- For any $\eth_1, \eth_2 \in \mathscr{D}$, a mereological overlap relation $O(\eth_1, \eth_2)$ is such a binary relation on $\mathscr{D}$ that there exists $\eth_3 \in \mathscr{D}$ such that $P(\eth_3, \eth_1)$ and $P(\eth_3, \eth_2)$.
- For any $\eth_1, \eth_2 \in \mathscr{D}$, if $PP(\eth_1, \eth_2)$, then there exists $\eth_3 \in \mathscr{D}$ such that $P(\eth_3, \eth_2)$ and not $O(\eth_3, \eth_1)$ (Supplementation) (Varzi [9, pp.51-52]).
- For any $\eth_1, \eth_2, \eth_3 \in \mathscr{D}$, a mereological product relation $PR(\eth_3, \eth_1, \eth_2)$ is such a ternary relation on $\mathscr{D}$ that $P(\eth_4, \eth_3)$ iff $P(\eth_4, \eth_1)$ and $P(\eth_4, \eth_2)$, for any $\eth_4 \in \mathscr{D}$.
- For any $\eth_1, \eth_2 \in \mathscr{D}$, then there exists $\eth_3 \in \mathscr{D}$ such that $PR(\eth_3, \eth_1, \eth_2)$ (Product).
- For any $\eth_1, \eth_2 \in \mathscr{D}$, we define $\eth_1 \bigotimes \eth_2$ as the uniquely existential object bearing the relation PR with $\eth_1$ and $\eth_2$, in symbols, $\imath \eth_3 PR(\eth_3, \eth_1, \eth_2)$ (Varzi [9, pp.51-52]).

Example 2 (Rodriguez-Pereyra-Yi Problem and Mereology). *In Rodriguez-Pereyra-Yi Problem, by means of a mereological parthood function P, we would like to describe the parthood between a particular and its parts referred to for determining the raking on resemblance relations with respect to carminity and vermillionity and triangularity. In this case, neither carminity, vermillionity nor triangularity themselves is reified.*

2.2.2.7 Final Step

By connecting *measurement-theoretic* concepts with *mereological* concepts, we define a *mereorogical additive difference factorial proximity structured model* $\mathfrak{M}$ of RMRL:

Definition 17 (Mereorogical Additive Difference Factorial Proximity Structured Model).

- The mereological additive difference factorial proximity structured frame *of* RMRL *is a structure*

$$\mathfrak{F} := (\mathscr{W}, R, \mathscr{D}, \{\precsim_F\}_{F \in \mathscr{P}}, \{\mathscr{D}_{\precsim_F}\}_{F \in \mathscr{P}}, P, \{\precsim_{F_1 \times \cdots \times F_n}\}_{F_1 \ldots, F_n \in \mathscr{P}}),$$

where
- $\mathscr{W}$ *is a non-empty class of worlds,*
- R *a binary accessibility relation on* $\mathscr{W}$,
- $\mathscr{D}$ *a non-empty class of particulars,*
- $\{\precsim_F\}_{F \in \mathscr{P}}$ *a family of such quaternary relations* $\precsim_F$ *on* $\mathscr{D}$ *that* $(\mathscr{D}, \precsim_F)$ *is an absolute difference structure and* $\precsim_F$ *satisfies* Maximality *of Definition 8,*
- $\{\mathscr{D}_{\precsim_F}\}_{F \in \mathscr{P}}$ *a non-empty class of* $\mathscr{D}_{\precsim_F}$ *which is a non-empty class of the parts of particulars referred to for determining the ranking on* $\precsim_F$ *and which postulates that there exists a unique F-part of a particular belonging to* $\mathscr{D}$,

- P *a mereological parthood relation on* $\mathscr{D} \cup \bigcup_{F \in \mathscr{P}} \mathscr{D}_{\precsim_F}$ *of Definition 16*
- $\{\precsim_{F_1 \times \cdots \times F_n}\}_{F_1 \ldots, F_n \in \mathscr{P}}$ *a family of such quaternary relations* $\precsim_{F_1 \times \cdots \times F_n}$ *on* $\mathscr{D}_{F_1} \times \cdots \times \mathscr{D}_{F_n}$ *that* $(\mathscr{D}_{F_1} \times \cdots \times \mathscr{D}_{F_n}, \precsim_{F_1 \times \cdots \times F_n})$ *is an additive difference factorial proximity structure.*

– *A function I is an* interpretation *of $\mathfrak{F}$ if I*

- *assigns to each $a \in \mathscr{C}$ and each $w \in \mathscr{W}$ some object that is a member of $\mathscr{D}$ that satisfies* Transworld Identity: *for any w, w',*

$$I(a, w) = I(a, w'),$$

and

- *assigns to each four-place resemblance predicate symbol $\leqslant_F$ and each $w \in \mathscr{W}$ such a quaternary relation $\precsim_F$, and*
- *assigns to each four-place resemblance predicate symbol $\leqslant_{F_1 \times \cdots \times F_n}$ and each $w \in \mathscr{W}$ such a quaternary relation $\precsim^*_{F_1 \times \cdots \times F_n}$ that it is defined as follows:*

  if, for any particular $\mathfrak{d}_1, \mathfrak{d}_2, \mathfrak{d}_3, \mathfrak{d}_4 \in \mathscr{D}$, $\mathcal{W}_{i+4}P(\mathfrak{d}_{i+4}, \mathfrak{d}_1)$, $\mathcal{W}_{i+5}P(\mathfrak{d}_{i+5}, \mathfrak{d}_2)$, $\mathcal{W}_{i+6}P(\mathfrak{d}_{i+6}, \mathfrak{d}_3)$, $\mathcal{W}_{i+7}P(\mathfrak{d}_{i+7}, \mathfrak{d}_4) \in \mathscr{D}_{F_i}$ are such uniquely existential parts of $\mathfrak{d}_1, \mathfrak{d}_2, \mathfrak{d}_3, \mathfrak{d}_4$ respectively, then

  $$(\mathfrak{d}_1, \mathfrak{d}_2) \precsim^*_{F_1 \times \cdots \times F_n} (\mathfrak{d}_3, \mathfrak{d}_4)$$

  iff

  $$(\bigotimes_{i=1}^{n} \mathcal{W}_{i+4}P(\mathfrak{d}_{i+4}, \mathfrak{d}_1), \bigotimes_{i=1}^{n} \mathcal{W}_{i+5}P(\mathfrak{d}_{i+5}, \mathfrak{d}_2))$$
  $$\precsim_{F_1 \times \cdots \times F_n}$$
  $$(\bigotimes_{i=1}^{n} \mathcal{W}_{i+6}P(\mathfrak{d}_{i+6}, \mathfrak{d}_3), \bigotimes_{i=1}^{n} \mathcal{W}_{i+7}P(\mathfrak{d}_{i+7}, \mathfrak{d}_4)).$$

  (Refer to Definition 16 for the definition of $\otimes$.)

– *A property class $I(F, w)$ is defined as a* maximal resemblance class *in terms of a resemblance relation $\precsim_F$: $A \subsetneq \mathscr{D}$ is a* property class $I(F, w)$ *iff $(\mathscr{D}, \precsim_F)$ is an absolute difference structure and for any $\mathfrak{d}_1, \mathfrak{d}_2, \mathfrak{d}_3 \in A$ and for any $\mathfrak{d}_4 \in \overline{A}$,*

$$(\mathfrak{d}_1, \mathfrak{d}_2) \prec_F (\mathfrak{d}_3, \mathfrak{d}_4) \quad (\text{Maximality}).$$

– *The mereological additive difference factorial proximity structured model of* RMRL *is a structure*

$$\mathfrak{M} := (\mathscr{W}, R, \mathscr{D}, \{\precsim_F\}_{F \in \mathscr{P}}, \{\mathscr{D}_{\precsim_F}\}_{F \in \mathscr{P}}, P, \{\precsim_{F_1 \times \cdots \times F_n}\}_{F_1 \ldots, F_n \in \mathscr{P}}, I).$$

Remark 5 $(\precsim^*_{F_1 \times \cdots \times F_n}$ **and** $\precsim_{F_1 \times \cdots \times F_n})$. *In this definition, we consider the comparison $(\precsim^*_{F_1 \times \cdots \times F_n})$ of differences of resemblance between particulars with respect to F_1-ness and ... and F_n-ness to be the comparison $(\precsim_{F_1 \times \cdots \times F_n})$ of difference of resemblance between the n-tuple products of parts of a particular referred to for determining the raking on resemblance relations with respect to F_1-ness and ... and with respect to F_n-ness, respectively.*

Remark 6 (Not Absoluteness But Conditionality). *The mereological additive difference factorial proximity structured model of* RMRL *does not require that $\precsim_F$ should absolutely satisfy such conditions above as Betweenness and the Archimedean Property and so on, but requires that if $\precsim_F$ satisfies them, then Theorems 1–4 below can be proven.*

Remark 7 (Nominalism about Universals). $\mathfrak{M}$ *is* nominalistic *both about such universals as properties and about $\precsim_F$ and R neither of which are reified, whereas it is* Platonistic *about such abstract objects as classes, functions, numbers and possible worlds. As Rodriguez-Pereyra [5] observes, Realism/Nominalism about universals is* independent *of Platonism/Nominalism about abstract objects.*

Remark 8 (Non-Circularity of Resemblance Relation). *Since a resemblance relation $\precsim_F$ depends* not *on a property class $I(F,w)$ defined by $\precsim_F$ but on a predicate symbol F, where $I(F,w)$ is the semantic value of F. In this sense, $\precsim_F$ is not circular.*

Remark 9 (Reducibility and Resemblance Nominalism). $\mathfrak{M}$ *is resemblance-nominalistic in the sense that $I(F,w)$ is reducible to $\precsim_F$.*

2.2.3 Satisfaction Definition

We define an (extended) assignment as follows:

Definition 18 ((Extended) Assignment).

- *We call $s : \mathcal{V} \to \mathcal{D}$ an assignment.*
- *$\tilde{s} : \mathcal{V} \cup \mathcal{C} \to \mathcal{D}$ is defined as follows:*
  1. *For each $x \in \mathcal{V}$, $\tilde{s}(x) = s(x)$,*
  2. *For each $a \in \mathcal{C}$ and each $w \in \mathcal{W}$, $\tilde{s}(a) = I(a,w)$.*
  We call $\tilde{s}$ an extended assignment.

We provide MRL with the following satisfaction definition relative to $\mathfrak{M}$, define the truth (at a world) in $\mathfrak{M}$ by means of satisfaction and then define validity as follows:

Definition 19 (Satisfaction).

- *What it means for $\mathfrak{M}$ to satisfy $\varphi \in \Phi_{\mathcal{L}}$ at $w \in \mathcal{W}$ with s, in symbols $(\mathfrak{M}, w) \models \varphi[s]$ is inductively defined as follows:*
  - $(\mathfrak{M}, w) \models (t_1, t_2) \leqslant_F (t_3, t_4)[s]$ *iff* $(\tilde{s}(t_1), \tilde{s}(t_2)) \precsim_F (\tilde{s}(t_3), \tilde{s}(t_4))$,
  - $(\mathfrak{M}, w) \models (t_1, t_2) \leqslant_{F_1 \times \cdots \times F_n} (t_3, t_4)[s]$ *iff* $(\tilde{s}(t_1), \tilde{s}(t_2)) \precsim^*_{F_1 \times \cdots \times F_n} (\tilde{s}(t_3), \tilde{s}(t_4))$,
  - $(\mathfrak{M}, w) \models F(t)[s]$ *iff* $\tilde{s}(t) \in I(F,w)$, *where $I(F,w)$ is defined by Definition 17,*
  - $(\mathfrak{M}, w) \models t_1 = t_2[s]$ *iff* $\tilde{s}(t_1) = \tilde{s}(t_2)$,
  - $(\mathfrak{M}, w) \models \top[s]$,
  - $(\mathfrak{M}, w) \models \neg\varphi[s]$ *iff* $(\mathfrak{M}, w) \not\models \varphi[s]$,

- $(\mathfrak{M}, w) \models \varphi \wedge \psi[s]$ *iff* $(\mathfrak{M}, w) \models \varphi[s]$ *and* $(\mathfrak{M}, w) \models \psi[s]$,
- $(\mathfrak{M}, w) \models \Box\varphi[s]$ *iff*   *for all* $w \in \mathscr{W}$ *such that* $R(w, w')$, $(\mathfrak{M}, w') \models \varphi[s]$,
- $(\mathfrak{M}, w) \models \forall x \varphi[s]$ *iff*   *for any* $\eth \in \mathscr{D}$, $\mathfrak{M} \models \varphi[s(x|\eth)]$, *where* $s(x|\eth)$ *is the function that is exactly like s except for one thing: for the individual variable x, it assigns the object* $\eth$. *This can be expressed as follows:*

$$s(x|d)(y) := \begin{cases} s(y) & \text{if } y \neq x \\ \eth & \text{if } y = x. \end{cases}$$

- *If* $(\mathfrak{M}, w) \models \varphi[s]$ *for all s, we write* $(\mathfrak{M}, w) \models \varphi$ *and say that* φ *is true at w in* $\mathfrak{M}$.
- *If* $(\mathfrak{M}, w) \models \varphi$ *for all* $w \in \mathscr{W}$, *we write* $\mathfrak{M} \models \varphi$ *and say that* φ *is true in* $\mathfrak{M}$.
- *If* φ *is true in any model based on the frame of* MRL, *we write* $\models \varphi$ *and say that* φ *is valid.*

The next corollary follows from Definitions 17 and 19:

Corollary 1 (Property Class and Resemblance Relation).

$$(\mathfrak{M}, w) \models F(t)[s]$$

iff

$$\tilde{s}(t) \in I(F, w)$$

iff for any $\eth_2, \eth_3 \in I(F, w)$ *and for any* $\eth_3 \in \overline{I(F, w)}$,

$$(\tilde{s}(t), \eth_1) \prec_F (\eth_2, \eth_3).$$

Remark 10 (Definability by Resemblance Relation). *The satisfaction clause of* $F(t)$ *can be defined by a resemblance relation* $\prec_F$.

2.2.4   Representation and Uniqueness Theorems Then the next theorems follows from Facts 1 and 2 and Definition 19.

Theorem 1 (Representation).
If $(\mathscr{W}, R, \mathscr{D}, \{\precsim_F\}_{F \in \mathscr{P}}, \{\mathscr{D}_{\precsim_F}\}_{F \in \mathscr{P}}, P, \{\precsim_{F_1 \times \cdots \times F_n}\}_{F_1 \ldots, F_n \in \mathscr{P}}, I)$ *is a mereological additive difference factorial proximity structured model of* RMRL, *then there exists a function* $f : \mathscr{D} \to \mathbb{R}$ *satisfying*

$$(\mathfrak{M}, w) \models (t_1, t_2) \leqslant_F (t_3, t_4)[s]$$

iff

$$(\tilde{s}(t_1), \tilde{s}(t_2)) \precsim_F (\tilde{s}(t_3), \tilde{s}(t_4))$$

iff

$$|f(\tilde{s}(t_1)) - f(\tilde{s}(t_2))| \le |f(\tilde{s}(t_3)) - f(\tilde{s}(t_4))|.$$

Proof.
Suppose that $(\mathscr{W}, R, \mathscr{D}, \{\precsim_F\}_{F \in \mathscr{P}}, \{\mathscr{D}_{\precsim_F}\}_{F \in \mathscr{P}}, P, \{\precsim_{F_1 \times \cdots \times F_n}\}_{F_1 \ldots, F_n \in \mathscr{P}}, I)$ is a mereological additive difference factorial proximity structured model of RMRL (Definition 17). Then because, by Definition 17, $(\mathscr{D}, \precsim_F)$ is an absolute difference structure (Definition 6), by Fact 1, there exists a function $f : \mathscr{D} \to \mathbb{R}$ satisfying

$$(\tilde{s}(t_1), \tilde{s}(t_2)) \precsim_F (\tilde{s}(t_3), \tilde{s}(t_4))$$

iff

$$|f(\tilde{s}(t_1)) - f(\tilde{s}(t_2))| \le |f(\tilde{s}(t_3)) - f(\tilde{s}(t_4))|.$$

On the other hand, by Definition 19, we have

$$(\mathfrak{M}, w) \models (t_1, t_2) \leqslant_F (t_3, t_4)[s]$$

iff

$$(\tilde{s}(t_1), \tilde{s}(t_2)) \precsim_F (\tilde{s}(t_3), \tilde{s}(t_4)). \square$$

Theorem 2 (Uniqueness). *The above function f is a quasi-interval scale.*

By Facts 7 and 8 and Definition 19, we can prove the following *representation* and *uniqueness theorems* for $\precsim_{F_1 \times \cdots \times F_n}$:

Theorem 3 (Representation).
If $(\mathscr{W}, R, \mathscr{D}, \{\precsim_F\}_{F \in \mathscr{P}}, \{\mathscr{D}_{\precsim_F}\}_{F \in \mathscr{P}}, P, \{\precsim_{F_1 \times \cdots \times F_n}\}_{F_1 \ldots, F_n \in \mathscr{P}}, I)$ is a mereological additive difference factorial proximity structured model of RMRL, then there exist functions $f_{\precsim_{F_i}} (1 \le i \le n) : \mathscr{D}_{\precsim_{F_i}} \to \mathbb{R}_{\ge 0}$ and monotonically increasing functions $g_{\precsim_{F_i}} (1 \le i \le n) : \mathbb{R}_{\ge 0} \to \mathbb{R}_{\ge 0}$ such that

$$(\mathfrak{M}, w) \models (t_1, t_2) \leqslant_{F_1 \times \cdots \times F_n} (t_3, t_4)[s]$$

iff

$$(\tilde{s}(t_1), \tilde{s}(t_2)) \precsim^*_{F_1 \times \cdots \times F_n} (\tilde{s}(t_3), \tilde{s}(t_4))$$

iff

$$(4) \quad \sum_{i=1}^{n} g_{\precsim_{F_i}} (|f_{\precsim_{F_i}}(\mathcal{m}_i P(\mathcal{o}_i, \tilde{s}(t_1))) - f_{\precsim_{F_i}}(\mathcal{m}_{i+1} P(\mathcal{o}_{i+1}, \tilde{s}(t_2)))|)$$

$$\le$$

$$\sum_{i=1}^{n} g_{\precsim_{F_i}} (|f_{\precsim_{F_i}}(\mathcal{m}_{i+2} P(\mathcal{o}_{i+2}, \tilde{s}(t_3))) - f_{\precsim_{F_i}}(\mathcal{m}_{i+3} P(\mathcal{o}_{i+3}, \tilde{s}(t_4)))|),$$

where $\mathcal{m}_i P(\mathcal{o}_i, \tilde{s}(t_1)), \mathcal{m}_{i+1} P(\mathcal{o}_{i+1}, \tilde{s}(t_2)), \mathcal{m}_{i+2} P(\mathcal{o}_{i+2}, \tilde{s}(t_3)),$
$\mathcal{m}_{i+3} P(\mathcal{o}_{i+3}, \tilde{s}(t_4)) \in \mathscr{D}_{\precsim_{F_i}}.$

Proof.
Suppose that $(\mathscr{W}, R, \mathscr{D}, \{\precsim_F\}_{F \in \mathscr{P}}, \{\mathscr{D}_{\precsim_F}\}_{F \in \mathscr{P}}, P, \{\precsim_{F_1 \times \cdots \times F_n}\}_{F_1 \ldots, F_n \in \mathscr{P}}, I)$ is a mereological additive difference factorial proximity structured model of RMRL (Definition 17). Then because, by Definition 17, $(\mathscr{D}_{F_1} \times \cdots \times \mathscr{D}_{F_n}, \precsim_{F_1 \times \cdots \times F_n})$ is an additive difference factorial proximity structure (Definition 15), by Fact

7, there exist functions $f_{\precsim_{F_i}}(1 \le i \le n) : \mathscr{D}_{\precsim_{F_i}} \to \mathbb{R}_{\ge 0}$ and monotonically increasing functions $g_{\precsim_{F_i}}(1 \le i \le n) : \mathbb{R}_{\ge 0} \to \mathbb{R}_{\ge 0}$ such that

$$(\tilde{s}(t_1), \tilde{s}(t_2)) \precsim^*_{F_1 \times \cdots \times F_n} (\tilde{s}(t_3), \tilde{s}(t_4))$$

iff

$$\sum_{i=1}^{n} g_{\precsim_{F_i}}(|f_{\precsim_{F_i}}(\eta_i P(\partial_i, \tilde{s}(t_1))) - f_{\precsim_{F_i}}(\eta_{i+1} P(\partial_{i+1}, \tilde{s}(t_2)))|)$$
$$\le$$
$$\sum_{i=1}^{n} g_{\precsim_{F_i}}(|f_{\precsim_{F_i}}(\eta_{i+2} P(\partial_{i+2}, \tilde{s}(t_3))) - f_{\precsim_{F_i}}(\eta_{i+3} P(\partial_{i+3}, \tilde{s}(t_4)))|).$$

On the other hand, by Definition 19, we have

$$(\mathfrak{M}, w) \models (t_1, t_2) \leqslant_{F_1 \times \cdots \times F_n} (t_3, t_4)[s]$$

iff

$$(\tilde{s}(t_1), \tilde{s}(t_2)) \precsim^*_{F_1 \times \cdots \times F_n} (\tilde{s}(t_3), \tilde{s}(t_4)). \quad \square$$

Remark 11 (Mereological Parthood Relation). *One of the points of this theorem is that it is formulated by the help of a mereological parthood relation P.*

Theorem 4 (Uniqueness). *The above functions $f_{\precsim_{F_i}}$ are interval scales and the above functions $g_{\precsim_{F_i}}$ are interval scales with a common unit.*

We define the degree of unresemblance and its weight in terms of Theorems 3 and 4:

Definition 20 (Degree of Unresemblance and Its Weight). *The degrees of unresemblance with respect to $\precsim_{F_i}$ are defined by*

$$|f_{\precsim_{F_i}}(\eta_i P(\partial_i, \tilde{s}(t_1))) - f_{\precsim_{F_i}}(\eta_{i+1} P(\partial_{i+1}, \tilde{s}(t_2)))|$$

and

$$|f_{\precsim_{F_i}}(\eta_{i+2} P(\partial_{i+2}, \tilde{s}(t_3))) - f_{\precsim_{F_i}}(\eta_{i+3} P(\partial_{i+3}, \tilde{s}(t_4)))|$$

of (4), and their weights are defined by

$$g_{\precsim_{F_i}}$$

of (4), where the existence and uniqueness of $f_{\precsim_{F_i}}$ and $g_{\precsim_{F_i}}$ are guaranteed by Theorems 3 and 4 respectively.

3   Concluding Remarks

Suppose that

$Cx := x$ is carmine,

$Vx := x$ is vermillion,

$Tx := x$ is triangular, and

$(x, y) <_{C \times V \times T} (z, w) := x$ resembles y more than z resembles w with respect to carminity and vermillionity and triangularity. Then the RMRL-logical form of (1) is

$$\forall x \forall y \forall z ((Cx \wedge Vy \wedge Tz) \rightarrow (x, y) <_{C \times V \times T} (x, z)).$$

Its semantic value (satisfaction condition) is given by the following corollary that follows from Theorem 3 and Definition 19:

Corollary 2 (Solution to Rodriguez-Pereyra-Yi Problem by RMRL**).** *If* $(\mathscr{W}, R, \mathscr{D}, \{\precsim_C, \precsim_V, \precsim_T\}, \{\mathscr{D}_{\precsim_C}, \mathscr{D}_{\precsim_V}, \mathscr{D}_{\precsim_T}\}, P, \{\precsim_{C \times V \times T}\}, I)$ *is a mereological additive difference factorial proximity structured model of* RMRL, *then there exist* $f_{\precsim_C} : \mathscr{D}_{\precsim_C} \rightarrow \mathbb{R}_{\geq 0}$ *and* $f_{\precsim_V} : \mathscr{D}_{\precsim_V} \rightarrow \mathbb{R}_{\geq 0}$ *and* $f_{\precsim_T} : \mathscr{D}_{\precsim_T} \rightarrow \mathbb{R}_{\geq 0}$ *and* $g_{\precsim_C}, g_{\precsim_V}, g_{\precsim_T} : \mathbb{R}_{\geq 0} \rightarrow \mathbb{R}_{\geq 0}$ *such that*

$$(\mathfrak{M}, w) \models \forall x \forall y \forall z ((Cx \wedge Vy \wedge Tz) \rightarrow (x, y) <_{C \times V \times T} (x, z))[s]$$

iff there is no $\mathfrak{d}_1, \mathfrak{d}_2, \mathfrak{d}_3 \in \mathscr{D}$ *such that* $\mathfrak{d}_1 \in I(C, w)$ *and* $\mathfrak{d}_2 \in I(V, w)$ *and* $\mathfrak{d}_3 \in I(T, w)$ *such that*

$$
\begin{aligned}
&(g_{\precsim_C}(|f_{\precsim_C}(\mathfrak{n}_4 P(\mathfrak{d}_4, \mathfrak{d}_1)) - f_{\precsim_C}(\mathfrak{n}_5 P(\mathfrak{d}_5, \mathfrak{d}_2))|) \\
&+ g_{\precsim_V}(|f_{\precsim_V}(\mathfrak{n}_6 P(\mathfrak{d}_6, \mathfrak{d}_1)) - f_{\precsim_V}(\mathfrak{n}_7 P(\mathfrak{d}_7, \mathfrak{d}_2))|) \\
&+ g_{\precsim_T}(|f_{\precsim_T}(\mathfrak{n}_8 P(\mathfrak{d}_8, \mathfrak{d}_1)) - f_{\precsim_T}(\mathfrak{n}_9 P(\mathfrak{d}_9, \mathfrak{d}_2))|)) \\
&\geq \\
&(g_{\precsim_C}(|f_{\precsim_C}(\mathfrak{n}_4 P(\mathfrak{d}_4, \mathfrak{d}_1)) - f_{\precsim_C}(\mathfrak{n}_{10} P(\mathfrak{d}_{10}, \mathfrak{d}_3))|) \\
&+ g_{\precsim_V}(|f_{\precsim_V}(\mathfrak{n}_6 P(\mathfrak{d}_6, \mathfrak{d}_1)) - f_{\precsim_V}(\mathfrak{n}_{11} P(\mathfrak{d}_{11}, \mathfrak{d}_3))|) \\
&+ g_{\precsim_T}(|f_{\precsim_T}(\mathfrak{n}_8 P(\mathfrak{d}_8, \mathfrak{d}_1)) - f_{\precsim_T}(\mathfrak{n}_{12} P(\mathfrak{d}_{12}, \mathfrak{d}_3))|)).
\end{aligned}
$$

We have the following conclusion: When we choose as the weight-assignment functions such functions $g_{\precsim_C}, g_{\precsim_V}, g_{\precsim_T}$ that the value of $g_{\precsim_T}$ is much greater than those of $g_{\precsim_C}$ and $g_{\precsim_V}$, Corollary 2 can give a solution to Rodriguez-Pereyra-Yi Problem by Definition 20 in terms of giving the satisfaction condition of (1) in RMRL so that

the weighted sum of the degrees of unresemblance of carmine particulars to triangular particulars may be greater than that of carmine particulars to vermillion particulars,

instead of using Definition 1 that is the main culprit of this problem. In so doing, RMRL obtains the capacity to deal with multidimensionality in general beyond Rodriguez-Pereyra-Yi Problem.

Acknowledgements. The author would like to thank the reviewers and the audience of LENLS19 for their very helpful comments.

References

1. Krantz, D.H., et al.: Foundations of Measurement, vol. 1. Academic Press, New York (1971)
2. Lewis, D.: On the Plurality of Worlds. Basil Blackwell, Oxford (1986)
3. Roberts, F.S.: Measurement Theory. Addison-Wesley, Reading (1979)
4. Rodriguez-Pereyra, G.: Resemblance Nominalism. Clarendon Press, Oxford (2002)
5. Rodriguez-Pereyra, G.: Nominalism in metaphysics. Stanford Encyclopedia of Philosophy (2015)
6. Rodriguez-Pereyra, G.: Resemblance nominalism and abstract nouns. Analysis **75**, 223–231 (2015)
7. Suppes, P., et al.: Foundations of Measurement, vol. 2. Academic Press, San Diego (1989)
8. Suzuki, S.: Measurement-theoretic foundations of resemblance nominalism. In: Mineshima, K. (ed.) Proceedings of the Seventeenth Workshop on Logic and Engineering of Natural Language Semantics (LENLS17). JSAI, Tokyo (2020)
9. Varzi, A.: Mereology. Stanford Encyclopedia of Philosophy (2019)
10. Yi, B.U.: Abstract nouns and resemblance nominalism. Analysis **74**, 622–629 (2014)
11. Yi, B.U.: Nominalism and comparative similarity. Erkenntnis **83**, 793–803 (2018)

Correction to: Logic and Engineering of Natural Language Semantics

Daisuke Bekki, Koji Mineshima⦿, and Elin McCready

Correction to:
D. Bekki et al. (Eds.): *Logic and Engineering of Natural*
Language Semantics, **LNCS 14213,**
https://doi.org/10.1007/978-3-031-43977-3

In the original version the surname of the last editor has been misspelled. The correct name is Elin McCready.
This has been now corrected.

The updated version of the book can be found at
https://doi.org/10.1007/978-3-031-43977-3

Author Index

© The Editor(s) (if applicable) and The Author(s), under exclusive license
to Springer Nature Switzerland AG 2023
D. Bekki et al. (Eds.): LENLS 2019, LNCS 14213, p. 233, 2023.
https://doi.org/10.1007/978-3-031-43977-3

Printed in the United States
by Baker & Taylor Publisher Services